Tunisia
a country study

Foreign Area Studies
The American University
Edited by
Harold D. Nelson
Research completed
January 1986

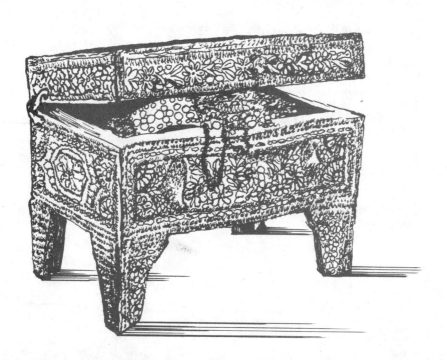

MTB

On the cover: Jewelry box of embossed silver and enamel, representing one of the proficiencies of Tunisia's artisans

Third Edition, 1986; First Printing, 1987

Library of Congress Cataloging in Publication Data

Tunisia : a country study.

    (Area handbook series) (DA pam ; 550–89)
    "Research completed January 1986."
    Bibliography: pp. 313–56
    Includes index.
    1. Tunisia.   I. Nelson, Harold D.,   II. American
University (Washington, D.C.). Foreign Area Studies.   III.
Series. IV. Series: DA pam ; 550–89.
DT245.T7955 1986 961'.1 86 3351

Headquarters, Department of the Army
DA Pam 550–89

For sale by the Superintendent of Documents, U.S. Government Printing Office
Washington, D.C. 20402

9/1/88

Foreword

This volume is one of a continuing series of books prepared by Foreign Area Studies, The American University, under the Country Studies/Area Handbook Program. The last page of this book provides a listing of other published studies. Each book in the series deals with a particular foreign country, describing and analyzing its economic, national security, political, and social systems and institutions and examining the interrelationships of those systems and institutions and the ways that they are shaped by cultural factors. Each study is written by a multidisciplinary team of social scientists. The authors seek to provide a basic insight and understanding of the society under observation, striving for a dynamic rather than a static portrayal of it. The study focuses on historical antecedents and on the cultural, political, and socioeconomic characteristics that contribute to cohesion and cleavage within the society. Particular attention is given to the origins and traditions of the people who make up the society, their dominant beliefs and values, their community of interests and the issues on which they are divided, the nature and extent of their involvement with the national institutions, and their attitudes toward each other and toward the social system and political order within which they live.

The contents of the book represent the views, opinions, and findings of Foreign Area Studies and should not be construed as an official Department of the Army position, policy, or decision, unless so designated by other official documentation. The authors have sought to adhere to accepted standards of scholarly objectivity. Such corrections, additions, and suggestions for factual or other changes that readers may have will be welcomed for use in future new editions.

Director
Foreign Area Studies
The American University
5010 Wisconsin Avenue, NW
Washington, D.C. 20016

Acknowledgements

The authors are grateful to those individuals in various international, governmental, and academic organizations who gave of their time, data, special knowledge, and authoritative perspective on Tunisia. Gratitude is also extended to members of the Foreign Area Studies support staff who contributed directly to the production of this book. These persons include Catherine L. Connor, Denise R. Barber, and Andrea T. Merrill, who edited the manuscript and the accompanying figures and tables; Harriett R. Blood and Gustavo Adolfo Mendoza, who prepared the graphics; Ernest A. Will, publications manager; Wayne W. Olsen, administrative assistant; Gilda V. Nimer and Karen Leitch, librarians; and Jesse L. Williams and Lisa C. Young, who keyboarded the manuscript. The book was indexed by Kathryne Kozak and phototypeset by Margaret Quinn.

The aesthetic touches that enhance the book's appearance are the work of Mr. Mendoza, whose illustrations appear on the cover and the title pages of the chapters. The inclusion of photographs has been made possible by the generosity of various individuals and public and private agencies. Special appreciation is extended to those persons who contributed original camera work not previously published.

Contents

NATIONAL INCOME—Economic Growth—Inflation and Prices—Income Distribution—THE ROLE OF THE GOVERN-MENT—Development Planning—The Domestic Budget—THE MONETARY SECTOR—The Central Bank and Monetary Policy—Other Banks and Savings Institutions—THE LABOR FORCE—AGRICULTURE—Land Use—Land Tenure and Reform—Crop Production—Livestock, Fishing, and Forestry—INDUSTRY—Hydrocarbons—Other Mining—Manufacturing and Handicrafts—Electricity—T O U R I S M—F O R E I G N TRADE—BALANCE OF PAYMENTS AND EXTERNAL FI-NANCE—TRANSPORTATION AND TELECOMMUNICA-TIONS

CONSTITUTIONAL DEVELOPMENT—STRUCTURE OF GOV-ERNMENT — Executive — Legislature — Elections—The Legal System—Regional and Local Government—POLITICAL DY-NAMICS—The 1981 Election: Opposition Parties Sanctioned—The Riots of 1984 and Their Aftermath—Presidential Succession—Bourguibism and Destourian Socialism—The Des-tourian Socialist Party—Opposition Groups—Interest Groups—Politics and the Information Media—FOREIGN RELATIONS—Maghribi Affairs—Other Arab Countries—France and the Euro-pean Community—United States—Communist Countries

INTERNATIONAL SECURITY CONCERNS—DOMESTIC SE-CURITY ISSUES AND POLICIES—Roots of Domestic Security Difficulties—Government Security Policy under Mohamed Mzali—ARMED FORCES—Military Tradition, Development, and Philosophy—The Military and Politics—Defense Costs and the Economy—Quality and Sources of Manpower—Military Structure and Training—Uniforms, Ranks, and Insignia—For-eign Military Assistance—INTERNAL SECURITY FORCES—Sûreté Nationale—Garde Nationale—Prisons

List of Figures

Preface

This third edition of *Tunisia: A Country Study* replaces the second edition, which was researched and written in late 1978 and published in 1979. At the time the second edition was finished, Tunisia was at the beginning of its third decade of independence from French administrative domination. Under the charismatic leadership of President Habib Bourguiba, the young republic had gained a significant international reputation as an Arab state seeking to achieve national development goals through a pragmatic course that borrowed liberally from the concepts of free and centrally planned Western societies. Now, seven years later, the third edition views the results that have been achieved as Tunisia nears the end of its third decade of sovereignty.

Like its predecessor, the third edition seeks to provide a compact and objective exposition of Tunisia's dominant social, economic, political, and national security institutions and, hopefully, to give the reader some appreciation of the forces involved in contemporary national life. In presenting this new study, the authors have relied primarily on official reports of governmental and international organizations, journals, newspapers, and material reflecting recent field research by scholarly authorities. Detailed information on many aspects of the society, however, was not always readily available, and gaps in the data as well as varying interpretations existed among some of the sources consulted. Where appropriate, these gaps and inconsistencies have been cited in the text. Should readers require greater detail on core area topics, the authors have noted the availability of amplifying materials in bibliographic statements at the end of each chapter. Full references to these and other sources used or considered are included in the detailed Bibliography.

The literature of Tunisia is frequently confusing because of the tendency to mix English and French transliterations of Arabic words, phrases, personal names, and place-names. For the most part, the authors of this study have attempted to reduce this confusion by adhering to the system of French transliteration, inasmuch as that is the form generally used in Tunisia, where half of the people speak French in addition to the official language, Arabic.

Arab personal names are often particularly confusing to the Western reader. A man's name includes his paternal genealogy and sometimes also indicates his family name, his tribal affiliation, and his village or region of origin. For example, a man named Abd al Rahman ibn (or ben) Qasim ibn Mohammed (or Mohamed) El (or Al) Hamma would be recognized as the son of Qasim, the grandson of Mohammed, and a native of the town of El Hamma. The man would be addressed as Mister (or his title, if any) Abd al Rahman. In spoken Arabic, names are elided, so that in this instance the name would be pronounced as if it were spelled Abdur Rahman. On many occasions the Western press spells such names as Abdel (or Abdul) Rahman, implying incorrectly that the man's first name is Abdel and that his last is Rahman. Many Arabic names, such as the one in this example, are designations of the attributes of God (Allah). *Abd al* means a slave or servant of, and *Rahman* means merciful; thus, the name literally means the slave or servant of the Merciful (God).

Where foreign and technical words and phrases have been used in this study, they have been defined briefly where they first appear in a chapter, or reference has been made to the Glossary, which is included at the back of the book for the reader's guidance. The dictionary used was *Webster's Ninth New Collegiate Dictionary*. All measurements are presented in the metric system, which is used in Tunisia. A conversion table will assist those readers who are not familiar with metric equivalents (see table 1, Appendix).

Country Profile

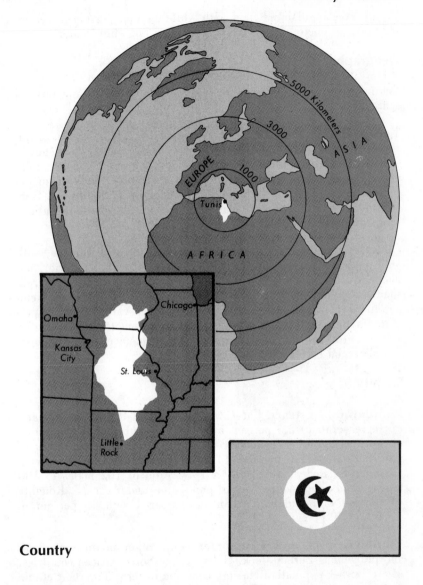

Country

Formal Name: Republic of Tunisia.

Short Form: Tunisia.

Term for Citizens: Tunisian(s).

Capital: Tunis.

Flag: Rectangular red field with white circular portion in center; red crescent encircles red five-point star within white center.

Geography

Size: About 164,000 square kilometers; 1,600 kilometers of coastline.

Topography: Dominant natural feature Dorsale mountain chain, which extends across north-central portion of country from northeast to southwest. North of Dorsale, terrain uneven and generally mountainous except where Mejerda River, country's only major perennial stream, passes through fertile floodplain. Southward from Dorsale, region of semiarid plateaus gives way in extreme south to Tunisian portion of Sahara.

Climate: Mediterranean climate prevails north of Dorsale, with only moderate seasonal variation. Occasional frosts in interior, but temperatures seldom drop below freezing. Dorsale acts as rain shadow; precipitation decreases progressively, and average temperatures increase southward. Extreme diurnal variation in temperature in Sahara. Heavy morning dew supplements scanty rainfall along central portion of eastern littoral to make possible prosperous olive and cereal culture.

Society

Population: Estimated at 7.2 million in mid-1985. Rate of natural increase about 2.6 percent annually, but substantial emigration of workers to other countries each year reduced actual rate of growth to about 2.5 percent. In 1983 number of Tunisians living abroad estimated at 300,000. In 1984 ratio of 102 males to 100 females and about 42 percent of population under age 15. Roughly 47 percent of population urban as compared with 40 percent in 1966 and 30 percent in 1956.

Ethnic Groups and Language: Population mixture of Arab and indigenous Berber stock. Unlike other North African countries, where Berber population clusters continue to form important ethnic minorities, arabization of Tunisian Berbers has long been virtually complete. Arabic official language, spoken by nearly all. French, however, spoken as second language by one-half of population, remains principal language of business.

Literacy: According to 1980 estimate, approximately 50 percent of population over age 15 considered literate. By gender, rate about 67 percent for males and 33 percent for females; gap closing rapidly with increasing female school attendance.

Health: Conditions of health and sanitation improving steadily, and most of formerly serious endemic diseases eliminated or under fair degree of control. Diseases of infancy and early childhood, however, remain major hazards; more than one-half of all deaths occur among children under age five. Shortage of medical personnel of all kinds prevails, particularly in rural areas.

Economy

Gross Domestic Product (GDP): In 1984 amounted to TD6.23 billion; real growth rate averaged around 7 percent in mid-1980s.

Agriculture: Largely traditional with small modern sector; major crops cereals, olives, olive oil, citrus fruits, potatoes, tomatoes, dates, and fish. Provided about 13 percent of GDP and 32 percent of employment in mid-1980s.

Manufacturing: Fast-growing sector; marked growth among those industries making textile, chemical, electrical, and mechanical products. Provides about 12 percent of GDP.

Mining: Petroleum dominant product followed by phosphates and natural gas. Provided about 10 percent of GDP.

Foreign Trade: Exports mainly petroleum, natural gas, phosphates, phosphate derivatives, textiles, and olive oil. Imports largely machinery, semifinished products, and foodstuffs. Imports exceeded exports in mid-1980s; tourism and remittances from Tunisians working abroad reduced deficit only slightly.

Currency: Tunisian dinar (TD—see Glossary).

Fiscal Year: Same as calendar year.

Transportation and Telecommunications

Roads: Network of about 23,700 kilometers of surfaced roads; most modern segments of system in north, particularly around Tunis.

Railroads: About 2,150 kilometers of track reaching most of country's main urban centers and phosphate mines in southwest.

Ports: Major ports at Tunis, Bizerte, Sfax, Sousse, Gabès, and Sakhira.

Airports: International airports at Tunis, Bizerte, Monastir, Sfax, and on Jerba Island.

Telecommunications: Major urban centers well served by telephones and telex, including automatic international dialing; member of Intelsat and Arabsat.

Government and Politics

Government: Republic under president, who serves as both head of state and head of government. Habib Bourguiba declared president for life in 1975 after having been elected unopposed four successive times. Day-to-day administration under Prime Minister Mohamed Mzali and Council of Ministers (cabinet), both responsible to president.

Legislature: Unicameral chamber of 136 deputies elected by direct suffrage for five-year term. Election to Chamber of Deputies in 1981 swept by National Front Coalition dominated by Bourguiba's Destourian Socialist Party (Parti Socialiste Destourien—PSD). Chamber generally approves president's legislative program and budget without significant change.

Legal System: Modern legal codes adopted after independence reflect influence of both French law and sharia (sacred Islamic law). Code of Personal Status, dealing with family, marriage, and divorce, considered radical by Arab standards, notably with respect to rights of women. Three tiers of courts with original and appellate jurisdiction; judgments subject to power of annulment by highest tribunal, Court of Cassation.

Administrative Subdivisions: 23 governorates (provinces), each composed of several delegations, in turn divided into sectors. In 245 communes and municipalities, local self-government exercised by elected councillors, subject to review by governor.

Politics: Influence of PSD, only legal party between 1963 and 1981, pervasive at all levels of government. Under Constitution, Mzali in line to succeed Bourguiba, although more conservative rivals within PSD likely to contest his leadership aspirations. Three opposition groups—Movement of Socialist Democrats, Popular Unity Party, and Tunisian Communist Party—officially sanctioned but impeded in efforts to campaign against PSD. Growing Islamist movement not yet legalized as political party.

Foreign Relations: Officially nonaligned but oriented toward West. Rejects policies of more radical Arab states, urging moderation on Israeli-Palestinian issue and other Middle Eastern problems. Stresses solidarity among northwestern African states (Maghrib). Relations with United States marked by warmth, although Washington regarded as too uncritical in its support for Israel.

National Security

Armed Forces: In 1985 armed forces, collectively known as Tunisian National Army, included army of 30,000, air force of 2,500, and navy of 2,600. Conscription for one-year tour of duty irregularly enforced for male citizens aged 20. Over 85 percent of army composed of draftees; career personnel dominated in other services.

Major Tactical Units: Army included two combined arms brigades (each with one armored battalion and two mechanized infantry battalions); one elite paracommando brigade; one brigade of desert troops; and reconnaissance, artillery, air defense, and engineering units. Air force maintained one fighter squadron formed in 1985, one light-attack squadron, one training unit, and one helicopter wing; inventory of about 20 combat aircraft. Naval forces included one frigate, eight fast-attack craft (six armed with surface-to-surface missiles), and several patrol vessels.

Foreign Military Assistance: United States major arms supplier providing bulk of armor and aircraft acquired in 1980s. France important source of equipment and training since Tunisian independence. Sweden and Italy also prominent suppliers of military equipment in 1980s.

Defense Expenditures: According to Tunisian government figures, appropriations for Ministry of National Defense in 1985 amounted to TD225.1 million. Of this figure, TD102.6 million allocated from current budget (9.8 percent of total) and TD122.5 million from capital budget (10.9 percent of total). Total defense costs 10.3 percent of total central government expenditures in 1985 and about 3.6 percent of GDP.

Internal Security Forces: All government internal security forces under authority of Ministry of Interior. Sûreté Nationale performed most urban police duties. Garde Nationale had responsibility for rural police affair and border patrol.

Figure 1. Republic of Tunisia, 1985

xviii

Introduction

TUNISIA FORMS PART of the region that its early Arab conquerors called the "island of the west" *(jazirat al maghrib)*—the land between the "sea of sand" (the Sahara) and the Mediterranean Sea. According to tradition, other regional members are Morocco, Algeria, and the northwest portion of Libya known as Tripolitania, but in more recent times Mauritania has often been included. Tunisia has stood throughout history as a bridge between this Arab west (the Maghrib) and the Arab east (the Mashriq). Jutting into the Mediterranean midway between Gibraltar and the Suez, the country's northeastern promontory commands the narrows between the African continent and Sicily that divide the great intercontinental sea into eastern and western basins. From this strategic location Tunisia has been depicted by its promoters as an important crossroads between Africa, the Middle East, and Europe.

Smallest of the Maghribi nations, Tunisia is roughly the size of the state of Missouri. Bounded on the north and the east by an extensive coastline, the small country shares its other frontiers with much larger Algeria and troublesome Libya (see fig. 1). Tunisians and their Maghribi neighbors have a common language, religion, and cultural heritage and, in large measure, a common history as well. The area has been a locus of trade and colonization almost since the beginning of recorded time. Its people are ethnically a mixture of Arab and indigenous Berber stock, but succeeding waves of Carthaginians, Romans, Spanish Muslims, Ottoman Turks, and—more recently—French and Italian settlers have had a profound effect on cultures, social structures, and values.

Independent since 1956 after 75 years as a French protectorate, Tunisia is regarded not only as the most modernized of the Arab countries but also as the most Westernized. Under the French, Tunisians were exposed to a progressive European society whose methods of government and business administration left indelible marks. Advanced plantation agriculture transformed the fertile coastal regions into export-oriented production centers. The French education system introduced foreign political concepts—most notably nationalism—to Tunisian youth. After 1934 an indigenous independence movement, the Neo-Destour (New Constitution) Party, began active resistance to the continuation of the protectorate. The movement was led by a forceful, charismatic Tunisian named Habib Bourguiba.

The new order drew its social and political values from the Sahil, a coastal plateau region heavily influenced by its continued exposure to foreigners. In marked contrast to the more arabized remainder of the country, the Sahilian community was intensely industrious, flexible in accepting new methods, independent and rather secular in spirit, and highly cooperative. Bourguiba and the vanguard of the nationalist movement were all of Sahilian origin. After independence, rather than fashion a nation based on pride and extremism, these men sought to accustom the people to a realistic assessment of the new republic's position in the world and to a pragmatic, flexible approach to the problems of national development. Many observers believed Tunisia not only would attain its goal but also would do so through a democratic governmental system and a free society. Certainly it enjoyed a combination of advantages rarely matched in other emerging sovereign states.

From the outset Bourguiba's leadership was a major advantage. Popularly hailed as the Supreme Combatant for his role in the struggle for national independence, he had no competitors in gaining public recognition as "father of his country." Widely regarded as capable, incorruptible, progressive, and committed to a compassionate, humanistic philosophy regarding the Tunisian people, the national leader was respected—even revered—by a citizenry eager to follow his lead. A popular political party already existed as a potential vehicle for mobilizing the masses in the development effort. An efficient, uncorrupted civil service and a well-trained cadre of technicians inherited from the protectorate period stood ready to administer the new state and its modernization plans. The issue of Tunisification (replacement of foreigners by Tunisians in the civil service and the education system) and arabization (replacement of foreign languages by Arabic as the official tongue) lacked the emotional and dysfunctional impact that had accompanied similar actions in newly independent neighboring states.

Although there was some geographic sectionalism, the deep tribal or ethnic cleavages with which other North African states had to deal were largely nonexistent. Moreover, Tunisia's independence struggle had been a political maneuver rather than a military encounter, and it had united the country without causing the mass destruction suffered, for example, by neighboring Algeria in its own agonizing war of independence. Particularly heartening was Tunisia's affinity for the Western cultural and social aspects of its heritage and its avowed friendship with the West, despite an official foreign policy of nonalignment.

The republican Constitution endorsed the separation of executive, legislative, and judicial powers; provided for regular elections; and included a bill of rights designed to protect individual freedoms. Although clearly democratic in its intent, the fundamental law permitted the president to exercise broad and unqualified executive powers within the context of a single-party state.

The political organization of Bourguiba and his fellow nationalists was renamed the Destourian Socialist Party (Parti Socialiste Destourien—PSD) in 1964. A populist party active at all levels of the society, its chief functions were to rally public opinion behind government policies and to channel local reactions upward to the national leadership. The PSD's goal was to ensure national unity, which in political terms meant confining free political competition within the framework of a single party; the habit of discipline among a large and stable majority could counterpose opposition minorities while providing them with a channel for the expression of their views. Formally the party—like the government—purported to be representative and democratic, but in practice it too was subject to executive guidance that transcended statutes. From its educated elite, the loyal party membership learned to accept this seeming contradiction as an example of pragmatic flexibility.

Bourguiba, the country's first president (and its only one since his assumption of that office in 1957), became a pioneer among Arab leaders in declaring his intention to bring about social modernization within the framework of Islam, the national religion. Postindependence history has in large part been a chronicle of progress achieved in this endeavor, and the reforms attained have amounted to a social revolution in a Muslim environment.

In most countries where Muslim Arabs are predominant, the fountainhead of traditional social and political values is Islam, the religion brought to Tunisia by the Arabs in the seventh century. The word of God (Allah), revealed to the Prophet Muhammad and recorded in the Quran, provides

Muslims with an integrated structure ordering all personal, social, and political aspects of life. After Tunisian independence, however, the traditional social order, particularly as it affected the family and women, was gradually supplanted by a system based on liberal values, and the government became the leader in effecting change. Responsibility for social security and education, formerly accepted as the duty of the extended family, was assumed by the state. With varying degrees of success, religious rituals, family law, and social customs became targets of official pressure and legislation in the name of equality and productivity—values regarded as critical to the goals of modernization and national development.

Significantly, the reforms and development planning as a whole were undertaken in the name of traditional concepts. For example, two of the fundamental social values preached by Islam—obedience to authority and protection of the helpless—reappeared in the principles of "guided democracy" and state welfare fostered by the Bourguiba regime. Assuring Tunisians that only the "outmoded and obscurantist" aspects of the traditional culture were being transformed because they stood in the way of national development, Bourguiba abolished the traditional sharia courts, reformed religious education, outlawed polygyny, legalized birth control and abortion, and brought about change in the religion-based system of landholding.

In the process of carrying out Tunisia's social revolution, the government gave great emphasis to the role of education in its design for national development. It plowed the largest single share of each annual budget into education; public school enrollments soared, and the national literacy rate advanced—particularly for women. Modern health and welfare programs also received prominent support from the government. Many of the reforms were opposed by conservatives and religious traditionalists, but modernization was seen by the Tunisian political elite as an adaptation of Islam to contemporary imperatives rather than as a denial of the religion's basic tenets. In the mid-1980s modernization had yet to penetrate the more remote parts of the countryside, where farmers and a few nomadic communities continued to live in the relatively traditional social environment. But in the cities the process had progressed so far that there were growing signs of reaction against it.

The cost of economic development has been a heavy burden on the national economy, as typified by an education system that provided free schooling for all Tunisians from the elementary through the university level. In 1985 about half of the country's 7.2 million people were under the age of 25—a statistic that demonstrated the scope of continuing budgetary requirements. Ironically, the economy was unable to provide jobs for the increasing number of graduates, a situation that had potentially serious political implications.

Although endowed with only a modest resource base, Tunisia achieved a remarkable record of economic progress during the 1960s and 1970s. Predominantly an agricultural country, it nonetheless made important strides toward industrialization as a result of extensive foreign aid, pragmatic planning, and little public resistance to the adoption of modern values. During the 1970s, economic growth averaged a phenomenal 7.6 percent annually, attributable to steady expansion of the hydrocarbons sector, an increase in manufacturing, and high receipts from phosphate exports and tourism. Per capita income rose substantially, earning for Tunisia the classification of a middle-income developing country, according to standards established by the World Bank (see Glossary). But when the economy became more narrowly based on petroleum in the late 1970s, a downturn in the country's prosperity was not long in coming. Foreign demand for oil weakened in the early 1980s, as did the market for phosphates, and a slump in tourism occurred as a result of economic sluggishness in potential travelers' own countries. Severe drought conditions brought poor harvests to Tunisia's agricultural sector, and food imports increased.

The resulting slowdown in growth revealed basic structural weaknesses in the economy, including substantial government subsidies for imported consumer goods. In the mid-1980s both the budget and the balance of payments current account suffered major deficits, inflation increased, and unemployment became one of Tunisia's most severe problems. The government attempted to redress its economic problems, but restrictive measures, such as reducing subsidies, increasing consumer goods prices, and freezing wages, sparked worrisome public disturbances.

In retrospect, there seems little doubt that the reforms introduced in the Tunisian society stemmed to some degree from Bourguiba's determination to neutralize long-standing conservative Muslim power. But his chosen path toward national development, modernization, and economic well-being carried with it certain inherent problems and dangers. The emphasis on national unity, centralization of power, and efficiency undermined local contributions to the development effort. In stressing uniformity, pluralism was shunned. The result has been an inability to accept nonconformity and criticism, as well as a refusal to permit—much less accommodate—political dissent, which the regime has equated with a lack of patriotism.

Long supported by popular consensus and a Tunisian tradition of strong central government, Bourguiba has consolidated his authority over all levels of political administration and has extended his personal influence to most aspects of national life. Adopting a paternalistic attitude toward the nation, he has ruled in a manner as authoritarian as that exercised by the bey of Tunis, who preceded him in the days of the preindependence monarchy. But he has made a practice of keeping political issues before the people and of explaining government policy through press conferences and speeches.

Internal political opposition generally has been kept in bounds by adroit personnel management. The president shuffles government and party officials frequently to discourage the development of factions and eliminates those regarded as threats to the status quo. Bourguiba's perception of his role as the primary molder of national solidarity is perennial, and, ever conscious of his place in Tunisia's history, he loses no opportunity to remind his fellow citizens of their debt to him. "There is not a Tunisian," he is fond of stating, "who does not owe being a free citizen in an independent country to me."

Despite his continued active participation in the affairs of state, the Tunisian leader in early 1986 was no longer the vigorous activist he had been in an earlier era. His age officially given as 83, Bourguiba has a long history of health problems for which he has sought repeated medical attention both at home and abroad. Still recovering from a heart attack suffered in late 1984, he has reduced his official schedule accordingly. Much of the burden of executive responsibility has been assumed by Mohamed Mzali, the PSD protégé Bourguiba chose for his prime minister in 1980. Having been declared president for life by the national legislature in 1975, the aging Supreme Combatant presides over a nation that is in the process of cultural, social, economic, and political transition.

There are signs that the ailing president may no longer be capable of providing the strong-fisted leadership that once characterized his government. Social unrest has been generated by rising unemployment, particularly among the youth in urban areas. Political rivalries have arisen within the PSD, which functions mainly as the medium through which the leadership's wishes are communicated to the people. Aspiring politicians have increased their maneuvering as hopeful contenders for the government's top office once its aged incumbent passes from the scene. Unrest stemming from a reawakening of Islamist (see Glossary) fervor has raised the public issue of whether Tunisians should abandon their support of the government's Western approach to nationbuilding and return instead to the traditional principles and practices of their religion. Many observers fear that the country's unity and stability have been threatened by pro-Western and anti-Western rivalries and that if they are not contained and managed intelligently, Tunisia could become the Lebanon of North Africa. Solutions to these problems have been difficult to achieve as the country has continued to exist in a political twilight zone awaiting the end of the Bouguiba era.

January 1986

Harold D. Nelson

As noted on the title page, the authors finished research and writing in January 1986. Because of protracted problems of phototypsetting, however, preparations for printing were not completed until late 1987. During the intervening period, Tunisia experienced significant political changes. The ensuing is a brief summary of some of the more important.

In July 1986 Bourguiba dismissed Prime Minister Mohamed Mzali, the person he frequently had identified as his chosen successor (see Presidential Succession, ch. 4). In addition, Bourguiba divorced his wife, Wassila, who for a long period had exercised considerable influence and who was believed to favor a gradual loosening of political controls. During the next fifteen months, Bourguiba continued to make abrupt personnel changes. Many observers concluded that a niece of Bourguiba, Saida Sassi, and others were encouraging Bourguiba in his reluctance to delegate decisionmaking power and expand the political process.

On October 2, 1987, Bourguiba suddenly replaced the incumbent prime minister with Minister of Interior Zine al

Abidine Ben Ali, a 51-year-old former army general. On November 7 Prime Minister Ben Ali announced over Radio Tunisia that a panel of six physicians had determined that Bourguiba had "become totally incapable of fulfilling the duties of the presidency." Ben Ali stated that "in accordance with Article 57 of the Constitution, we . . . assume the presidency and the supreme command of the armed forces." The new president asserted that the time had arrived for "a republican regime that respects the institutions and provides the prerequisites for a responsible democracy." Although Ben Ali was lavish in his praise of Bourguiba's contributions to the nation, he declared that "there is no room for a life presidency, nor for an automatic succession in which the people are not involved." Ben Ali also announced that his government would propose new legislation on parties and the press so that Tunisians could participate in "political activities that truly rely on a plurality of political parties and popular organizations."

Later in the day Ben Ali assumed the chairmanship of the PSD, the third major post that Bourguiba had filled. Ben Ali appointed Hedi Baccouche, formerly minister of social affairs and director of PSD, prime minister and secretary general of the party. In interviews with foreign correspondents, the new prime minister emphasized that the new cabinet included only four ministerial changes. Observers noted one important change, however, in the designation of Mahmoud Mestiri as foreign minister. Mestiri had served in the previous cabinet as secretary of state for the Ministry of Foreign Affairs; he had previously been posted as Tunisia's ambassador to Paris, Moscow, and the United Nations. Baccouche confirmed that although Ben Ali had been critical of the succession procedure by which he assumed the presidency, he intended to adhere to the provisions of the Constitution by serving until the next election, which was scheduled for 1991.

A few hours after taking power, Ben Ali announced the promotions of several military officers, including the elevation of the army chief of staff, Youssef Baraket, to general and Major General Said el Kateb to lieutenant general. A Colonel Youssef Ben Slimane reportedly also was promoted to lieutenant general, as was Idaa Netar, who became the new chief of staff of the air force, replacing a nephew of Bourguiba, who along with several other relatives and close associates of Bourguiba was placed under temporary house arrest.

President Ben Ali retained Slaheddine Baly as minister of state in charge of national defense and appointed Ali Nourddine as director general of national security, a position that Ben Ali had held in the mid-1980s (see Internal Security, ch. 5).

November 23, 1987

Chapter 1. Historical Setting

Punic mausoleum at Dougga built in second century B.C. as a tomb for a Numidian prince

Tunisia has a long and distinct history as a politically and culturally unified country despite subjection to a variety of rulers and the impulses of contrasting civilizations over a period of nearly 3,000 years. The modern state derives its name from Tunis, originally a Phoenician settlement and since the thirteenth century the country's capital and principal city. But to the Romans and later the Arabs, this relatively small region was known as *Africa*, whose name was eventually extended to the whole of the immense continent that lay beyond.

History-conscious Tunisians point to Carthage and Kairouan as the sources of their continuous development as a people and a nation. Carthage built an empire that dominated North Africa and the western Mediterranean until it fell before the might of Rome. Destroyed by its conquerors and then rebuilt as the administrative center of Roman Africa, the city of Carthage became in time the spiritual center of Latin Christianity in North Africa. Kairouan, founded in the seventh century A.D. by advancing Arab armies, is one of the holy cities of the Muslim world and the wellspring from which Arab culture flowed across North Africa.

Tunisia was once part of great medieval Berber empires and, from the sixteenth century, was an autonomous province of the Ottoman Empire ruled by dynasties of Turkish beys. Tunisia was occupied by France in 1881 and remained a French protectorate for 75 years. The French impact on Tunisia was profound, imposing French institutions, leaving the imprint of French culture and technology, and creating a gallicized elite to whom leadership passed when the protectorate was ended in 1956.

The dominant factors of Tunisia's political life have been the power and personality of President Habib Bourguiba and the influence of the Destourian Socialist Party, which embodies his philosophy of government and society. Born in 1903 at Monastir in the Sahil region, Bourguiba—often referred to as the Supreme Combatant—is one of the last surviving Third World nationalist leaders who guided their countries to independence in the post-World War II era. His strength derived from his great popularity as the founder and ideological mentor of the Destourian movement. After independence he used his prestige to institutionalize presidential dominance of the governmental system and to secure for the party supremacy over most aspects of national life.

Many foreign observers regarded Bourguiba's Tunisia as a model for emerging nations attempting to build modern societies.

The republic made outstanding progress in areas of social development, particularly in education, while maintaining political stability in a one-party state. The social unrest that surfaced in the late 1970s was laid to resentment at the uneven distribution of the benefits of economic development and the persistent problem of unemployment. Political opposition focused on demands for party pluralism as an alternative to dominance by the Destourian Socialist Party. Another serious source of resistance to the regime was posed by the Islamic renewal that challenged the secularization of Tunisian society promoted by Bourguiba.

Early History

The coastal regions of Tunisia shared in an early neolithic culture that was common to the whole Mediterranean littoral. Artifacts left by hunters and fishermen who excelled in making stone blades and tools are plentiful, and evidence points to the early domestication of cattle and the cultivation of crops in the area. South of the Atlas range, nomadic hunters and herders roamed a vast savanna, well watered and abounding in game, that 8,000 years ago stretched across what is now the vast desert known as the Sahara. Their culture flourished until the region began to desiccate after 4000 B.C. Scattering before the encroaching desert and invading horsemen, some of the savanna people migrated northward, where they were subsequently absorbed by the Berbers.

Linguistic evidence suggests southwestern Asia as the point from which the ancestors of the Berbers began their migration into North Africa early in the third millennium B.C. Over succeeding centuries they extended their range from Siwa in Egypt to the Niger Basin. The Berbers present a broad range of physical types, and the affinity of various groups seems based almost entirely on linguistic grounds. Berber tradition told that they were descended from two unrelated families, and modern scholars believe that the Berbers did indeed cross North Africa in two simultaneous waves—one that entered the region from the southeast after a long sojourn in Black Africa and another that took a northerly route. The Berbers were well known to classical writers. Sallust, a Roman historian and politician living in the first century B.C., described their way of life, elements of which still exist in the twentieth century.

Carthage

Minoan seamen from Crete may have set up depots on the coast of present-day Tunisia before 2000 B.C., but it was only with the arrival of Phoenician traders, who penetrated the western Mediterranean before the twelfth century B.C., that the region entered into recorded history. Safe harbors on the African coast, equipped to service, supply, and shelter their ships, were the links in a maritime chain that reached to Spain. Tunis, Bizerte, Sousse, Monastir, and Sfax originated as Punic (see Glossary) trading posts where the merchants of Tyre (in present-day Lebanon) developed commercial relations with the Berber tribes of the interior and paid them tribute to ensure their cooperation in securing raw materials. The greatest of the Punic colonies, Carthage (Qart Hadasht, the New Town), was founded, according to tradition, in 814 B.C. by a Phoenician princess whose name has come down to Western readers through Virgil's *Aeneid* as Dido.

Carthage was governed by a mercantile oligarchy that exercised power through a senate, composed of elder statesmen, under a constitution praised by Aristotle for providing a perfect blend of monarchy, aristocracy, and democracy. Joint executive authority was vested in two *suffetes* (consuls), chosen annually by an electorate that was also called upon to decide on difficult questions by referendum. The coastal countryside was closely settled with self-governing towns dependent on Carthage for foreign affairs and defense.

Carthaginian seamen developed a thriving trade in the Mediterranean as they contested control of the sea-lanes with the Greeks from Italy and Sicily. Settlers on the Atlantic coast bartered merchandise for gold from the western Sudan (see Glossary), in the quest of which the Carthaginian admiral Hanno made his fabled voyage to the mouth of the Senegal River. Successful merchants, seamen, and craftsmen, the Carthaginians turned to agriculture as well, raising grain and introducing the cultivation of olive trees in the region on estates that employed Berber workers.

Beyond the Punic enclaves and plantations, the Berber tribes prevailed, but the influence of Punic civilization among them was deep-seated. The Berbers displayed a remarkable gift for cultural assimilation, readily synthesizing Punic religious cults with the nature worship, magic, and holy places of folk religion and adopting the Phoenicians' Semitic language, which was still spoken by Berber farmers in the coastal countryside in the late Roman period.

When the mother-city, Tyre, fell under Persian domination, the western Phoenician colonies looked for leadership to Carthage, which by the fifth century B.C. extended its hegemony along the coast of North Africa from the Atlantic Ocean to Cyrenaica as well as to Sardinia and western Sicily (see fig. 2). Carthage and its dependencies formed defensive alliances with the Berber tribes in the hinterland, from whom they regularly extracted payments of tribute. Essentially a maritime power, Carthage hired Berber mercenaries for its overseas military expeditions and imported mercenaries from abroad to man African garrisons. Carthage contended for generations against Syracuse and the other Greek city-states in Sicily and, as an ally of the Etruscans, resisted the expansion of their Greek commercial rivals in Corsica and Italy.

The growth of Carthaginian influence in Italy and commercial dominance in the western Mediterranean drew the Punic city-state into a confrontation with the emerging power of Rome in the third century B.C. Defeated in the first Punic war (264–241 B.C.), Carthage was forced to surrender its colonies in Sicily and Sardinia, but under the leadership of the Barcids—Hamilcar, Hasdrubal, and Hannibal—it rapidly built a new and larger empire in Spain to compensate for its losses. Claiming Roman interference in Carthaginian colonial affairs, Hannibal led an army of 40,000—many of them Berbers—out of Spain, crossing the Alps into Italy with a baggage train of elephants in 218 B.C. to exact revenge against Rome for previous humiliations. Hannibal remained in Italy for 16 years, defeating every army that the Romans threw against him, but his goal—the capture of Rome itself—eluded him. In the meantime, Roman forces occupied Spain, cutting him off from reinforcements and ultimately compelling him to abandon Italy by bringing the war to Africa. In 202 B.C. the Romans, under Scipio Africanus, defeated Hannibal at Zama (present-day Sidi Youssef) and dictated a harsh peace to Carthage, bringing an end to its days as a major power.

Berber Kingdoms

The basic unit of social and political organization among the Berbers was the extended family, usually identified with a particular village or with traditional grazing grounds. Families in turn were bound together in the clan. An alliance of clans, often tracing their origins to a common ancestor as a symbol of unity, formed a tribe. Courts and representative assemblies guided by customs peculiar to the group functioned at each level of organization. Berber

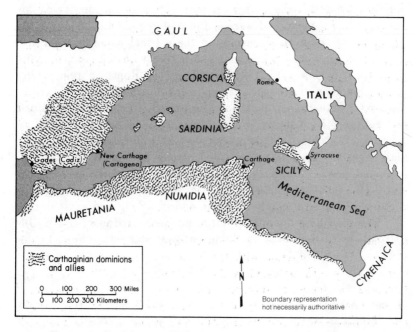

Figure 2. Carthaginian Hegemony, Fourth and Third Centuries, B.C.

folk law and government, like Berber folk religion, were highly personalized and therefore most effective at the lowest levels of their application. Ultimately, each household or tent was its own republic.

For mutual defense, kindred tribes joined in confederations, which, because war was a permanent feature of tribal life, were in time institutionalized. Some chieftains, successful in battle, established rudimentary territorial states by imposing their rule on defeated tribes and allies alike, but their kingdoms were easily fragmented, and the dynasties that they sought to found rarely survived more than a generation. By the third century B.C., however, several large, although loosely administered, Berber kingdoms had emerged behind the coastal areas controlled by Carthage. These monarchies were supported by the sedentary farmers who looked to the kings to protect them from the raids of the nomadic pastoralists. The Berber kings adapted Punic and Greek ceremonial forms to the usage of their courts, and treaties of friendship with Carthage were often sealed by a king's marriage to a woman from the family of a Carthaginian notable. The Berber kings ruled in the shadow of Carthage and later Rome, sometimes forming alliances with one or another of the great powers. After Carthage was vanquished by Rome, they threw in their lots with factions vying for power in the Roman civil wars of the first century B.C.

One of the most illustrious of these tribal monarchs was Masinissa (ca. 240–148 B.C.), who had served with the Carthaginians in Spain. Masinissa shifted his support to Rome in time to be counted among the victor's allies when Carthage surrendered in 202 B.C. With Roman patronage he united Numidia and extended his authority from the Moulouya River to Cyrenaica, a territory he governed from his Hellenistic court at Cirta (Constantine in present-day Algeria). Numidia was divided among several heirs after Masinissa's death. Rome intervened when his grandson, Jugurtha (118–105 B.C.), attempted to revive Masinissa's Berber kingdom. Betrayed by a rival chieftain at the end of a long and exasperating war in which he pinned down large numbers of Roman troops, Jugurtha was carried away to Rome and was starved to death in the Capitol.

Roman Africa

Rome dictated a hard peace to Carthage after the battle of Zama, imposing a stiff indemnity and prohibiting Carthage from making war without Roman consent. When Carthage succeeded in paying the indemnity levied against it, voices were raised in the Roman Senate warning against a revival of Carthaginian might and urging that Carthage be destroyed. Masinissa had in the meantime taken advantage of the restrictions placed on Carthage's war-making powers to invade its territory. When Carthage chose to defend itself, Rome declared war, charging a breach of the peace agreement. Carthage surrendered to a besieging Roman army in 146 B.C. Its population was dispersed, the city razed to the ground, and its earth sown with salt. Carthaginian territory was annexed by Rome and eventually organized as the province of Proconsular Africa, governed by a civilian official (proconsul) appointed annually by the Senate. Julius Caesar subsequently ordered the rebuilding of Carthage as a Roman city and the capital of the province. The royal house of Masinissa continued to rule Numidia as a Roman protectorate until 46 B.C., when Caesar deposed its king, who had sided with Pompey in the civil wars, and attached a part of it to Proconsular Africa (see fig. 3). For 400 years the province was peaceful and prosperous, part of a cosmopolitan world state whose citizens shared a common language, legal system, and Roman identity.

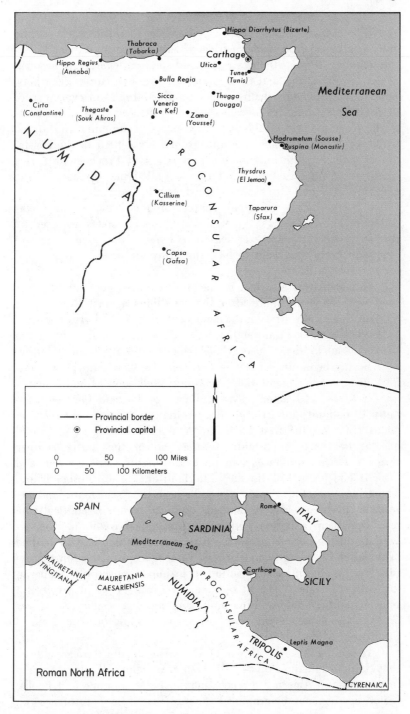

Figure 3. Proconsular Africa, Second Century A.D.

9

The Roman ruins seen in present-day Tunisia attest to the civic vitality of Proconsular Africa, where populous cities and even the smaller towns, their streets laid out in characteristic grid design, enjoyed the amenities of urban life—the forum, markets, public entertainments, baths, and fountains—found in every corner of the Roman Empire. Merchants and craftsmen from many parts of the Roman world established themselves in the cities and towns, while army veterans and migrants from Italy settled in the coastal countryside: but the bulk of the population of Proconsular Africa consisted of punicized Berber farmers. Called the "granary of the empire," Roman Africa was valued for its agricultural exports, which were Italy's principal source of food. Slave labor was common, but on the vast imperial domains and estates acquired by Roman aristocrats, land was leased to tenants who paid taxes and rent with grain that went to feed the army and provide free bread for the dole in Rome.

Roman Africa also had a substantial Jewish population. Many Jews were deported there after the rebellions against Roman rule in Palestine in the first and second centuries A.D., but others had come with earlier Punic settlers. Converts were made among the Berbers, and in some cases whole tribes may have been Judaized.

By the beginning of the second century, Christianity had been introduced among the Jewish community and soon gained converts in the towns and among slaves. Carthage became the center of Latin Christianity in Africa, and Tertullian, a convert born there in about 150, was the first Christian theologian writing in Latin and one of the most important. By the end of the fourth century Rome's African provinces had been thoroughly Christianized, and inroads had been made in the hinterland among the Berber tribes. The tribes sometimes converted en masse, but schismatic and heretical movements also developed, often as forms of political protest. Donatism, a heresy within the puritanical tradition, won adherents during periods of severe Roman persecution and flourished again after Christianity was officially recognized in the fourth century by the empire, in opposition to bishops accused of collaborating with the state. The sect became a vehicle for social revolt at a time of political deterioration and economic depression, and it was an example of the religious enthusiasm that would be seen again in the history of the Berbers.

It was against the threat of Donatism to the African church that Saint Augustine (354–430), bishop of Hippo Regius (Annaba in present-day Algeria), directed many of the sermons and books, including his autobiographical *Confessions*, whose influence on Christian thought has continued undiminished through the centuries. Born in Thegaste (Souk Ahras in present-day Algeria), Saint Augustine is recognized as one of the Latin Fathers of the Church. In *The City of God* he sought to demonstrate that the future of the church was not dependent on the survival of the Roman state (or, by extension, on any secular authority), as many contemporary Christians feared it was, and thereby to prepare his people for the onslaught of the Vandals.

Invited to North Africa by a rebellious Roman official, the Vandals, a Germanic tribe, crossed from Spain in 429, seized power, and under their war leader, Gaiseric, established a kingdom that made its capital at Carthage. Although the Roman Empire eventually recognized their overlordship in much of North Africa, the Vandals confined their rule to the most economically profitable areas in Proconsular Africa. There they constituted an isolated warrior caste, concerned with collecting taxes and exploiting the land. Civil administration was left in Roman hands, but the Vandals, who were Arian Christians, vigorously attempted to destroy Roman Catholic ecclesiastical influence. From their African base they conquered Sardinia and Corsica and launched raids on Italy, sacking the city of Rome in 455. In time, however, the Vandals lost much of their warlike spirit, and their kingdom fell to the armies of Belisarius, the Byzantine general who in 533 began the reconquest of North Africa for the Roman Empire.

Effective Byzantine control in the old Roman province was restricted to the coastal area, and even there the newly walled towns, strongholds, fortified farms, and watchtowers called attention to its tenuous nature. The region's prosperity had diminished under Vandal domination. Unpopular Byzantine governors imposed burdensome taxation, while towns and public services—including the water system—were left in decay. The old Roman political and social order, disrupted by the Vandals, could not be restored, but Byzantine rule in Africa did prolong the Roman ideal of imperial unity there for another century and a half and prevented the ascendancy of the Berber nomads in the coastal region. In outlying areas neglected by the Vandals, the inhabitants had sought the protection of tribal chieftains and, having grown accustomed to their autonomy, resisted reassimilation into the imperial system, but no coherent form of political organization evolved there to take the place of Roman authority.

Islam and the Arabs

By the time of his death in A.D. 632, the Prophet Muhammad and his followers had brought most of the tribes and towns of the Arabian Peninsula under the banner of the new monotheistic religion of Islam (literally, submission), which was conceived of as uniting the individual believer, the state, and the society under the omnipotent will of God. Islamic rulers therefore exercised both temporal and religious authority. Adherents of Islam were called Muslims ("those who submit" to the will of God).

Within a generation Arab armies had carried Islam north and east from Arabia in the wake of their rapid conquests and westward across North Africa as far as Tripoli. There, stiff Berber resistance slowed the Arab advance, and efforts at permanent conquest were resumed only when it became apparent that the Maghrib could be opened up as a theater of operations in the Muslim campaign against the Byzantine Empire. In 670 the Arabs surged into the Roman province of Africa (transliterated as Ifriquiya in Arabic), where their commander, Uqba ben Nafi, founded the city of Kairouan as a military base about 150 kilometers south of Byzantine-held Carthage. The selection of this encampment in the midst of a plain, separated from both the Roman cities on the coast and the mountains in Numidia, where the Berber tribes continued their stubborn resistance, was a deliberate act of policy by Uqba, who reportedly announced that he was founding a city that would serve "as a strong point for Islam until the end of time." The name chosen for the new Arab capital, derived from the Persian word *karwan* (caravan), also suggests that Uqba was aware of the commercial possibilities of the site located at a crossroads of the trade routes.

Carthage fell in 693, but the last pockets of Byzantine resistance on the North African coast were wiped out only after the Arabs had obtained naval supremacy in the Mediterranean. The Arabs cautiously probed the western Maghrib, and in 710 the governor of Ifriquiya, Musa ibn Nusair, invaded Morocco and carried their conquests to the Atlantic. In 712 they mounted an invasion of Spain and in three years had subdued all but the mountainous regions in the extreme north. Muslim Spain (called Andalusia) and the Maghrib, which had been conquered within 50 years of the founding of Kairouan, were organized under the political and religious leadership of the Umayyad caliph of Damascus.

Arab rule in Ifriquiya—as elsewhere in the Islamic world in the eighth century—had as its ideal the establishment of political and religious unity under a caliphate (the office of the Prophet's successor as supreme earthly leader of Islam) governed in accord with a legal system (sharia) administered by qadis (religious judges), to which all other considerations, including tribal loyalties, were subordinated. The sharia was based primarily on the Quran and the sayings of the Prophet and was derived in part from Arab tribal and market law.

Arab rule was easily imposed on the towns, which prospered again under their new patronage, and in the coastal farming areas. People in the former valued the security that permitted them to practice their commerce and trade in peace, while the punicized farmers recognized an affinity with the Arabs to whom they looked to protect their lands against the nomadic Berber tribesmen. The Arabs abhorred the tribal Berbers as barbarians, while the Berbers often saw the Arabs only as an arrogant and brutal soldiery bent on collecting taxes. Communal and representative Berber institutions also contrasted sharply and frequently clashed with the personal and authoritarian government that the Arabs had adopted under Byzantine influence.

The Arabs formed an urban elite in Ifriqiya, where they had come originally as conquerors and missionaries, not as colonists. Their armies had traveled without women and married among the indigenous population, transmitting Arab culture and Islamic religion over an extended period to the townsmen and farmers; but conversion to Islam was also rapid among the nomadic tribes of the hinterland that stoutly resisted Arab political domination. Many Berber converts were opportunists, however, and tribes that accepted Islam under Arab pressure often abandoned it once the intimidating Arab tax collectors and slave traders had moved on. Some tribes had records of repeated apostasy and reconversion. Once established as Muslims, however, the Berbers, with their characteristic love of independence and impassioned religious temperament, shaped Islam in their own image. They embraced schismatic Muslim sects—often traditional folk religion barely disguised as Islam—as a way of breaking from Arab control with the same enthusiasm that their Christian forebears had accepted Donatism in opposition to Rome.

The heretical Kharidjite movement surfaced in Morocco as a revolt against the Arabs in 739. The Berber Kharidjites (seceders; literally, those who emerge from impropriety) proclaimed their belief that any suitable Muslim candidate could be elected caliph without regard to his race, station or descent from the Prophet. Taking a position directly paralleling that of the Donatists, the Kharidjites maintained that a sinner could no longer be a believer because faith was not possible without purity, and they thereby regarded all other Muslims as heretics. The attack on the Arab monopoly of the religious leadership of Islam was explicit in Kharidjite doctrine, and Berbers across the Maghrib rose in revolt in the name of religion against Arab domination. Kairouan was sacked and its mosques desecrated. In the wake of revolt, Kharidjite sectarians established a number of theocratic tribal kingdoms, most of which had short and troubled histories. The rise of the Kharidjites in the Maghrib coincided with a period of turmoil in the Arab world during which the Abbasid dynasty overthrew the Umayyads and relocated the caliphate in Baghdad.

In the countryside the ulama (Islamic scholars and teachers) of the mosques were replaced as the spiritual guides of the people by wandering holy men (*al murabitun*), or "those who have made a religious retreat" (transliterated as marabouts). The marabouts were mystics and seers, miracle workers endowed with a charisma (*baraka*), whose tradition antedated Islam in the Maghrib and was as old as religion itself among the Berbers. They were incorporated into intensely local cults of saints whose domed tombs dotted the countryside and who were venerated by Muslims and Jews alike. The marabouts had traditionally acted as arbiters in tribal disputes, and, whenever the authority of government waned in a particular locale, the people turned to them for political leadership as well as for spiritual guidance. Maghribi Islam thus took shape as a coexisting blend of the scrupulous intellectualism of the ulama and the sometimes frenzied emotionalism of the masses. In general, however, Ifriquiya was not as susceptible to the heterodoxy that characterized popular Islamic practices farther west. Two factors account for this: first, Ifriquiya came more directly under the orthodox influence of the mosques and schools of Tunis and Kairouan, and, second, its larger urban and sedentary population had been more thoroughly arabized than was the case elsewhere in the Maghrib.

Aghlabids

After the Arab conquest, Ifriquiya was governed by a succession of amirs (commanders) who were subordinate to the caliph in Damascus and, after 750, in Baghdad. In 800 the caliph appointed as amir Ibrahim ibn Aghlab, who established a hereditary dynasty and ruled Ifriquiya as an autonomous state that was subject to the caliph's spiritual jurisdiction and nominally recognized him as its political suzerain. The ninth century has been described as the region's "golden age," from which it developed as a politically and culturally distinct entity within the Islamic world.

Ruins of the ancient Roman capitol at Dougga,
Tunisia's largest and best preserved archaeological site.
Courtesy Embassy of Tunisia, Washington

In 827 the reigning amir, Ziyat Allah, diverted the energies of the restless Arab military caste to Sicily, where rebellious subjects of the Byzantine emperor had invited Aghlabid intervention. The Arabs seized part of the island and conquered the rest piecemeal over the next 75 years. For a time they held Sardinia and gained a foothold in southern Italy as well, and in 846 Arab raiders plundered the suburbs of Rome and sacked the basilica of Saint Peter. The Aghlabids contested control of the central Mediterranean with the Byzantine Empire and played an active role in the internal politics of Italy (see fig. 4). Palermo, noted for its wealth and cosmopolitan culture as the capital of Aghlabid Sicily, was one of Europe's largest cities.

Meanwhile, in Ifriqiya the Aghlabid amirs repaired the neglected Roman irrigation system, rebuilding the country's prosperity and restoring the vitality of its cities and towns with the agricultural surplus that was produced. At the top of Ifriqiya's political and social hierarchy were the court, the military caste, and an Arab urban elite that included merchants, scholars, and government officials who had come to Kairouan and Tunis from many parts of the Islamic world. Members of the large Jewish communities that also resided in those cities held office under the amirs and engaged in commerce and the crafts. Converts to Islam often retained the positions of authority held traditionally by their families or class in Roman Africa; but a Christian community, speaking the provincial Latin dialect of Africa, lingered on in the towns until the twelfth century.

During the golden age Aghlabid patronage transformed Kairouan into the center of Maghribi religious and intellectual life. Kairouan was a great market for books in Arabic and Hebrew that had been copied by scribes. Its mosques and schools attracted pilgrims and scholars—Jewish and well as Muslim—from all parts of the Islamic world. So important was the reputation of Kairouan as a holy city that, according to custom, seven pilgrimages made there by a devout Muslim were the equivalent in merit of the required hajj (pilgrimage) to Mecca. The most outstanding cultural figure of the golden age was the poet-scholar Ibn Rachiq, renowned for his literary commentaries and historical works. His contemporary at Kairouan, Ibn Zeid, codified the Malikite branch of Islamic law that applied throughout the Maghrib, and more than 40 volumes on jurisprudence are attributed to him.

The Aghlabids established a tradition of intellectual excellence that survived the dynasty. In the tenth century Constantius Africanus, a Christian from Carthage knowledgeable in medicine, natural science, and astronomy, introduced Arab learning in those

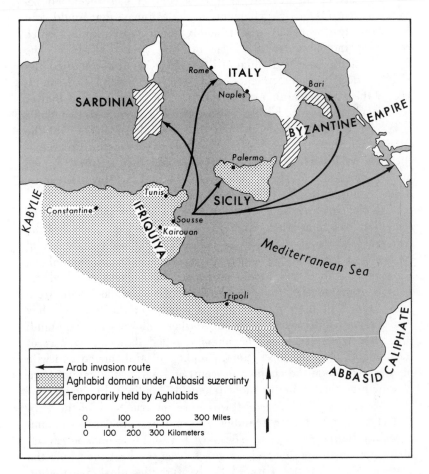

Figure 4. Aghlabid Domains, Ninth Century A.D.

fields to Europe from the Benedictine abbey of Monte Cassino in Italy, where he translated works of Arabic scholarship into Latin. It was primarily through Arabic texts that classical Greek learning in science and philosophy was transmitted to the scholars of Europe over the next two centuries. The tension and interplay between the Islamic and Christian worlds—most evident on the frontiers in Sicily and Spain, where the two cultures were in constant conflict—was a major stimulus for Europe's twelfth-century renaissance.

Fatimids

Already in the seventh century a conflict had developed between supporters of rival claimants to the caliphate that would split Islam into two branches—the orthodox Sunni and the Shia—which continued thereafter as the basic division among Muslims. The Shia (from the so-called Shiat Ali, or Party of Ali) supported the claim of the direct descendants of Ali, the fourth caliph and son-in-law of the Prophet Muhammad, whereas the Sunni favored that of Ali's rival, Muawiyah, leader of a collateral branch of Muhammad's tribe, the Quraysh of Mecca, and the principle of election of the fittest from the ranks of the *shurfa* (descendants of the Prophet—literally, nobles; sing., sharif). The Shia had their greatest appeal among non-Arab Muslims, who were scorned by the aristocratic desert Arabs.

In the closing decade of the ninth century, a missionary of the Ismaili sect of Shia Islam, Abu Abdullah al Hussein, converted the Kutama Berbers of the Kabylie region to that militant brand of Shiism and led them on a crusade against the Sunni Aghlabids. Kairouan fell in 909, and the next year the Kutama installed the Ismaili grand master from Syria, Ubaidalla Said, as imam (religious leader) of their movement and ruler over the territory they had conquered. Recognized by his Berber followers as the Mahdi (the divinely guided one), the imam founded the Shia dynasty of the Fatimids, (named for Fatima, daughter of Muhammad and wife of Ali, from whom he claimed descent) and moved the capital from Kairouan to a coastal stronghold renamed Mahdia in his honor.

Merchants of the coastal towns were the backbone of the Fatimid state that had been founded by religious enthusiasts and imposed by Berber tribesmen. The slow but steady economic revival of Europe created a demand for goods from the East for which the ports of Ifriquiya and Fatimid Sicily were the ideal distribution centers. Trading houses in Ifriquiya opened branches in Egypt, and their merchants, some of whom ventured as far as India in search of trade goods, won a reputation for their daring. The warehouses in the ports of Ifriquiya stored and shipped out grain, drugs, spices, lacquer, and dyes, as well as *susiyyat*, the cloth woven in Ifriquiya from Egyptian flax for export back to Egypt.

Fatimid rule was harsh and intolerant, persecuting the Sunni ulama of Kairouan and the Kharidjite sectarians alike. For many years the Fatimids threatened Morocco with invasion, but eventually they turned their armies eastward toward Egypt, where in the name of religion the Berbers took their revenge on the Arabs. The Fatimids completed the conquest of Egypt from the Abbasids by

969 and moved their capital to the new city that they founded at Cairo, where they established a Shia caliphate to rival that of the Sunni caliph at Baghdad.

The Fatimids left the Maghrib to their Berber vassals, the Zirids, but the Shia regime had already begun to crumble outside Ifriqiya as factions struggled indecisively for regional supremacy. The Zirids neglected the country's economy, except to pillage it for their personal gain. Agricultural production declined, and farmers and herdsmen took to brigandage. The depletion of the gold supply and the shifting of trade routes gradually depressed Ifriqiya's once thriving commerce. In an effort to hold the support of the urban Arabs, the Zirid amir, Al Moezz ibn Badis, defiantly rejected the Shia creed in 1049, broke with the Fatimids, and initiated a Berber return to Sunni orthodoxy.

In Cairo the Fatimid caliph invited beduin tribes from Arabia (known collectively as the Hilalians, who had ravaged Egypt for years) to migrate to the Maghrib and punish his rebellious vassals. The Arab nomads spread over the region, in the words of the historian Ibn Khaldun, like a "swarm of locusts," impoverishing it, destroying towns, and turning farmland into steppe. In 1057 they looted and destroyed Kairouan. Over a long period they displaced Berber farmers from their land and converted it to pasturage. Many Berbers, driven from their traditional lands, joined the Hilalians as nomads. The Hilalian impact on the Maghrib was devastating in both economic and demographic terms, altering the face and culture of the region and completing the arabization of Ifriqiya.

In the meantime, the Norman rulers of southern Italy took advantage of the Zirids' distress in North Africa to invade Sicily in 1060 and return it to Christian control. In 1134 Norman knights occupied the island of Jerba to use it as a base for attacks on the African mainland; by 1150 Roger II, Norman king of Sicily, held a string of ports and fortresses along the coast between Tunis and Tripoli and dominated the narrow straits of the central Mediterranean. Norman interests in North Africa, however, were essentially commercial rather than political, and no effort was made to extend their conquests inland.

Hafsids

The eleventh and twelfth centuries witnessed the rise in Morocco of two rival Berber tribal dynasties—the Almoravids and Almohads, both founded by religious reformers—that dominated the Maghrib and Muslim Spain for more than 200 years. The founder of the Almohad (literally, "one who proclaims" the oneness of God) movement was a Sunni *alim*, Ibn Tumart (d. 1130), who preached a doctrine of moral regeneration through the reaffirmation of monotheism. As judge and political leader as well as spiritual director, Ibn Tumart gave the Almohads a hierarchical and theocratic centralized government, respecting but transcending the old representative tribal structure. His successor, the sultan Abd al Mumin (1130–63), subdued Morocco, extended the Muslim frontier in Spain, and by 1160 had swept eastward across the Maghrib and forced the withdrawal of the Normans—with safe passage—from their strongholds in Ifriqiya, which he added to the Almohad empire.

Abd al Mumin proclaimed a caliphate at Cordova, giving the Almohad sultan supreme religious as well as political authority within his domains, but religious reform gradually gave way to dynastic politics as the motivating force behind the movement. The Almohads had succeeded in unifying the Maghrib, but as its empire grew and the Almohad power base shifted to Spain, the dynasty became more remote from the Berber tribes that had launched it. By 1270 the Almohads in Morocco had succumbed to tribal warfare and in Spain to the steady advance to Castile.

At the eastern end of the Almohad empire the sultan left an autonomous viceroy whose office became hereditary in the line of Mohamed ben Abu Hafs (1207–21), a descendant of one of Ibn Tumart's companions. With the demise of the Almohad dynasty in Morocco, the Hafsids adopted the titles of caliph and sultan and considered themselves the Almohads' legitimate successors, keeping alive the memory of Ibn Tumart and the ideal of Maghribi unity. Their dynasty survived in Tunisia—as Ifriqiya came to be known—until the sixteenth century.

The poet-prince Abu Zakariya al Hafs (1228–49) moved his captial from Kairouan, which had never recovered from its sacking by the Hilalians, to Tunis, which then became the cultural and political capital of the country. The Hafsids' political support and Tunisia's economy were rooted in the coastal towns, while the hinterland was effectively given up to the tribes that had made their nominal submission to Tunis. The Hafsid sultans encouraged trade with Europe, forged close links with Aragon and the Italian maritime states, and dispatched embassies as far afield as the court of King Haakon of Norway.

The Maghrib and Spain, linked under the Almohads, shared a common culture—called Moorish—that transcended dynastic lines and political boundaries in creating new and unique forms of art, literature, and architecture. Its influence spread eastward from

Spain as far as Tunisia, where the return of order and prosperity made possible a second flowering of Arab culture and scholarship. Under the Hafsids the school of the Zituna Mosque in Tunis was recognized as the leading center of Islamic learning in the Maghrib, but Hafsid Tunisia's culture was essentially a phenomenon of the court, dependent on the patronage of its sultans. One of the greatest intellectual figures of the Hafsid age was Ibn Khaldun (1332–1406), the historian and critic, who attempted to formulate historical laws to explain the rise and fall of dynasties in the Islamic world in his encyclopedic *Al Muqaddima*, (Prolegomena or "Introduction" to universal history), a work that remains an important source of information about early Maghribi history.

Despite commercial and diplomatic ties, Hafsid relations with the European powers eventually deteriorated. In 1270 Louis IX of France (Saint Louis) led the Eighth Crusade to Tunisia, where he died of the plague. The Aragonese intrigued in the dynasty's increasingly troubled and complex internal politics, backing rival claimants to the Hafsid throne. Marabout republics, tribal states, and the coastal enclaves seized by Andalusian and renegade Greek pirates defied the sultan's authority and by the fifteenth century had supplanted it in large parts of Tunisia. The Hafsids periodically attempted to revive the dynasty's fortunes, only to exhaust their resources in the effort; but during the Hafsid era, spanning more than 300 years, Tunisia acquired a distinctive character and defined its place within the Islamic world.

Ottoman Regency

Piracy lured adventurers from around the Mediterranean to the Maghribi coastal cities and islands. Among them were two brothers, Aruj and Khair al Din, the latter known as Barbarossa (Redbeard) to Europeans. Muslims from the Greek island of Lesbos, they reached Tunisia in 1504 and sailed from Jerba Island under Hafsid patronage. In 1510, however, the brothers were invited by the maritime republic of Algiers to defend it against the Spaniards. Instead they seized Algiers and used it as a base of operations not only for piracy but also for conquests in the interior. Khair al Din subsequently recognized the suzerainty of the Ottoman sultan over the territory that he controlled and was in turn appointed the sultan's regent in the Maghrib, bearing the title beylerbey (commander in chief). He was forced to abandon Algiers temporarily (1519–25) to the Hafsids, who resisted Ottoman penetration in the Maghrib, but with Turkish troops Khair al Din was able to consolidate his position in the central Maghrib and in 1534 mounted a successful seaborne assault on Tunis.

The Hafsid sultan, Hassan, took refuge in Spain, where he sought the aid of the Habsburg king-emperor, Charles V, to restore him to his throne. Spanish troops and ships recaptured Tunis in 1535 and reinstalled Hassan. Protected by a large Spanish garrison at La Goulette, the harbor of Tunis, the Hafsids became the Muslim ally of Catholic Spain in its struggle with the Turks for supremacy in the Mediterranean, making Tunisia and the waters around it the stage for repeated conflict between the two great powers.

In 1569 a Turkish force operating out of Algiers retook Tunis, only to lose it again in 1573 to Don Juan of Austria. The next year, however, the Turks returned with a large armada and 40,000 troops, compelling the Spanish garrison to abandon Tunis. The last of the Hafsids was carried off to Constantinople, and Tunisia became a province of the Ottoman Empire, governed by the beylerbey in Algiers, with Turkish as the language of administration.

Pashas, Deys, and Beys

In 1587 the Ottoman Maghrib was divided into three regencies—at Algiers, Tunis, and Tripoli. In Tunisia the authority of the beylerbey as regent gave way to that of a pasha (governor) appointed by the sultan for a one-year term. The regency was provided with a corps of janissaries, recruited from Anatolian peasants who were committed to a lifetime of service in Tunisia. The corps numbered 4,000 infantrymen and was organized into 40 companies, each commanded by a junior officer with the rank of dey (literally, maternal uncle). It formed a self-governing military guild, subject to its own laws, whose interests were protected by the Divan, a council of senior officers. Real power came to rest with the army, and the pasha's role was reduced to that of ceremonial head of state and figurehead representative of Ottoman suzerainty.

While the mission of the janissaries in Tunisia was to maintain order and collect taxes, the Barbary corsairs supplied the regency's treasury with a steady income from piracy and waged war at sea against Spain. Piracy was a highly disciplined business, calculated as an extension of overall Turkish naval strategy in the Mediterranean. Operations were conducted by the *raïs* (pirate captains), who preyed on shipping and raided the European coasts of the western Mediterranean to capture and carry away hostages to be held for ransom or as merchandise for the slave markets of North Africa. The *raïs*—many of them European renegades who had apostatized and become "Turks by profession"—were banded together in a self-regulating *taifa* (guild) to further the corporate interests of their trade and to counter the influence of the Turkish military garrison in the affairs of the regency.

Mutinies and coups were frequent, and generally the janissaries were loyal to whomever paid and fed them most regularly. In 1591 the deys staged a successful coup against their superior officers in the divan and forced the pasha, acting as regent for the sultan, to appoint their chosen leader as head of government—in which capacity he continued to bear the title of dey. The deys, their Turkish infantry reinforced by spahis (locally recruited cavalry), were secure in their control of the cities and the coastal region but relied on a civilian official, the bey, to oversee the government of the tribes and to collect taxes in the hinterland with his private army of Tunisian auxiliaries. Such was the strength in the countryside of one of these officials, the Corsican renegade Murad Bey (d. 1631), that he secured a hereditary title for his family both to the beylicate and also to the office of pasha. The political history of seventeenth-century Tunisia thus became one of the struggle between the dey, backed by the janissaries and the Turkish bureaucracy, and the bey-pasha, who increasingly came to be identified with the interests of the old Arab elite for control of the apparatus of government.

After 1666 the bey-pasha dictated the choice of the dey and gradually relieved him of his duties as head of government. The beylicate, in the meantime, had established itself as the representative of order and stability against tribal anarchy and military indiscipline. Tunisian naval units were dispatched to reinforce the Turkish navy in time of war, and the sultan as caliph was recognized as the spiritual leader of Islam; but, although it remained nominally part of the Ottoman Empire, Tunisia had in fact become an autonomous state governed by a hereditary ruling house.

By the late seventeenth century, trade had become a more important source of income than piracy. Commercial agreements were entered into with European trading partners, particularly France, and concessions for the development of trade were granted to foreign interests. Tunisia imported finished manufactured goods in exchange for a variety of commodities—grain, olive oil, dates, hides, textiles, and sponges. Tunisian hatters enjoyed a monopoly on the sale of the shashiya, the red fez worn throughout the Ottoman world, which they made of Spanish wool imported by Jewish merchants in Tunis.

Husseinids

Continually troubled by the truculence of the janissaries and beset by unrest in the tribal areas, Tunisia in the seventeenth and eighteenth centuries was also threatened by armed intervention from Algiers, whose dey claimed hegemony over the other autonomous Ottoman regencies in the Maghrib. In 1702 a janissary officer, Ibrahim al Sharif, murdered the bey-pasha, Murad III, together with his family, and seized control of the government in Tunis, but his regime was short-lived. Janissaries from Algeria invaded Tunisia in 1705 on the pretext of restoring legitimate government and took Ibrahim prisoner. Hussein ben Ali, an officer of Greek origin who had organized the defense of Tunis against the Algerian janissaries, assumed the title of bey with the army's backing and subsequently secured the sultan's appointment as pasha. Hussein then defied the dey of Algiers, who plotted to reinstate Ibrahim in Tunis as his puppet, and named a member of his own family to succeed him as bey-pasha. A move by the Porte (Ottoman government) to install a regent in Tunis of its own picking when Hussein died in 1715 was thwarted when religious and military leaders rallied behind the Husseinid Dynasty and the concept of Tunisian autonomy it represented.

The bey-pasha was an absolute monarch who directed the government in Tunis with the aid of a small cabinet. It was clear that he governed Tunisia for, and in the name of, the Turkish elite, who with officials recruited from the class of Mamluks (literally, slaves; non-Turkish subjects of the sultan conscripted for life into the service of the Ottoman Empire), to which Hussein belonged, monopolized positions of authority in the central government. After Hussein, title to the beylicate remained within the ruling house according to a system by which the Husseinid prince regarded best qualified to rule was designated heir apparent during the lifetime of the reigning bey. The choice of a successor was determined by the janissary officer corps, whose periodic coups in support of one or another rival Husseinid claimant were routinely legitimized in decrees issued by the Porte. A relatively strong ruler like Ali Bey (1759–82) assured the stability of his regime by acceding to the demands of the janissaries, but he also courted Arab support to counterbalance their power. Increasingly, the dynasty's policies came to reflect concern for the interests of the Arab urban elite in Tunis and the towns of the north and the Sahil.

Local government devolved on about 60 qaids (governors), appointed by the bey from Arab notables. Working beneath the qaids were approximately 2,000 sheikhs who were responsible for collecting taxes and maintaining order in tribal areas and provincial towns with the aid of Arab spahis put at the qaïd's disposal. At the end of the eighteenth century, however, tribal leaders commanding the loyalty of more than one-third of the bey's subjects in the highlands, steppes, and far south acted quite independently of his government's authority. Neglected as a fighting force, the army refrained from venturing into these areas to collect taxes; as state finances deteriorated, the beylicate was forced to look abroad for loans.

Whatever internal problems may have afflicted the Husseinid regime, European travelers reported that the Tunisians were the "most civilized people who inhabit the coast of the Mediterranean," superior in their politics and culture to the Algerians and given to commerce rather than to piracy. Although piracy was discouraged by the Husseinids, corsairs armed and sheltered in Tunisian ports continued to threaten trade and the security of seamen, and European maritime powers regularly paid tribute to the bey of Tunis and rulers of the other Barbary States (Morocco, Algiers, and Tripoli) to purchase immunity from attacks on their shipping. American merchant ships, no longer covered by British protection, were seized by Barbary pirates in the years that followed United States independence, and American crews were enslaved in North Africa. In 1800 the United States ratified a treaty with the bey, guaranteeing him payment of tribute in return for a promise that Tunisian-based corsairs would not molest American shipping. In 1805, however, a Tunisian mission visited Washington to modify the treaty, and the annual tribute was eliminated in return for a trade agreement. An Anglo-French fleet imposed acceptance of a protocol on Tunisia in 1818 that prohibited further arming of corsairs and the enslavement of Christians.

Ahmed Bey

The French occupation of neighboring Algeria in 1830, displacing the Ottoman regency there, was not a cause for alarm in Tunisia. It was considered a temporary measure and for a time held out the promise that Husseinid princes would be called on to rule in Oran and Constantine. French annexation of Algeria four years later, coupled with the reassertion of Turkish sovereignty in Tripoli in 1837, discouraged Tunisian optimism, however. The overriding concern of Ahmed Bey (1837–55) was to avoid giving an excuse for foreign intervention in Tunisia. Slavery was completely abolished and privateering suppressed in response to European objections, while steps were taken to put the beylicate's sovereignty and Tunisian autonomy beyond challenge.

The key to nationbuilding was the modernization of Tunisian institutions. Reformism, however, was an elite movement, totally lacking in popular support. Lacking as well the resources to finance reform or the machinery to manage it, the political elite had no clear idea of what its goals ought to be. Without considerable success, administration was strengthened in an effort to bring all areas of the country under the control of the government in Tunis and to provide a more efficient tax collection system.

Building a modern army was seen as an appropriate and realizable starting point for the reform movement. A military academy was established at the beylical palace at Bardo to provide officers, still predominantly of Turkish background, for a 26,000-man army that was intended to stand as a symbol of Tunisia's sovereignty. The new army was modeled on the recently re-organized Turkish army and was trained by French officers. The bey's government took out large loans from French banks to pay for the military buildup.

Ahmed Bey's mentor was his prime minister and treasurer, Mustafa Khaznader, who survived the bey and served continuously as head of the Tunisian government from 1837 to 1873. A Greek by origin, he had been carried off as a small child from Khios by the Turks when they ravaged that island during the Greek war for independence. Raised as a Muslim, Mustafa Khaznader had been Ahmed Bey's companion since their boyhood together and encouraged his master in debilitating debauchery. Occupying a position of trust in the beylicate, Khaznader was an embezzler on a large scale who ultimately led Tunisia into bankruptcy and opened the door for French economic and political penetration. Encouraged by the French, he promoted an ambitious public works program and accumulated an immense personal fortune by arranging loans to pay for it at exorbitant rates of interest in collusion with French banking houses.

Despite the bolstered armed forces and reformed administration that his regime offered as evidence of its modernity, Ahmed Bey's fear that Tunisia would be swallowed up by France or Turkey dictated the content of his foreign policy. The greater the threat from France was perceived to be, the closer Tunisia drew toward its nominal suzerain, the Ottoman sultan. The more persistent Turkey's pressure on Tunisia for formal recognition of the sultan's suzerainty, the more avidly French support was cultivated.

Foreign policy was an issue that divided Turkish and Arab elites within the reform movement. France encouraged Tunisia's assertion of its independence from the Ottoman Empire, a policy favored by the Turks in Tunis because it assured the continuance of the bey's authoritarian regime and their privileged position with it. During the same period, however, Britain backed the formal restoration of Ottoman sovereignty in Tunisia. Committed to propping up the Ottoman Empire as a barrier against Russian expansion, the British not only guaranteed its territorial integrity but also looked for opportunities to draw parts of the diffuse empire toward Constantinople and away from the influence of other European powers. Tunisia's Arab elite preferred the British approach, believing that the connection with a reformed and revitalized Ottoman Empire would promote internal reform in their own country that would extend to them greater participation in government.

Ahmed Bey pawned the family jewels to send 4,000 Tunisian troops to the Crimean War (1854–56) and to become in one stroke an ally of all the contenders for influence in his country. Tunisia was represented at the peace conference in Paris, where the Ottoman Empire agreed to further constitutional and legal reforms proposed by its European allies, Britain and France, whose consuls in Tunis picked up the theme by recommending extension of similar reforms to Tunisia "so as to be"—in the words of the British consul—"as modern as Turkey." Tunisian reformers were receptive and saw in suggestions for the constitutional restructuring of the government a means for achieving rapid modernization and economic development. Unquestionably, however, the immediate purpose of the European consuls in proposing specific legal reforms was to make it easier for European commercial interests to function in a country where Islamic codes prohibited equal application of the law to non-Muslims engaged in business there. In this divergence of interests lay the essential contradiction in the reform movement. For the Tunisian elite, reform was necessary to maintain the country's independence. But reform and modernization also led inevitably to greater European participation in Tunisia's political and economic affairs.

Constitution of 1861

In 1857 Ahmed Bey's successor, Mohamed Bey (1855–59), issued the so-called Fundamental Pact, which spelled out the principles regulating relations between the bey and his subjects and foreigners residing in Tunisia. The document, dictated to the beylicate by the French consul in Tunis, also allowed foreigners to own property in Tunisia and guaranteed them equal protection under the law.

The Fundamental Pact paved the way for the appointment of Kherredin Pasha, a Circassian Mamluk with long service in Tunisia and the son-in-law of Mustafa Khaznader, to draw up a constitution. Promulgated by Mohamed al Sadok Bey (1859–73) in 1861, it was the first written constitution in the Islamic world. Prefaced by a declaration of rights, the constitution of 1861 provided for a limited and hereditary monarchy in which the bey served as head of state and the government was headed by the prime minister of the bey's cabinet. The government was not directly reponsible to the bey, however, but to the newly established Supreme Council, consisting of 60 members chosen on a rotating basis by the bey. The Supreme Council initiated legislation, approved tax measures, supervised the military establishment, and appointed public officials. Kherredin, author of the constitution, was chosen to be the body's first president. In what was a major innovation for a Muslim country, the constitution of 1861 also created the secular Supreme Court, empowered to review decisions of the sharia courts.

The constitutional reforms responded to the demand of an urban elite whose political and economic interests they clearly favored, but they held less appeal for the rest of Tunisia. The introduction of constitutional government was associated in the popular mind with new and burdensome taxes, including levies on date and olive trees, that were more efficiently collected than in the past by qaids, appointed by the Supreme Council, who were often strangers in their jurisdictions. Opponents of the constitution also objected to concessions granted by the government to European companies to operate public services. Despite constitutional restraints imposed on the executive power of the beylicate, Kherredin resigned his office in frustration over the Supreme Council's inability to check the excesses of Mustafa Khaznader.

The most serious criticism of the constitutional government came from provincial notables and tribal chiefs—the traditional leadership in the countryside—who recognized the constitution of 1861 for what it was intended to be, an attack on local and tribal autonomy that from the standpoint of the reformers was essential for the creation of a modern nation-state. Regional interests were therefore set in opposition to the influence of Tunis and the Sahil, where reform and the foreign investment it encouraged had been welcomed. Opponents of the constitution appealed over the bey to the Ottoman sultan for relief. Rising popular resentment was capped by a serious tribal rebellion that forced the suspension of the constitution in 1864. Although Tunisia's experiment with constitutional government had failed for want of deep-rooted popular support, the modern nationalist movement was premised on the demand for the restoration of the constitution in 1861.

Kherredin

Mustafa Khaznader's policies and the corruption of his government had by 1864 plunged Tunisia into an economic crisis. When money became scarce, new currency was issued that was so devalued that foreign traders refused to accept it as a medium of exchange. Devaluation depressed the export price of Tunisian grain and at the same time made it impossible for Tunisian buyers to import necessities. These difficulties were compounded by bad harvests, famine, and plague, which afflicted the country in 1867 and for several years thereafter. By 1868 Tunisia was bankrupt, and the government was unable to meet its financial commitments abroad. That same year, the bey agreed to the establishment of the International Financial Commission (IFC) in Tunis, whose members included French, British, and Italian controllers charged with reorganizing Tunisia's finances to ensure payment of the country's existing debt and to curb further expenditures. Kherredin served as the Tunisian representative on the commission.

In 1871 Tunisia reaffirmed the suzerainty of the Ottoman sultan, thereby obtaining a British guarantee of its territorial integrity. Control of foreign relations was surrendered to the Porte. Although the IFC retained jurisdiction over economic affairs, absolute authority over all other internal matters was left to the bey and his ministers. Mustafa Khaznader was finally removed in 1873 from the office that he had held for over 36 years and was succeeded as prime minister by his son-in-law and long-time political rival, Kherredin.

Kherredin had begun his career in Tunisia as a soldier and, after rising rapidly in the beylicate's administration, was entrusted with diplomatic missions abroad. He was already a leader of the reform movement when chosen to draw up the constitution and, after its suspension, wrote a learned treatise dealing with the question of political and social reform in Muslim states. Positive in his expectations of what could be achieved, Kherredin was also realistic in his aims for Tunisia.

As prime minister, Kherredin faced the problem of satisfying the European powers represented on the IFC, while working to preserve Tunisia's independence and, although he was a modernizer, the Muslim character of its society. Like Ahmed Bey, he was concerned with maintaining the army as a symbol of sovereignty, but he also saw the practical need for overhauling the bureaucracy. Perhaps the outstanding achievement of his regime was the founding of the Sadiki College, a secondary school with a modern curriculum intended to train candidates for the civil service.

Cooperating closely with the IFC, Kherredin introduced fiscal reforms that markedly improved Tunisia's financial position, but European opposition stymied other essential reforms. Tunisia's export trade in grain was locked into the European market system and was monopolized by French and Italian merchants. Land exploitation by foreigners, allowed after 1857, was capital-intensive rather than labor-intensive and had led to the eviction of peasants from their farmsteads, resulting in severe rural unemployment. Kherredin's efforts at agrarian reform to correct the situation drew him into conflict with entrenched European landowning interests.

Having spent his life as a professional servant of the state dependent on the bey's patronage, Kherredin was without a political base of his own in the country. As a reforming prime minister he met with opposition from the followers of Mustafa Khaznader, whom he had deprived of office, and from traditionalists who had marked him as the candidate of the Europeans. Kherredin had indeed been given a mandate by the European powers to make Tunisia safer for foreign investment, but when he appeared to be succeeding all too well in modernizing the country's political and economic structure, they cooled toward his regime and finally withdrew support. Under French pressure, Kherredin was dismissed from office in 1877 and replaced by Mustafa ben Ismail, a French puppet who compounded corruption with incompetence in office.

Kherredin was called to Constantinople, where he was made grand vizier to the Ottoman sultan, Abd al Hamid. It is one of the ironies of the history of Tunisia that a Circassian Mamluk came to be regarded as the father of Tunisian nationalism.

The French Protectorate

At the Congress of Berlin in 1878, Britain agreed to allow France a "free hand" in Tunisia in exchange for French acquiescence to the leasehold on Cyprus that the British had acquired from Turkey. It was accepted among the European powers that France planned to occupy Tunisia, but no excuse for French intervention presented itself until April 1881, when a punitive expedition was launched into Tunisian territory, ostensibly in pursuit of

Khumiri tribesmen who had raided across the border into Algeria. The considerable force of more than 40,000 men—which the French explained was necessary to avoid undue bloodshed—was more effectively used in overawing the Tunisian government, however, than it was in hunting down nomadic tribesmen. French cavalry advanced on Tunis while seaborne units landed in Bizerte and occupied the port, considered potentially the best naval base in North Africa but far from Khumiri country.

As French troops were poised near the capital, the French representative in Tunis confronted the bey at the Bardo Palace with a treaty, a draft of which reportedly had lain for years in the files of the French Foreign Ministry, that sanctioned the temporary military occupation of strategic points in Tunisia to put an end to disorders there. Theoretically, Tunisian sovereignty was left unimpaired, although a resident minister was posted to Tunis to represent France and to advise the bey. Sadok Bey signed the Bardo Treaty on the condition that French troops not enter the city.

Long-range French political and economic interests in Tunisia went well beyond the momentary question of frontier security. Sadok Bey's tilt toward Italy had given substance to French alarm at Italian claims to a sphere of influence in Tunisia that were based both on geography and on the presence of a well-established colony of Italian settlers in the country. The French action was understood, therefore, as preemptive intervention. In the economic sphere the French argued that Tunisia was a backward and impoverished country incapable of coping with its indebtedness.

Once the Khumiri had submitted, most of the French forces were promptly withdrawn, leaving behind only small garrisons to enforce the treaty's provisions. No sooner had the French pullout begun, however, than the bey, influenced by Mustafa ben Ismail, disavowed the treaty on the grounds that he had signed it under duress. In the belief that a show of force would bring Turkish aid, the Tunisians attacked the French garrisons. Reacting swiftly, the French invaded Tunisia for the second time in a matter of weeks, occupied Tunis, and subjected Sfax to a naval bombardment. By the end of October resistance in the north had been crushed, and in November Gabès fell to the French. In the south, however, Ali ben Khalifa, a tribal chieftain assisted by the Turks in Tripoli, held out through the winter of 1882–83. In June 1883 a humiliated Ali Bey (1882–1900) agreed to the Al Marsa Convention, which confirmed Tunisian acceptance of the Bardo Treaty and added provisions whereby "in order to facilitate to the French Government the exercise of its *protectorate* His Highness the Bey of Tunis engages to make such administrative, judicial, and financial reforms as the French Government considers useful."

Under the protectorate Tunisia was governed according to a system of dual sovereignties in which the de facto sovereignty of France was superimposed on the de jure sovereignty of the beylicate. Tunisia remained what it had been for 300 years, the "Regency of Tunis." The preexisting form of beylical government was maintained intact, and the established political elite continued to function within it. Although the elite readily assimilated French values, Tunisian society retained its own social standards and a tradition of higher culture that were the core of the country's sense of nationhood. The demographic impact of the protectorate was not severe in Tunisia, where European corporate development of the land rather than European settlement remained the rule.

The protectorate succeeded where Tunisian reformers had not in modernizing administration and providing Tunisia with a government that could collect taxes efficiently, ensure the rule of law applied throughout the country, and stimulate the growth of a modern economic and social service infrastructure. Fiscal affairs were rigorously supervised, and gradually Tunisia achieved financial stability and even prosperity. Railroads, port facilities, hospitals, schools, and sanitation works were constructed under French direction. Corporate investment from France created a modern agricultural sector, specializing in olive and grape production, that turned Tunisia once again into a net exporter of foodstuffs. Tunisia's phosphate reserves were exploited and ancillary industries developed.

The standard for French administration in Tunisia was set early by Pierre Paul Cambon, resident minister from 1882 to 1885, then resident general until 1886. Cambon, who distinguished himself as a diplomat later in his career, pressed for the formal declaration of a protectorate after the breakdown of the Bardo Treaty and is credited with drafting the Al Marsa Convention, in which the term *protectorate* was used for the first time to describe the relationship between Tunisia and France. An ardent republican suspicious of the military, Cambon firmly established civilian control over the protectorate. On his recommendation, Tunisia's foreign debt was consolidated in a single 125 million franc loan from France, which eliminated the need for the multinational IFC and, with it, direct British and Italian influence on Tunisia's financial affairs.

Cambon, more than most of his successors, was scrupulous in observing the legal prerogatives of the bey as a sovereign monarch who had contracted with France to develop his country's administrative institutions and economy. He was conscious that France had definite reponsibilities in Tunisia beyond colonial aggrandizement. Despite the acknowledged contributions made by France in Tunisia after 1881, however, it must be recognized that they were accomplished primarily for the benefit of France—or, more specifically, to protect French investment in Tunisia—and that Europeans, not Tunisians, were the primary beneficiaries of Tunisia's economic development under the protectorate. An economic infrastructure was built that served the French markets to which Tunisian production was tied and bore little relation to the basic needs of the traditional sector of the economy to which the majority of Tunisians were restricted. Tunisian tax revenues paid for government-sponsored projects that improved transportation, marketing facilities, and utilities, but the income generated by these expenditures ultimately accrued to a handful of French-owned companies and large landowners and to French building contractors.

Administration of the Protectorate

After the Al Marsa Convention the bey continued to appoint a cabinet, but its members were named on the advice of the resident general, whose approval was required to validate every action taken by the beylical government. The resident general, who was responsible directly to the French foreign minister, was ex officio foreign minister in the Tunisian government, and his control over its foreign affairs was unquestioned. He was both the political representative of the French Republic in Tunisia and the protectorate's chief administrative officer, assisted in that task by a council of ministers composed of the bey's prime minister and two other Tunisian cabinet officers, as well as by 10 to 12 French department heads seconded for service in the Tunisian government. Although the bey was legally the source of all authority, the resident general, who was usually given considerable latitude by Paris in determining policy, exercised the beylical authority through a highly centralized administration operated by a staff of French bureaucrats whose influence stretched from the bey's palace to the lowest level of local government. After 1896 the Consultative Conference, a body composed of Tunisian delegates appointed by the resident general and representatives elected by French residents, was impaneled to advise the resident general on a broad range of topics, but it did not have the power either to introduce measures or to question executive actions. French legislation did not apply in

Tunisia, although laws enacted in France were often introduced by beylical decrees.

Reformed local government followed recognizably traditional patterns but was made more systematic and became uniform in its organization in most parts of the country (see fig. 5). Five regions (provinces) were created (Tunis, Bizerte, Kef, Sousse, and Sfax) and were administered by French regional chiefs. The regions were subdivided into 19 districts, each under a French civil controller. These were further divided into the traditional qaidats and, in the countryside, shaykhats. Special status was given to 59 municipal communes that provided local government for the cities and larger towns in each district. In the south the so-called military territories came under the jurisdiction of French army area commanders, whose mission it was to keep the peace in the sparsely settled hinterland as well as to defend the ill-defined border with Turkish-controlled (and, after 1911, Italian-controlled) Tripolitania.

The functions of the qaids and shaykhs under the protectorate were unchanged—to collect taxes and maintain order in the countryside. A native gendarmerie served under the orders of the qaids, who worked closely with French police superintendents. Appointed by the bey on the recommendation of the resident general, the qaids and shaykhs were intended to be an important link between the French authorities and the rural population. French policy favored these secular officers over the ulama and the qadis, who had been indifferent, when not openly hostile, to the reform movement. Although drawn from the traditional leadership in the countryside, the shaykhs were increasingly resented as being agents of the French and became alienated from the people whom they governed.

The Tunisian court system, like the central administration and local government, was reformed and then operated under French tutelage. Sharia courts administered law affecting the personal status of Tunisians in such areas as marriage and inheritance, but, through usage, principles of the French legal code were gradually imposed on Islamic law. Laws of property in particular were modified in this manner. Decisions of the sharia courts affecting Europeans were automatically subject to review by civil magistrates, and all criminal cases were reserved for French courts. Appeals from both the sharia courts and the French courts in Tunisia were made in the first instance to the Court of Appeal in Algiers and ultimately to the Court of Cassation (French superior court of appeal) in Paris.

Before World War I the French army routinely stationed about 25,000 men, including units of the Foreign Legion, in Tuni-

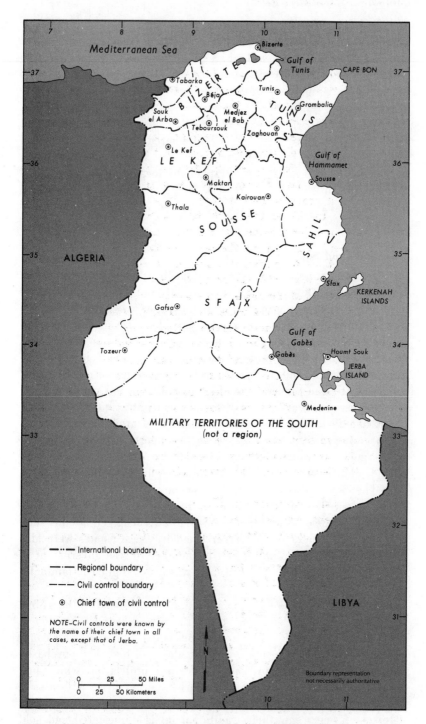

Figure 5. Tunisia under the French Protectorate, 1881–1956

sia. Tunisians as well as all French citizens resident in Tunisia were subject to French military service, although in practice few Tunisians were called because volunteers were so plentiful. Tunisian infantry regiments—*tirailleurs* (riflemen)—and mounted spahis served under French officers as part of the regular French army in Tunisia and in various parts of the French colonial empire. The bey's own French-trained "army" numbered only about 600 men and was employed for ceremonial purposes. Bizerte was developed as a major French naval base strategically located at the narrows of the Mediterranean. Observers testified that possession of Bizerte alone would have made the Tunisian protectorate worthwhile.

Economic and Social Development

Traditional patterns of landholding in Tunisia were collective. No individual title existed for *arch* (tribal land), which was considered the inalienable property of the tribe as a whole. It did not have definite boundaries but might expand in size or shift location as the needs of the tribe, the climate, or the condition of the land changed. Under other kinds of tenure, more common in the north and in the Sahil, land was the collective possession of a family or a village. Extended use was proof of ownership, and continued use was necessary to retain it. In the mid-nineteenth century, however, about one-third of Tunisia's most productive farmland, concentrated in grain-growing areas, was *habus*—property held in perpetuity by religious institutions as endowments to maintain mosques and shrines and to support public welfare and religious education.

The bey derived part of his income from beylical or crown lands, extensive tracts acquired over the years by conquest and confiscation that, according to Muslim law, belonged to the state and passed by right to whomever ruled it. Large estates were also assigned to Turkish families and to members of the government in clientage from the bey. Beylical land was also assigned to landholders on long-term leases.

As the government's financial situation worsened in the 1850s and 1860s, beylical land was sold for ready cash and converted to freehold. The growth of a class of peasant proprietors who could operate above the subsistence level on the land that they purchased was paralleled by the increase of a rural proletariat, which had been disposed of the land confiscated by the bey to be put on sale. In 1859 sale of land to Europeans was made legal. In some cases Tunisian farmers saw their traditional lands sequestered and sold to French-owned companies whose managers in turn hired them as laborers.

The famine and cholera epidemic that struck Tunisia in 1868 hit hardest in the most populous and productive areas. The countryside lay empty where fields had been abandoned and villages deserted. The population in marginal areas reverted to nomadism, while others fled the country. The demographic impact was devastating: Tunisia's population, estimated at 1.6 million in 1867, stood at only 900,000 in 1881 and showed no marked growth as late as 1890.

French buyers took advantage of Tunisia's distress and the beylicate's bankruptcy to acquire land abandoned during the plague years, including them in the growing European-operated modern agricultural sector that specialized in olive and grape production for export. As a result of investment by French-owned companies, France had established its economic domination over Tunisia years before the protectorate imposed political control as well.

French law recognized only individual ownership of a property, a practice that was at variance with Tunisian traditions of collective holdings. Because so much Tunisian land could not be alienated from its collective ownership under Muslim law, a legal framework was constructed through which European landowners could ensure their title to property that they had acquired. In 1885 the beylicate published a decree requiring registration of titles to land. An application for a title was then advertised. If it was not claimed by another party within a given period, the applicant received undisputed title to the property in question. Challenges to an application were considered by a mixed tribunal of Tunisian and French magistrates. The latter formed the majority on the tribunal, which usually decided in favor of European applicants. Tunisians also took advantage of the new law, however, to lay claim to tribal and other collectively held land.

By 1892 more than one-fifth of Tunisia's arable land, concentrated in the north, was French owned, but 90 percent of it was in the hands of only 16 landowners and companies engaged in capital-intensive agriculture. Less than 10 percent of the French residents were engaged in farming. In 1897 a fund was established to pay the cost of settling French colons (colonists), and the next year the beylicate allowed *habus* land to be put on the market. But, despite inducements offered by the French government and by private colonization societies in France, there was no rush of colons to Tunisia as there had been to Algeria.

More than 10,000 Italians lived in Tunisia in 1881 as compared with fewer than 4,000 French residents, and they remained the largest ethnic group within the European community throughout the period of the protectorate. By 1901 the size of the European community had increased to approximately 130,000, of which two-thirds was Italian and among which were included a large number of Maltese. The Europeans were occupationally differentiated: the Italians, mostly Sicilians, were blue-collar workers, public utilities workers, or small farmers. The Maltese, who were British subjects, were the proverbial shopkeepers. Tunisians rubbed shoulders constantly with these Europeans, confronted them in the marketplace, and competed with them for jobs. Shut out from the social and economic advantages that were reserved for French citizens, the Italians were held in contempt by both the Tunisians and the French. Except for members of the elite, Tunisians seldom had contact with the French—the administrators, supervisors, managers, and owners—and even the elite did not meet them on a social level.

Traditional education in Tunisia was highly developed before 1881, and the school of the Zituna Mosque in Tunis was recognized as one of the leading centers of classical Islamic studies. Under the protectorate the French residency continued to emphasize education, patronizing the Zituna Mosque school and the Muslim schools as well as Kherredin's Sadiki College. The latter was accredited as a lycée and set the standard for a bilingual, bicultural school system, offering instruction to a mixed student body, that was extended throughout the country. Many Tunisian graduates of these schools went on to complete their education in France. Within a generation a class of well-educated, gallicized Tunisians—the *évolués* (literally, the evolved ones)—had been created that formed a new social elite among their countrymen. Strongly influenced by French culture and political attitudes—and particularly attracted by a Cartesian, or rationalistic, inquiry, which was alien to the Islamic tradition—they nonetheless became the core of a highly motivated nationalist movement.

Rise of Nationalism

Tunisian nationalism was elitist in its origins and was rooted in the schools rather than in a popular mass movement. After 1881 Kherredin's disciples at the Sadiki College continued their emphasis on political and economic modernization, which could be accomplished under French auspices, they urged, without Tunisians either approving the protectorate or openly attacking France. The nationalists in the schools initially reacted to the particular form of the protectorate that excluded Tunisians from full participation in their own government, but they stopped short of advocating a break with France. Ali Bash Hambak, an intellectual leader of graduates of the Sadiki College, argued for the selective adoption of Western scientific rationalism not only for political reform but for reinvigorating Tunisia's Arabic and Islamic culture as well. In 1896, however, Bashir Sfar, a member of Hambak's circle, broke with him and established the revivalist Khalduniya Institute, named in honor of Ibn Khaldun, which was dedicated to restricting the influence of French culture and restoring traditional Arab-Islamic culture in its pure form. Both Hambak's group from the bilingual Sadiki College and Sfar's followers at the Khalduniya Institute were eventually associated with the embryonic nationalist movement, providing it with public platforms and with an influx of articulate converts. Subsidized by the French residency, as were other Islamic institutions, the Khalduniya Institute undertook to give instruction in modern subjects to graduates of the Zituna Mosque school to enable them to compete for positions in the civil service and to enter the professions.

In 1908 the Hambak and Sfar factions reunited to form a nationalist political organization, the Young Tunisians. They were a small group, interested in efficiency rather than representative government, whose newspaper, *Le Tunisien*, was aimed at convincing liberal French readers that the Tunisian elite was capable of taking over a greater share of responsibility for the country's management. Proud of their education and accomplishments, their liberal politics, and their competence in French, they were conscious of their distinct Tunisian nationality. But popular feeling responded to bread-and-butter issues. To broaden their appeal, the Young Tunisians became involved in a labor dispute in 1912 that focused on obtaining jobs for Tunisians in the public transportation system reserved for Italians. Implicated in the rioting that resulted, the Young Tunisians were disbanded, and many of their leaders were sent into exile. Despite growing discontent with the protectorate and residual pro-Turkish feeling, more than 60,000 Tunisians served in the French army during World War I, and many more tens of thousands were recruited for work in France.

Postwar Tunisian nationalism drew its inspiration as much from the French liberal thought imbibed at the schools as from the pan-Arab movement and the native traditions of Kherredin. Nationalist activists gravitated toward the Destour (literally, Constitution) Party, founded in 1920 by Abdelaziz al Thalibi, a graduate of the Zituna Mosque school who had been one of the leaders of the Young Tunisians exiled in 1912. Typically, they came from the traditional elite—Turks from Tunis, civil servants, businessmen, merchants, and professionals—who were social conservatives and economic liberals. The Destour Party, from the start, was consciously urban and middle class in its orientation, standing aloof from working-class movements and holding few ties to the countryside. Although the nationalist movement was also Muslim in character, it met with the antipathy of the ulama as well as with the court party around the bey. The French made the error of overrating the party's importance, attempting to link it at one time with the Communists, and thereby contributed to Thalibi's prestige as a nationalist leader.

Although Thalibi denounced the protectorate, he did not propose severing Tunisia's links with France completely but advocated a formal association between the two sovereign states. In collaboration with Ahmed Saqqa, he wrote *La Tunisie martyre*, a book published in Paris in 1921 that served as the party's manifesto. It was the seminal work of Tunisian nationalist political literature. Thalibi held that there was a viable Tunisian state, capable of modernization under its own constitution, before the French occupation and that France, whose political ideals were admired, had betrayed its own liberal values in depriving Tunisia of its independence. He looked to the Fundamental Pact and the constitution of 1861 as the basis of which Tunisian independence could be restored.

The Destourian reform program was gradualist, and, in order to reassure the French, Thalibi reiterated that the party was not revolutionary in its aims. In fact, time and events caused the Destourians to modify Kherredin's constitution. They called for a deliberative assembly composed of both Tunisian and European representatives elected by universal suffrage. The bey's government was to be responsible to the assembly, which would have complete control over finances. Basic freedoms were to be guaranteed, and education was to be compulsory within a bilingual school system. More immediately, the Destourians, whose constituency included many civil servants, demanded appointment of Tunisians to the government positions that they were capable of filling and "equal pay for equal work" with their French colleagues.

The French residency used both the carrot and the stick in its response to the demands of the Destour Party. Minor reforms were quickly instituted to pacify Tunisian sentiment, and the Ministry of Justice was opened to Tunisian applicants; but repressive measures were taken against the most outspoken of the nationalists, and restrictions were imposed on political activities. Nasir Bey (1906–

22), provoked by the French crackdown, threatened to abdicate in solidarity with the nationalists. In 1922 the residency acquiesced further in the formation of the Grand Council, which replaced the Consultative Conference and gave Tunisians a greater voice in government, together with local councils that duplicated its work at the regional level.

Hardly comparable to the legislature envisioned by the Destourians, the Grand Council was composed of two sections—one Tunisian, elected indirectly through the regional councils, and the other European, whose delegates were elected directly or took their seats as representatives of the Chamber of Commerce. Voting by section rather than by individual delegates ensured the preponderance of the European section. To become effective, actions recommended by the Grand Council had to be ratified by the resident general, who also cast the deciding vote in case of split decisions. A mixed committee from the Grand Council was also selected to join the cabinet in its deliberations. The resident general prepared the budget in consultation with the Grand Council, but the government was in no way responsible to it for its actions.

The reform package, intended by the French to mollify nationalist sentiment and to disarm support for the Destour Party, was capped in 1923 by an offer to grant French citizenship to Tunisians who qualified by education or service. The nationalists, as well as members of the bey's entourage and religious leaders, were incensed at the insensitivity of the proposal, which was recognized as an infringement of Tunisian sovereignty. To become French citizens, Muslims in Tunisia were required to accept the full jurisdiction of the French legal code, including laws affecting personal status, and to reject the competence of the religious courts. Because of the unitary nature of Islam, this meant, in effect, that a Muslim had to renounce his religion. Few Tunisians applied for French citizenship, and those who did—for the most part *évolués* who were part of the French administration—were ostracized by the Muslim community at large.

The palliative offered by minimal reform failed to stall the nationalist movement. The Destourians' demand for implementation of their full constitutional program increased in intensity during the late 1920s and early 1930s. The economic depression, which fell heavily on Tunisia, served as a catalyst for politcal activism. Although it had been nonviolent in its origins, the party now took Tunisian discontent into the streets. The residency was harried by strikes and by demonstrations that were put down with severity by the French police. In 1933 the resident general ordered the disbanding of the Destour Party.

Leadership of the nationalist movement was already passing to a new generation of French-educated Tunisians, more at ease in French than in Arabic, who crystallized ideas of national identity and populism, which the old leadership had been unable and unwilling to do, and who adopted tactics that emphasized constant activism and violent resistance to the protectorate. Younger members of the Destour Party had argued that nationalism, to be effective against the French, had to break loose from its traditional power base among the urban elite and mobilize mass support. Among the more impatient of the party activists were Mahmoud Materi, Tahar Sfar, and a lawyer named Habib Bourguiba. They came from the Sahil, an area less affected by European landholdings than the north, more North African in character, and less cosmopolitan than Tunis. But they were more Westernized than the older Destourian leaders and lacked their strong religious sympathies. All had been educated at the Sadiki College and in France, where they had been profoundly influenced by the ideas of the intellectual left. In 1934 Bourguiba and his colleagues formed the Neo-Destour Party and called in the pages of their newspaper, *La Voix du Tunisien*, for responsible constitutional government. Like the old Destourians, they advocated the creation of a legislature representing Tunisians and Europeans on an equal basis and an end to the protectorate. Although supporting the beylicate as a necessary expedient during the hoped-for transition to independence, they looked forward to the establishment of a Tunisian republic.

Support for the Neo-Destour Party came from artisans, shopkeepers, and peasant proprietors, who in the midst of the depression of the 1930s were more interested in maintaining their standard of living than in expelling French, as well as from students and members of the professional class who had backed the old Destourians. The new party's cadres were highly disciplined and organized in cells throughout the country. Working relations were formed with student, labor, and agricultural organizations. French authorities and the colons were terrified by the appeal and effectiveness of the new nationalist party, and its organizers, including Bourguiba, were arrested and jailed. But the Neo-Destour Party cells continued to function underground and to recruit new members.

The victory of the Popular Front in France in 1936 and the formation of a left-wing government under Léon Blum held out hope to the Tunisian nationalists, who redoubled agitation for political and economic reforms and abolition of the despised citizenship law. Released from prison, Bourguiba resumed leadership of the Neo-Destour Party. Faced with opposition within the nationalist movement from a revived moderate Destour Party, Bourguiba's party became more radical, promoting labor unrest, work stoppages, and demonstrations through the summer of 1937. Blum's government fell after 15 months in power, having achieved little in the way of reaching a settlement in Tunisia, except to have aroused nationalist anticipation of reform. The colons, who had become increasingly defensive as they saw their privileged position threatened, petitioned the new government in Paris to take effective action against the nationalist demonstrations. On April 9, 1938—commemorated in Tunisia as Martyrs' Day—122 Tunisians were killed in nationalist-inspired rioting. The nationalist parties were outlawed once again, and Bourguiba was arrested.

France and Italy

The "Tunisian question" had remained alive as an issue in Italy after 1881. Although Italy reluctantly acquiesced to the French occupation of Tunisia, a country that it also coveted, Italian public figures periodically gave voice to a lingering resentment of France for having "cheated" them of Tunisia. Complaints by Italian settlers against the French administration were a continuing irritant in relations between France and Italy, but Italians retained a special position in Tunisia, operating a separate school system sponsored by the Italian government. Italy's occupation of Libya in 1911 gave it a common colonial border with the French in Tunisia. France and Italy were allies in World War I, but relations steadily deteriorated after the rise of Benito Mussolini's fascist regime in Italy in 1922. Italian settlers in Tunisia came to be viewed as a potential security threat.

Legislation in 1921 provided that all Europeans born after that date in Tunisia would automatically have French nationality. Protests were lodged by both Italy and Britain against compulsory naturalization, which would entail liability for conscription, and in 1923 the British put the matter before the Permanent Court of International Justice in The Hague. The court found that Tunisian-born children of British subjects—the Maltese—would be entitled to reject French nationality, although that right could not be applied to succeeding generations. Some Italians, made uneasy by the rise of fascism in their homeland, voluntarily sought and received French citizenship, however. As a result, the 1924–25 period marked the point at which for the first time French citizens accounted for more than half of the European community in Tunisia, numbering nearly 200,000. Italians were also under economic pressure to become French citizens, which made them eligible for better pay—particularly in public utilities, where many of them were employed.

In 1935 Mussolini, who was anxious to ensure French noninvolvement in his Ethiopian campaign, agreed to a treaty proposed by French premier Pierre Laval that would have gradually rescinded the special legal status of Italians in Tunisia and phased out their autonomous school system. The treaty also determined that after a 30-year transitional period, all Tunisian-born offspring of Italian parents would become French citizens. It is doubtful if Mussolini, who at that time already had reason to anticipate a radical alteration of the balance of power in Europe, considered these concessions to be permanently binding.

While on tour in Libya two years later, Mussolini proclaimed himself the "Sword of Islam" and offered Italy as the protector of Muslims under French and British rule. Italy became more reckless in putting forward its claim to Tunisia—as well as in citing its irredentist aspirations for Corsica and Nice—and in 1938 openly denounced the French protectorate. Frightened at the prospect of an Italian invasion, Tunisians rallied behind France as Europe moved toward war, and they demonstrated their support on the occasion of French premier Edouard Daladier's visit to Tunis in January 1939.

World War II

After the fall of France in June 1940, Tunisia's border with Libya and the large naval base at Bizerte were demilitarized. Tunisian ports and airfields were used, however, to give logistical support to Axis forces in Libya. The French colons were generally sympathetic to the Vichy regime, and Mussolini's Fascists had for years been building areas of support in the Italian community. Shortly after the French surrender, a pro-Vichy naval officer was appointed resident general in Tunis and given broad responsibilities for defense.

Allied landings in Algeria and Morocco in November 1942, code-named Operation Torch, had as an objective the speedy occupation of Tunisia, with the cooperation of French authorities and armed forces there. Admiral Jean Darlan, the French high commissioner in North Africa, who had initially offered resistance to the landings, ordered a cease-fire when word reached him that the Germans had moved into Vichy-controlled France, and he surrendered Algiers to Allied commander Lieutenant General Dwight D. Eisenhower. In Tunis the resident general hesitated to act on Darlan's orders and awaited confirmation from Vichy. His delay allowed quick-moving German forces to relieve the French garrisons and occupy key positions in Tunisia ahead of the Allies.

American airborne units took Gafsa in mid-November, but Allied attempts to mount a concentrated drive on Tunis before German reinforcements could be introduced failed. Allied air and naval power cut off supplies to the Axis forces by sea, but between December 1942 and March 1943 more than 40,000 German and Italian troops were ferried by air from Sicily to Tunisia. Supported at one point during the campaign by an estimated one-quarter of the total German tactical air force, 'they held nine American, British, and Free French divisions along a line that stretched from the north coast down the spine of the Eastern Dorsale to the desert, while 14 divisions of General (later Field Marshal) Erwin Rommel's Afrika Korps retreated westward across Libya and into Tunisia before the advancing British Eighth Army (see fig. 6).

In January Rommel hurled an armored attack at the untried United States II Corps and broke through at the strategic Kasserine Pass, throwing Allied forces to his rear offbalance while the Afrika Korps prepared to defend the Mareth Line in the south. The Mareth Line was a 35-kilometer-long defense system constructed by the French before the war against the threat of an Italian invasion. When frontal assaults against the Axis positions were turned back, Eighth Army commander Bernard Montgomery sent the New Zealand Division on a wide end run around the German defenses, attacking through the narrow defile at Djebel Tebaga and compelling General Jürgen von Armin, who had succeeded the ailing Rommel in command of the Afrika Korps, to abandon the Mareth Line in March. Early in April, units of II Corps advancing from the west linked up with the Eighth Army at the Wadi al Akarit. Von Armin's skillful withdrawal, however, saved the bulk of his army to take up the defense of Tunis along a new line at Enfidaville. The Enfidaville front held firm, but at the end of April the Allies opened an offensive from the west. On May 7 the British took Tunis and II Corps entered Bizerte, trapping tens of thousands of Axis troops between their pincers. Meanwhile, a British sweep through Cape Bon cut off the remaining Germans and Italians facing the Eighth Army at Enfidaville. Axis resistance in Tunisia ceased on May 13, and the North African phase of the war was brought to a close. Fewer than 700 of the 250,000 German and Italian troops engaged in the battle of Tunisia escaped death or capture. Control of air bases in Tunisia and the naval facility at

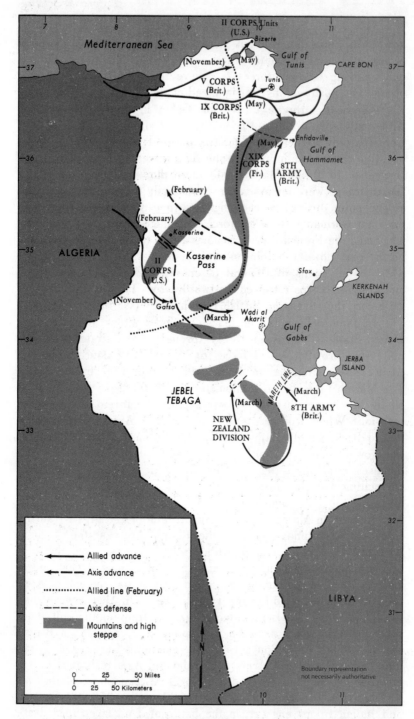

Figure 6. The Battle for Tunisia, November 1942 to May 1943

Bizerte was crucial to the success of the subsequent Allied invasion of Sicily and the mainland of Italy.

Bourguiba's Tunisia

When it was dissolved for the second time in 1938, the Neo-Destour Party had an active membership of approximately 100,000. Its underground activities were directed after Bourguiba's imprisonment by an executive committee, the Political Bureau. Some nationalists at the lower level of party echelons urged support for Germany in 1939, contending that "the enemy of my enemy is my friend," but their enthusiasm for the Axis waned when Italy, which had annexationist designs on Tunisia, entered the war shortly before the fall of France. More significant, Bourguiba had spoken from prison in favor of cooperation with France from the outset of the war. He continued to oppose collaboration after the French defeat in 1940, when he was transferred to a more secure prison facility in Marseilles by the Vichy regime. The Germans freed Bourguiba after the Allied landings in North Africa, lionized him and other nationalist leaders in Rome, where they were brought for talks, and then repatriated him to Axis-occupied Tunisia.

Bourguiba anticipated the Allied victory in the European war and swung his support behind the Free French. An instinctive liberal, he expressed confidence that "the whole of France, once liberated from the Nazi yoke, would not forget . . . her true friends, those who stood by her in the days of trial." Once the Free French were established in Tunisia, Bourguiba, together with Musif Bey (1926–43), proposed a gradual evolution toward internal autonomy for the country. Ignored by French authorities, Bourguiba appealed to the British and Americans to bring influence to bear on Free French leader Charles de Gaulle to grant political reform in Tunisia. Through the United States consul in Tunis, Hooker Doolittle, who had advocated United States support for Tunisian independence, Bourguiba made direct contact with President Franklin D. Roosevelt. Late in 1943 Musif Bey was deposed by the French on the pretext that he had collaborated with the enemy. Fearing that similar charges would be leveled against him, Bourguiba spent the years until 1950 pleading the case of Tunisian independence in Europe, the Middle East, and the United States.

Agitation for political reform continued to mount in Bourguiba's absence as Tahar Ben Ammar, moderate president of the Tunisian section of the Grand Council, joined a group of 80 "notables" to petition the French government for internal autonomy. In 1946 an autonomous trade union, the General Union of Tunisian Workers (Union Général des Travailleurs Tunisiens—UGTT), backed by the American Federation of Labor (AFL), broke away from the communist-dominated French labor organization. Led by a onetime trolley driver, Ferhat Hached, the UGTT cooperated closely with the Neo-Destour Party in efforts to redefine Tunisia's relationship with France.

Toward Independence

In 1950 Prime Minister Mohamed Shanniq formed a new government, one that for the first time since the Al Marsa Convention had a Tunisian majority in the cabinet. Salah Ben Youssef, the Neo-Destour secretary general, joined the government as minister of justice, but it was Bourguiba who went to Paris to lay before the French government a program for independence that included provisions to create a national legislature and emphasized demands for civil rights. The Tunisian proposal also insisted on maintaining cultural, economic, and military ties with France. The French government refused out of hand to give up direct participation by French officials in the Tunisian government, but Foreign Minister Maurice Schuman confirmed that a newly appointed resident general "had been given the task of leading Tunisia to independence."

The residency offered only minor reforms, all of them eventually rejected by the nationalists. Terrorist groups directed attacks against French authorities and colons, who in turn formed counterterrorist vigilante units. The residency retaliated with a crackdown on all nationalists, including moderates as well as those extremists who had engaged in terrorist activities. In January 1952 the French demanded that Al Amin Bey (1943–57) dismiss Shanniq as prime minister and, when the bey refused to comply, arrested Bourguiba, Shanniq, and most of his ministers. Ben Youssef, however, escaped the French net and fled to Egypt, where he fell increasingly under the influence of the pan-Arab nationalism of Gamal Abdul Nasser. In exile, Ben Youssef became a vocal exponent of violent revolution.

The arrests intensified nationalist bitterness toward the protectorate and produced two years of terrorist violence, rioting, and strikes. The UGTT's Hached, a voice of moderation, was murdered by colon vigilantes, who thereby cut off a valuable channel for dialogue between the nationalists and the residency. Meanwhile, France's ability to cope with the growing unrest was compromised

by its own political instability that had brought down five governments in two years and had left the country without a government
for more than three months during that period. Tunisia, however,
was a minor concern in Paris when compared with the debacle in
Indochina in the spring of 1954.

Early in 1954 Bourguiba was released from prison to negotiate with French premier Pierre Mendès-France. The nationalists
and the French government were still deadlocked between Tunisian
demands for full independence and the French plan, which called
for internal autonomy despite vigorous objections from the colons.
But Bourguiba showed a willingness to accept what France was
prepared to offer while pressing for further concessions. In July
Mendès-France, who had just concluded the dismantling of the
French colonial empire in Indochina, flew to Tunis and issued the
dramatic Declaration of Carthage, which recognized Tunisia's internal autonomy. The French preferred to have leaders of the old
Destour Party guide the new semi-independent country, but continuing violence persuaded them to bring in Bourguiba, who made
it clear that he accepted autonomy only as the first step toward full
independence. Although he functioned as the power behind the
new government, he refused to take part in it formally while the
French presence remained.

The next major step toward the fulfillment of Bourguiba's
demand for full independence came in June 1955, when French
premier Edgar Faure and Tunisian premier Tahar Ben Ammar
signed a series of agreements in Paris. The six agreements covered
internal administration, status of residents, judicial reform, administrative and technical cooperation, cultural relations, and economic
and financial relations. The most significant aspect of the agreements was the abrogation of Article I of the Al Marsa Convention
of 1883, which gave the French resident general control over internal government. However, the Bardo Treaty of 1881, by which
France obtained responsibility for Tunisia's foreign affairs and defense, remained in force.

Bourguiba endorsed the agreements as part of his pragmatic
strategy for achieving independence with measured steps, but Ben
Youssef, a close collaborator for many years, broke with him on
the issue. Ben Youssef, who had returned to Tunisia, and the left-
wing faction supporting him held out for immediate independence
and contested Bourguiba's leadership of the Neo-Destour Party.
When the party congress backed Bourguiba's gradualist policy, Ben
Youssef returned to Cairo to lead an opposition movement from
exile. Guerrilla units loyal to him conducted military operations
against both the French and the new Tunisian government.

The agreements, as they affected relations between the bey as monarch and the French government, required certain changes in Tunisia's governmental structure. By decree in September 1955, Al Amin Bey reaffirmed his absolute power but agreed to accept the advice of his prime minister, who was the president of the Council of Ministers (cabinet). While legislative and executive power remained formally in the hands of the bey, in effect the decree required the bey to have the approval of the full Council of Ministers before issuing a law. It also authorized elections for a constituent assembly and gave that assembly the right to establish the form of government that it chose for Tunisia.

The bey, aware of the threat to the monarch posed by a popularly elected assembly that was likely to be republican in its sympathies, was pressured into signing the decree for the Constituent Assembly by Bourguiba, who threatened to expose the bey's request that the French remain in Tunisia. Shortly thereafter the bey ratified Bourguiba's electoral law, which provided for voting for party lists rather than for individual candidates. The law meant that party headquarters would select the candidates and that party lists would sweep the elections, although some effort was made to represent other interests in the assembly by consultation with labor, professional, and farmer organizations and by formation of the so-called National Front.

Independent Tunisia

An agreement between France and Morocco early in 1956 indicated that Morocco, which had been a French protectorate since 1912, would soon gain complete independence, and it was hoped that the forthcoming election of the Constituent Assembly would provide a means for pressing Tunisia's case for independence. On March 20, 1956, the patience of the Neo-Destour Party leaders was rewarded by the signing of a protocol that abrogated the Bardo Treaty of 1881 and recognized Tunisia as an independent state. The portfolios of the two ministries vacated by French officials—foreign affairs and defense—were taken by Bourguiba.

With independence the Neo-Destour Party, which had been jarred by the dissent from Ben Youssef's faction, faced the problem of consolidating its leadership and replacing the struggle for national independence with the building of national consensus as the party's primary goal. Expelled from the party for his opposition to Bourguiba, Ben Youssef organized a leftist opposition party that continued the guerrilla war against the Neo-Destour government.

The crisis ended only when a French military operation forced the Youssefists to lay down their arms in June, three months after independence. Ben Youssef, who had earlier been condemned to death in absentia for having plotted against Bourguiba's life, was assassinated in Frankfurt in 1961.

On March 25, 1956, some 84 percent of the registered voters went to the polls to elect candidates of the National Front, who were for the most part members of the Neo-Destour Party, to the Constituent Assembly. Bourguiba was elected president of the assembly by acclamation at its first session held two weeks later, and Ahmed Ben Salah was elected vice president. The assembly then divided its 98 members into a number of committees, each charged with drafting a part of the new constitution. Within a week Article I had been unanimously adopted. It declared Tunisia to be a free, independent, sovereign state, with Islam its official religion and Arabic its official language. On April 15 the bey called on Bourguiba to form the new government.

Independence and the election of the Constituent Assembly left the constitutional base of the Tunisian government as it had been at the time of the decree of September 1955: The bey promulgated laws as decrees with the unanimous consent of his Council of Ministers. The Western-educated leaders of the Neo-Destour Party were instinctive republicans who had little affection for the beylicate, and they were far from satisfied with this arrangement. The aged Al Amin Bey himself did not command much respect. He had increasingly withdrawn from public activity as the nationalists took charge of Tunisian politics after the 1955 conventions so that he counted little as a political force, and the ostentatious living of members of his family further detracted from his reputation. In July 1957 the Constituent Assembly, which had authority to determine the form of government, unanimously voted to depose the bey and abolish the monarchy, declaring Tunisia a republic. Bourguiba was named president of the republic and given the bey's full executive and legislative powers as head of state until the assembly could produce a constitution.

During the two years of his provisional presidency, Bourguiba promulgated by executive decree a number of far-reaching reforms that fulfilled—and went beyond—the promises made by the Neo-Destour Party before independence. The Party had been a secular nationalist movement, and, although it had not rejected traditional Islam, its program had not invited the participation of religious leaders. Once in power Bourguiba set about to eliminate religious regulations and customs that were considered "obsolete" in a modern country. Religious courts were abolished, even though this

President Habib Bourguiba,
Tunisia's Supreme Combatant
Courtesy Embassy of Tunisia,
Washington

meant the forced retirement of many socially prominent judges. Laws governing marriage and the status of women were revised, giving Tunisian women legal rights comparable to those pertaining in France. At a later date, abortion and birth control were legalized. The Zituna Mosque school was absorbed into the new University of Tunis, which was to be the showplace of Tunisia's modernization. The *habus* system of landholding was abolished and agrarian reform instituted. A personal status law required all births and deaths to be registered and required each Tunisian national to adopt a surname, a rationalization that even the French had not proposed, thus reducing the confusion of names common in traditional Arab society. In his zeal for reform, however, Bourguiba occasionally appeared to overstep the bounds of propriety in a Muslim society. He was compelled by popular resistance, for instance, to relax his public effort to push a 1961 recommendation that Tunisians abandon fasting during Ramadan, a practice that is one of the traditional five pillars of Islam.

Meanwhile, the Constituent Assembly committees had revised the draft of the constitution along lines that would make Tunisia a presidential republic. The crisis generated by the French bombardment of Algerian rebel positions inside Tunisia in 1958 interrupted plenary discussions in the assembly, providing Bourguiba with the necessary time to consolidate his power and shape an answer to the crucial constitutional question—that of the relationship between the executive powers of the president and the legislative powers of the new National Assembly. When the Constitution was finally promulgated on June 1, 1959, its most striking feature was the strong position accorded the president of the republic, an office that critics charged had been tailored expressly for Bourguiba.

Relations with France

In spite of its many links with the West, independent Tunisia was fundamentally nonaligned in its foreign policy. Tunisia attached great importance to its membership in the United Nations (UN). Although it sought to increase economic cooperation in the Maghrib and was a member of the League of Arab States (Arab League), the Bourguiba regime was intensely suspicious of appeals for Arab unity and avoided a close identification with regional blocs. After independence Tunisia retained its closest ties with France.

More than 3,000 French officials remained behind in Tunisia to assist in the transition to independence. French nationals were sent to give technical assistance and to staff schools and medical facilities. The French armed forces retained bases in Tunisia, and the status of French-owned businesses and property remained unchanged.

Despite his working relationship with France, Bourguiba simultaneously lent his support to Algerian nationalists whose war of liberation had broken out only a few months after Tunisia was granted its independence. The Algerian government-in-exile had headquarters in Tunis, and about 25,000 Algerian rebel troops were based in sanctuaries inside Tunisia. Tens of thousands of Algerian refugees fled to Tunisia to escape the war. In 1957 France halted economic assistance and arms deliveries to Tunisia, and the French army constructed a heavily patrolled system of electrified barbed-wire fences—known as the Morice Line—along the Algerian border with Tunisia to discourage infiltration from Tunisian sanctuaries.

In February 1958 French aircraft bombed the Tunisian border town of Saqiyat Sidi Youssef, which the Algerians reportedly used as a base of operations. The popular reaction to the incident among Tunisians was intense, and French troops in Tunisia were confined to their bases. Tensions were eased a few months later after de Gaulle came to power in France, and the two governments agreed in June that French troops would be withdrawn gradually from all areas except the base at Bizerte.

For a time, French-Tunisian relations ran smoothly, despite the continuing war in Algeria. In 1959 the customs union between the two countries was abolished, but Tunisia was allowed preferential tariffs and remained in the Franc Zone. Tunisia also pursued associated status in the European Economic Community (EEC) with French backing. Over the objections of the Algerian nationalists, Tunisia allowed a French-owned pipeline to be constructed across the country to transport Algerian oil. In early 1961 Bourguiba met with de Gaulle in France to discuss a variety of topics, including Algeria and the status of Bizerte.

As French-Algerian negotiations moved toward acceptance of Algerian independence, however, Bourguiba apparently became concerned that Tunisia would be charged with softness for having allowed French forces to remain on its territory during the hostilities. He took the occasion of a French move to extend the runways of the military airfield at Bizerte to call for complete French withdrawal. Popular demonstrations were staged throughout the country to echo his demand, and a number of French nationals were arrested. Then, in July 1961, Tunisian irregulars attacked the base at Bizerte and fired on French aircraft. Reinforcements were flown in, and the French launched a counterattack that threw back the Tunisians, leaving about 1,000 of them dead. In the meantime, Tunisian "volunteers" had moved against the French post at Garet al Hamel in the Algerian Sahara, 15 kilometers south of Tunisia's extreme southern limits, intending to extend the country's claims in that region.

The French-Tunisian dispute was submitted to a special session of the UN General Assembly, which in August adopted a resolution recognizing Tunisia's right to demand the French withdrawal from Bizerte and called on France and Tunisia to enter immediately into negotiations. France refused to participate in the General Assembly debate; however, later in 1962 talks began on all outstanding questions troubling relations between the two countries. The atmosphere was eased by a voluntary French undertaking, completed in October 1963, to evacuate Bizerte. Negotiations led to an agreement that permitted the takeover of French-owned land with compensation from Tunisia and a guarantee for the protection of French citizens resident in Tunisia and of French investments there. France, in turn, consented to a large loan to finance Tunisian development.

Unexpectedly, however, on the next anniversary of the Bardo Treaty (May 12, 1964), Bourguiba, standing before the table on which that treaty had been signed in 1881, announced that henceforward lands usable for farming could be held only by physical persons, i.e., not companies or corporations, of Tunisian nationality. This new law affected approximately 275,000 hectares owned by French nationals, including much of the best farmland in the country, which was nationalized without indemnity. Its enactment set off an exodus of Europeans, many of whom had been born in Tunisia. The French government reacted promptly by canceling the development loan, suspending technical assistance, and subjecting Tunisian imports to strict quotas. Only gradually were relations normalized and close French-Tunisian ties restored.

Destourian Socialism: Tunisia in the 1960s

A motion was introduced at the 1955 party congress supporting the principle of economic planning, without identifying the form it was to take. The next year, however, Ben Salah, speaking as head of the UGTT, formally advocated centralized state economic planning as the basic approach for Tunisia's development effort. Bourguiba promptly rejected the idea, perhaps on the grounds that he would have to delegate too much authority to the planning agency that it envisioned, and Ben Salah was forced from the union leadership. Despite Bourguiba's opposition to centralized planning, the issue remained the subject of debate within party circles.

The economic sluggishness of the late 1950s convinced many in the party and the government of the need for long-term planning on pragmatic grounds. By 1960 the UGTT had revived its campaign for centralized state economic planning. Proponents of the scheme eventually succeeded in persuading Bourguiba that state planning offered a solution to the country's outstanding problems, and on the basis of the president's decision an entirely new course was set for its economic development. In January 1961 Ben Salah was appointed to the government as minister of state in charge of the newly created planning department. Later in the year Bourguiba formally introduced "Destourian socialism," announcing that the state would assume an interventionist role in economic affairs. Ben Salah's concept of socialism, however, proved to be much more comprehensive and far-reaching than that outlined by the president.

In the months that followed his appointment, Ben Salah increased the areas of economic activity subject to centralized planning, and as the influence of his ministry expanded, his political power became second only to that of Bourguiba.

Ben Salah's rise to prominence coincided with the apparent decline of the Neo-Destour Party's influence as a mass movement. Popular support for the regime was grounded on Bourguiba's immense personal prestige rather than on the guidance of the party. Meanwhile, within the party itself the president's handling of the Bizerte crisis had caused some important figures to question his judgment and leadership. Consequently, Bourguiba came to lean on Ben Salah for support and reassurance, and Ben Salah in turn infused the party with what passed for a dynamic ideology. Bourguiba's reliance on him increased after a plot to assassinate the president was uncovered in 1962. Youssefists and Communists were implicated in the plot, leading to the proscription of the Tunisian Communist Party (Parti Communiste Tunisien—PCT) and the discrediting of the political opposition on Ben Salah's left. By the mid-1960s Ben Salah was widely spoken of as the ailing Bourguiba's obvious successor.

Ben Salah's planning goals anticipated augmented state control of the economy and the elimination of all foreign participation. The process of economic "decolonization" included isolating the country not only from foreign investments but also from imports. Under the planning scheme, agriculture was regarded as the priority sector and was expected to satisfy the bulk of domestic food demand. Raw material exports, led by phosphates, would be relied on to earn foreign exchange for reinvestment in development. Although discouraging foreign investment, Tunisia sought and received grants and loans from multilateral sources for development projects from the United States and other countries as well as unilateral aid that financed programs in education, health care, energy, irrigation, and transportation.

From its inception, Ben Salah's brand of centralized planning, which carried with it the implicit threat of state control of the economy, was inimical to landowning and business interests that still carried some weight in the party. Attempts by Bourguiba to foster open discussion of proposed reform measures within the party broke down in the backlash of the Bizerte crisis. With a deft sense of timing, however, Bourguiba announced a major reorganization of the party in 1963 that was designed to improve the dialogue between the national leadership and local and regional branches in preparation for the next party congress, the first to be held in more than five years. Convened in October 1964, the Congress of Destiny, as it was advertised, endorsed centralized state planning and approved Destourian socialism as the party's official

Small craft along a wharf at the port of Bizerte

ideology, attempting to reconcile Bourguiba's political ethics with Ben Salah's collectivism. In keeping with its new image, the congress voted to rename the party the Destourian Socialist Party (Parti Socialiste Destourien—PSD). In November, running unopposed under its banner, Bourguiba was elected to a second term as president.

While Ben Salah tightened his control over economic policy and consolidated his position in the PSD, Bourguiba turned his attention to foreign affairs and attempted to use his prestige on the international scene as a moderate Arab leader to promote a negotiated settlement of the Palestinian question. In April 1965 he proposed an Arab reconciliation with Israel, in return for which Israel would allow the return of refugees and would cede territory for the creation of a Palestinian Arab state on the basis of the 1947 UN plan. Although Israel welcomed the opportunity for direct negotiations with concerned Arab states, it rejected the 18-year-old plan for a settlement on the grounds that it was not relevant to contemporary conditions in the region. Meanwhile, Egypt and Syria denounced Bourguiba for breaking ranks with Arab solidarity by recommending a course of action that would have implied recognition of Israel. Tunisia kept a low profile officially during the Arab-Israeli June 1967 War, although rioting in Tunis was directed against Jewish residents, and the United States and British embassies were attacked by mobs. The following year, Tunisia broke relations with Syria after Damascus had condemned Bourguiba for his conciliatory attitude toward Israel. The Tunisian government also cited contacts between Syrian agents and radical groups in Tunisia as evidence of attempted subversion.

The Tunisian government had initiated agricultural cooperatives, using former *habus* land, as early as 1956. These cooperatives coexisted alongside a private sector that included peasant smallholders as well as large-scale farm proprietors. Under Ban Salah's direction, the program was enlarged by adding communal property sequestered by the government and again in 1964 to include foreign-owned land that was nationalized that year. Individual farmers, mostly smallholders, had also been allowed to buy expropriated land put up for sale by the government, but as more and more property was brought into the public sector, it became clear that the cooperative system would be developed at the expense of private ownership.

By 1968 agricultural production had fallen drastically in the public sector, in large measure as a result of unrealistic planning, incompetent management, and a reluctance among farmers to join the cooperatives. The structural failure of the cooperative system was compounded by drought conditions and a series of extremely poor harvests. Negative reports from the World Bank (see Glossary), highly critical of the planning program and cooperative system, further embarrassed the regime. Resentment in liberal circles within the party over Ben Salah's continued accumulation of power came to a head when Ahmed Mestiri resigned abruptly as defense minister to protest his policy of collectivization. Mestiri, who had held important cabinet, party, and diplomatic posts, was at the time considered one of the most promising of a new generation of leaders—including Ben Salah and Mohamed Masmoudi—and was a member of the party's governing Political Bureau. Although carefully explaining his withdrawal in terms of an objection to the methods by which current policies were applied rather than to their substance, Mestiri also suggested that the PSD was not being true to its own principles in pursuing collectivization. After his resignation he was expelled from the party.

Ben Salah reacted to opposition from party liberals by attempting to broaden his already extensive bureaucratic authority and accelerating plans for collectivization. In January 1969 he announced the organization of the National Union of Cooperatives, a superagency that consolidated all aspects of the cooperative sector under his immediate control. Because the cooperative system had been so successful, he argued, it would be extended under the agency's guidance from 1 million hectares to 4 million by collectivizing private landholdings, particularly in the Sahil, where opposition to his policies had been most pronounced. Some observers argued that the agency's establishment was an act of desperation on Ben Salah's part, representing a last-ditch effort to ensure the survival of the cooperative system. Others have pointed out, however, that he was strengthening his bureaucratic power base, from which he managed the greater part of the Tunisian economy, in order to eliminate his opponents. Bourguiba, who was ill at the time, was not in a position to block Ben Salah's moves, even if he disapproved of them.

During the spring and summer of 1969, violent demonstrations against collectivization broke out in the Sahil, where large landholders and peasants alike organized to resist the confiscation of their land. Stocks of sheep and cattle were halved as farmers slaughtered their animals or smuggled them into Algeria rather than turn them over to the state farms. It was their determined resistance to collectivization—more than the opposition of liberal politicians or Bourguiba's ultimate intervention—that led to Ben Salah's removal from the planning ministry. In September Ben Salah was transferred during a cabinet reshuffle to the education ministry, a shift that marked the end of the collectivist experiment and was correctly interpreted as the beginning of Ben Salah's political downfall.

Intraparty Politics in the 1970s

The turmoil caused in the countryside by collectivization and the serious divisions that were developing within the PSD over Ben Salah's role had compelled Bourguiba to reassert his authority over political decisionmaking. His action responded in part to warnings from veteran politicians who were concerned that public faith in Bourguiba's judgment would be compromised as much by his failure to control Ben Salah as by the support he had given to the minister's unpopular policies. Bourguiba also had reason to worry that Ben Salah's bureaucratic empire had become so extensive that it posed a threat to the presidency itself. Bahi Ladgham, who as general coordinator of state affairs had presided over the executive office during the frequent periods when Bourguiba was indisposed by illness, announced that a change in the government's political and economic orientation was required "if catastrophe is to be averted." The edifice of centralized state planning and control of the economy, of which Ben Salah had been the architect, was dismantled virtually overnight.

In November 1969 Bourguiba was elected to a third term as president. Before leaving for prolonged medical treatment abroad, he appointed Ladgham to the newly created post of prime minister and head of government. Ben Salah was left out of the government in the cabinet reorganization that followed, was deprived of his party post, and finally was expelled from the PSD. He was later arrested and in June 1970 was convicted of abuse of power and mismanagement of funds after a long trial at which peasants were brought in to describe the hardships caused by collectivization. In his own defense Ben Salah testified that he had only tried to interpret the president's directions and to implement a policy that had originated with him. The judgment of the court was that Ben Salah had misled Bourguiba with "false statistics" and had concealed from him the discontent aroused by the land program in the countryside. Although it was not proved that he had plotted to take over the government, the implication that such a plan existed was strong. Acknowledging the extent of the power base Ben Salah had constructed, Bourguiba boasted that "without me no one would have been able to rid the country of him." The court sentenced Ben Salah to 10 years of hard labor. In 1973, however, Ben Salah, presumably with assistance from supporters still highly placed in the government, escaped from prison and fled to exile in France, where he remained an outspoken critic of Bourguiba and the focus of left-wing opposition to the regime.

Bourguiba regrouped his support in the liberal wing of the party, which had opposed Ben Salah. Mestiri was rehabilitated, and when Ladgham formed a new government in June 1970, he was named interior minister and given responsibility for internal security. Hedi Nouira, formerly director of the National Bank, accepted the portfolio for economic affairs in the same government. Ladgham soon became involved in mediating the cease-fire in Jordan between the forces of King Hussein and the Palestine Liberation Organization (PLO). Consequently, he was replaced as prime minister by Nouira, whose emphasis on economic liberalization would characterize government policy in the 1970s.

Most of those who had opposed Ben Salah could be classified as economic liberals who, like Nouira, favored a return to private-sector initiative in economic development and the lifting of restrictions on trade and investment. Some, like Mestiri, who had championed economic liberalization, also subscribed to liberalization of the political system, by which they had initially meant greater democracy within the PSD rather than political pluralism. And they were encouraged when Bourguiba spoke publicly of the need for democratization of the political process. Addressing this question, an advisory committee chaired by Mestiri proposed a constitutional amendment in October 1970 that would have allowed for a government led by a prime minister who was responsible to the National Assembly. Nouira submitted the proposal to the legislature, but when no action was taken on it, Mestiri demanded that a party congress be called to take up the matter of constitutional reform, including the sensitive issue of the presidential succession.

Citing the delay in setting a date for a party congress, Mestiri offered his resignation in June 1971 from both the government and the party. Bourguiba, who had been undergoing medical treatment abroad during most of the time that the debate on the constitutional questions was taking place, refused to accept Mestiri's resignations and convinced him that liberalization of the political system was on his agenda and would proceed.

An October date was eventually set for the party congress, at which Mestiri was expected to play a leading role. Just before it was convened, however, Nouira appointed several officials to posts in Mestiri's interior ministry without prior consultation with the minister. The action was considered to be a calculated provocation, and when Mestiri took the bait and complained, Bourguiba dismissed him. The defense minister, Hasib Ben Ammar, resigned in protest. Despite this prelude, the liberal faction at first appeared successful in gaining concessions at the party congress. When the central committee was elected, Ladgham and Mestiri finished first and second, respectively, in the voting. Ladgham's compromise proposal carried, deferring discussion of the constitutional amendment on parliamentary responsibility in exchange for an agreement on enlarged popular participation in the election of party officials. Against Bourguiba's wishes, the congress formally recommended that presidential succession be based on an open vote of the party.

The departure of Mestiri and other liberal ministers left Nouira in a commanding, although not entirely uncontested, position as head of government. Bourguiba placed increasing confidence in the prime minister's management of the government and deferred more and more decisionmaking responsibility to him. Inci-

President Habib Bourguiba (right) and
Prime Minister Hedi Nouira at Monastir in 1974.
Courtesy Embassy of Tunisia, Washington

dents occurred, however, that indicated that other ministers were competing for access to the ailing president. Bourguiba also seemed to suffer periodic lapses in judgment, during which he made ill-advised departures from his usually levelheaded approach to foreign policy. In July 1973, for instance, Bourguiba called on King Hussein to abdicate his throne in order to convert Jordan into a Palestinian state. Jordan severed relations with Tunisia for a time in protest. In 1972 Bourguiba had brushed aside Libyan leader Muammar al Qadhaafi's overtures for a Maghribi union. At the conclusion of a subsequent meeting in Tunis in June 1974, however, Bourguiba and his Libyan guest announced agreement on a plan for the federation of their two countries. Nouira, who was out of the country at the time of the meeting, rushed home to take control of the situation, and the agreement was formally disavowed by the Tunisian government. The foreign minister, Mohamed Masmoudi, whom Nouira considered a potential political rival, was summarily dismissed from the government for his role in influencing Bourguiba to agree to the Libyan union in the prime minister's absence. Relations between the two countries soured after the episode, and Libya was thereafter regarded by Tunisia as the primary threat to its security.

Bourguiba seemed once more in charge at the September 1974 party congress. He blamed the excesses of the previous party gathering on those whom he said had mistakenly believed he was "about to die and that the presidency would soon be vacant." Ignoring a renewed appeal by liberals for direct election of his successor, the president declared that he had "now come back in full strength and in very good health to be at the helm of this congress, which is to adopt resolutions to put matters in order." The congress dutifully approved a plan put before it whereby the prime minister, appointed by the president, would automatically succeed to the presidency in case of the demise or permanent disability of the incumbent. Bourguiba thereby confirmed Nouira as his heir apparent. In November Bourguiba was elected to a fourth term as president, running unopposed. The following May the National Assembly unanimously approved a constitutional amendment naming him president for life.

Economic Liberalization

If those who had looked for political liberalization were disappointed by the outcome of the 1971 party congress, others who had limited their expectations for reform to economic liberalization came away satisfied. The congress endorsed the measures that had been taken to reverse Ben Salah's collectivization policy. Although it reaffirmed Tunisia's official commitment to maintaining a mixed economy that included a significant cooperative sector, party delegates also approved previously enacted legislation that had decisively shifted emphasis from the public to the private sector in order to generate economic development. Among those measures had been the lifting of restrictions on trade and foreign investment. Priority was also shifted away from raw materials to agriculture, tourism, and manufacturing as the chief sources of foreign earnings.

The first and most important step in the program of economic liberalization, however, had been the liquidation of state farms. Nearly 300,000 hectares of collectivized farmland were scheduled for redistribution to smallholders. *Habus* land taken by the state was returned to the original benefactors, and additional property remaining in the public sector was rented to large landholders. Agricultural production, which was regarded as the prime element in increasing economic growth, rose 70 percent in value in the first half of the 1970s, stimulated by improved marketing, modernization of equipment, and good harvests.

Although agriculture prospered as a sector, serious contradictions also developed. Increased production was accounted for primarily by larger, increasingly mechanized holdings that provided fruit and vegetables for export. Smallholdings proved inefficient and uneconomic for producing cash crops, and peasant owners reverted to subsistence farming and production for local markets. A pattern soon developed in which peasants, who lacked capital for tools, animals, and seeds, sold their small plots to larger landholders and either migrated to the cities or hired out as farmworkers. Tunisia enjoyed a favorable balance of trade in agricultural goods in the early 1970s, but its farm production, geared to export markets, was unable to keep pace with the growth in domestic demand for foodstuffs. Overall output fell sharply in the late 1970s, largely as a result of drought conditions. Furthermore, Tunisia's export-oriented agriculture was highly susceptible to fluctuations in the West European markets that it supplied. Because of the deterioration of trade and poor harvests, by 1980 imported foodstuffs were almost twice the value of cash-crop exports.

Tunisia's industrial base had been small before the turnabout in economic orientation in 1969. Under the new policy, foreign companies and other potential investors were offered generous tax advantages to locate in the country. A liberal trade environment also allowed them to import capital equipment duty free. Later legislation sought to generate domestic investment as well. This policy contributed to significant growth in the industrial sector during the 1970s, especially in assembly plants for reexports, food processing, textiles, and leather goods. The tourist industry, which owed more than any other sector to foreign participation attracted by liberal incentives, accounted for 20 percent of all foreign exchange earnings by 1980. During the same period, however, the cost of capital goods for manufacturing and tourism, imported under liberalized trade policies, exceeded returns for exports and services from those sectors.

Opposition and Unrest

Social and political discontent, in reaction to the failure to achieve political liberalization and to the social costs of economic liberalization, became increasingly apparent during the 1970s. Particularly evident was dissension on the part of students and organized labor. By the mid-1970s, student demonstrations and strikes protesting education policies and official interference in student governmental bodies had become annual events. Left-wing groups, which won control of student government away from the PSD, also organized students to join trade unionists in their strike actions.

One of the advantages that Tunisia offered to prospective investors was a plentiful supply of cheap labor. Likewise, one of the aims of economic liberalization was to encourage the development of industrial and service sectors that would stimulate new jobs in areas where unemployment had been intractable. But rapid growth in these sectors did not cut into unemployment as deeply as expected, and the low wages paid those who were employed lagged behind rises in the cost of living. Unemployment and demands for higher pay were the major causes of labor unrest, which in the 1970s found sympathizers among the urban working class swollen by migrants from rural areas and among jobless youths.

The unrest grew in intensity in 1976 when textile and metal workers were joined by public sector employees in utilities, transportation, hospitals, and the postal service in a strike over wage demands that had not been sanctioned by the UGTT. Habib Achour, who was a high-ranking PSD official as well as leader of the trade unions, was caught in a dilemma: the government expected the UGTT to enforce the labor peace necessary for economic development to proceed undisturbed, and at the same time militants in the unions pressured him to demand wage and employment policies more favorable to workers. Achour condemned wildcat strikes led by the militants, but he was also publicly critical of the government's policies.

Prime Minister Nouira was anxious to ensure the UGTT's cooperation in controlling labor costs during the five-year development plan that began in 1977. Achour had initially approved a social pact under which periodic wage revisions were tied to increased productivity as well as to the cost of living. Union militants, however, refused to recognize Achour's authority to commit them to the social pact, and wildcat strikes continued in various parts of the country throughout the year. In October an illegal strike by workers at Qasr Hellal turned violent, and the army was called in to break it. The incident at Qasr Hellal marked the first time since independence that the military was deployed to quell a civil disturbance. Although the UGTT had not sanctioned the strike, Achour nonetheless condemned the government's use of the army against workers. Other critics of the regime, including Mestiri, Masmoudi, and Ben Salah, all publicly supported the UGTT in its widening dispute with the government.

When regime critics took up the cause of the unions, the dispute between the government and labor went beyond bread-and-butter economic issues and became political in character. Labor unrest thereafter was more than a threat to the government's economic program. The UGTT had a power base that was separate from the party, and its opposition was viewed as a direct challenge to the government's authority. Relations were further strained when a threat was made against Achour's life.

Nouira's cabinet was divided on how to deal with the UGTT. When the interior minister, Taher Belkhodja, came out in favor of conciliation with the union, he was removed from office. Shortly afterward, six fellow cabinet ministers resigned to protest his dismissal. Those appointed to replace them supported sterner action to force the UGTT into compliance with government policy.

Tension mounted after the UGTT's national council meeting on January 10, 1978, adopted a resolution critical of certain economic liberalization initiatives and alleging that Nouira's government was oriented toward the "consolidation of a capitalist class" whose interests were linked to those of "foreign exploiting capital." The same day that the UGTT issued its attack on the government, Achour resigned from the PSD Political Bureau and Central Committee, although not from the party itself. He explained that his action indicated disagreement only with the current government, to which the government responded that an unrepresentative radical minority had taken control of the UGTT.

The long anticipated confrontation between the government and the UGTT occurred two weeks later on January 26, when a general strike was called as a demonstration against the government to protest the arrest of a union official and attacks on union offices. It was estimated unofficially that 150 people were killed when strikers and their supporters clashed with police, soldiers, and PSD militia on what became known as Black Thursday. The scale of violence was unprecedented in the history of independent Tunisia. A state of emergency was declared, and hundreds were arrested, including Achour and virtually the entire leadership of the UGTT.

The government characterized the Black Thursday strike as a calculated attempt to incite rebellion against the state. Earlier contacts between UGTT officials and Qadhaafi were cited as proof of Libyan involvement. Achour was convicted on charges of sedition and sentenced to 10 years of hard labor. Progovernment appointees were subsequently installed on a new union executive council.

During the 1970s several political organizations surfaced and were openly critical of Bourguiba and the PSD and hostile to the government. In 1973 Ben Salah consolidated noncommunist, leftwing opposition in the Movement of Popular Unity (Mouvement d'Unité Populaire—MUP), which was organized in exile in Paris.

An internal branch also operated in Tunisia. The MUP's program advocated a socialist economy and called for the formation of a transitional government that would organize free parliamentary elections. In contrast, the outlawed PCT was small, never numbered more than a few hundred active members at home and abroad, but it exercised an influence disproportionate to its size in student circles. The PCT and the MUP were believed by the government to have collaborated in events leading up to the Black Thursday incident.

Early in 1977 a large number of liberal dissidents, including Mestiri and several other former cabinet ministers, appealed to Bourguiba to halt the deterioration of civil liberties in Tunisia and called for the convocation of a national conference for the same purpose. The proposal was couched in such a way as to allow the president to distance himself from the actions of the Nouira government. The conference was banned by authorities, but in October Mestiri proposed a National Pact to be signed by representatives of all political tendencies working within the constitutional system that would guarantee freedom of political activity. The preamble of the pact, to which Ben Salah gave his qualified support, was highly critical of the one-party system and recommended movement toward political pluralism. Prime Minister Nouira emphatically rejected the pact and attacked the liberals for what he termed their negative attitude. Lacking a positive response from the government, Mestiri formed the Movement of Social Democrats (Mouvement des Democrats Sociales—MDS) as a liberal opposition group in June 1978.

An area of serious concern for the regime was the emergence of political groups rooted in an Islamic revivalist movement that condemned the regime's secularism and attributed a decline in traditional values and moral standards to Western influence. The most important of these groups was the Islamic Tendency Movement (Mouvement de la Tendence Islamique—MTI). The MTI was committed to the establishment of an Islamic state, integrating all aspects of national life in conformity with Islamic law and custom, and it fused religious zeal with a program of economic reform. At its inception, religious revivalism was almost exclusively a student movement that had its base of support at the University of Tunis, where in the early 1980s the MTI had wrested control of student government bodies and organizations from previously dominant left-wing groups (see Religious Life, ch. 2; Opposition Groups, ch. 4).

In January 1980 about 50 Tunisian insurgents, trained and armed in Libya, seized the police barracks at Gafsa. The attack coincided with the anniversary of the Black Thursday strike, and it was apparently intended to spark a nationwide uprising to bring down the government. Gafsa was a stronghold of the militant mineworkers' union, and its economy was heavily dependent on re-mittances from Tunisian workers in Libya. Some locals joined the insurgents in resisting army and police units that retook the area after three days of bloody fighting. All of the insurgents were killed or captured in the engagement. Thirteen of those captured were subsequently sentenced to death and executed. France sent military assistance to Tunisia, and French naval units demonstrated off Jerba Island to discourage Libyan intervention (see Internation-al Security Concerns, ch. 5).

Toward Pluralism

In February 1980 Prime Minister Nouira was incapacitated by a stroke, and Bourguiba turned to Mohamed Mzali, the minister of education, to serve as acting prime minister. Mzali, a moderate, was named prime minister when it became apparent that Nouira would not be able to resume his duties, and in December he was authorized by the president to make changes in the cabinet that strengthened the hand of party liberals. Two of the new ministers had been among those purged from the party during the 1970s. The next month the PSD rescinded the expulsion of some former party and government officials who had crossed over into the liber-al opposition. Although Achour remained under house arrest, other union leaders, jailed after Black Thursday, were released from prison. The apparent shift in the attitude of the government deflat-ed the opposition, and Mzali's openly conciliatory policy toward the dissidents persuaded many disaffected liberals and trade unionists to seek reinstatement in the PSD (see Interest Groups, ch. 4).

An extraordinary congress of the PSD was summoned in April 1981 to approve a move toward political pluralism. Opposition par-ties, including the MDS and the MUP, were given permission to participate in the next election, although full legal status was with-held from them. The long-standing ban on the PCT was also lifted, but the MTI and other Islamic groups were explicitly excluded from the political process. Likewise, Islamic political leaders who had been imprisoned were not included in the amnesty granted to the trade union leaders. Bourguiba himself explained that the Is-lamic groups were committed to using religion for political ends, contrary to the secular nature of Tunisian political institutions dic-tated by the Constitution.

Tunisia's first multiparty elections were scheduled for November 1, 1981. In preparation for the campaign, the PSD and the UGTT put a seal on the reconciliation between the party and the trade unions by agreeing to present candidates as partners on a coalition slate, called the National Front, and issuing a joint election manifesto. In previous elections, union nominees had been included on the PSD list. Just before the November election Achour was released from house arrest and was restored to the leadership of the UGTT.

Despite the options offered on the ballot in the November election, the National Front gained 95 percent of the total vote and won all 136 seats in the Chamber of Deputies, as the national legislature was redesignated. Mestiri's MDS, winning about 3 percent of the vote, led other opposition parties. Ben Salah, who had been denied amnesty, dismissed the election as a "maneuver designed to reduce pluralism to a simple election operation." From Paris he held out for nothing less than power-sharing with the other parties, but he was unsuccessful in persuading the internal branch of the MUP to boycott the election. Mzali, regarded as Bourguiba's appointed successor, formed a new government, and in the months after the election the prime minister pushed for greater liberalization both in politics and in the economy (see The 1981 Election: Opposition Parties Sanctioned, ch. 4).

* * *

The history of Tunisia can be profitably studied, particularly for the preprotectorate period, as part of the general history of the Maghrib. Jamil M. Abun-Nasr's *A History of the Maghrib* is the most accessible narrative survey available in English of Maghribi history from earliest times to the present. Abdallah Laroui's *The History of the Maghrib* is a critical interpretive work recommended to readers with some background in the history of the region. Charles-André Julien's *History of North Africa*, edited and extensively revised by Roger Le Tourneau, provides a clear, scholarly treatment of Tunisian history up to 1830. Julien's *L'Afrique du Nord en marche* brings the coverage up to independence. The late medieval period is the subject of Robert Brunschvig's *La Berbérie orientale sous les Hafsides des origines á la fin du XV siécle*. Leon Carl Brown's *The Tunisia of Ahmad Bey, 1837–1855* views the period during which Tunisia made its initial attempt to come to grips with the influence of Europe, and Lucette Valensi's *On the*

Eve of Colonialism tries to demonstrate that Tunisia and neighboring Algeria possessed viable political institutions that were disrupted by French intervention. David C. Gordon's *North Africa's French Legacy* is a study of the intellectual conflict posed by the French presence. Jacques Berque's *French North Africa: The Maghrib Between Two World Wars* covers social and cultural developments during the interwar period.

Tunisia was for a time a popular area of research by American scholars, who in the 1960s saw it as an example of a single-party state that was successfully modernizing its political and economic institutions by means of an indigenous brand of socialism. Their research, however, has not been updated to take into account the failure of the socialist experiment there. Surveys of Tunisian history and postprotectorate policies from that period include Dwight L. Lings's brief *Tunisia from Protectorate to Republic*, Clement Henry Moore's *Tunisia since Independence*, and Wilfrid Knapp's *Tunisia*, all of which are dated. Among more recent scholarship in English is Norma Salem's revisionist biography *Habib Bourguiba, Islam, and the Creation of Tunisia*, published in 1984. (For further information and complete citations, see Bibliography).

Chapter 2.   The Society and Its Environment

Sidi Uqba mosque in Kairouan

TUNISIA IN THE MID-1980s had the appearance of a society in transition from one set of guiding principles to another. To a noticeable degree, it was also increasingly divided against itself, pitting those devoted to modernization along Western lines against those favoring a more traditional society in conformity with Islamic norms and precepts. The middle class and governing elite—mostly urban, relatively well-off economically, and successful professionally—had fared well during the years since independence in 1956. French-educated and West European-oriented, this class was well-represented in government circles. The lower classes lived in rural areas and villages or in slums surrounding major cities. Considerably poorer than the middle class and composed of subsistence farmers, herders, and the unemployed, the lower classes were less receptive to Westernization and were oriented more toward the Arab world and Islam.

The upper classes had controlled the nature and direction of the Tunisian society since independence, but over the past few years they had come under strong challenge from their more tradition-minded countrymen. In the mid-1980s the future course of the nation and society was not at all clear. What seemed certain, however, was a new emphasis on indigenous Muslim norms and values together with a movement to restructure the society along those lines at the expense of Western-inspired ideals and life-styles.

Tunisia, like its neighbors Algeria and Morocco, had a high rate of population growth. While the rate was substantially lower than it had been a decade or more earlier, population control remained a major problem that affected all aspects of national life. It slowed socioeconomic development, stimulated internal and external migration, produced high rates of unemployment, and caused shortages in housing, educational facilities, and health services. The demographic situation, while serious, was more encouraging than elsewhere in the Maghrib because of a well-established family planning program, rising marriage ages among the young, and a growing awareness of the advantages of smaller families.

A majority of the population were under the age of 25 and posed a challenge to the government in terms of their impact on housing, education, and employment. Many young people found themselves without employment or the opportunity for social advancement and had become frustrated and resentful of the wealth and status of the middle class. They were also questioning the value of the elite's modernization policies. These discontented youth, particularly the educated among them, were instead finding in Islam and Tunisian identity an alternative to the West European-inspired values of the upper classes. They were also joining organizations opposed to the government and were becoming more inclined to reject the contemporary social order.

The nuclear family continued to gain in popularity at the expense of the patriarchal extended family of the past. This trend was especially significant in that it favored lowered birth rates and improvement in the status of women. Over the last 30 years women had been granted legal rights and protections in matters of family law and had taken advantage of educational opportunities in order to move out of the home and into the workplace and even the political arena. It was not always easy to exercise the new freedoms or to assume different roles, however, because women's emancipation offended deeply held beliefs about the proper place and behavior of females in a male-dominated Islamic society, even one as receptive to change as that of Tunisia. As part of the recent popularization of Islamic precepts, some younger women were returning to traditional dress or attempting in other ways to conform to the more normative standards of Muslim behavior.

In the mid-1980s Tunisia remained in many ways a moderate, socially progressive state virtually unique among its Muslim contemporaries. Its society was homogenous and possessed a high degree of ethnic and cultural unity. The governing elite had in the past demonstrated its capacity to recognize problems and to devise solutions to meet them. The challenge in the 1980s from the young, the Islamists, and the have-nots indicated that the elite's resilience and convictions would continue to be put to the test as the country prepared for an uncertain future.

Physical Setting

Together with Algeria, Morocco, and the northwestern portion of Libya known historically as Tripolitania, Tunisia is part of the Maghrib (see Glossary), a region in which fertile coastal lands give way to the great Atlas mountain chain of North Africa and, finally, to the interior expanses of the Sahara (see fig. 7). Tunisia has an area of approximately 164,000 square kilometers and a coastline of about 1,600 kilometers indented by the gulfs of Tunis, Hammamet, and Gabès.

The Atlas mountain system, which begins in southwestern Morocco, terminates in northeastern Tunisia. Most of northern Tunisia is mountainous, but elevations average less than 300 meters and rarely exceed 1,000 meters. The Atlas Mountains in Algeria and Morocco, however, reach much higher elevations.

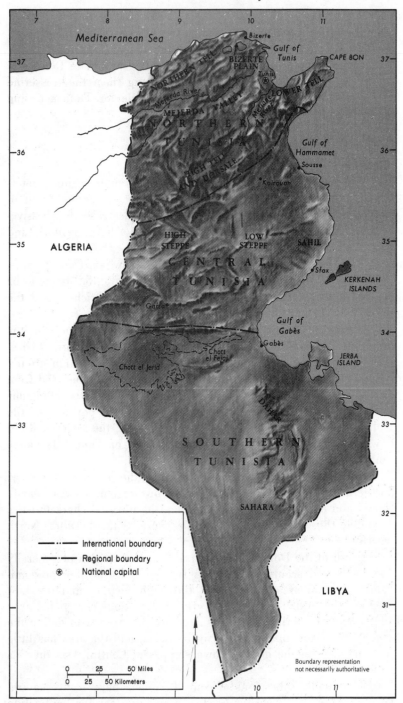

Figure 7. Terrain and Drainage

75

The principal mountain chain, the Dorsale, slants northeastward across the country and plunges into the sea at Cape Bon, an area famed among early Mediterranean navigators. The Dorsale is cut by several transverse depressions, among them the Kasserine Pass, which figured significantly in the battle for Tunisia during World War II.

Geographic Regions

Tunisia is divided into three major geographic regions, determined in part by topography and the quality of the soils and in particular by the incidence of rainfall, which decreases progressively from north to south. The regions are northern, central, and southern Tunisia.

The Dorsale mountains form a rain shadow separating northern Tunisia from the remainder of the country. Rainfall tends to be heavier north of this mountain barrier, soils are richer, and the countryside is more heavily populated.

Northern Tunisia is a generally mountainous region and is sometimes referred to as the Tell, a term peculiar to North Africa. It is generally defined as a heavily populated area of high ground located close to the Mediterranean Sea. The region is bisected from east to west by the Mejerda River and is divided into subregions made up of the Mejerda Valley and the several portions of the Tell. Rising in the mountains of eastern Algeria, the Mejerda River flows eastward and discharges into the Gulf of Tunis. Its valley contains Tunisia's best farmland.

Comprising less than one-fourth of the national territory, northern Tunisia is a generally prosperous region. It was heavily settled and exploited by the French, and its physical characteristics resemble those of southern Europe more than those of North Africa.

South of the Dorsale lies central Tunisia, a region of generally poor soils and scanty rainfall. Its interior consists of a predominantly pastoral area made up of the High Steppes and the Low Steppes, the former occurring at greater elevations near the Algerian border. The term *steppes* was used by the French to define the semiarid interior highlands of North Africa, and the area has little in common with the better known steppes of Central Asia than its name.

The steppe subregions of central Tunisia have scanty natural vegetation and are used for pasturage and the marginal cultivation of cereals. Eastward the Low Steppes give way to a littoral known

Sand dunes surround an oasis in the Sahara of southern Tunisia

as the Sahil, an Arabic term meaning coast or shore. Rainfall is
not appreciably heavier there, but heavy dew has made possible
the intensive cultivation of olive and other tree crops, and there is
considerable cereal production. The Sahil is customarily regarded
as including Jerba Island and the Kerkenah Islands in the Gulf of
Gabès. Jerba Island has been heavily populated since antiquity.

Southward from the steppes, the arid expanses that constitute
southern Tunisia commence with an area where elevations are
lower and where the landscape is marked by numerous chotts (salt
marches, sometimes known as *shatts*) that lie below sea level. On
higher ground around these depressions are various oasis settlements and valuable groves of date palms. Farther to the south, the
land rises to form the plateaus and occasional eroded hills that
make up the Tunisian portion of the Sahara. Fringed by lagoons
and salt flats, the narrow gravelly coast of this region formed the
traditional access route to the Maghrib from the east. The coast is

77

sparsely settled, and the interior is almost totally empty except for a few nomads and inhabitants of oases that occur along a line of springs at the foot of an interior escarpment.

Climate and Hydrology

The most significant natural features that influence the climate are the Mediterranean Sea, which moderates climate conditions; the Atlas mountains; and the Sahara with its hot and dry sirocco winds, which blow northward over much of the country. A Mediterranean climate is characteristic of the northern coastal zone. Temperatures are higher in the interior and the south. Seasonal changes are moderate, although humidity increases in winter. In the desert, enormous diurnal changes are registered, the thermometer plummeting after dusk. Even in the coldest winter months the freezing point is reached only at high elevations in the interior. Winter nights are damp and chilly, however. Tunis is at about the same latitude as San Francisco, and its more expensive new homes are equipped with central heating.

Most of the precipitation occurs during the rainy season, between December and March. Tunisia is generally less favored than the other Maghribi countries with respect to rainfall, and agriculture is heavily dependent on the irregular climatic conditions. In central Tunisia in particular, droughts are frequent, and a two-month-long drought means the loss of 30 to 50 percent of the crops. In the north, in contrast, the Mejerda River is subject to frequent flooding. Rainfall decreases from north to south, ranging from 1,000 to 1,500 millimeters annually in the northwest highlands near the Algerian frontier to less than 100 millimeters in the southern portion of the Sahara zone. The 400-millimeter and 200-millimeter rainfall zones extend between east and west, roughly corresponding to the northern and southern limits of central Tunisia, respectively.

The Mejerda River is the country's only major perennial stream. Other watercourses are seasonal, and the volume of flow even in the Mejerda in June and July is less than one-twelfth of that in February, thus minimizing the river's potential as a source of hydroelectric power.

In the central Tunisian steppes, occasional watercourses flow southward out of the Dorsale after heavy rains but evaporate in salt flats without reaching tidewater. The Chott el Jerid, the largest of southern Tunisia's salt lakes, is dry during half of the year but is flooded to form a shallow salt lake during the winter months.

Even intermittent streams are rare in the Sahara, but rich artesian sources make possible numerous fertile oases. In a large part of the region slightly brackish but usable water from enormous aquifers can be brought to the surfaces, but at prohibitive cost.

Vegetation

True Mediterranean vegetation is found only in northern Tunisia, where the mountains were once abundantly forested, principally in cork, oak, and pine. Cork production, tree felling for firewood and charcoal, and clearing of land for agriculture have severely depleted the reserves, however, and have brought about widespread erosion.

There is no continuous ground cover in central Tunisia. Esparto grass grows on the steppes, and there are occasional jujube trees, members of the blackthorn family. Meager forests of pine and helm oak are found on the approaches to the Dorsale mountains, and red juniper grows at higher elevations elsewhere in the region. In the Sahil almost all of the land has been cleared.

Southern Tunisia is largely devoid of vegetation, except where date palms and planted crops grow around oases. Saharan species, such as acacia and saltbush, enter the natural pattern, however, and at higher levels of the desert occasional patches of scrub grass provide meager food for camels.

Population

In mid-1985 it was estimated that Tunisia's population totaled some 7.2 million. Based upon projections from the 1984 census that counted over 6.9 million Tunisians, this figure indicates that the population had nearly doubled in the three decades since 3.8 million were counted at the time of independence. Since the 1956 census—the last conducted by the French—the Tunisian government has counted the national population in the general censuses of 1966, 1975, and 1984. Although the fertility rate fell significantly—especially in the 1966–75 period—Tunisia's rate of natural increase (crude birth rate minus crude death rate) remained nearly constant, i.e., in the region of 2.6 or 2.7 percent each year between the late 1960s and the early 1980s. During this period, the crude birth rate fell 22 percent to 32.9 births for every 1,000 Tunisians. At the same time, however, improved health services and nutrition led to a simultaneous decline in the crude death rate from 15.2 to 7.3 deaths for every 1,000 Tunisians.

The 1984 census indicated that there were about 102 males to every 100 females in the population. Improving health conditions that lowered maternal death rates and changing social patterns were believed to have contributed to a decline in female mortality since 1966, when the census indicated that there were 104 males to every 100 females. The change between the 1966 and 1984 figures, however, had taken place by the mid-1970s. Some observers attributed the lack of change after that time to a stagnation in economic and social progress, whereas others thought that the census procedure might have resulted in undercounting women.

The population in the early 1980s was a young one in which some 42 percent of all Tunisians were under the age of 15. Although this figure was slightly lower than it had been in previous years, it was far higher than the level of 23 percent under the age of 15 that existed in Western Europe and North America, a level that Tunisian planners hoped eventually to reach. The large proportion of people too young to earn a living placed a burden on those in the economically active age brackets. Moreover, the youthful age structure of the national population built into the society significant momentum for future growth. Thus, even if the future rate of natural increase declined, the large number of Tunisians who had not yet reached childbearing age and the small number of older Tunisians who might be expected to die sooner ensured that the number of births would continue to far outstrip the number of deaths for at least another generation.

Although the country's natural rate of increase was about 2.6 percent annually in the 1975–84 period, emigration of Tunisians to other countries made the overall growth rate somewhat less. Between 1975 and 1984 the annual rate of population growth averaged 2.5 percent. This reflected a decrease in net emigration over the 1966–75 span, when net population growth averaged only 2.3 percent per annum, significantly less than the 2.7 percent annual rate of natural increase during that time.

Emigration had been a major factor in Tunisia's population dynamics since independence. At first, the largest number of emigrants consisted of European residents, the great majority of whom left in the 1950s and 1960s. The census figures showed that the number of foreign residents declined from over 341,000 in 1956 to fewer than 67,000 in 1966 and to under 38,000 in 1975. Tunisia's Jewish community has all but disappeared because of emigration (see The Peoples of Tunisia, this ch.).

Large numbers of Muslims have also emigrated, most of them to seek temporary employment abroad. In the 1966–75 period, some 19,000 Tunisians emigrated each year, but the flow of migrants slackened after the mid-1970s as changing economic conditions reduced the demand for labor abroad. In 1983 it was estimated that 300,000 Tunisians were living in foreign countries, down from 350,000 in 1979. Much of the outflow went to Western Europe, where in 1981 some 180,000 Tunisians resided in France alone. Large numbers also went to neighboring Libya to seek employment in an economy that had benefited from the oil price rises of the 1970s. Because many of the Tunisians in Libya traveled without documentation, their actual number was not known. Estimates ranged as high as 200,000 in the 1970s, but in early 1985 there were thought to be roughly 90,000 to 100,000 Tunisians living there. The expulsion of some 25,000 of them later that year resulted in a major crisis between the two countries (see Foreign Relations, ch. 4; International Security Concerns, ch. 5).

Most of the country's cities and its densest rural populations were in the northeastern coastal lowlands and the Sahil (see table 2, Appendix). This zone, comprising less than 20 percent of the country's territory, contained over one-half of its inhabitants in 1984. The remainder of the country, often referred to generally as the "interior," was for the most part rural and scantily populated. A single exception was the governorate of Kairouan, which in 1975 was one of the most heavily populated. Its ancient capital city was established in the seventh century A.D. as an armed camp and transport center, and it early became an important center of Muslim culture (see Islam and the Arabs, ch. 1).

The prevailing pattern of rural settlement varied by region, although in all parts of the country most of the sedentary population lived in nuclear villages rather than on farms. The rural population of northern Tunisia usually lived on large, mechanized farms (operated either collectively or individually) or on small ones. The big farms, most of them former properties of the European colonists, were found in the lower Mejerda Valley and in the coastal lowlands. The rest of the region was made up of mountainous terrain where small farm villages were scattered on the mountainsides and in the valleys.

In the steppes of central Tunisia the scanty population made a meager livelihood from tending livestock and from farming. The Sahil consisted of closely arrayed farm villages given over to olive growing and other tree culture. The farms in the area were already so heavily concentrated at the beginning of the protectorate period that the French and Italian colonists found little land available for the taking and consequently settled elsewhere.

The bulk of the population of southern Tunisia was clustered in the palm-grove oases surrounding the salt lakes in the pre-Saharan zone. In the Sahara a few populated oases were scattered in the higher elevations (Dahar), southeast of Gabès. The Sahara was the land of the nomads, but beginning in the 1960s drought, overgrazing of the scanty sources of pasturage, declining demand for camels, and declining trade opportunities progressively reduced nomadism. At the same time, the government encouraged the settling of nomads on artificial oases in a process that began with the sinking of a well and took shape through the erecting of fences and the planting of date palms or crops. The process of cultivation, however, remained repugnant to many nomads, and some chose the alternative of urban migration.

According to the 1984 census, urban residents made up 47 percent of the national population. Substantially unchanged since 1975, this figure compared with 40 percent in 1966 and 30 percent in 1956. Urban localities were generally defined as administrative communes with populations of 2,000 or more inhabitants. Growth of the cities and towns quickened during the years after independence with the increasing migration of country people. Between 1966 and 1975 the urban population sector increased annually at a rate of about 4.2 percent as compared with 0.5 percent in the countryside, but this narrowed to 3.0 and 2.0 percent, respectively, in the ensuing nine-year period.

Some migration took place between rural localities, most frequently from a depressed agricultural zone in the interior to a more prosperous one in the coastal area. Most of the movement, however, has led into the cities and towns. Poverty, underemployment at home, excitement, and job prospects in the cities have motivated the migrants. A majority of the migrants have been young men traveling alone; all but a few returned from time to time to their villages of origin, and many married local women. Ultimately they might return permanently to their villages or relocate their families in their new urban homes.

The pattern of urban settlement was one of a few cities and a great many large and small towns. Only Tunis had more than 500,000 inhabitants, and in 1984 Sfax was the only other city with more than 100,000 (see table 3, Appendix). A total of 31 communes had a population of more than 25,000.

Tunis was a magnet for migrants. It had the best schools and the only really good hospitals. The country's best-trained government and private-sector workers resided in it, and its factories con-

Tunis, the national capital.
Courtesy Embassy of Tunisia, Washington

Minaret of the Sidi
Ben Arous Mosque in Tunis
and the Medina (background)

Avenue Bourguiba in the
center of Tunis; Roman
Catholic Cathedral on left

tributed one-half of the national industrial output. Even the prosperous Sahil had contributed its share of migrants to Tunis.

The metropolitan zone of the city of Tunis extends far beyond the limits of the city itself. The district of Tunis, in which the city is located, had nearly 1.4 million inhabitants in 1984, over 90 percent of whom were urban dwellers. The pattern of settlement in Tunis was uneven. In the mid-1980s it was estimated that one-third of the population was crammed into the medina, the oldest part of the city. One-third resided in correspondingly crowded *gourbivilles*, the squatter settlements of urban migrants scattered around the urban periphery, and the remaining one-third lived for the most part in the spacious *ville nouvelle*, the new city built by the French colonists.

Ethnic Groups and Languages

The Peoples of Tunisia

Modern-day Tunisians are a mixture of Berber and Arab stock. The Berbers, the indigenous people of North Africa, have no generic name for themselves. The Romans called them *barbari*, or "barbarians," the term applied to those peoples who lived outside the framework of Greco-Roman civilization and from which the designation *Berber* probably comes. Of stocky physique and having a high incidence of light hair and blue eyes, the Berbers are Caucasians akin to other Mediterranean peoples.

The Arab component of the society was introduced during the conquests of the seventh, the eleventh, and succeeding centuries. Racially, the Arabs brought a slender build, dark eyes and hair, and darker skin to the community from which most modern Tunisians are descended. The Berbers quickly accepted the religion, language, and culture of the invaders and intermarried with them. In modern times most Tunisians claim Arab ancestry, speak Arabic, profess Islam, and find only traces of Berber culture in their lives.

In this respect Tunisia contrasts with Algeria and Morocco, where in the 1980s people still ethnically identifiable as Berbers made up substantial minorities of the population. The relative completeness, as well as the early date, of the arabization of the Tunisian Berbers may have been in part because most of the Berbers occupied a relatively compact geographical area. It may also have been because long before the coming of the Arabs, the Berbers had undergone a substantial degree of assimilation under the Carthaginians and the Romans. In the 1980s small Berber communities were still found on the island of Jerba, in a few villages and oases on the edge of the Sahara, in highlands along the Libyan border, and in the mountainous northwestern corner of the country. The Berbers numbered about 180,000, or less than 3 percent of the total population, of which less than one-half had retained their native Berber speech.

The Arab-Berber population is dispersed over the whole country. Subtle racial distinctions, however, are discernible: the coastal and northern peoples tend to have the stocky Berber physique, while those of the inland and southern regions where Arab concentration has been highest are slender and darker skinned. Cultural differences are also noticeable between inhabitants of the coastal region and those of the hinterland. Since the time of the Phoenicians, Tunisia has had a sedentary coastal civilization and a nomadic interior populace (see Early History, ch. 1). The Arab invasions increased the cultural and linguistic homogeneity of the population but sharpened this ancient division, which remains visible in the form of dialects, in the sedentary versus the nomadic life, and in the rate of acceptance of modernization in the two areas.

Since the end of the Arab invasion the ethnic composition of the population has changed little. Black Africans, once widely used as household slaves and concubines, have affected the composition of the population only slightly, although skin color ranges from bronze to black in the southern oases. In the fifteenth century the Tunisian population received an infusion of Spanish blood with the expulsion of the Muslims from Spain. Intermarriage between Tunisians and Balkan peoples, Greeks, Turks, and European Christians made a significant social and commercial impact on the coastal society but did little to alter the Arab-Berber population as a whole. With the disappearance of these foreign elements, their characteristics have diffused in the ethnic majority.

Jews, indigenous and foreign born, were once far more numerous in Tunisia. Their numbers have declined steadily over the last few decades, from about 86,000 at the time of independence in 1956 to some 60,000 in 1966, to perhaps 5,000 in the early 1980s. About 2,500 still reside in Tunis, and others live in Zarzis and elsewhere in Tunisia; but probably the most interesting enclaves are the tiny communities on Jerba Island. Numbering about 1,200 in the early 1980s, the Jews of Jerba were one of the last remnants of once extensive Jewish communities that were scattered across the Maghrib. Most of them were merchants or skilled

crafts-people. They have lived according to age-old cultural traditions and have preserved a form of theocratic republican government under the tutelage of a leading rabbi.

Both Tunisian and foreign-born Jews left in large numbers at
national independence and have continued to do so in smaller
numbers in response to tensions arising from events in the Middle
East. At the time of the Arab-Israeli June 1967 War, anti-Jewish
demonstrations in Tunis resulted in heavy damage to the principal
synagogue. Rioting in three southern towns occurred in 1982 after
the murder of Palestinian refugees in Lebanon, and two Jerban
Jews were killed when anti-Jewish sentiment again ran high in late
1985 in the wake of an Israeli bombing raid on Palestinian headquarters south of Tunis (see International Security Concerns, ch.
5).

Throughout the years of the protectorate the population included a large number of Europeans, French and Italians predominating. The two groups were sociologically distinct, the French constituting a well-to-do elite and the bulk of the Italians consisting of
working-class people from southern Italy and Sicily. In 1956 the
European colony totaled more than 341,000 people, the majority
of whom were French.

During the first two years after independence about one-half
of the Europeans departed, but their departure was less hurried
than that from Morocco and Algeria. For a time the new government continued to employ more than 3,000 former French officials
and a great many schoolteachers, and the replacement of French
bureaucrats and business leaders was generally orderly. By 1966,
however, the census showed that the population included only
66,834 foreigners, of whom only 32,520 were not Arabs. The size
of the non-Tunisian population in the early 1980s was estimated at
about 50,000, but some sources placed it significantly below that.

Language and the Society

Arabic is the official language of Tunisia and in its North African Maghribi form constitutes the native language of virtually
entire population. Berber, the indigenous tongue, is spoken by substantial ethnic minorities in Algeria and Morocco, but in Tunisia
only about 1 percent of the population use it as their mother
tongue. Berber speakers, who numbered about 70,000 in the mid-
1980s, occupy villages on the edge of the desert in such areas as
Sened, Matmata, Jerba Island, and Nefusa on the Libyan border.
They also inhabit the oasis of Ghadames. Half of the population

speaks French as a second language, and many French-educated Tunisians find themselves more at ease with French than with Arabic. French has declined somewhat in both usage and status since independence. Although it is widely used in government, education, and commerce, it is no longer an official language, as it was before independence.

The apparent simplicity of language-use patterns is illusory. While Berber and French can be clearly identified, Tunisian Arabic is not a single language but rather a complex of different forms and dialects. Arabic is a Semitic tongue related to Amharic, Aramaic, and Hebrew. The predominant language throughout North Africa and the Middle East, it was introduced by Arab invaders and conquerors in the seventh, eleventh, and succeeding centuries (see Islam and the Arabs, ch. 1). Written Arabic is psychologically and sociologically important as the vehicle of Islam and Arab culture and as the link with other Arab countries.

Four varieties of Arabic are in use in Tunisia: classical, modern literary (or modern standard), colloquial (or dialectical), and intermediary (or "educated"). The classical Arabic of the Quran is the basis of Arabic and the model of linguistic perfection, according to orthodox Islamic precepts. It is the vehicle of a vast historical, literary, and religious heritage, and individuals with a knowledge of classical Arabic can converse with their counterparts throughout the Middle East. Classical Arabic is employed for religious purposes or sometimes for literary or rhetorical emphasis.

Modern literary Arabic is a derivation and simplification of classical Arabic in wide use throughout the Middle East in newspapers, magazines, and government communiqués. In Tunisia modern literary Arabic is the official language of the mass media, formal government documents, and literature and is taught in the schools. For most Tunisians, however, it is a language as foreign as French, knowledge of which comes through education, especially in its written form. As a consequence, the form of Tunisian Arabic known as intermediary enjoys much wider popularity. A mixture of modern literary and colloquial Arabic, intermediary Arabic is increasingly employed by the media, the bureaucracy, and intellectuals.

The popular dialects that make up colloquial Arabic occur in bewildering variety. They vary from village to village, although for the most part they are mutually intelligible within Tunisia. One of these dialects is called Franco-Arabic. A high-level dialect into which numerous specialized French terms and turns of speech have been woven, it is most commonly used by students, government officials, and professionals. The urban and coastal dialects resemble those spoken in other North African cities and are closest to classical Arabic. Dialects of the interior differ more substantially from the classical and have relatively low prestige. They are heavily infused with Berber words, particularly place-names taken from Berber terms for flora, fauna, and tools.

In all Maghribi countries since independence, language and language policy have commanded a great deal of attention as a result of the colonial experience. The French sought to undermine Arabic and to impose French in their North African colonies as one way of "civilizing" the population and of isolating it from the larger Arabic-speaking world. As a reaction to this policy, independent governments in the Maghrib have sought to restore Arabic to the status and level of usage it enjoyed before the colonial era through policies that have aimed at the gradual substitution of Arabic for French. Known as arabization, this effort has entailed an official commitment to the use of modern literary Arabic in the media, education, and government administration at the same time that French has continued to be widely used. Compared wth Algeria or Morocco, the issue has been somewhat less emotionally charged in Tunisia, where President Habib Bourguiba has decided upon only partial arabization and upon the retention of French as an integral component of Tunisian identity.

The pace of arabization has been gradual, but it has faced the same problems as elsewhere in the Maghrib—too few trained teachers and a lack of teaching materials, resistance on the part of the French-educated elite, and the difference between modern literary Arabic and the colloquial Arabic spoken by a majority of the population. Nonetheless, by the mid-1980s arabization had begun to make a significant impact. In the education sector, Arabic was the language of instruction in primary schools, and French was introduced as a second language in the third year. On the secondary level, students could choose a bilingual option in which subjects such as history and philosophy were taught in Arabic while mathematics and the sciences were taught in French. At the University of Tunis, the only university in the country, French remained the chief medium of instruction; only in the faculties of theology, law, and Arabic language and literature was Arabic dominant.

Arabic was increasingly used in public administration and in most government ministries (especially the Ministry of Justice), and proficiency in modern literary Arabic was a requirement for employment in the government. Even so, French was widely employed in both oral and written communications in most ministries and was essential in the fields of science, technology, and medicine. A similar situation applied in the armed forces. Although they had been completely arabized, there was a marked preference for

Artisans loading camels with pottery produced on Jerba Island

French among the members of the officer corps, some of whom had been educated in France. Arabic was also making inroads in commerce and business, once the exclusive domain of French.

More important than either the education system or the bureaucracy in promoting modern literary Arabic were radio and television. Because of this, French programming on government-controlled radio and television networks had declined over the last two decades while programming in Arabic, modern literary as well as colloquial, had increased. Current figures were roughly 60 percent Arabic and 40 percent French, with locally produced programs almost completely in Arabic. In addition to general programming, literacy campaigns employing radio and television had been designed to increase competence in modern literary Arabic among adults without access to formal instruction.

In Tunisia as elsewhere in the Maghrib, the degree and pace of arabization have been debated extensively. Aside from the seeming remoteness of modern literary Arabic, another obstacle to rapid arabization has been the cost of language substitution. This has meant that however committed planners might be to the policy, it has had to be a gradual one, and individual steps have required a decade or more to be implemented. This certainly has been true in Tunisia, where arabization was not yet an accepted national goal.

Whatever the obstacles, other factors may prove decisive to the success of arabization over the long run. Because of the departure of most of the French-speaking community, lessened emphasis upon French in the schools, and a general repression of French throughout the society, school-age youth have had fewer opportunities to speak French. The consequence has been a decline in proficiency in that language. At the same time, the upsurge in emphasis on Islam and Muslim culture, the inflow of funds from wealthy Arab countries, and the presence in Tunis of international institutions such as the League of Arab States (Arab League) have created a demand for Tunisians trained in a standard form of Arabic. The situation has produced a change in attitude toward learning modern literary Arabic based on cultural as well as economic grounds. In the mid-1980s developments such as these favored the continuation of arabization in Tunisia and could lead to pressures for intensifying the pace and scope of the program beyond what the Bourguiba government had envisioned.

The Social System

Throughout North Africa the population originally was made up of tribes, the basic unit of social organization for both Berbers and Arabs. In the 1980s a number of tribes were still to be found in rural parts of Algeria and Morocco, but in Tunisia they had all but disappeared. The foreign influences that had made the Tunisian society a cosmopolitan one at an early date had operated also to break down tribal organization, and under the French administration a deliberate and at least partially successful effort was made to bring the primarily nomadic tribal people into the mainstream of national life. Tribal shaykhs were made civil servants, and tribespeople were encouraged or coerced into becoming sedentary farmers.

Soon after independence the remaining tribal lands were nationalized. In the 1980s a few tribes and remnants of tribes were still to be found in the more remote central and southern parts of the country, but the tribal system, as a significant element in the Tunisian social complex, had given way to more modern forms of organization.

Traditional Social Groups

Under the Turkish regency and later under the French protectorate, traditional Muslim society evolved as a class hierarchy consisting of four elements. At the top were the *baldi*, the urban aristocracy; other town dwellers were the *tunsi*. The *afaqi* were sedentary rural villagers, and the *arabi* were the nomadic and seminomadic people of central and southern Tunisia, some of them still organized in tribes. These traditional class distinctions have become increasingly blurred, only the *baldi* exhibiting significant class consciousness after independence. Important remnants of all four remained, however, either as elements of new social groups or as centers of resistance to modernization.

Sometimes referred to as the traditional aristocracy or as the old upper class, the *baldi* traced their ancestry to the Prophet Muhammad or to one of his important followers and regarded themselves as the guardians of Islamic civilization. They rarely married outsiders, although for several centuries particularly wealthy commercial families strengthened the *baldi* ranks through arranged marriages.

Children of the *baldi* received a strict religious education culminating in studies at the old Zituna Mosque school in Tunis (now the Faculty of Theology and Religious Science at the University of Tunis). The prestige of the *baldi* was based in large part on their administering *habus* land (the numerous large agricultural estates held in trust for religious and charitable works), other religious charities and the mosques, and through their positions in the Islamic court system. Thus the domain of the *baldi* extended far beyond the agricultural properties and the commercial establishments they owned individually.

The *baldi* families were related to and closely associated with the ulama, the religious scholars and notables who elsewhere in the Maghrib formed an important elite element in traditional society. The ulama played a much less significant role in Tunis, however, where in addition to being conservative and intellectually uninspired, they tended to be servile in their dealings with the French administrators. Since independence the ulama have disappeared from view as an identifiable social element, and the loss of *baldi* wealth and influence has severely restricted the role of that group. The postindependence nationalization of *habus* land, the reduction in the size of the estates, and the general modernization of society have combined to force the *baldi* to give way to a new elite.

Seldom heard since independence, the term *tunsi* was formerly applied to all town dwellers other than the elite. Wealthy as well as poor and educated as well as illiterate, the *tunsi* represented an extremely fluid element in urban society, where much upward mobility could be attained. The *tunis* also represented a channel of interaction between town and countryside, and the group's relatively open and liberal social values made it natural for the better educated and wealthier among its ranks to associate and sometimes ally with the Europeans. With the flow of migration that commenced in the 1930s, they have given way to other social groups, but the *tunsi* contributed many leaders to the independence movement.

Afaqi, or sedentary villagers, had their archetype in the prosperous farmers of the Sahil. Looked down on by the *tunsi* as well as by the *baldi* for their social aggressiveness and lack of sophistication, they were highly industrious, thrifty, and forward looking. Few Europeans took up residence in the already heavily populated Sahil, but it was the *afaqi* from this subregion who showed the greatest adaptability to Western values and institutions. Many were prosperous peasant proprietors able to send their children to French schools, and these young people played a leading role in the developing nationalist movement early in the twentieth century. Later a disproportionately large number of postindependence party leaders and civil servants were *afaqi* of Sahilian origin.

The populations of the relatively underdeveloped interior of the country were generally described as the *arabi*. Newly arrived but still unassimilated migrants to the cities as well as nomads and seminomadic villagers, these people occupied the lowest rung of the social ladder. Their customs and life-styles, however, were too diverse for them to have developed a sense of belonging to a society larger than that of their own village or nomadic tribe.

The term *arabi* is now seldom heard. A corresponding lower social element, however, continues to possess many of the characteristics of the *arabi*. In the countryside much of the population still lives by subsistence farming outside the mainstream of national life. In the cities and towns, newly arrived migrants continue to be identified with their villages of origin rather than with their new homes.

Social Stratification in Modern Tunisia

By the time of national independence Tunisian society, especially its uppermost echelons, had undergone significant modification as a result of French colonial influence. Among the most important innovations were Western-style education and the use of examinations to fill lower positions in the colonial service. These innovations provided a new avenue for social and political mobility and permitted the slow emergence of a new class of administrators and professionals alongside the older aritstocratic families and large landowners. According to one estimate, one-third of the population at independence was clearly in the modern sector, which could be found almost entirely in the cities and larger towns and in the Sahil. Another one-third was transitional, moving out of the traditional stage and consisting principally of urban migrants. The remaining one-third, including the rural population of central and southern Tunisia, remained almost untouched by the modernizing social and economic forces that were changing the rest of the society.

Four broad socioeconomic groupings could be distinguished in the 1980s, all with roots clearly discernible in the colonial period. The first grouping consisted of the country's rulers and the upper middle class, who comprised an elite that dominated the country politically and economically. Here were found members of the old aristocratic families, the new class of Western-educated civil servants and professionals who governed the country, prominent businesspeople, and large landowners. The second grouping was the lower middle class, consisting of low-level civil servants, secondary- and primary-school teachers, small businesspeople and shopkeepers, skilled workers in industry and the service sector, and small independent farmers in the Sahil, Cape Bon, and Bizerte. The third grouping included subsistence farmers and agricultural workers, who resided in the interior and the south of the country and who formed the largest proportion of the working population. The fourth grouping consisted of the day laborers, the unemployed, and the underemployed—a sizable group that resided both in rural areas and in shantytowns around the major towns and cities.

Members of the elite were linked by common values and experiences. Education served as a principal denominator and a strong tie traceable in many cases to shared experiences in French secondary schools. Many of its members had received advanced education abroad, usually in France, although a few possessed only a secondary education or were products of the traditional Zituna Mosque school. Among older members, a preponderant majority had attended the prestigious Sadiki College, which in the years before independence managed with considerable success to synthesize Arabic and French culture. A decade after independence the University of Tunis, founded only in 1958, began to contribute substantial numbers to this group.

For the most part Western-educated, the Tunisian elite admired Western institutions and values and had a special attachment to French culture and life-styles. Having adapted themselves quickly to Western customs and ways of dressing, they were for the most part strongly committed to rapid modernization and an egalitarian national society. They were united in their rejection of the precolonial social order.

In terms of social background, some were urban-born professionals, but many came from important commercial or landowning families. Others were of lower middle-class origins; their fathers were merchants, shopkeepers, bureaucrats, or small farmers of the Sahil. In all cases their families could afford the cost of education, the prerequisite for membership in the uppermost stratum of independent Tunisia. The elite came disproportionately from the Sahil, with significant additions from Tunis, other large urban centers, and Jerba Island. Bourguiba himself was perhaps the ideal example of a Sahilian of poor but respectable origin who achieved prominence through ability, education (provided by the Sadiki College and university studies abroad), intense patriotism, and adroit political activity.

The decade from 1956 to 1966 witnessed a great expansion of the Tunisian middle class. This was an era of unprecedented social mobility, brought about by the departure of the French, Italian, and Jewish foreign communities. Because these groups had monopolized most important positions in business, commerce, and government, their departure opened up immense opportunities. In the first few years after independence, Tunisians scrambled to fill tens of thousands of jobs vacated by Europeans in such fields as industry, transportation, large and small businesses, skilled trades, and government service. Those with education and skills established themselves firmly in the middle class, henceforth being in a position to determine the future of the country together with the already existing national elite.

At the top of the elite structure were the leaders of the Destourian Socialist Party (Parti Socialiste Destourien—PSD), bound together by old student-day friendships, by intricate political ties, and to some extent by marriage. They had studied in France and, speaking French fluently, tended to look down on those not familiar with the French language and customs. In the years just before independence the leading members of the party were young men devoted to changing the Tunisian society. In the mid-1980s these men were in their sixties or older and were entrenched in positions of authority.

Beginning in the mid-1960s a new group of technically trained men began to join the government and the elite. Graduates of the University of Tunis or Tunisian technical schools, these technocrats in the 1980s were aged 40 to 60 and played a commanding role in managing the affairs of state under the tutelage of the oldest generation of political leaders. Behind them, however, there was a sharp drop-off in the number of youthful members of the party and the government. According to one source, only about 15 percent of the elite was less than 40 years of age at a time when roughly one of every two Tunisians was age 20 or younger.

The lower middle class also expanded greatly after national independence and had both urban and rural components. It was predominantly urban, however, and included middle- and lower-grade civil servants; members of labor unions; self-employed individuals, such as taxi drivers, shopkeepers, and tailors; and the more substantial wage earners. In Tunis, in particular, members of this class were often reported to be recent migrants who retained strong ties with their villages of origin and who identified with the traditional town dwellers only in the second or third generation. However, they looked up to the Westernized elite, whose life-styles they sought to emulate. The most upwardly mobile of Tunisians, these people had high aspirations for their children. Occasionally an entire migrant group was successful in establishing itself in a particular occupation that lifted it into the middle level of society. This process occurred, for example, when migrants from Jerba Island were generally successful in establishing themselves as grocers on the mainland.

The farmers and villagers of the Sahil and the northeastern coastal lowlands formed the nucleus of the rural lower middle class. Probably more than any other social group, they had taken advantage of opportunities in the social and political realms in the three decades since independence. Although small merchants or olive growers and of only moderate means, they nonetheless managed to afford Western-style education for their children, many of whom went on to staff the bureaucracy or to assume positions of importance in politics and business. Despite obvious links with the political elite, they remained fiercely independent and opposed governmental interference in rural affairs that ran counter to their best interests, such as the abortive attempt to institute widespread cooperative farming in the 1960s (see Land Tenure and Reform, ch. 3).

The situation of the farmers and merchants of the Sahil, miners and factory workers, school teachers, civil servants, and other members of the lower middle class was definitely preferable to that of the lowest strata of Tunisian society—subsistence farmers and paid agricultural workers in rural areas, day laborers in the *gourbivilles* around Tunis and other major urban centers, and the underemployed and the unemployed in both settings. These people constituted the bulk of Tunisia's labor force. Subsistence farming was concentrated in the interior and the south; day laborers, who often came from the poorest rural areas, shared many characteristics with middle-class migrants but differed from them in their general lack of education and skills. Underemployment was common in both groups. Least enviable were the unemployed, a substantial category of unfortunates. Often but not necessarily uneducated or unskilled, they constituted a class of economically marginal people without a useful role to play in the society. Composed to an ever increasing degree of disenchanted youth, the plight of the unemployed posed a troubling challenge to the established social and political order.

For the rural population in general, socioeconomic changes that commenced during the protectorate years have continued to disrupt the age-old pattern of life without replacing it with a clearly identifiable alternative. Education, health care, and welfare services have spread throughout the countryside, and there have been attempts at land reform and land redistribution in the years since independence. Even so, the more capable and ambitious of the rural population have shown a marked inclination to migrate to urban centers such as Tunis, Béja, and Kasserine rather than to remain on the land and work for social improvement there. Change has been slowest in the desert lands of southern Tunisia and in the semiarid interior. Both have become areas of out-migration in which only women, the old, and the very young have remained at home.

Over the years since independence Tunisian society has often been described as open, equitable, dynamic, modern, and democratic, especially in comparison with neighboring states in North Africa and those of the Middle East. While there has been cause for such description, the situation since the mid-1970s has become less sanguine, and the cleavages inherent in the country's social structure have become more pronounced. What formerly appeared to be one of the most politically stable and socially progressive states of the region has yielded evidence over the past few years of tensions and oppositons that if left unaddressed by responsible authorities portended an unsettled future.

Two major dichotomies underlay contemporary Tunisian society, one an old phenomenon, the other more recent. The older dichotomy was the regional opposition between the interior and the coast, which coincided economically with the division between the

underdeveloped and the developed sections of the country and socially with that between the rural and the urban segments of the
population. The opposition between the interior and the coast can
be traced to antiquity; since then the tribesmen and small villagers
of the central area and the south have been pitted against the ur-
banized population of the coastal lowland. The manifestation of
this opposition in the mid-1980s lay in the regional distribution of
the membership of the PSD and the General Union of Tunisian
Workers (Union Générale des Travailleurs Tunisiens—UGTT). On
the one hand, most of the party's membership and the country's
political leadership came from an axis stretching from Bizerte to
Jerba Island, and the peoples of the interior and the south were
poorly represented. Trade union membership and leadership, on
the other hand, were heavily concentrated in the interior. Hence
one encountered a basic geographic division between Tunisia's politicians and wealthy middle class and its small farmers, miners, and
shepherds. It was no accident that a preponderance of the political
upheavals the country experienced after the mid-1970s originated
in the interior or in trade union activity (see Political Dynamics,
ch. 4).

The second major dichotomy was the generational gulf that
separated those under 25 years of age from the generation over 40
years of age. This split had its roots in contemporary demographic
reality: more than one of every two Tunisians was under the age of
20. As with the regional dichotomy already noted, this generational
division was of enormous economic and political significance. From
the point of view of the young, the age-group from 40 to 60 controlled the government and the economic life of the country and
monopolized nearly all desirable positions associated therewith.
While new positions were being created, they were far too few to
satisfy the demands and expectations of those newly arrived on the
employment scene. As a result, approximately one-half of the population—overwhelmingly young, often educated, and aspiring to careers in statecraft, business, and commerce—saw itself as excluded
from any meaningful role in the country for the indefinite future.
Those under 25 increasingly seemed to have little in common with
their elders, and the hallmarks of the post-1956 era—independence, Bourguiba, and the PSD—had largely ceased to be relevant
to their concerns.

Several factors were at work in Tunisia that helped to perpetuate or to exacerbate these two overiding dichotomies. The first
was long-term population pressure. Since the mid-1970s Tunisia's
population has been growing at an annual rate of about 2.5 per-

Elderly Tunisian resident of Teboulba in the Sahil

Tunisian housewife in Teboulba

Tunisian farmer from Menzel Bourguiba in the
Bizerte Plain of the north

Farm youngster near Menzel Bourguiba
Photos courtesy John Metelsky

cent. While this was less than the growth rate of the 1960s and better than in either Algeria or Morocco, it was still quite high, given the meager natural resources and industrial base of the country. Through the mid-1970s the economy barely managed to contain the increase; since then, even that modest accomplishment has been impossible to maintain, despite efforts on the part of the central government to create new jobs.

Directly related to the high birth rate was the rate of unemployment. High by any standard and characteristic of all age-groups and locales, unemployment and underemployment fell especially hard on young people and the poorly educated, running at rates of 20 percent and more among these groups. In many cases the young and the unemployed had despaired of ever finding satisfactory occupations. They survived on the margins of a society that often appeared not to care about them or their welfare, eking out a meager living incommensurate with their hopes, expectations, and education and resentful of the wealth and success of the middle classes and the elite.

Poverty was another source of social and political malaise. It was especially widespread in the center and the south of the country, where the farming potential was limited and industry was non-existent. These regions had long suffered from neglect on the part of economic planners and from a standard of living considerably lower than that of the neighboring Sahil. As a consequence of its destitution, the poverty-stricken hinterland has produced a steady flow of young migrants to the larger towns and cities, to neighboring countries, and to Western Europe. Partly as a result of internal migration, the annual growth rate of the urban population in recent years has been in excess of 4 percent, leading to a severe housing shortage and the relentless extension of slums around Tunis and other urban centers.

Finally, there were the inequalities in the distribution of income and wealth. An enormous gap in income existed between the elite and the middle classes on the one hand and the lower classes and the unemployed on the other. The general consensus in the mid-1980s was that both the differential in incomes and the level of poverty continued to grow. This disparity was well established at the time of independence, but it widened measurably during the 1970s when government-sponsored economic reforms caused an expansion of the middle class and fostered the emergence of a new class of small-scale entrepreneurs and businesspeople. Wealthy upper-class Tunisians benefited disproportionately from public and private sector employment and government spending programs, and they were often accused of corruption, dodging taxation, using their positions for personal enrichment, and obstructing reforms. The gap in income and wealth between them and the poorer segment of the population played a major role in fomenting the violence that convulsed Tunisia in 1978 and again in 1984.

Social Values

Islam is at the root of the traditional system of values. People's power to influence their destiny or environment is believed to be limited or nonexistent, and the harshness and unreliability of the climate in most of the Muslim world have strengthened this belief among nomadic tribespeople. Even among sedentary people, pestilence and other misfortunes are often attributed to the will of God.

To be respected a person must, above all, be a good Muslim. A believer must publicly profess the faith, pray at established times, and give alms. The strong resistance encountered by Bourguiba in 1960, when he moved to discourage fasting during the sacred month of Ramadan, bore witness to the surviving strength of traditional religious values in modern-day Tunisia. The same could be said of the more recent upsurge of interest and devotion to Islam among the young, the Islamists (see Glossary), and others.

At an early date Tunisia became divided into two cultural regions, and the distinction between these two can still be readily observed. The first one consists roughly of the cities and the coastal rural zone, including the Sahil, and the second one encompasses the rural interior. The differences between these two regions correspond generally to the historical division between settled life and nomadism; and their roots go back to pre-Arab times when Berbers settled in the ancient cities under the suzerainty of Carthaginians or Romans.

In the more remote localities, values associated with tribal life have tended to survive. In the past the people of nomadic tribes were highly individualistic, and tribal and family loyalties were considered values of the highest order. Raids and counterraids were frequent. Tribal warfare was suppressed by the French, and over the years a majority of the nomads either became sedentary farmers or migrated to the cities. Values associated with tribal organization have persisted, however, and probably have contributed to the strong resistance encountered by the government in its efforts to aid landless farmers and to introduce modern farming techniques.

The primordial acceptance of mankind's helplessness and complete dependence on God has been considerably modified in the cities and the coastal plains since early times. City people came to stress intellectual and political acumen, commercial success, and wealth. In the Sahil, whose population came to share values more in common with those of Tunis than with those of the peoples of the interior, town and village life have been marked by a considerable sense of security, right to property, and material progress, and a middle-class value system developed at an early date.

Throughout the nineteenth and early twentieth centuries contact between Tunisia and the Western world increasingly brought modernizing influences, but their full impact came to bear only with the establishment of a large European community and the opening up of opportunities in French universities for significant numbers of Tunisian youth who had attended the already prestigious Sadiki College in Tunis. The emergence of this educated elite left an old social hierarchy badly shaken and had an important influence on the spread of modern values. In part because of its middle-class background and in part because of its intense nationalism, self-confidence, and sense of political security, the new elite lent its wholehearted support to the modernization of society, thus creating an atmosphere of mobility that encouraged many of the less educated and less privileged to adopt the new way of thinking.

During the first years after independence enormous efforts were made to transform attitudes and values and to reduce psychological and social impediments to investments in human resources, such as new schools and hospitals, which far outstripped investment in capital goods. The new values were secular ones, justified not in terms of religious precepts and traditional values but in terms of natural law and rationalism that assumed the probability of material and social progress to an extent that appeared to contradict the traditional Islamic acceptance of man's situation as not susceptible to change. However, there remained a strong emotional attachment to Islam that stressed the cultural rather than the strictly dogmatic aspect of the religion.

In the years that followed, modern values and their reflection of higher expectations made parents highly ambitious for their children. Those still on the fringes of modern society became anxious for their children to become civil servants or teachers, the only modern occupations with which they were familiar. Those better integrated in modern society wanted their children to enter a profession or, perhaps, to become a minister in the government. Education was regarded as the key to achievement of aspirations, and the government's phenomenal success in expanding and improving the educational system during the 1950s and 1960s made it possible for young people of the 1970s to entertain high educational and occupational goals. High aspirations were the product of the government's encouraging a massive transformation in attitudes and values by creating a shared commitment to modernization.

By the mid-1980s, however, such optimism had been considerably tempered in view of the difficulty of finding professional or white-collar employment in a low-growth economy. Indeed, many young people found themselves in the ironic situation of having benefited from the state education system but of being unable— albeit willing—to repay the social cost of the investment through productive activity. Finding upward channels blocked and their hopes of joining the middle class and the elite thwarted, many young Tunisians had become disillusioned, cynical, alienated from their parents and elders, and contemptuous of the Westernized middle class they formerly had envied.

Rejecting middle-class values and ostentatious display of wealth and seeking alternatives to consumerism and the "get rich quick" ethic of the 1970s, a sizable portion of the younger generation had withdrawn from participation in state functions and political organizations. Instead they had turned to the religious sphere for inspiration, guidance, and self-fulfillment. This movement was especially pronounced among secondary-school and university students who came from the poorer strata of society and who were without real hope of upward social or economic mobility. Hence, there were low levels of participation in state- or party-sponsored student organizations such as the General Union of Tunisian Students (Union Général des Étudiants Tunisiens—UGET) on the university level or the National Organization of Students and Youth (Organisation Nationale de Jeunesse Étudiante) for secondary-school students but ever growing interest in Islamic social and cultural values and adherence to religious organizations. For example, significant numbers of the young were joining the Islamic Tendency Movement (Mouvement de la Tendance Islamique—MTI), which condemned contemporary society as morally depraved and sought to replace it with an Islamic-based society and a strict code of behavior. The MTI drew most of its support from coastal regions, including Tunis, the same locales where the PSD and the middle classes were concentrated. This regional congruence of two fundamentally opposed sets of values accentuated in yet another way the divergence between the older and younger generations that contained the potential for further protests in the future.

The Individual, the Family, and the Sexes

Personal status and interpersonal relations in the Tunisian society were dictated traditionally by the precepts of the Quran and sharia, the Islamic system of law. The Muslim system is a generally stern one, but from an early date it was modified somewhat in Tunisia by relatively liberal attitudes and by a sense of national identity that long predated independence. With the attainment of national independence, moreover, Bourguiba and the political elite who supported him undertook to bring Tunisian society fully into the modern world, and the chief instrument in this respect was the Code of Personal Status, enacted only five months later.

The Code of Personal Status stands as a landmark in Tunisian legislation and possibly as the most remarkable code of conduct ever enacted in a Muslim country. Because it profoundly altered the legal bases for family matters and the status of women, it received strenuous opposition from conservative Islamic elements, but the new educated elite gave it their unqualified support. Moreover, the opposition of the conservative elements was anticipated by the drafters of the code, and the thrust of opposition was blunted by careful retention of traditional Islamic concepts where it was feared that their rejection might arouse too much opposition. Similarly, certain modernizing precepts were not contained in the original code but were added later as amendments.

The code was presented not as a rejection of Islamic teaching but as Islam in modern dress. Moreover, it was offered as something for all Tunisian people, regardless of religion. Previously, the sharia courts had applied only to Muslims; Jews had their own rabbinical courts, and Tunisians who were neither Muslim nor Jewish had been governed by the French Civil Code. This situation continued until late 1957, after which the code's provisions applied to all Tunisians without exception.

Conservative opposition to the code gradually abated, and by the late 1970s its provisions were generally accepted in the cities. Implementation was still far from complete in the more remote parts of the countryside, where the new system was least understood and where attachment to traditional ways was the strongest. But in the Tunisian society in general it was being accepted and was considered a success.

Family and Household

Throughout the Arab world the traditional social unit has been the extended family, a patrilineal grouping headed by a father and including his wife or wives, their unmarried and married sons with their families, and their unmarried daughters. This family unit consists of a dozen or more members who reside in a single house or in adjoining dwellings with a common courtyard. Property is held in common by the family, which acts as an economic unit. The men work together in joint ventures; all expenditures are defrayed from the common fund.

In Tunisia, however, the intrusion of Western customs and values in the cities during the nineteenth century led to the gradual displacement of the extended family group by the nuclear family, consisting only of the spouses and their unmarried children. The extended family has persisted with greater tenacity in the rural interior of the country, but the policy of the government since independence has been to encourage the nuclear form of family organization at the expense of the extended form.

The 1966 population census indicated that the average family consisted of only slightly more than five members, and fewer than 10 percent of the families included relatives other than spouses and children. Moreover, the census showed that more than 10 percent of the family heads were women, an arrangement that would have been unheard of in traditional Muslim society. Surveys in the early 1980s showed that the ideal family size was six among one-half or more of the urban and rural respondents, a figure that had not changed for two decades. In many cases, however, it remained only an ideal, because nuclear families often numbered seven or more members.

The decline of the extended family, however, has not necessarily meant the corresponding decline of all values and practices associated with it. For example, marriage between close relatives continued to enjoy high esteem, especially in rural areas, although the number of such marriages was decreasing. In one survey about 90 percent of the marriages in a seminomadic community and 60 percent of those among Tunis factory workers were endogamous. In addition, urban working-class neighborhoods were traditionally organized on the basis of kinship, and recent urban migrants have sought to preserve this pattern to the extent that housing shortages permit. Indeed, such a tie often represents the only secure social factor available to them in the highly complex and competitive urban environment.

Although the Tunisian father no longer exercises absolute authority over his children, he is still regarded as the household head, and the relationship between father and son remains a peculiarly important internal family tie. Reserve and formality mark the relationship of the son with his parent, who remains an authoritarian figure. Greater informality and an almost conspiratorial friendship marked the relationship between mother and daughter in the extended family, and something of this spirit survives. The mother was traditionally responsible for the care and supervision of sons until they reached the age of about six. A warm relationship developed, but all discipline remained the responsibility of the father, who assumed supervision of older male children.

Children commence their education at home as early as the age of four. Rural daughters help their mothers with household duties, and sons work in the fields and olive groves. Tasks become more difficult as the children grow older, so that youngsters of 12 and 13 are virtually fully prepared for adult work. It is more difficult for sons to assist their fathers when they live in towns, and prominent families even consider this practice inappropriate. The sons, therefore, learn a trade or continue in school. Moreover, education for daughters is increasingly favored, particularly in urban areas. As a result, most girls attend school for at least a few years before marriage.

After independence the guardianship of children was clarified and formalized within the legal system. Under a 1956 law women were considered to be the best guardians for younger children. A listing of preferred relatives for legal guardianship was also established. In 1959 the law was modified to permit the court to appoint the person most qualified. If the father is not appointed guardian, guardianship by the mother or a relative lasts until a boy is seven and a girl nine. The father remains responsible for his children's education and may, upon termination of the mother's guardianship, take the children into his home.

In addition to performing its normal domestic functions, the household frequently serves as a business and labor unit. In villages and oases the household is a cooperative work unit in which animals and land are distributed to and managed by household members. In towns many small businesses, especially those of craftspeople, are family enterprises in which the son is trained by his father and eventually takes over the business from him, a system reminiscent of the traditional guilds of artisans in which membership was handed down from father to son.

The Code of Personal Status struck directly at the patriarchal family system and sought to strengthen the nuclear family by outlawing polygyny and by bringing divorce into the courts. Before the code it had been the husband's unrestricted right to take up to four wives, whom he could divorce at will by repudiation—the traditional Muslim practice whereby the husband could rid himself of an unwanted spouse by saying "I divorce thee" three times before witnesses. When repudiated, the wife was required to abandon her children and return to her father's household. The code abolished polygyny and gave to wives rights corresponding to those of husbands in seeking court-ordered divorces. The act of marriage became legally a voluntary one rather than the traditional agreement between families. Legal strictures such as these tend to weaken paternalistic authority and control by kin groups while at the same time heightening the emotional commitment between husband and wife and parent and child.

The legal age for marriage was set by the code at 15 years for females and 18 years for males, but a 1964 amendment raised the ages to 17 and 20, respectively. This amendment, which effectively outlawed child marriage, serves as an example of the cautious and gradual manner in which the government's planners sought modernization. Census data show a sharp rise in the percentage of singles between the ages of 15 and 24 over the period from 1956 to 1980. While the mean age at first marriage in 1980 was 22 for women and 27 for men, data for 1978 indicated that the most popular ages for first marriages were 17 for women and 26 for men.

Status of Women

The traditional Muslim cultural pattern, which countenanced polygyny and permitted the maintenance of an unrestricted number of concubines, had the inescapable side effect of placing a high value on masculine virility. Women were restricted to the home and in all ways required to play a subordinate role. The husband held a position of unquestioned authority and moderated all family quarrels. In his absence, authority was delegated not to the wife but to the eldest or best educated son.

The most reliable basis for trust between men was traditionally considered to be kinship, and the ties of friendship, no matter how strong, remained inferior to blood tie. This kinship value, common throughout the Muslim world, probably harked back to the time of tribal existence when all members of the tribe bore a real or ascribed relationship to one another, or at least to a time when all or most of the residents of a village or quarter were related.

Since independence the performance of kinship ties has abated somewhat but is still an important factor governing interpersonal relationships. The tendency to draw a distinction between relatives and friends has led to the survival of behavior patterns sometimes difficult for Westerners to understand. Men are unlikely to bring their wives to mixed functions that include business associates, and they are even less likely to discuss their families or family life with outsiders.

The subordinate nature of the status of women is spelled out in sharia, although not in the Quran. The status of women, however, has always been somewhat higher in Tunisia than in most other Muslim countries, and with the enactment of the Code of Personal Status their civil status became almost equal to that of men with respect to such matters as inheritance, ownership of property, custody of children, and divorce. Indeed, since national independence the general status of women has undergone a significant transformation, in part because of the provisions of the code. But other factors have also been at work, among them urbanization, increased mobility, industrialization, and new educational opportunities, the same developments that were behind the breakdown of the patriarchal extended family. The altered status of Tunisian women increased the tension and conflict that existed between the sexes, because Tunisian men found it difficult to adjust to the demands of their liberated wives and sisters.

One major goal of Bourguiba and the modernizing elite behind him at independence was to bring Tunisian women out of seclusion and into the modern world. To do this, new laws were passed, and the leadership used the organizations and local cells of the PSD to institute novel concepts about women. In 1956 the party supported the founding of the National Union of Tunisian Women (Union Nationale des Femmes Tunisiennes—UNFT) to give voice to women's problems and aspirations and in general to promote female participation in the political and social life of the country. The organization has served as a useful forum for expression of feminine concerns in employment, health, literacy, and family planning.

Whatever the efforts of the party and the UNFT, women have found it difficult to play roles in public life or to provide high-level administrative leadership. In 1971 there were 83 women town councillors in local town halls, and four women deputies sat in the Chamber of Deputies, a number that rose to seven in 1981. Not until 1985, however, did women gain entry to the top echelons of the government, when two—one of them the wife of Prime Minister Mohamed Mzali—joined the cabinet as minister of family and women's advancement and minister of public health. The gulf in status and achievement between urban and rural women, however, remained wide, and even in the cities women were timid about experimenting with their newly acquired liberty. For example, while urban upper- and middle-class women had largely abandoned Is-

Young brides at a traditional wedding in the south
Courtesy Embassy of Tunisia, Washington

lamic dress, including the veil, it was still worn in villages and
rural areas by women who wished to preserve their modesty and
live within the strict dictates of Islam.

The change in women's rights and roles has affected almost
every aspect of Tunisian life. In terms of marital relations, marriage required the consent of both parties. A woman could not be
legally married against her will, and child marriages, popular in
the past, were outlawed with the establishment of age minimums
for both males and females. It was also permissible for women to
marry outside the Muslim faith, but in practice this privilege, along
with some other newly won rights, was often difficult to exercise.
Polygyny, formerly practiced only by a tiny percentage of Tunisian
men, was forbidden, as was the husband's former right to repudi-
ate his wife unilaterally and without recourse to outside authority.
Marriages could only be dissolved before a civil court, and wives

exercised equal rights with husbands in divorce proceedings. With passage of the Code of Personal Status, the divorce rate rose dramatically over the next decade, but since the mid-1960s it has leveled off somewhat. Women have initiated a high percentage of these divorces.

Despite traditional preferences for the marriage of cousins and parental selection of prospective spouses, many young Tunisians—especially those who were educated—expected to select their own marriage partners. Young men often expressed a preference for a wife who was educated and who could contribute to the welfare of the family through her own employment. Educated young women also preferred an educated husband and entertained high expectations of their future spouses. Once married, however, spouses sometimes experienced difficulty reconciling expectations with reality, a situation that could lead to frustration, friction, and all too often divorce among newlyweds.

During the years since national independence Tunisian parents have continued to encourage sons far more than daughters to develop modern attitudes and aspirations, but school attendance has had a much more profound modernizing effect on girls than on their brothers. It has provided the primary, and sometime sole, opportunity to develop friendships outside the home and to achieve new self-concepts and aspirations. In the early 1980s girls made up nearly one-half of the students in primary schools and more than one-third of the secondary and vocational school enrollments, and, although male students continued to predominate in higher education, 40 percent of the 40,000 students enrolled in the University of Tunis and other institutions of higher education were women.

Employment outside the home was another realm in which Tunisian women had made significant gains. The prejudice against employment of unmarried women had largely abated, but opinions about married women who worked were at best mixed. According to official figures based on a 1982 survey, some 244,700 women were engaged in full-time paid employment. This represented 7 percent of the total working population and a gain of 76 percent over similar labor statistics in 1977. More than 64 percent worked in administration and services, 14 percent in industry, and 3 percent each in agriculture and in transportation and communications. Female teachers numbered 71,605, whereas women in the medical field totaled 14,897, accounting for 35 percent of both professions.

Some 60,000 women were listed as partially paid laborers, an increase of nearly 57 percent over 1977, while another 37,000 were seeking paid positions. Part-time employment usually meant agricultural work in rural areas or seamstress jobs in cities, mostly within family enterprises. A large number of widows, divorcees, and unmarried women were found in this category. On the one hand, the sampling showed that the higher the level of education, the more likely a woman was to be employed. On the other hand, it failed to report the sizable amount of unpaid female labor in rural areas and in craft industries that was most often performed in a family setting. According to other government statistics, women constituted about 20 percent of the Tunisian labor force in the mid-1980s (see the Labor Force, ch. 3).

Since the beginning of the 1980s a reaction against the more excessive aspects of postindependence Westernization has slowly been gaining strength at the same time that official commitment to planned social change—including female status—has waned. This reaction was especially popular among Islamic activists, who tended to feel that the emancipation of Tunisian women had come at the expense of the family. As a result of this renewed stress upon Islamic identity, some younger women were beginning to resume the wearing of traditional dress and even to surrender their jobs in order to devote themselves to familial matters. Further, a 1983 survey documented the enduring conservatism among Tunisians with respect to family patterns and male-female roles in the face of three decades of state-sponsored social change. Survey researchers reported that men particularly felt that "women's status still depends largely on women having children, and their outside employment is considered unimportant or contrary to their primary roles."

Family Planning

Before independence Tunisia did not have a family planning program. The Quran contains no injunction against birth control, but tradition-minded families, in particular, felt that having large families was in keeping with God's will. Perhaps more important, in families with limited income, numerous children were considered important for the work they could perform in assisting their parents and as assurances of security for their parents' old age. In a survey of selected Arab countries in 1965, Tunisia ranked at about the average in crude birth rate. (Arab countries regularly rank among the highest in the world.)

Soon after national independence, however, the new government determined that if Tunisia were to be brought into the modern world, a modern posture toward population control had to be adopted. Birth control measures were legalized in 1961, and in

1964 the government commenced family planning studies with the assistance of several foreign agencies, becoming the first Arab or African country—and only the fifth nation in the world—to adopt an official policy of birth control as a means of spurring socioeconomic development. In 1973 the government provided centralized leadership for already well-established planning activities by establishing the National Office of Family Planning and Population as a semiautonomous agency of the Ministry of Health and by legalizing abortion during the first trimester of pregnancy.

Between 1966 and 1976 the average number of births per woman fell from 7.1 to 5.7, a significant decline, but over the next five years the fertility rate edged down only to 5.2. By 1981 there were 726 local centers, 20 regional centers, five clinics, and 50 mobile teams administering the family planning program nationwide. The percentage of married women aged 15 to 49 using traditional or modern contraceptive methods rose from 3.2 percent in 1966 to 41 percent in 1983; intrauterine devices and birth control pills were the most widely used techniques.

On the surface, Tunisian family planning seemed to be relatively successful, yet a number of problems had come to the fore by the early 1980s. The availability of services varied widely, and most women using them lived in urban, not rural, areas. There was concern that the fertility rate appeared to have leveled off after an initial period of decline, and in searching for the cause, researchers found that the decrease in fertility was attributable largely to marriage at somewhat later ages rather than to application of birth control techniques. Further, while births were fewer among women in the 15-to-25 age bracket, once married they tended to make up for this deficiency, with the result that the total fertility rate remained almost unchanged. Researchers also discovered that the decline in births was matched by a fall in the overall death rate because of improved health care, so the rate of natural increase in Tunisia's population—birth minus deaths—scarcely varied from about 2.7 percent from 1967 to 1982. At that rate of growth, the population would double in less than 30 years, considerably sooner than government projections.

One of the most important obstacles to population control was a general lack of commitment on the part of the people. Men in particular continued to have trouble accepting any role for women other than as wives and mothers. The burden of family planning thus fell to women, many of whom expressed an interest in the concept but found it difficult to persevere in the face of opposition from their husbands or of suspected health risks. Another problem was that women often resorted to contraception only after having borne several children, using it to stop births rather than to space them.

But there was cause for at least some optimism. The government's commitment to family planning remained strong, and plans were afoot to encourage wider participation. Demographic planners were encouraged by the lower infant mortality rates; the inclination to marry at a slightly older age, reinforced by education and urbanization; an ideal of four children per family, although couples often had more; and the popularity of the nuclear family. The age structure of Tunisia's population, however, of which 40 percent or more were under age 15 in the early 1980s, argued in favor of continued high population growth for the foreseeable future.

Religious Life

In the mid-1980s virtually all Tunisians who professed the Muslim faith were Sunnis adhering to the Malikite rite. The only exceptions were about 40,000 Berber-speaking Ibadi on Jerba Island, who kept austere Kharidjite beliefs (see Islam and the Arabs, ch. 1). In recognition that Tunisia was a Muslim country, the preamble to the Constitution opened with the invocation "In the name of God, the Compassionate, the Merciful" and proclaimed that the Tunisian people were resolved "to remain faithful to the teachings of Islam." Article 1 stated that Islam was the official religion of the republic, and a subsequent provision required that the chief of state be a Muslim. Since independence, however, the Tunisian government has been decidedly secularist in its orientation, attempting to divorce Islamic practices from the country's political life. The Constitution also guaranteed free exercise of conscience to all Tunisians and allowed all residents freedom of worship.

The Christian community, composed mainly of Roman Catholics among French and Italian expatriates, numbered less than 30,000 in the mid-1980s. Before independence, there were about 300,000 communicants residing in Tunisia, and many churches were converted to mosques after their departure.

Tenets of Islam

In A.D. 610 Muhammad (later recognized as the Prophet), a merchant belonging to the Hashimite branch of the ruling Quraysh tribe in the Arabian town of Mecca, began to preach the first of a series of revelations granted him by God through the angel Gabriel. A fervent monotheist, Muhammad denounced the polytheistic paganism of his fellow Meccans. Because the town's economy was based in part on a thriving pilgrimage business to the shrine called the Kaabah and numerous pagan religious sites loacated there, his vigorous and continuing censure eventually earned him the bitter enmity of the town's leaders. In 622 he and a group of followers were accepted into the town of Yathrib, which came to be known as Medina (the city) because it was the center of Muhammad's activities. The move from Mecca, or hijra, also known as the hegira, marked the beginning of the Islamic era and of Islam as a force on the stage of history. The Muslim calendar, based on the lunar year, thus begins in 622. In Medina, Muhammad continued to preach, eventually defeated his detractors in battle, and consolidated both the temporal and the spiritual leadership of all Arabia in his person before his death in 632.

After Muhammad's death his followers compiled those of his words regarded as coming directly from God into the Quran, the holy scriptures of Islam; others of his sayings and teachings and precedents of his personal behavior, recalled by those who had known him during his lifetime, became the hadith. Together they formed the Sunna, a comprehensive guide to the spiritual, ethical, and social life of the orthodox Sunni Muslim.

The *shahadah* (testimony, creed) succinctly states the central belief of Islam: "There is no god but God (Allah), and Muhammad is his Prophet." This simple profession of faith is repeated on many ritual occasions, and recital in full and unquestioning sincerity designates one a Muslim. The God preached by Muhammad was not previously unknown to his countrymen, for Allah is Arabic for God rather than a particular name. Rather than introducing a new deity, Muhammad denied the existence of the many minor gods and spirits worshiped before his ministry and declared the omnipotence of the unique Creator. God is invisible and omnipresent; to represent him in any visual symbol is a sin. Events in the world flow ineluctably from his will; to resist it is both futile and sinful.

Islam means submission (to God), and one who submits is a Muslim. Muhammad is the "seal of the prophets;" his revelation is said to complete for all time the series of biblical revelations received by the Jews and the Christians. God is believed to have remained one and the same throughout time, but people had strayed from his true teachings until set aright by Muhammad. Abraham, Moses, and Jesus (known in Arabic as Ibrahim, Musa, and Isa, respectively) are recognized as prophets who were inspired vehicles of God's will. Islam, however, reveres only the message as sacred, rejecting Christianity's deification of the messenger Jesus. It accepts the concepts of angels, the Day of Judgment, general resurrection, heaven and hell, and eternal life of the soul.

The duties of the Muslim form the five pillars of the faith. These are the recitation of the *shahadah,* daily prayer (*salat*); almsgiving (*zakat*); fasting (*sawm*); and hajj, or pilgrimage. The believer is to pray in a prescribed manner after purification through ritual ablutions each day at dawn, midday, midafternoon, sunset, and nightfall. Prescribed genuflections and prostrations accompany the prayers, which the worshiper recites facing toward Mecca. Whenever possible men pray in congregation of the mosque with the imam, or prayer leader, and on Fridays are obliged to do so. The Friday noon prayers provide the occasion for weekly sermons by religious leaders. Women may also attend public worship at the mosque, where they are segregated from the men, although most commonly those who pray do so at home. A special functionary, the muadhdhin, intones a call to prayer to the entire community at the appropriate hour; those out of earshot determine the proper time from the sun.

In the early days of Islam the authorities imposed a tax on personal property proportionate to one's wealth; this was distributed to the mosques and to the needy. In addition freewill gifts were made. Almsgiving, however, although still a duty of the believer, has become a more private matter. Many properties contributed by pious individuals to support religious and charitable activities, or institutions, were traditionally administered as an inalienable endowment, called *habus* in the Maghrib.

The ninth month of the Muslim calendar is Ramadan, a period of obligatory fasting in commemoration of Muhammad's receipt of god's revelation, the Quran. Throughout the month all but the sick, the weak, pregnant women, soldiers on duty, travelers on necessary journeys, and young children are enjoined from eating, drinking, smoking, and sexual intercourse during daylight hours. Those adults excused are obliged to endure an equivalent fast at their earliest opportunity. A festive meal breaks each daily fast and inaugurates a night of feasting and celebration. The pious well-to-do usually do little or no work during this period, and some businesses close for all or part of the day. Because the months of the lunar calendar revolve through the solar year, Ramadan falls at various seasons in different years. Though a considerable test of discipline at any time of year, a fast that falls in summertime imposes severe hardship on those who must do physical work. Frayed tempers and poor work performance, concomitants of the fast, were an early cause of concern to the Bourguiba regime.

At least once in their lifetime all Muslims should, if possible, make the hajj to the holy city of Mecca to participate in special rites held there during the twelfth month of the lunar calendar. The Prophet instituted this requirement, modifying pre-Islamic custom, to emphasize sites associated with Allah and with Abraham, founder of monotheism and father of the Arabs through his son Ishmael (Ismail). Once in Mecca pilgrims from all over the world, dressed in white seamless garments called *ihram*, abstain from sexual relations, shaving, haircutting, and nail paring for the duration of the hajj. Highlights of the pilgrimage include kissing the sacred black stone; circumambulating the Kaabah, the sacred structure reputedly built by Abraham that houses the stone; running seven times between the hills of Safa and Marwa in imitiation of Hagar, Ishmael's mother, during her travail in the desert; and standing in prayer on the Plain of Arafat. The returning pilgrim is entitled to the honorific haji before his name. Id al Adha, a major festival celebrated worldwide, marks the end of the hajj month.

The permanent struggle for the triumph of the word of God on earth, the jihad, represents an additional duty of all Muslims. Although this has been used to justify holy wars, modernist Muslims interpret the concept in a broader context of divine and personal action. The Bourguiba regime has encouraged this outlook. In addition to specific duties, Islam imposes a code of ethical conduct encouraging generosity, fairness, honesty, and respect and forbidding adultery, gambling, usury, and the consumption of carrion, blood, pork, and alcohol.

Early Development of Islam

During his lifetime Muhammad held both spiritual and temporal leadership of the Muslim community; he established the concept of Islam as a total and all-encompassing way of life for people and society. Islam teaches that Allah revealed to Muhammad the immutable principles governing decent behavior, and it is therefore incumbent on the individual to live in the manner prescribed by revealed law and on the community to perfect human society on earth according to the holy injunctions.

After Muhammad's death the leaders of the Muslim community consensually chose Abu Bakr, the Prophet's father-in-law and one of his earliest followers, to succeed him. At that time, some persons favored Ali, the Prophet's cousin and husband of his daughter Fatima, but Ali and his supporters recognized the community's choice. The next two caliphs, Uman and Uthman, enjoyed the recognition of the entire community, although Uthman was murdered. When Ali finally succeeded to the caliphate in 656, Muawiyah, governor of Syria, rebelled in the name of his kinsman Uthman. After the ensuing civil war Ali moved his capital to Baghdad, where a short time later he too was murdered.

Ali's death ended the last of the so-called four orthodox caliphates and the period in which the entire Islamic community recognized a single caliphate. Muawiyah then proclaimed himself caliph from Damascus. Ali's supporters, however, refused to recognize Muawiyah or his line, the Umayyad caliphs; they withdrew in the first great schism and established a dissident sect known as the Shias (or Shiites)—the party of Ali—in support of the claims of Ali's line to a presumptive right to the caliphate based on descent from the Prophet. The larger faction of Islam, the Sunnis, claims to follow the orthodox teaching and example of the Prophet as embodied in the Sunna.

Originally political in nature, the differences between Sunni and Shia interpretations rapidly took on theological and metaphysical significance. Ali's two sons, killed in the wars after the schism, became martyred heroes to the Shias and repositories of the claims to Ali's line to mystical preeminence among Muslims. The Sunnis retained the doctrine of leadership by consensus, although Arabs and members of the Quraysh, Muhammad's tribe, predominated in the early years. Reputed descent from the Prophet still carries great social and religious prestige throughout the Muslim world. Meanwhile, the Shia doctrine of rule by divine right became more and more firmly established, and disagreements over which of several pretenders had the truer claim to the mystical power of Ali precipitated further schisms. Some Shia groups developed doctrines of divine leadership far removed from the strict monotheism of early Islam, including beliefs in hidden but divinely chosen leaders whose spiritual powers equaled or surpassed those of the Prophet himself.

The early Islamic policy was intensely expansionist, fueled both by fervor for the new religion and by economic and social factors. Conquering armies and migrating tribes swept out of Arabia, spreading Islam with the sword as much as with suasion. By the end of Islam's first century Islamic armies had reached Asia and North Africa, occupying present-day Tunisia in 670 (see Islam and the Arabs, ch. 1).

Although Muhammad had enjoined the Muslim community to convert the infidel, he had also recognized the special status of the "People of the Book," Jews and Christians, whose own revealed scriptures he considered perversions of God's true word but nevertheless in some sense contributory to Islam. These peoples, approaching but not yet having achieved the pefection of Islam, were known as dhimmis and were spared the choice offered the pagan: conversion or death. Jews and Christians in Muslim territories could live according to their own religious laws and in their own communities if they accepted the position of tolerated subject peoples. This status entailed recognition of Muslim authority, additional taxes, prohibition of proselytization among Muslims, and restrictions on political rights.

Islamic Institutions

Islam is a comprehensive religion that played an all-encompassing role in a traditionally oriented Muslim society such as that existing in Tunisia before its independence. As traditionally constituted, therefore, Islam is far more than a creed. It is a way of life, the ramifications of which affect political, economic, and social behavior and cultured outlook as well as religious belief and individual morality. For the devout believer, the dichotomy between the sacred and the secular is a specious one, and to accept it bespeaks a failure of religious commitment.

In keeping with this concept of society, all Muslims have traditionally been subject to sharia (Islamic jurisprudence, but in a larger sense meaning the Islamic way). A comprehensive legal system, sharia developed gradually during the first four centuries of Islam, primarily through the accretion of precedent and interpretation by various judges and scholars. Within this context, several rites, or systems of interpreting sharia, had developed in accordance with the interpretations. The form adopted in Tunisia and in the rest of the Maghrib was that of the Malikite rite derived from the teaching of the eighth-century scholar Malik Ben Abas. Its outstanding feature was that the interpretation resisted expansion or revision of revealed texts. During the tenth century legal opinion began to harden into authoritative doctrine, and the figurative *bab al ijtihad* (gate of interpretation) gradually closed. Thenceforth, rather than encouraging flexibility, Islamic law emphasized maintenance of the status quo.

The Muslim's relationship to God is personal and direct. The Quran does not recognize the evidence of clergy or other intermediaries. Those who lead prayers, preach sermons, and interpret the law do so by virtue of their superior knowledge and scholarship in the community that they serve rather than because of any special powers or prerogatives conferred by ordination. Furthermore, there is no Muslim "church" in the conventional Western understanding of that term.

Although a formal ecclesiastical organization is absent in Islam, a variety of officials perform many of the duties usually associated with a clergy. One particularly influential group, the ulama, interpreted and administered Islamic law in urban centers that under their leadership became the strongholds of orthodox, Quranic Islam. In Tunisia they were often graduates of the Zituna Mosque school and also taught there. In the courts the *qadis* (judges) heard cases in accordance with sharia, and difficult legal questions were referred to the even more learned muftis. The mufti of Tunis presided over the sharia court until the system was abolished in 1956.

The title of imam can have many meanings. Informally, it is conferred on the leader of the prayer ritual. So used, anyone can be an imam. In a more formal sense, it refers to a paid official who is in charge of a mosque, collects its revenues, leads the prayers, and delivers the weekly sermon. He also serves as a consultant on points of Islamic law and is called on to officiate at religious functions, marriages, and funerals. When the mosque is used as a Quranic school, the imam is the teacher. In the larger urban mosques, the imam might be highly respected as a figure of learning and distinction. The typical village imam, however, has had at most a few years of schooling, and his scholarship is usually exhausted by the reading of prayers, passages from the Quran, and prepared sermons. According to custom, the imam held office by the consensus of the community, but in practice the position often became hereditary. In Tunisia, imams are paid by the state, and the government prescribes topics of sermons to be preached.

Popular Islam and Folk Beliefs

Popular Islam is based overwhelmingly on oral tradition; however limited their formal education, it is not uncommon for an imam—to say nothing of blind storytellers who travel from village to village—to memorize the entire Quran. Religious tales are told and retold at village festivals as well as at the individual villager's rites of passage. The basic tenets are deeply held; everyone believes there is no god but God and Muhammad is his Prophet; everyone wishes to make the pilgrimage to Mecca; Ramadan fasting is commonly observed; and almsgiving is an integral part of the village rituals and celebrations. There is a strong fatalistic component to popular Islam, a sense that all is the will of God and to seek to avoid misfortune is only to kick against the goad and invite worse affliction. Monotheism merges wth a belief in magic and spirits.

Although Islam preaches the unique majesty of God and the equality of all believers before him, a heterodox North African view has for centuries entailed a belief in the coalescence of special spiritual powers in particular human beings. This special charisma is known as *baraka*, a transferable quality of personal blessedness and spiritual force said to reside in certain individuals.

The human being to whom God granted the most powerful *baraka* is said to have been Muhammad. Its possession was also ascribed, however, to holy men or saints known as marabouts, whose claims to the possession of *baraka* could be substantiated through performance of apparent miracles, exemplary spiritual insight, or genealogical connection with a recognized earlier possessor of *baraka*.

Tunisian marabouts at one time were highly influential, particularly in the countryside, but in the postindependence period they continued to function only in a few of the more remote localities in the central and southern parts of the country. Previously, however, their religious prestige made them useful as arbiters of disputes between families or tribal groups. They built centers, called *zawayiate*, that combined the functions of school, living quarters for the marabouts, and—ultimately—the tombs of the holy men. Although the French government was tolerant toward the marabouts, their religious role was never approved by the regular religious authorities during the colonial period, and the government of independent Tunisia has been unsympathetic toward them.

Marabouts were the most frequent, though by no means the only, founders of brotherhoods, religious fraternities in which membership was formerly widespread. The members of each group followed a common discipline called *tariqah* (path) in the pursuit of further closeness to God. The teachings of the founder were carried on by his disciples after his death, and the brotherhoods achieved considerable political and social prominence. Certain forms of popular worship were identified with them. The brotherhood system had commenced to decline even before independence and, like the system of marabouts, was not encouraged by the postindependence government.

A few folk beliefs and customs, probably pre-Islamic in origin, persist in modern Tunisia, particularly among the poor and in the more remote parts of the countryside. Some of these concern evil spirits called djinns, which frequently take the guise of animals such as snakes. Wearing verses from the Quran on an amulet is believed to provide protection against these creatures. The evil eye is widely feared, but according to belief it can be warded off by holding out the fingers of the right hand. Certain stones are believed to have magic properties; a bloodstone, for example, is considered useful in preventing a toothache. The imam himself may be the source of the charms.

Folk beliefs are dying out with the spread of public education and the general modernization of society. They remained widespread enough at the time of independence, however, for Bourguiba to devote part of an important speech to denouncing belief in the evil eye, avoidance of the numbers 10 and 15, and the custom of tossing bits of meat into dark corners to placate the djinns. Tunisians were urged by Bourguiba to discard these outmoded ideas, which were unworthy of a monotheistic religion such as Islam.

Islam in Contemporary Tunisian Society

Both as a nationalist leader opposing the French protectorate and as the president of an independent country imposing modernization on a sometimes reluctant population, Bourguiba regularly invoked the precepts of Islam in his public exhortations. To the masses, he explained proposed reforms that were offensive to observant Muslims as a defense of Islam "by modern means." In the same series of legislation shortly after independence by which the sharia courts were abolished and replaced by a uniform legal code based on secular norms, the Code of Personal Status also was introduced, which drastically altered family law and paved the way for the legal emancipation of women. Family planning was encouraged and abortion legalized. Religious endowments in the form of *habus* land, inalienable according to Muslim tradition, were nationalized and absorbed into state farms. The famous school of the Zituna Mosque was made a faculty of the University of Tunis, subject to regulation by the government.

Bourguiba blamed the backwardness of Tunisian society and the stagnation of its economy on the influence of traditional Islam. Tunisia might be a Muslim country, but in Bourguiba's vision of its future it would be a secular state that rejected "any fanaticism that is the product of centuries of ignorance and obscurantism." He strictly prohibited the incorporation of any religious elements into the ruling party and refused to permit any group from attempting to promote a political program based on Islam. Despite the official status accorded Islam, religion was to be a private

121

matter for those who cared to observe it. Although Islamic studies was a required subject in the primary and secondary schools, there could be no question that the education system to which the regime committed a large share of the national budget was supposed to advance the secularist outlook that characterized Bourguiba's attitude and that of the party elite to the country's youth.

French sociologist Jacques Berque defined Bourguiba's objective as being the "desacrilization" of Tunisia, by which he explained that Bourguiba intended to end Islam's undifferentiated role in a modernized Tunisian society and to force its withdrawal from all activities except that of leading the country at prayer, allowing the state to preempt all those other functions that Islam performed in a more traditional society. Even prayer, Bourguiba acknowledged on one occasion, was useful for developing a sense of national unity, and, in the years following independence, the government financed the opening of hundreds of new mosques. The imams who cared for them and for other mosques were licensed and paid by the state and often provided with the text of the sermons they were to deliver. Those who refused to cooperate or who spoke against the policies of the government were systematically deprived of access to mosques.

The aim of "desacrilization" was incompatible with the beliefs of observant Muslims and the traditional practices of Islam. Bourguiba suffered a major setback in his plans to modify customs and attitudes that to his mind stood in the way of modernization when, in 1960, he urged his countrymen to dispense with the month-long fast of Ramadan. He argued that religious observance should not be an obstacle to the country's development and that workers should abstain from fasting if it impaired their productivity, which invariably it did. But Bourguiba framed his appeal in religious terms by proclaiming a jihad against economic underdevelopment and explaining that—like warriors in a holy war—workers should thereby be excused from fasting. Public employees and students were ordered to keep their schedules, and restaurants were kept open during the day for those who wished a meal. Denouncing the "debauchery" that followed the hours of fasting, he likewise closed those establishments where allnight feasting and entertainment took place.

Observance of Ramadan was lax among the Westernized elite, who often flaunted their nonobservance at sidewalk cafés, but the overwhelming majority of Tunisians disregarded Bourguiba and maintained the fast. Most also ignored the scientific determination of the lunar calendar substituted by the government for the traditional method of reckoning the beginning of Ramadan, thus putting the popular observance of the fast at odds with the official date.

It has been noted that the practice of Islam had always been less rigorous in Tunisia than elsewhere in the region and that the bourgeois values of an important element in Tunisian society had never satisfactorily accommodated those of traditional Islam. Superficially at least, the intermingling of French with Arab culture had worked its way relatively far down the socioeconomic scale in the cities, where it was reflected in language and dress. Sympathetic Western observers commented approvingly in the late 1950s and 1960s of the impressive strides made by the Bourguiba regime in sweeping away the barriers to modernization set up by custom and tradition. Outside the small but very conspicuous circle of a Westernized elite, however, the secularism that it promoted had not struck roots, even among the young who were supposed to be the beneficiaries of modern education, economic growth, and a liberalized social environment that had dispensed with the strictures of Islam. Beneath the surface traditional values persisted or awaited renewal.

By the early 1970s it was evident that an Islamic renewal was underway in reaction to official secularism and that it was gaining considerable support, particularly among the educated youth of the country. The Islamist movement sought to reassert religious influence in areas from which the regime had attempted to exclude it, including the political process. Islamists, popularly referred to by Western sources as fundamentalists, decried the identification of modernization, which they did not generally oppose, with Westernization, which they blamed for the alleged decline of moral values in Tunisian society.

The earliest form of popular protest to what Islamists regarded as the regime's trifling with religious practices came from groups organized by the devout to determine the beginning of Ramadan by traditional methods. The impetus for a more intellectually oriented Islamic renewal came from the activities of the Society for the Preservation of the Quran. Branches of the society had existed in most cities for many years, but after 1970 its membership grew impressively, attracting young people who felt that their secular education had neglected their spiritual heritage as Muslims. Among those who joined the Society was Rachid Ghanouchi, later to be regarded as the ideological leader of the Islamist movement and its principal spokesperson.

The society was able to put some pressure on the government to give more attention to Islamic studies in the state-run schools, emphasizing an expanded understanding of scripture rather than the rote memorization of passages from the Quran, as had been the practice in traditional religious schools. Reform and improvement in the quality of religious education advocated by the Society remained one of the principal aims of Islamic renewal in Tunisia. The Society's supporters denied charges by opponents that they wanted to repeal secular laws, admitting only that they were seeking "a more Muslim society."

An even more important contribution to the Islamic renewal that blossomed in the 1970s was made by informal seminars that were held by the Islamists in various mosques, most prominently the Sidi Youssef Mosque in Tunis. Early participants were teachers, students, and graduates active in the professions, who were influenced by the lectures of theologian Ahmed Ben Miled. The seminars were often led by graduates of the Zituna Mosque school and by others who had studied abroad, particularly at Al Akzar University in Cairo. Among these were Ghanouchi and Abdelfattah Mourou. The seminars concentrated on building ideological awareness by methods that systematically analyzed Western concepts offered by secular education, attempted to demonstrate the superiority of Islamic concepts, and offered Islamic alternatives.

The Islamic renewal spurred by the activities of the Society for the Preservation of the Quran and the mosque seminars soon went beyond concern for religious observance and education. The seminars eventually focused on a vision of creating an Islamic order in Tunisia. In rejecting both Marxism and liberal capitalism, the Islamists also rejected conventional secular analyses of their country's socioeconomic problems. Poverty and underdevelopment, they argued, were the consequences of spiritual failures—religious laxity, secularism, and the like—and the solutions lay in a return to the simplicity of Muslim community life, cooperativeness, austerity, hard work, and piety.

The Islamist movement, in which Ghanouchi and Mourou have played leading roles, has been described as being "integrist" in that its primary concern has been to integrate Islamic values into every aspect of national life, including the political process. The Tunisian Islamists took inspiration from the Islamic revolution in Iran in 1979 because it demonstrated the power latent in Islam to mobilize a population but accepted neither its methods nor its aims. The two countries, they noted, had different spiritual traditions and historical experiences, and they were careful to draw a distinction between their movement and that of the Iranian leaders.

Although it sought support from a broad constituency, the Islamist movement was essentially academic in character and orientation. The vanguard of the movement was largely composed of teachers who had built followings in the mosque seminars among students and recent graduates of the university and the secondary schools. Support for the movement was therefore strongest in Tunis and other large cities that had faculties of the university and advanced schools and weakest in the smaller provincial towns where political control by the regime was tighter. The Islamists considered the University of Tunis, where they had ousted the leftists from control of student organizations during the 1970s, as "our stronghold." Identification with the movement was particularly strong among science and engineering students, who as a group were considered academically the most gifted. These students, who made up the movement's core, were typically from rural families and the lower rungs of the urban population and were among those who would seem to have benefited most from Bourguiba's program to expand educational opportunities. A great percentage were the first in their families to receive an education. The movement also attracted large numbers of well-educated women, many from the middle class, whose emancipation had also been one of Bourguiba's most important goals.

The effects of the movement were manifested in renewed sensitivity toward religion in the population at large and a greater respect for Muslim customs on the part of government authorities. Attendance at mosques for prayer noticeably increased. In the late 1970s a survey among university students who were the products of a secular education indicated that over half considered themselves "very" or "rather religious" and 30 percent "somewhat religious," while about 60 percent observed the fast strictly during Ramadan. Later polls showed that the considerable rise in the number of Tunisians admitting to personal religious attachments, to being religiously observant, and to holding respect for the imams was found to have grown at the same rate among all classes, age-groups, and levels of education.

Several theses have been advanced to explain the apparent interest, particularly among students and other young people, in the movement for Islamic renewal. The thesis drawn from economic considerations explained that students for whom education was no longer a guarantee of employment were resentful of the Westernized elite who had graduated in the 1960s and were secure in jobs that were being denied the next generation. A political thesis spoke of young Tunisians who were disillusioned with Bourguiba's secular nationalism, Marxism, and Pan-Arabism, all of which were foreign imports, and who had filled the void with Islamic nationalism. A third thesis emphasized the psychological effects of their disappointment with secular values, which led them to look to religion as a refuge from despair. In each thesis, Islam was also seen as providing a way out of the political, economic, and social malaise that they perceived. Many students reported that the price of receiving a modern education and being accepted in a secular environment had been the repudiation of their own origins and heritage. Ghanouchi, for example, said that he had been made to feel like a stranger in his own country and yearned for an identity that he could find only in Islam.

The first highly visible manifestation of the Islamist discontent that was centered in the university was the dramatic appearance of a young female instructor, dressed in traditional garb, on a nationally televised program marking the beginning of Ramadan in 1975, during which she challenged government policies in the presence of Bourguiba and then-Prime Minister Hedi Nouira. Unrest grew at the university, where Islamist students clashed with leftists. Violent confrontations with police also occurred at religious observances. In a widely reported incident in 1981 that was seen as a challenge to the government, a state-run tourist hotel was attacked by Islamists, who had frequently decried the demeanor of foreign vacationers as offensive to Muslim sensitivities. Tourism, which was an important element in the government's development plans, was regarded by Islamists as an unwholesome intrusion.

As an expression of their sympathy for the Islamist movement, many male students began to go unshaven, and many university women took to wearing the *hijab*, a traditional headdress that Bourguiba had barred from the schools many years before. It was understood, however, that many of the women who identified with the movement also acknowledged that they did not wish to see rescinded the laws that had allowed their legal emancipation. Nor did they feel that wearing the *hijab* was necessary for a woman to be a good Muslim. It was an option that was as much a sign of protest against the government and solidarity with other students as it was an expression of piety.

Government authorities tended to minimize the influence of the religious renewal. It was a transitory phenomenon, they explained, which by the mid-1980s had already peaked within the student community and had had little real impact outside the university. They were attempting to rebuild bridges to students in the university whom they expected would join the mainstream once they had begun their careers. Members of the university faculty, however, including some who were not identified with the Islamist movement, did not dismiss its continuing influence among students so lightly and believed that the Islamic renewal would remain an important factor at the university and in the country (see Opposition Groups, ch. 4).

Education

The administration of Tunisia's primary and secondary education system in the mid-1980s was highly centralized under the Ministry of National Education. The ministry had overall responsibility for the formulation and implementation of the government's education policy and for the supervision of curricula, teaching, and maintenance of facilities. The minister, a cabinet-rank official, was assisted by a permanent director general of the ministry, who coordinated the work of directorates supervising each level of instruction. Local officials in each governorate oversaw the day-to-day operation of schools in their jurisdictions but were directly responsible to the ministry in Tunis. Higher education was administered by the Ministry of Higher Education and Scientific Research. Other ministries also sponsored specialized schooling, either independently or in collaboration with the two ministries involved primarily with education.

The Tunisian school system was modeled on the French system and offered a uniform curriculum at each level in schools across the country. These consisted of a six-year primary-level cycle that was followed at the secondary level by a three-year comprehensive cycle and a four-year cycle of specialized academic or technical education. Paralleling the latter was a three-year vocational cycle intended to prepare students for employment as skilled workers. Higher education was provided by the University of Tunis, which had branches in several cities, and by university-level advanced schools.

The 1958 basic law of education, although subsequently amended, remained the legal foundation for Tunisia's education system. The law specified that public education was tuition free at all levels and that, although schooling beyond the age of 12 was not mandatory, equal access to education should be ensured to all regardless of gender, class, or ethnic background. All schools at the primary level and most secondary schools were coeducational in the mid-1980s.

Private schools, which accounted for only about 2 percent of primary- and secondary-school enrollment, had to be approved by the Ministry of National Education and had to conform to the ministry's regulations on curriculum and staffing. Most private schools were operated under the auspices of Muslim groups and were locat-

127

ed in the Tunis area. Several schools were also conducted by Roman Catholic religious orders. All were financed chiefly by their sponsoring bodies and by tuition fees, although most also received some government assistance. In addition, the French University and Cultural Mission, a section of the French embassy, operated primary and secondary schools for the children of French nationals resident in Tunisia. A large part of their enrollment, however, was composed of Tunisian students.

Modern education was introduced in Tunisia at the Sadiki College, founded by Kherredin Pasha in 1875 on a European model to train candidates for the civil service. Before that date, education beyond elementary instruction in Arabic and in the Quran was restricted to traditional religious schools (*madrasahs*), where at different levels teachers, prayer leaders, and Islamic judges studied theology, philosophy, law, and literature. The most important center of Islamic scholarship was at the Zituna Mosque school in Tunis. The Khalduniya Institute, established in 1896, attempted to combine instruction in modern subjects with traditional Islamic education. Under the French protectorate, the French school system was transplanted to Tunisia. Although intended primarily to provide education for Europeans, French schools also accommodated a limited number of Tunisian students. There was no corresponding development of modern Arabic-language education (see Economic and Social Development; Rise of Nationalism, ch. 1). At the time of national independence, less than one-quarter of Tunisian children were in primary schools, and under 5 percent of the school-age population had been exposed to modern secondary education. The 1958 law integrated the various kinds of schools then operating into a unified and essentially secular school system.

The government of newly independent Tunisia regarded an expanded and improved education system as the precondition for its transformation into the modern state envisioned by Bourguiba. Education was officially viewed as the primary vehicle for effecting social change and the basic ingredient for economic development. The stated aim of the government's vigorous educational expansion program in the late 1950s and 1960s was to provide trained personnel to replace departing Europeans in government offices, schools, public services, and the professions and also to create an educated work force to fill new jobs in a rapidly growing economy. But the schools were also expected to forge great national unity by instilling respect for the ruling party and by affirming Bourguiba's personal role in leading the country to independence. By implication, the modernization of the country through education was also expected to promote the secularization of its society.

Young woman of Tunis dressed
in the traditional white hijab
Courtesy Jack and Micaela Mendelsohn

Emphasis in education policy was initially put on quantitative development in the terms of the number of schools built, teachers trained, classroooms added, and the increase in the number of students enrolled to fill them. By 1970 approximately 70 percent of all children in the 6-to-12 age bracket were receiving primary schooling, and 20 percent of those in the appropriate bracket were students in secondary and vocational schools. Gains in enrollment were particularly impressive among females, who composed nearly 40 percent of the total number of students enrolled at all levels. Increased opportunities for the education of Tunisian women had been a matter of particular concern for Bourguiba.

Quantitative improvement in the ·schooling rate during the 1960s, however, had been achieved in part by shortening the school day in order to permit double shifts. The output of teachers was increased so rapidly to meet the needs of expanding enrollments that many were introduced into the classroom before being fully qualified. Likewise, the labor market experienced difficulty in absorbing the larger number of graduates being turned out. In the early 1970s, therefore, the government reached a decision that may have been unique in the annals of education in developing countries. Enrollments at the secondary level were stabilized and, in some cases, deliberately cut back. This was accomplished by restricting the number of times that a student was permitted to repeat grades and by raising academic admission standards for secondary schools. No corresponding budget reductions were made, however, and reforms were publicized as marking a shift in emphasis from quantitative to qualitative improvement in education. Greater attention was placed on technical education, for instance, and on providing vocational training in marketable skills. Steps were also taken to improve the quality of teacher education, producing fewer but better-trained primary school instructors. Unqualified teachers were upgraded through in-service training classes or were reassigned as social workers.

Despite the reorientation from a primary concern with quantitative development toward higher quality education in the 1970s, the number of children attending primary schools had risen to more than 90 percent of those in the 6-to-12 age bracket by the mid-1980s. More than 30 percent of the total in the 13-to-19 age bracket were enrolled in secondary schools. In addition, about 6 percent of those in the 20-to-25 age bracket were receiving some form of higher education. But response to expanded opportunities for vocational training at the secondary level had been disappointing, and, because of increased competition for admission to academic and technical tracks in secondary schools, reforms may have discriminated against students from rural and lower socioeconomic backgrounds. Enrollment was also unevenly distributed; much higher schooling rates were found in the Tunis area and in the Sahil than in other parts of the country. Parents, particularly in rural areas, were still much more likely to withdraw their daughters than their sons from school.

In addition to tuition-free education, the state also provided books for all students, as well as other school supplies, clothing, and meals for those who were needy under the government's "Democratization of Education" program. Financial aid in the form of cash grants was also made available at all levels. About 80 percent of all secondary-school students and nearly 90 percent of university students, including many of those studying abroad, received stipends that were roughly equivalent to the minimum wage for an industrial worker.

Since Tunisian independence education has been the priority item in the national budget. In the mid-1980s about 20 percent of government spending was being allocated for education, representing more than 60 percent of total social expenditures and an average of 7 percent of the gross domestic product (GDP). The percentage of the budget devoted to education was lower than in the early 1970s, when education accounted for as much as one-third of government spending, but the amount in gross terms and the average expenditure per student had increased substantially since that time. Tunisia has also relied heavily on unilateral foreign aid and multilateral assistance to support its education program. For many years after Tunisia became independent, France supplied teachers under a bilateral cultural agreement, and, although that program had drawn to an end by the mid-1980s, France continued to provide assistance in teacher-training programs. The United States, through its Agency for International Development (AID), contributed direct aid for improvements in technical and vocational education and for school construction. Funds from the United States were also used to equip laboratories and to enhance the physical plant of the University of Tunis. Food aid was directed to the support program for needy students in Tunisia, and advanced training at universities in the United States was provided for technical students. Peace Corps volunteers assisted in teaching English at the secondary-school level. Technical assistance, funding, and loans for education projects also came from various agencies of the United Nations (UN).

Tunisia was heavily dependent on foreign—mainly French—assistance in providing teachers at all levels during the period its school system expanded rapidly. The progressive replacement of expatriate teachers by Tunisian personnel—a process referred to as Tunisification—was an important goal but one that was less emotion laden then similar programs undertaken in Morocco and Algeria. By the mid-1970s, however, Tunisians filled almost all teaching positions at the primary level, and the number of expatriates at the secondary level had been reduced to about one-fourth of the total. Nearly full Tunisification of secondary-school teachers had become a reality by the mid-1980s, partly as a result of French cooperation in setting up advanced teacher-training schools. At the university level, however, the number of foreign teachers was still significant, and Tunisification of the faculties and institutes remained a distant goal to which not much immediate attention was attached.

Instruction in schools at all levels was bilingual in Arabic and French. The latter language was introduced in the third year of primary school and became the language of instruction in some subjects by the fourth year. At the secondary level, except in vocational schools, one-half to three-fourths of all instruction was in French, the proportion varying with the kind of program. University courses were conducted almost entirely in French, except in the Arabic literature and theology and Islamic studies faculties and in sections of teacher-training schools preparing students to teach Arabic.

One of the announced goals of the education system has been a gradual switch to the use of Arabic in courses that have been taught in French. According to official sources, the transition awaited the training of teachers in sufficient numbers to teach technical subjects in Arabic and the availability of Arabic-language textbooks that were considered adequate. Arabization of some subjects has proceeded at the primary level, but the trend in the mid-1980s, particularly because of greater emphasis on technical courses, has been to add more hours of instruction in French at both the primary and the secondary levels.

Primary Education

During the 1984–85 academic year, some 1.2 million Tunisian children were enrolled in nearly 3,200 public primary schools across the country. The enrollment figures represented a 10-percent increase in the number of students at the primary level from the previous year. Although the rate of attendance among females (approximately 85 percent) was considerably lower than that of males, girls constituted over 40 percent of overall enrollment and matched that of boys in many urban districts. Girls were also entering primary schools at a faster rate of increase than boys.

The six-year primary school cycle was designed to allow students to achieve literacy in both Arabic and French. It was also intended to reveal the potential for advancement to the secondary level in some students and to develop skills needed for employment in the others. In addition to language studies, primary-school students received instruction in arithmetic, elementary science, social studies, art, music, physical education, and religion. Instructional programs were uniform in all schools at that level.

A high rate of failures and repetition of classes has been experienced in primary-level grades. This situation was considered to result in some measure from the inability of students to cope with instruction in French. Repeaters, who constituted approximately one-third of the total enrollment in primary grades, caused overcrowding and increased the per-unit cost of education. The large number of repeaters also created difficult age disparities in classrooms. Many students, particularly females, who have not completed the six-year program because of academic deficiencies, leave school at the age of 12.

Perhaps as a result of upgrading the quality of primary-school instruction and of efforts to reduce the incidence of grade repetition, the trend since the mid-1970s has been toward an improvement in pass rates and grade promotion. In the mid-1980s about three-fourths of all students entering primary school at the age of six completed the six-year program by age 14, and the proportion of graduates continuing their education in secondary and vocational schools was greater than 40 percent. Vocational courses, extending primary-school training by an additional two years, have been instituted in some areas for pupils who failed secondary-school entrance examinations.

Secondary Education

Entrance to secondary schools was determined by highly selective competitive examinations and by the age of the student. Applicants for places in secondary schools providing academic and technical educations outnumbered those applying to vocational schools by a two-to-one margin, but of those taking the entrance examination in the mid-1980s only about one-third were admitted. Students over the age of 14 who had completed primary school were automatically directed to vocational schools (see Vocational Education, this ch.).

The secondary school system was patterned closely on the French model and consisted of a three-year preliminary cycle, the *tronc commun* (common track), equivalent to the French *collège*, and a four-year "long" cycle, comparable to the French *lycée*, which led to a *baccalauréat* (secondary-school degree required for admission to a university). Specialized schools at the secondary level also offered a four-year teacher-training program leading to a pedagogical diploma and three-year commercial and technical programs that conferred professional diplomas on completion to students entering from the *tronc commun*. Nearly 400,000 students were enrolled in secondary-level courses of all kinds during the 1984–85 academic year. This figure represented a very rapid expansion of about 17 percent in the number of students since 1982–83. During the same period, more than 40 new secondary schools were opened, bringing the total in operation nationwide to nearly 350.

The long cycle, essentially an academically oriented program of studies preparing students to continue their education at the university level, was composed of tracks in letters, science and mathematics, and technical studies, each having specialized course options. All students were exposed with differing degrees of intensity to social studies, mathematics and science, Islamic studies, Arabic, French, and another modern language, usually English. Those in the first track followed a modern liberal arts program that emphasized language, literature, and social studies while those in the scientific track concentrated on natural and experimental sciences and advanced mathematics, specializing in either mathematics or one of several branches of science in the fourth year. The technical track included separate programs in pre-engineering and economics, stressing applied mathematics and specialized subjects in addition to the general courses. The choice of a track in secondary school generally dictated the university faculties or specialized institutes to which recipients of the *baccalauréat* would apply for admission. A shift in preference among students from the liberal arts program to the scientific and technical tracks has occurred since the 1970s. About 70 percent of secondary-school students were enrolled in these tracks in 1985.

Parallel three-year secondary-level programs offered diplomas in commercial and technical studies. Students in the commercial track combined a general program that included Arabic, French, and another modern language with specialized courses in accounting, economics, and business administration. Those in the technical track added applied mathematics and specialized courses in either industrial technology or basic civil engineering to the general program. The training prepared students for mid-level employment in business or industry upon graduation, and diplomas also led to admission to engineering or other advanced technical schools. In exceptional cases, promising graduates were permitted to go into the fourth year of the technical track and qualify for the *baccalauréat* and university admission.

Higher Education

The country's only university, the University of Tunis, was founded in 1958, incorporating several existing institutions of higher education. Initially an autonomous institution, the university was brought under the administrative control of a government min-

Primary school students
in the classroom

istry in 1967. In 1976 a process of decentralization of the university was initiated, in which new faculties were established and some existing facilities were relocated outside of Tunis. One rationale for the move was to allow students, particularly in technical fields, to be trained in the regions where their skills were most needed. The measure was also intended, however, to break up the heavy concentration of students in the city of Tunis, where the government considered they had become a threat to public security. A separate ministry responsible for higher education was set up in 1979.

In 1984 the University of Tunis was composed of 12 faculties, each containing several departments, and numerous affiliated institutions and schools. Specialized professional education was provided at advanced schools, some of which offered degree programs equivalent to those at the university level. Of a total of 53 advanced schools, 34 were funded by the Ministry of Higher Education and Scientific Research and the remainder by other ministries. Among the most important was the National School of Administration, which provided postgraduate courses for civil servants. Others included advanced schools for agriculture and veterinary medicine, fine arts, architecture, telecommunications, and the performing arts. In 1985 nearly 40,000 students were enrolled in institutions of higher education that were producing about 5,000 graduates annually.

Requirements for degrees in letters, law, Islamic studies, science, and mathematics and from most specialized institutes of the University of Tunis could be fulfilled in four years. A two-year preliminary stage qualified students for a terminal diploma or for promotion to a more specialized second stage leading to a university degree. In science departments, a third stage was devoted to research. Degree requirements in other faculties and specialized institutes and at advanced schools depended on the field of study. A degree in fine arts, for instance, required three years; in engineering, five years; and in medicine and architecture, seven years.

In the mid-1980s more than 40 percent of all students at the University of Tunis were enrolled in the Faculty of Letters and the smaller Faculty of Law. After national independence these faculties had turned out much needed teachers and civil servants, but 20 years later they were educating students in fields that offered increasingly limited possibilities for employment. An earlier effort to attract students to study agricultural sciences had failed to meet its goals; but the government continued to expand opportunities for students in technical fields, offering training in marketable skills, and undertook to attune university admission policy to the country's economic needs. Slightly more than half of all university-level students were engaged in scientific and technical studies in the mid-1980s.

As a result of reforms introduced in the mid-1970s, admission to each department was regulated on the basis of an annual assessment of employment opportunities for graduates in particular disciplines and projected requirements for technically trained personnel. During their final year of secondary school, applicants to the university and advanced schools selected from five to 10 fields of study for which they wished to be considered for admission. There were about 130 fields to choose from in 1985. Acceptance was determined by scores in the *baccalauréat* examination, the highest ranking students being given preference for places in the departments of their choice. Each year a percentage of applicants failed to be accepted in any of the fields of study they had listed, and they were forced to make new choices if they expected to be considered for the university.

Because of the restricted admissions policy, some students chose to go abroad for higher education to study in their chosen field of interest. Others sought out foreign universities where they could pursue courses of study not offered in Tunisia. Approximately 10,000 Tunisians were studying abroad in 1985, about one-third of them on government scholarships. The largest number attended universities in France and the United States.

Teacher and Teacher Training

In the 1984–85 school year an estimated 35,000 teachers, all Tunisian, were employed in the public primary-school system. Annual increases in the number of primary-school teachers were gradually improving the teacher-student ratio and were allowing for the elimination of double-shift school days. Teachers in secondary schools numbered nearly 19,000 and increased at a rate that kept pace with the growth in enrollment at that level. University instructors of all ranks totaled 4,600 in 1985, representing an increase in full-time teachers of more than 10 percent in two years. More than 1,500 university lecturers were retained on a part-time basis. Tunisia exported teachers to a number of other Arab and African countries.

Classroom hours for teachers at the primary and secondary levels were reduced from 30 to 25 hours per week in a move that was designed to improve the quality and effectiveness of teaching. While teacher-training facilities have been expanded to make up for understaffing caused by the change, standards for admission to teacher-training programs were simultaneously upgraded in line with the general policy emphasizing improved quality in education.

Most primary-school teachers received their training at secondary-level normal schools. The four-year course, which admitted about 1,000 new students in 1985, provided pedagogical courses in addition to a general secondary-school education. Teachers were accepted as fully qualified after a one-year probationary period following graduation, during which they combined teaching with further study at one of several regional teacher-training centers. A number of teacher-candidates who had taken the *baccalauréat* were also recruited for the primary schools each year and allowed to begin teaching after completing a short training course.

Secondary-school teachers were educated at an advanced teacher-training school (*école normale supérieure*), of which three operated in conjunction with the University of Tunis in 1985. Teacher-trainees, who were required to hold either the *baccalauréat* or a secondary-level normal school diploma, followed a five-year program, during which they took courses in an academic field of study at a university faculty before going on to complete their pedagogical training at the advanced school. After receiving a degree in secondary education, candidates were subject to a one-year probationary period before being certified to teach at that level. A parallel four-year course in teaching technical and vocational subjects at the secondary level was also provided. Scholarships for students entering this program were larger than those awarded students in other university faculties and schools, but trainees were required to make a commitment to teach in the secondary-school system for a minimum of 10 years. Some university graduates, holding degrees from other faculties, were also accepted to teach at the secondary level after appropriate professional training.

Vocational Education

The government's education policies laid emphasis on improving vocational education and increasing its acceptance as an alternative to a strictly academic education. Vocational training was provided in separate systems at the secondary level in industrial arts and agriculture. Efforts were being made to upgrade vocational education by extending the length of programs, and plans were also discussed for conferring a degree on vocational graduates that was equivalent to an academic *baccalauréat*. Vocational training was being introduced at the primary level in some areas.

A three-year vocational course intended to train workers immediately employable in the industrial sector in skilled trades was open to primary-school graduates, and those older than 14 were invariably directed to vocational schools. In addition to a general education and specialized vocational training, students were also given practical work experience as part of an apprenticeship program. Successful completion of a fourth year of vocational training earned students a professional diploma and improved credentials for employment. Exceptional students were permitted to move into the final three-year cycle of the technical secondary school.

The Ministry of Agriculture operated four secondary-level vocational boarding schools in 1985. Three were for boys only, and one was reserved for girls. Students out of primary school entered a three-year middle school, equivalent to the *tronc commun* and, depending on their academic performance at the level, were allowed to continue with a three-year course leading to a technical diploma or to pursue a four-year *baccalauréat* in agricultural sciences.

Training in both the diploma and the degree programs included general academic as well as technical courses. The *baccalauréat*, however, entitled graduates to apply to the advanced schools of agriculture and veterinary medicine or to enter a two-year program at one of several other specialized schools.

Adult vocational training was sponsored at different levels by the Ministry of Labor and several other ministries. These programs were generally targeted at providing workers for areas of known need and had a good record of placing participants in jobs on completion of training. Diplomas in nursing, paramedical skills, and laboratory technology were offered in schools conducted by the Ministry of Public Health. Courses provided by the Ministry of Tourism and Handicrafts taught traditional handicraft skills, while the Ministry of Youth and Sports operated preapprenticeship training centers in manual arts and social services for school leaders and unemployed young people. During the early 1980s, the government initiated a US$47 million project, partially financed by the World Bank (see Glossary), to establish a number of new vocational training centers and to enlarge existing facilities. Eight new centers were scheduled to open in 1986.

Literacy and Adult Education

According to a 1980 estimate, approximately 50 percent of the Tunisian population over the age of 15 years was considered literate. By comparison, the rate of literacy at the time of independence in 1956 was only 30 percent. Broken down by gender, the 1980 estimate reported rates of literacy of about 67 percent for males and 33 percent for females. This compared with rates of 47 percent for males and only 18 percent for females estimated in 1967. Literacy rates varied regionally from over 70 percent in the Tunis metropolitan zone to 30 percent in some rural areas. Overall literacy in the urban population, however, exceeded 80 percent.

For the most part, Tunisia has relied on an expanding public school system both for the reduction of illiteracy and for adult education. Literacy classes, however, were made available at special centers located throughout the country. Classes were also established for workers by business enterprises, by the armed forces, and by women's organizations.

In addition to job training programs, government ministries also sponsored adult education that included courses in such varied subjects as literature, civics, and child care. Increasing use was also being made of television as a means of giving instruction in family planning techniques, providing schooling outside the regular education system, and promoting literacy.

Health and Welfare

Tunisia not only inherited a health system from the French protectorate that was inadequate for the needs of its population but after independence the country also suffered the loss of most of its European medical personnel, who included well over half of the physicians practicing there in 1956. The "right to the protection of health" was guaranteed to Tunisians in the 1959 Constitution, however, and in the years since achieving independence the government has extended considerable effort in implementing that provision. Public expenditures per capita for health service exceeded those of most countries, and in 1985 allocations for the Ministry of Public Health absorbed 7 percent of the national budget, funding second in size only to that for education and representing about 3 percent of GDP. Foreign assistance also contribued to health projects in Tunisia.

Initially, the public health program was directed principally toward the physical expansion of the system, concentrated on providing curative medical care in urban-based facilities. Under a so-called pyramid system that continued to function in the mid-1980s, inpatients were referred upward for treatment from rural dispensaries and small auxiliary hospitals to regional hospitals in each of the country's four public health regions and, finally, to about 25 general and specialized hospitals located in the large cities, which handled more than 70 percent of total inpatient admissions. About one-third of all admissions to hospitals in Tunis were referred from other parts of the country. By the late 1970s, however, great emphasis was being placed on preventive medicine and the more extensive use of local health care centers and paramedical personnel, particularly in rural areas.

The results of improvement in medical care, as well as in nutrition and sanitation, were reflected both in mortality statistics and in quantitative indicators of the expansion of the public health system. Nationally, the infant mortality rate was reduced from 200 deaths per 1,000 live births in 1956 to 85 per 1,000 in 1985, and the overall death rate dropped from 20 per 1,000 population annually to under eight per 1,000. The average life expectancy for Tunisians during the same period rose from 40 to 61 years. According to a 1981 survey, inpatients were treated at 98 hospitals, providing 21 beds per 10,000 population, and outpatients received medical attention at approximately 1,000 health care centers, including more than 500 rural dispensaries. All were public facilities.

Official sources estimated that 80 percent of the population received medical care annually under the public health system. Treatment and services provided by the system were free. Hospital care was also covered for employed persons and their families insured under the social security system, and costs to others were nominal.

In 1981 about 1,800 physicians were practicing in Tunisia. Physicians were allowed to maintain private practices and to treat patients in private clinics, but all were required to contribute their services under the public health system. Paramedical personnel included 5,000 trained nurses and about 800 licensed midwives. The country's first medical school was established in 1964 as a faculty of the University of Tunis and graduated its first class in 1970. Medical faculties were subsequently opened in Sfax and Sousse. Training for nurses and paramedicals was provided in schools operated by the Ministry of Public Health. There were more than 300 practicing dentists and nearly 800 pharmacists working in Tunisia in 1981. Many were graduates of the dental and pharmacy schools that opened in Monastir in the 1970s.

Despite the progress made in improving the quality and outreach of the public health system, serious disparities still existed in the mid-1980s in the medical resources available to urban and rural populations. Outside Tunis and other large cities and the Sahil, quantitative indicators of medical care delivery declined sharply. About 60 percent of the country's physicians, for instance, practiced in the Tunis area, which had a physician-to-patient ratio that was five or six times greater than that of some rural governorates. Perhaps the most striking reflection of the urban-rural health care differential was the significantly higher incidence of infant mortality rates in rural areas, where, outside the Sahil, an estimated one-half of all deaths recorded were among children under the age of five years and where the infant mortality rate was nearly double that of Tunis. Tunisian authorities recognized the problem as essentially one of inadequate distribution of available public health system services. Reports in the early 1980s by international organizations indicated that the rural population was often excluded from ready access to those medical resources under the pyramid system because of bureaucratic bottlenecks at the local level in referring patients to regional and urban hospitals. Importance was therefore attached by both sources to augmenting the number of health care facilities in rural areas. A US$41 million project, assisted by the World Bank, for the construction, remodeling, and equipping of several hundred rural health centers was scheduled for completion in 1986.

By the 1980s inoculations and other preventive measures had brought under control some major communicable diseases, such as smallpox, diphtheria, polio, and typhus. The Ministry of Public Health conducted regular campaigns against malaria, trachoma, and schistosomiasis, and it assigned personnel to combat outbreaks of other diseases, particularly cholera. It was responsible for providing inoculations and for the detection and treatment of communicable diseases.

For the population as a whole, the principal health hazards were intestinal infections and parasites, skin infections, trachoma, hepatitis, tuberculosis, syphilis, schistosomiasis, typhoid, and paratyphoid. Rural people were particularly susceptible to respiratory ailments, while digestive disorders were principally urban complaints. Although polio, diphtheria, and whooping cough were on the decline, as a result of widespread inoculation, gastrointestinal and upper respiratory infections remained major causes of mortality among young children. The incidence of measles was of serious concern.

About 70 percent of the population had access to potable water, but the water supply was inadequate in parts of the country, particularly during the summer. Piped water to residences, waterborne sewage, and central treatment facilities for waste were available in Tunis and other large urban centers, but systems were generally overtaxed. Public sanitation in rural areas and in the older quarters of cities was poor or inadequately maintained. Food intake nationally was 116 percent of the basic requirement recommended by the UN's Food and Agriculture Organization. Malnutrition was still apparent in some parts of the country, but this was largely because of inefficient distribution rather than insufficient supplies of food.

Legislation enacted in 1960 created a social security system and the Social Security Fund, charged with the management of the system's benefits. Initially applicable to employees of industrial and commercial establishments of a certain size, the program was subsequently extended to some of the nonagricultural workers and to university students, and in 1970 a separate insurance system was instituted for farmworkers. Benefits under the program for industrial and commercial workers included hospital care, medical equipment, and treatment abroad when necessary. Payments to the fund consisted of a 5-percent tax on individual wages and a 15-percent wage tax contributed by employers. Contributions paid by agricultural workers were nominal. The social security system operated several hospitals separately from the general public health system for the exclusive admission of patients covered by medical insurance paid through its fund.

* * *

Richard Parker surveys major social trends in Tunisia in his *North Africa: Regional Tensions and Strategic Concerns.* An earlier but more detailed introduction to contemporary Tunisian society is found in Clement Henry Moore's *Tunisia Since Independence: The Dynamics of One-Party Government.*

A body of literature is developing on the subject of the religious renewal in Islam and its social and political implications. Articles dealing specifically with Tunisia include Susan E. Waltz' "The Islamist Challenge In Tunisia" in the *Journal of Arab Affairs,* Mark A. Tessler's "Political Change and Islamic Revival in Tunisia" in the *Maghreb Review,* and those by Michel Camau and Mohamed Elbaki Hermassi in the French journal *Maghreb-Machrek.* In his book, Parker devotes a chapter to an assessment of the Islamic Tendency Movement.

Margaret McFerren's *Arabization in the Maghreb* discusses linguistic biculturalism in Bourguiba's Tunisia and the status of arabization in the bureaucracy, schools, and the media. James Allman describes social stratification and analyzes education policy in *Social Mobility, Education, and Development in the Middle East.* A more timely critique of the effects of official attitudes in these areas is provided by Marie Thourson Jones' "Politics and Social Policy in Tunisia" in the *Maghreb Review.* In his essay "Tunisia: A Single Party System Holds Change in Abeyance," Russell A. Stone describes the structure and values of the country's elite.

Jeswald W. Salacuse examines the Code of Personal Status in *An Introduction to Law in French-Speaking Africa, II: North Africa.* Lorna Durrani's article in the *Maghreb Review* and Tessler's essay in *Women in the Muslim World* explore the degree to which enactment of the code has affected family life and the status of women. Roderic Beaujot and Mongi Bchir's *Fertililty in Tunisia: Traditional and Modern Contrasts* is based on recent field surveys. (For further information and complete citations, see Bibliography.)

Chapter 3. The Economy

Orange blossoms from a Tunisian citrus grove

IN LESS THAN 30 years of independence, Tunisia has grown out of economic subordination and poverty and into a middle-income state. A small country with a modest resource base, it had used its diverse assets to move from a purely agricultural economy to one in which hydrocarbons, manufacturing, and to a lesser extent, banking and tourism were also important contributors to national income and growth. The management of the economy was recognized internationally as sensible and had earned the country considerable financial assistance. The economic role of the government was alternatively limited or intrusive according to the principles of Bourguibism, a term referring to attributes of the regime of Tunisia's president for life, Habib Bourguiba, and one that was defined as pragmatic and moderate, though also flexible and opportunistic.

The foundation of the economic infrastructure was built during the period of the French protectorate, and later the Tunisian authorities made improvements, shaping it to the needs of modern Tunisia. Administrative procedures, technical methods, and the financial system, however, have retained an essentially French character.

When compared with the performance of the previous decade, growth in the 1980s has been slow. Indeed, Tunisia has struggled with quite a few problems. The agricultural sector had been afflicted by a severe drought, and imports of food increased substantially to satisfy the demands of a fast-growing population. The international markets for petroleum and phosphate, Tunisia's major foreign exchange earners, were weak, and at the same time the sales of textiles and olive oil faced fierce competition and trade barriers. Inflation and unemployment were running very high, but the Tunisian authorities could not take the necessary steps, i.e., cutting down on wage increases and price subsidies, because of the political sensitivity attached to such actions. All of these factors aggravated trade and budget deficits, and loans from foreign sources soared.

Tunisia may have freed itself from economic subordination in a literal sense, but its economy was an open one and remained, as could be observed in 1985, extremely vulnerable to external factors. To remedy the situation, the government reduced capital imports and selectively used limited funds to modernize agriculture and develop alternative sources of foreign exchange. But the capacity of the Tunisian people to tolerate the resultant austerity had become uncertain.

National Income

Although only 3 percent of the land was arable, the country had traditionally been an agricultural one with a majority of the labor force engaged in agriculture and production sufficiently abundant to allow the export of fruits, vegetables, and olive oil. Agriculture gradually lost its predominant role in the economy with the discoveries of oil, natural gas, and phosphates and with the growth of the services sector and the commercialization of tourism (see fig. 8). Official data in the late 1970s and early 1980s reflected the evolution toward a more diversified economy (see tables 4 and 5, Appendix). In the early 1980s annual gross domestic product (GDP—see Glossary) was roughly TD4.3 billion (for value of the Tunisian dinar—see Glossary). Of this total, 15 percent came from agriculture, 12 percent from oil and gas, 4 percent from textiles, 10 percent from manufactured products, 7 percent from construction and public works, and 4 percent from tourism.

Economic Growth

Since independence, Tunisia has experienced growth rates seldom encountered elsewhere in Africa. National GDP grew at an annual average of 4.7 percent during the 1960s and 7.6 percent during the 1970s. The exceptional income growth that Tunisia witnessed during the 1970s was attributed largely to surging oil prices. But in neighboring Algeria, a far larger oil producer and exporter, the GDP growth rate during the same period averaged only 5.8 percent a year, a comparison that revealed that Tunisia's lucrative oil revenues were by no means the only contribution to growth. Other contributing elements were favorable weather for agricultural production, an improvement in the investment climate through an easy credit policy, a drive for industrial development (particularly in the export industries whereas Algeria emphasized import-substitution industries), an initially receptive export market, and a move toward a more liberal market-oriented economy.

The first half of the 1980s did not present the same bright picture. The annual growth rate slowed considerably, falling to nearly zero in 1982, when a severe drought led to a disastrous agricultural harvest. Additionally, oil and phosphate revenues were lower because of depressed world prices and lower domestic production resulting from impoverished reserves and technical problems. Moreover, a recession in Western Europe led to a decrease in Tunisian exports and in West European tourism abroad.

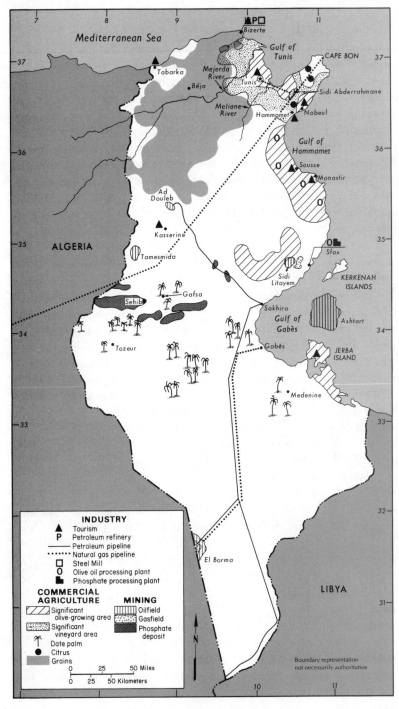

Figure 8. Economic Activity, 1985

149

It was difficult, in the mid-1980s, to foresee which economic sectors had the best prospects. Agriculture and the food-processing industry were subject to erratic weather conditions, and the future of the production of minerals and energy appeared uncertain because of pessimistic estimates of deposits. The services sector was growing consistently but slowly. The irrigated agriculture and manufacturing sectors were among the most promising. The mechanical and electrical industries showed an average yearly growth rate of 15 percent in the mid-1980s; the chemical, construction materials, and textiles industries followed with growth rates of 12 percent, 12 percent, and 5 percent. All of these industrial activities were assured a relatively healthy market demand either domestically or abroad.

Inflation and Prices

General investment and consumption each rose by more than 100 percent between 1979 and 1983, aggravating an existing inflationary trend. An inflation rate at around 7.8 percent per year between 1977 and 1981 grew to 13.6 percent in 1982. Subsequently, price and wage controls brought inflation down to around 9 percent in 1983. The wages and salaries of civil servants were frozen in 1984–85 despite increasing pressure from the labor unions. Retail prices were kept under control despite the growing financial burden of subsidies, remaining lower than those in other countries of the Maghrib (see Glossary). Algerians, in particular, often crossed the border to purchase goods in Tunisia.

A comprehensive system of price controls was formulated in several ways. For consumer necessities, such as bread, meat, flour, oil, and tea, as well as for public transportation, lodging, and cement, the maximim retail prices or fares were set directly by the government. The prices of some items were determined by adding fixed maximum profit margins to the wholesale or retail costs of the products. Prices of some commodities were established by proposals to the government from the manufacturer, supported by data. Other items constituting about one-third of consumers' expenditures had freely fluctuating prices. Because of the heavy reliance on the maximum profit margin technique and because of the readiness of the government to adjust fixed prices in response to underlying market forces, the Tunisian price control system was not considered terribly distorting.

Income Distribution

As is often the case when a country experiences important and rapid growth, the gap between the rich and the poor in Tunisia widened. The government became increasingly aware of acute regional income disparities during the 1970s and began a reorientation of investment funds to help create jobs in the poorer areas and to upgrade living standards by developing facilities such as hospitals, and systems of electricity, running water, sewerage, and roads. About 13 percent of total investments in the 1982–86 development plan were allocated to regional development, and about 16 percent of GDP in the early and mid-1980s annually went to social programs. Official sources proudly cited statistics indicating the per capita income in the country was the comfortable equivalent of US$1,200—a result, to an important extent, of a few high income levels—and that the percentage of people living below absolute poverty standards was reduced from 17 percent in 1975 to 13 percent in the early 1980s. However, data from the early 1980s suggested that a large percentage of Tunisian households lived just above the poverty level.

Tunisians remained dissatisfied with the size of the investment funds allocated to regional development and were growing increasingly sensitive to the issue of equity. The most deprived people were those residing in the northwest, the central area of the country, and the south, where living conditions were Spartan. A marked contrast could be observed in the capital city of Tunis between the modern opulence of upper-class residential areas and suburban shantytowns, called *gourbivilles*. Articles appearing in Tunisian periodicals in the mid-1980s reflected concern—sometimes resentment—over the means by which "colossal fortunes" had been accumulated. Widespread corruption was imputed to the upper management of the state-owned enterprises. The government prepared a preliminary plan of action in 1985 to fight what it termed "inefficient management in public enterprises." Corrective measures included selling many of the state's shares to spread ownership to more private interests, giving greater power to the board of directors (rather than management) in budget financing, and implementing hiring laws whereby people would be employed on the basis of competence and integrity rather than family ties and contacts.

The Role of the Government

The Tunisian government has not dominated the economy as conspicuously as have the governments of the other Maghribi countries, but in the mid-1980s there was no economic sector in which the state did not intervene either directly or indirectly. As the source of regulatory legislation and as the author of comprehensive planning for development, the state was supreme. It acted as lawmaker, planner, investor, manager, and owner. Its role varied widely between industries ranging from sole ownership, as in the transportation industry, to a partnership arrangement with private foreign or domestic owners, as in manufacturing. The role of the public sector in agriculture and manufacturing had been declining since the shift in emphasis toward encouraging private investment. In the field of finance the government exercised a broad role, controlling the money supply, investments, and prices. For enterprises that were wholly private and deemed to be important to development of the economy, the state offered direct investment services through public lending institutions.

The government employed roughly 18 percent of the total work force. Its most important goals in the mid-1980s were to develop a wider economic base that would not rely solely on hydrocarbons and phosphates, to create enough jobs to solve the unemployment problem and reduce income disparities, and to make a more equitable division of the economic pie.

Development Planning

In its role as planner and investor, the government traditionally relied on the framework set forth in the various development plans. The first attempt was the 1962–71 Ten-Year Perspective Plan of Development, which was only a long-range policy statement. By 1985 there had been six medium-term plans, the first three of which attempted to implement the policy of the ten-year plan. Originally overoptimistic, these subsequent plans became more pragmatic by the end of the decade. The first medium-term plan for 1962–64 emphasized modernizing the country's infrastructure. Its performance fell well below plan goals, and most of the country's foreign exchange holdings were later used up to pay for the projects that were started. The authorities borrowed from the domestic banking system to help finance completion of the projects, which only added to inflationary pressures. Part of the difficulty of the first plan was that the statistics upon which it was based were sparse and unreliable.

The second medium-term plan was called the 1965–68 Four-Year Plan and was based on more detailed and accurate statistics. It continued the development policy of the first plan but with some modifications in objectives and financing. It focused more upon developing heavy industrial projects. Most goals of the next plan, called the 1969–72 Third Development Plan, were met because of a very favorable growth rate in 1972 that pulled the average growth for the period above the projected rate. The 1969–72 plan's total investment funds were equal to TD676 million, 53 percent of which was financed by foreign assistance. The plan stressed investment in agriculture and in sectors having a comparative advantage over foreign competitors, such as light industry.

By the end of the decade, the planning process in Tunisia had become more sophisticated and realistic. Plans were periodically reviewed and were designed to create a climate conducive to development by enabling many agencies and individuals to share in drawing up the plan. After 1975 a minister in the cabinet was in charge of planning. Alternative broad objectives were drawn up by the planning authorities; from these the National Planning Council, a body that included representatives from many ministries and agencies, selected a major objective to be pursued in the next plan. This objective was then expanded and transmitted to ministries and sectoral and regional committees that would specify detailed sectoral and local projects compatible with the main objective. A final draft was synthesized and forwarded to the National Planning Council for approval and submission to the Chamber of Deputies for passage into law.

The 1973–76 plan, a much more elaborate one than its predecessors, called for investment funds of TD1.2 billion. The oil price hike of 1973, however, secured nearly TD400 million more than planned. The high investment subsequently made under the plan paid off in the creation of an estimated 164,000 jobs (only 119,000 were planned) and the attainment of most goals. The average annual growth during that plan period was 6 percent. Most important, only 16 percent of the investment was financed with external funds. The subsequent 1977–81 development plan was financed largely (78 percent of TD4.2 billion) by domestic savings.

Both the 1973–76 plan and the 1977–81 plan had sufficient funds to allow investment in various sectors of the economy while particularly promoting chemicals and export industries, such as petroleum and phosphate processing. The 1977–81 plan, officially designated simply the Fifth Plan, further included in its priorities the modernization of the transportation system and the development of water resources.

The 1982–86 plan reflected the efforts of the Tunisian government to shift the economy away from petroleum-based growth and to solve the rising unemployment problem. Emphasis was put on promoting agriculture and small private industrial activities. Development funds totaling TD8.2 billion were channeled to generate an annual growth rate of 6 percent and to create 300,000 jobs. The adverse weather of the early 1980s, however, caused poor agricultural harvests, and the recession in Western Europe resulted in lower remittances and tourism receipts; the combination of these conditions led to growth rates well below those targeted—an average of 3.5 percent per year in the first three years of the plan—and provided little opportunity for the creation of jobs. Agricultural output improved significantly in 1984–85, and efforts to boost manufacturing were commendable; but overall economic growth remained slow.

Preparation of the 1987–91 plan, Tunisia's seventh development plan, was underway in 1985. Its main objectives related to the three challenges the Tunisian economy faced: improving the balance of payments, solving the unemployment problem, and reducing interregional disparities. The 1987–91 plan would introduce technical committees to the planning process that were created to sustain and provide the national and regional committees with documents and studies on the sectors they covered.

The Domestic Budget

When the government in the mid-1960s adopted a centrally directed economic and social development plan, the budget became a major instrument in the planning and execution of the development effort. In the mid-1980s budgets were geared to the objectives of the plan, and annual adjustments were made in the plan after an assessment of the economic situation of the previous year.

Responsibility for drafting the annual budget rested with the planning authorities. The ministries and separate governmental agencies annually submitted expenditure estimates and justifications to that office, which after review and consolidation forwarded them to the Budget Service and the Public Expenditure Control office under a minister responsible directly to the president. These offices examined the proposals for feasibility and conformity with governmental policy. Any modifications proposed by the reviewing offices were submitted to budget committees consisting of representatives from each of the ministries.

The budget committees ironed out any interministerial differences over proposed appropriations that might have developed, and the budget thus established was then forwarded to the Economic and Social Council of 42 members representing various sectors in the economy for approval and subsequent introduction in the Chamber of Deputies to be enacted into law. Although subjected to the scrutiny of the legislature to an increasing extent, the budgets were generally approved after modification.

In the 1980s the budget specified both the expenditures and the revenues of the central government and was operative for the fiscal year, which coincided with the calendar year. It was drawn up in two parts: an ordinary or administrative budget and a capital or investment budget. In addition there were special treasury accounts and extrabudgetary accounts. The ordinary budget allocated funds to cover the usual current expenses of government (such as salaries, purchase of goods and services, and transfers), including those of any state-owned business enterprises that were not fully self-supporting. The capital budget was the vehicle for funding investment expenditures and other nonrecurring, extraordinary governmental obligations. It also included some current expenditures related to investments and some lending to public enterprises.

The special accounts received certain earmarked revenues and were used for specific purposes: current, capital, or lending operations. The various special accounts were large enough to exert an important effect on the economy. The single most important special account in the mid-1980s was the Price Stabilization Fund, which paid for subsidies on selected foodstuffs and certain basic raw materials. Some extrabudgetary accounts reflected the receipts and expenditures from foreign grants and loans.

Government expenditures increased rapidly between 1960 and the late 1970s, reflecting the growing role played by the state in the country's economic activity. By the early 1980s, however, an era of stringency began, and while annual budgets grew larger in absolute terms, they were increasing at a slower rate than that of the 1970s. Moreover, budget funds began to be allocated in a different way. The share of current expenditures decreased from around two-thirds of the total budget in the 1970s to hardly more than one-half. The larger capital expenditures' shares reflected the increased planned investment in the 1982–86 plan. Priorities were given to social sectors, such as education, health, employment, and housing, by significantly increasing their shares in both current and capital expenditures. Purchases of defense matériel and other equipment remained, however, among the most important capital expenses.

Tax receipts in the 1980s provided around 70 to 72 percent of the government's revenue. The system of taxation was complex, and the tax structure was modified annually to accommodate the needs of the development plan. If projected receipts were smaller than planned expenditures, certain taxes were raised or new ones were added, although care was taken to ensure that the new fiscal measures did not burden lower income groups disproportionately. Increasingly, direct taxes included levies on business profits, which also applied to certain self-employed individuals, such as lawyers and physicians; an individual income tax; and a professional income tax that was assessed against noncommercial individuals and companies. An agricultural property tax was paid on the basis of an estimated value of certain crops and products, and an agricultural income tax was levied at a flat rate on the gross sales of agricultural products. Dividends and interest were taxed as well as inheritances.

Among the various indirect taxes in effect in the mid-1980s were customs duties, a production tax, excise taxes, and a service tax. Customs duties were levied on most imports, although an import tax surcharge, applied to most commodity categories, was not applied to essential items. Special export duties were levied at one of three rates. Excise taxes were imposed only on specific products, such as petroleum and beverages. There were also stamp taxes on a number of documents and registration taxes on various corporate activities.

Profitable state-owned enterprises, such as oil companies and state property, provided the balance of government revenues. The oil glut in the mid-1980s, however, resulted in minimal growth in such government revenues.

While petroleum revenue fell, public investment subsidies, wages, and salaries were rising. As a result, the early 1980s saw a deteriorating budgetary situation, which improved somewhat after a freeze in government wages and salaries in 1984. Nevertheless, the deficits remained significant in 1983, 1984, and 1985 at TD251 million, TD400 million and TD485 million, respectively. Attempts to decrease the cost of subsidies on cereals in late 1983 resulted in violent riots in January 1984, forcing the government to rescind its decision (see The Riots of 1984 and Their Aftermath, ch. 4). Instead, a number of measures to raise revenues were introduced, including value-added taxes on luxury items, higher prices on cigarettes and petroleum, higher taxes on alcohol, and a departure tax imposed on Tunisians for travel abroad.

The largest contribution to meeting budget deficits came from domestic borrowing. Additionally, joint Arab-Tunisian development banks and sometimes international organizations offered soft loans and government grants, and around 20 percent of the total amount applied to the deficit was raised through private foreign borrowing.

Local and municipal governments were permitted to have an investment budget financed partly from their own sources of income—they could levy their own taxes—and partly by the central government. Local governments financed their own payrolls and public services. Budgets were prepared annually by the governorates and municipalities and were voted upon by the governing councils. If they exceeded a specified level, however, they had to be approved by the Ministry of Finance.

Income for local budgets came from charges for services, license fees, fines, subsidies from the central government, and taxes the local governments were authorized to collect. The principal tax was that on real property, based on its assessed rental value. Local governments also collected taxes on vacant lots; taxes to support building maintenance, sanitation inspections, and services; and a tax on slaughterhouses. Other sources consisted of income earned from city-owned land and buildings and from concessions.

The Monetary Sector

The country's formal banking system dated from 1879, two years before the establishment of the French protectorate, when a monopoly for granting loans on gems and precious metals was given to a French national in Tunis by decree of the bey (ruler). To exercise the monopoly, the Franco-Tunisian Bank (still operating in the 1980s) was organized as a limited liability company. French banking interests opened branch houses or organized new ones in Tunisia after the protectorate was established, and strong financial ties between the governments and the business communities of Tunisia and metropolitan France developed. Control of monetary affairs in the country, including the management of currency, remained almost wholly in French hands and centered in Paris until 1958.

After 1958 a series of agreements brought financial autonomy, and the banking system grew considerably. In 1985 it consisted of the treasury, the Central Bank of Tunisia, nine development consortia, 10 offshore banks, 12 commercial deposits banks, two investment banks, about 45 agricultural mutual credit banks, two savings funds, a postal checking system, and several insurance companies. In the late 1970s several of the Tunisian commercial banks formed a joint bank, the Tunisian Union of Banks, based in Paris, to serve as a channel for foreign loans to Tunisia and for Tunisian investments in other countries. A small yet dynamic stock exchange was functioning in Tunis, and many companies were able to raise needed funds by issuing securities. The demand for securities often exceeded the supply, and the prices quoted for existing securities sometimes rose rapidly.

The Central Bank and Monetary Policy

The treasury carried out central banking functions for government agencies and public enterprises. The Central Bank of Tunisia was established in 1958 as a state institution to assume the functions of the Bank of Algeria and Tunisia, which previously performed most of the functions of a central bank and was the fiscal agent for the Tunisian government but followed the monetary policy dictated by the Monetary Committee of the franc zone in Paris. The Central Bank of Tunisia carried out the functions normally performed by most central banks. It was responsible for issuing and regulating the country's currency. The basic monetary unit was the Tunisian dinar, divided into 1,000 millimes, which replaced the Tunisian franc in 1968.

As of 1985, the Tunisian dinar was a nonconvertible currency, and the import and export of bank notes was strictly prohibited. The exchange rate between the dinar and foreign currencies was determined daily by the central bank in accordance with a basket of currencies. Transactions involving foreign exchange were controlled by the central bank with the exception of a few authorized banks handling payments for imports and invisibles.

The major responsibility of the central bank was that of implementing the government's monetary policy. It was charged with regulating the volume and cost of bank credit in accordance with the needs of economic development. The central bank had the power to make advances to the commercial banks and the quasi-public specialized credit institutions and was the main source of long-term equity and finance. Its principal means of controlling the money supply was through changing the rediscount rates and prescribing liquidity and reserve ratios applicable to the commercial banks. To ensure liquidity, a certain percentage of short-term obligations had to be covered by vault holdings or other quick assets. As a further requirement, the commercial banks had to retain in their portfolios government securities equal to at least 30 percent of their demand deposits.

In the early 1980s credit policy had been rather liberal to encourage investment, the money supply was growing at an average rate of 20 percent each year, and interest rates remained low. Gross investment grew from a share of around 20 percent of GDP in the early 1970s to about 30 percent in the mid-1980s. The International Monetary Fund (IMF), along with the World Bank (see Glossary), expressed the urgency of finding a solution to the trade deficit problem and preventing a foreign debt crisis. They recommended raising interest rates to curb loans (and consequently further imports) and devaluing the dinar to improve export prospects, acknowledging that these measures would slow economic growth. The Tunisian authorities were reluctant to do either. Imports of production machinery and materials were essential to local manufacturing and increasing output, and a devalued dinar would make such imports very costly. Moreover, devaluation would not be beneficial to the major Tunisian exports, hydrocarbons and phosphates, which were paid for in United States dollars. However, Tunisia did not totally reject the devaluation option because of the declining importance of hydrocarbons and phosphates relative to exports such as textiles and other manufactured products and to tourism.

Other functions of the central bank included supervising the country's gold and official foreign exchange assets and administering the government's foreign exchange regulations. The central bank also acted as fiscal agent for the treasury and the government's public entities and advised the government on financial and economic matters.

Other Banks and Savings Institutions

Banking was a growing sector in Tunisia in the mid-1980s, stimulated by the expansion of joint banks with other Arab interests and offshore banks. The first was brought about by the increased participation of Arab capital to form, along with Tunisian partners, a consortium of development banks. Except for the Economic Development Bank of Tunisia (Banque de Développement Économique de Tunisie—BDET), founded in 1959 under its previous name, the Société Nationale d'Investissement, the other six development banks were formed in the early 1980s and were funded largely by Arab capital, which never exceeded 50 percent of the

159

total. Development banks secured long-term loans and financed investment projects in the various sectors of the economy.

In 1985 the BDET was an important source of medium- and long-term loans for manufacturing and tourism. It had increased its capacity for mobilizing capital resources by receiving time deposits. Nearly one-third of the BDET's equity was owned by the Tunisian government and the balance by private Tunisian citizens and the International Finance Corporation, a member of the World Bank group.

Encouragement of offshore banking had been sought by a 1976 law permitting the establishment of foreign banks and other financial institutions and granting them a 10-year tax holiday. Their operations were restricted to nonresidents of Tunisia. A few foreign banks had begun operating in Tunisia by the early 1980s but were growing frustrated with the little freedom they were given in their currency exchange transactions. One offshore banking unit closed, and others were reducing their operations. The central bank, keen to see Tunis develop as an international commercial center, introduced significant changes in 1985. Accordingly, offshore banking units were allowed to do business in dinars with Tunisian residents, such as issuing guarantees in local currency, and to carry out some foreign exchange transactions. The changes were welcome but remained short of the demands of the offshore banking units, which were pressing for full equality with local banks and for making the dinar a convertible currency.

The leading commercial deposit banks in 1985 were the Tunisian Banking Company (Société Tunisienne de Banque—STB) and the National Bank of Tunisia (Banque Nationale de Tunisie—BNT). In addition to engaging in the usual commercial operations, the STB was an important source of credit for development projects offering medium- and long-term loans. It also made equity investments in new or expanding enterprises, primarily industrial ones. Founded in 1957, the STB was jointly owned by state and private investors. The BNT was established under its current charter in 1959 as a consolidation of several institutions that had dealt in agricultural credit since the early 1900s, and it remained a specialized agricultural bank in the 1980s, reaching its customers, insofar as seasonal credit was concerned, through a growing network of local mutual credit funds. Not registered as banks, the mutual credit organizations were supervised by the BNT and operated as private cooperatives extending credit to their members at reasonable rates and performing certain marketing functions. In another role, the BNT was the agent for the government in administering the complex program of farm price subsidies.

The National Savings and Housing Fund was a specialized credit institution that accepted deposits from individuals for home construction. The post office checking and savings account system provided an important banking service for many of the people who lived far from the branch offices of the commercial banks.

The Labor Force

In 1985, from a population of around 7.2 million people, the total labor force was estimated at 2.1 million. The low participation rate was attributable to the omission of unpaid labor in the statistics, the very low average age of the Tunisian population, and the low rate of participation of women in the work force. At about 20 percent, the rate of participaton among women was still considerably higher than that of neighboring countries, and many employed women, particularly those in farming, worked full-time but were not recorded in official labor statistics.

Official estimates for 1985 indicated that members of the labor force who had jobs numbered around 1.8 million, a figure which placed the number of unemployed at around 300,000. Although less important than a decade earlier, agriculture remained the largest employer with 32.4 percent of the total. About 23.4 percent of the labor force worked in industry, including manufacturing, mining, and energy (see table 6, Appendix). The subsectors in which job creation was most successful were fishing and public administration, particularly public education and public health.

Employment was governed by the amended and modernized 1966 Labor Code—considered by the International Labour Organisation (ILO) as among the most progressive pieces of legislation affecting work standards—and by the collective bargaining conventions used by employers, the sectoral unions, and the government. Both sources determined wage levels; enforced minimum wages; protected the right to unionize; and established worker grievance procedures, social security contributions, disability insurance, maternity leave, length of the workweek, and overtime pay. As of mid-1985 minimum wages were TD2.64 daily in agriculture and TD95.06 per week in industry for a 48-hour week. Unionized labor generally earned higher wages, sometimes 40 percent more than did laborers. Actually many farm members earned below the minimum official wage, particularly those living in the poor regions of the central and southern parts of the country. The authorities tended to overlook such infractions because the unemployment situation was somewhat relieved thereby. Salaries varied greatly; low-level government workers earned TD110 per month, a middle-income government worker was paid about TD300 to TD400, and cabinet ministers or company presidents received about TD3,000 per month plus benefits. The government raised salaries and wages every year by about 30 percent in the late 1970s and early 1980s, a policy consistent with the principle that workers ought to share in economic gains. Inflation, however, caused the authorities to raise wages by only 12 percent in 1983 and to freeze them in both 1984 and the first half of 1985; at the same time, nonwage benefits were raised substantially.

Unemployment was one of the most severe internal problems and hazardous challenges Tunisia faced in the mid-1980s. The official Tunisian figures estimated the unemployment rate at between 13 and 15 percent while the ILO placed it at 20 percent. Indeed, all surveys that led to these estimates did not cover the 15 to 17 age-group—25 percent of whom were searching for jobs—or those over the age of 59. Considered unemployed were only those working less than 14 hours one week before or at the time of the survey and not those who were underemployed or performing essentially unproductive work or those who were very poorly remunerated. Had such factors been taken into consideration, an alarming 30 percent of the labor force might have been revealed as unemployed.

Unemployed Tunisians were concentrated in the northwest part of the country and generally in more urban than rural areas. A large percentage of the rural work force, however, was underemployed or only temporarily working. During the 1970s the unemployed element of the population was primarily composed of unskilled or semiskilled labor but, in the 1980s, increasingly included educated people, such as physicians and engineers.

The problem was a natural result of an annual population growth rate at 2.4 percent but also partly a result of the government's investment policies. Many investments in the 1970s were made in areas such as tourism and petroleum production and other mining activities for which large numbers of workers were not required. Capital-intensive production, which was dominant in the manufacturing sector, was encouraged partly by the unselective grants and subsidized interest rates offered by the government and also by the reduced income duties on capital equipment imports. The protective labor laws also contributed to investors' preferences for nonlabor-intensive production. Some of these measures were reversed by the mid-1980s; employment-generating investment was particularly encouraged and protected, and the government had made progress in setting aside specific funds for creating new jobs every year. Around 45,000 jobs were created annually in the 1980s, a number that fell short of the 60,000 jobs projected in the context of the 1982–86 development plan as necessary to accommodate the growing labor force.

Many Tunisians have dealt with the local unemployment problem by working abroad. Since the early 1960s Tunisians have been going abroad for work, mainly to France, the Federal Republic of Germany (West Germany), and Italy, and later to Libya and the Persian Gulf states. Remittances traditionally constituted significant contributions to the balance of payments and continued to do so in the 1980s, reaching TD132 million in 1982, TD235 million in 1983, and TD265 million in 1984. Generally, those with fewer skills emigrated and took jobs abroad as laborers or construction workers; nevertheless, they were generally more skilled than their Moroccan or Algerian counterparts. More recently, in the mid-1980s, émigrés included physicians, engineers, and teachers. The latest estimate indicated that 300,000 to 350,000 Tunisians were working abroad, half in France and one-quarter in Libya. When the economic conditions in receiving countries deteriorated in the late 1970s, however, prospects for work abroad declined. France encouraged migrants to return to Tunisia, and about 6,000 workers had returned home by 1982. In 1980 and again in 1985, during periods of strained political relations, large numbers of Tunisians were forced to leave Libya. In 1985 about 30,000 Tunisian workers were expelled from Libya. Estimates of people returning to Tunisia in the 1980s ranged from 20,000 to 60,000 annually; at this rate around 350,000 people would be added to the labor force by 1990, further intensifying pressures for the creation of jobs.

Agriculture

In the mid-1980s the agriculture sector employed about 32 percent of the labor force and supported roughly one-half of the Tunisian population. Agricultural output had been growing at a satisfactory 7 percent rate per year during the 1970s and early 1980s until a severe drought affected all of North Africa in 1982–83. Since then output has grown at only 1 to 2 percent each year. Because of much higher growth rates in the other economic sectors, agriculture's share of GDP declined steadily from about 22 percent in 1970 to 15 percent in 1984.

Foodstuffs were by far the largest part of Tunisia's agricultural output. Crops and products included cereals, olive oil, wine, citrus and other fruits, dates, vegetables, and sugar beets. In the early 1980s the fairly new cotton and tobacco plantations began to yield crops. In general, Tunisia was 90 percent self-sufficient in meat, 60 percent in cereals, and 40 percent in milk. But rapid population growth, the growing preference for a more expensive diet, and the effects of the recent drought had caused a severe food trade deficit in the mid-1980s.

The agriculture sector's potential was underdeveloped, and realization of the full potential of the country's farmlands was hampered by low-yielding, traditional farming practices that were just beginning to give way to more productive modern techniques in 1985. Farming relies heavily on rainfall, which historically has been unreliable, often causing virtual crop failure. Agriculture also suffered from problems of erosion and an underdeveloped storage and marketing infrastructure; only a few farm operators made use of chemical fertilizers or modern equipment to prepare the soil.

The near-stagnation of the sector in the early to mid-1980s had far-reaching effects on the socioeconomic balances of the country; the government had to allocate significant amounts of money to subsidize food prices, the balance of payments deteriorated because of insufficient national production, and the rural-to-urban migration of the past 15 years increased. Accordingly, the government increased the agriculture sector's share of total development funds from 13 percent in the 1977–81 plan to 19 percent in the 1982–86 plan. The latter plan aimed to increase employment in agriculture, reduce regional disparities, balance trade in foodstuffs, and achieve a minimal annual growth rate of 5 percent. The investment in agriculture in the 1970s had resulted in the addition of 70,000 hectares of irrigated land, the planting of new trees on 315,000 hectares, the construction of greenhouses on 1,000 hectares, the reforestation of 30,000 hectares, and water and soil conservation work on 120,000 hectares. Most of the funds in the 1982–86 plan went to irrigation and the construction of dams to improve production in the rainfed areas, as well as to projects involving fishing, tree crops, livestock breeding, and storage amenities. The employment-generating subsectors received more than they did in the previous plan; the share of livestock increased from 12 percent of total agricultural funds to 15 percent, that of fruit tree plantations grew from 8 percent to 17 percent, and the share of farm machinery decreased from 17 percent to 11 percent.

Understandably, Tunisia has been very concerned about the enlargement of the European Economic Community (EEC). The impact on its agricultural exports would be almost fatal, particularly in the case of olive oil. Also threatened were citrus fruits and some vegetables. At best, Tunisia would still export oranges, which

Irrigation pipes bring water for agricultural use
to semiarid southern Tunisia
Courtesy World Bank/William Graham

had a two- to three-week yield advantage over the West European
produce, as well as apricots and a few vegetables. Regardless,
export prices were expected to be much lower, resulting in higher
subsidies to producers. In the mid-1980s Tunisia was negotiating a
special export treaty with France to retain its exports of olive oil,
despite the fact that the EEC will be nearly self-sufficient, similar
to the treatment extended to the countries of the Commonwealth of
Nations to market sugar in the EEC.

Land Use

Of the total land area of 164,000 square kilometers, about 52
percent was arable. The arable surface, equivalent to 85,280
square kilometers, or 8.4 million hectares, was distributed to 1.2
million hectares of forests and esparto grass, 2.2 million hectares
of grazing land, and 4 million hectares of cultivated land, planted

mostly to cereals and tree crops, and 1 million hectares of fallow land. Only 200,000 hectares were irrigated. Tunisia's potential of irrigable land itself was estimated in the early 1980s to be very low, and it was believed that only 25,000 to 50,000 more hectares could be made arable by irrigation.

The northern region of the country receives around 70 percent of the annual rainfall. The north also has more rivers and lakes and accounts for two-thirds of Tunisia's surface water resources. The central region of the country receives about 22 percent of the rainfall while the south is dry, sandy, and the water frequently saline. In the mid-1980s assessments of underground water in the center and the south revealed abundant quantities, and, although they did not provide a new estimate of the potential surface of irrigable land, they questioned the previous meager one. However, the cost of developing the supply of underground water would be very high.

All water resources in the country are under the jurisdiction of the Ministry of Agriculture. Initially, the government refrained from sponsoring irrigation schemes but permitted individual farmers to install water channels and wells. Public investment of large sums of money began in the late 1960s, however, and has continued since then. Around 23 percent of agricultural investment in the 1970s went to irrigation, and in the 1982–86 plan, water resources development was allocated a sizable 40 percent of overall agricultural investment. The benefit of irrigation was evident; in the early 1980s the irrigated sector (only 4 percent of the cultivated land) produced 25 percent of the total agricultural output.

To preserve the limited water supply for public use, three master water plans covering the north, central, and southern parts of the country had been implemented. The North Tunisia Water Master Plan was the most advanced of these plans as of 1985. It was a long-range project, which had begun in the late 1970s and involved the building of several dams and related facilities to develop irrigation and electricity and to supply drinking water to the coastal towns. A number of dams, of crucial importance to Tunisian agriculture, had been built by the mid-1980s. There were about seven major ones in the north and four in the central area. Five additional dams should come into operation, again in the north where most of the surface water lies, before the end of 1988. The government was investing heavily in extracting the underground water, having estimated that the high cost of drilling wells would be outweighed by the benefits. Around 800 deep wells, provided by the private sector, were operative as of 1985. Under the Southern Water Resources Plan, projects were under way in the mid-

1980s to drill new wells to supply water to the Jerid, Nefzaoua, Gabès, Medenine, and Tataouine areas and to increase irrigated land in the south by 4,500 hectares before the end of the decade.

The problem of erosion was a serious one, threatening 90 percent of the soil. It was caused by violent desert rainstorms, windborne sand and clay, seasonal rivers, and overgrazing. In an effort to eliminate the losses, the government emphasized reforestation and soil conservation programs. A government decree issued in 1958, and still being applied in the 1980s, made obligatory contour-plowing of all planted slopes of more than 2 percent incline and planting of trees on at least 2 percent of each farm. Land drainage operations centered in the northern coastal region. In the central and the southern areas of the country, the problem of diminishing natural vegetation was addressed. The vegetation served as animal fodder, and its reduction encouraged the advance of the desert. Projects involving soil and forest conservation amounted to as much as TD100 million during the 1982–86 plan and were expected to provide about 40,000 jobs each year. Antierosion measures were to cover around 60,000 hectares each year during the plan period.

Five agricultural regions could be discerned on the basis of prevalent crops. The banks of the Mejerda River in the north, blessed with high rainfall and the country's most fertile soil, were prime grain land and also supported livestock. Traditional farming was predominant except on the large units in the upper Mejerda Valley, the areas around Béja, Kef, and Siliana. Perennial crops could be found on the hillsides. The northeast was best suited to fruits and vegetables, and it produced 80 percent of the citrus output. Vegetable output was increasing there because of larger amounts of irrigated land. The Cape Bon region was also a major production area for grapes and wine. The eastern plateau region along the coast between Sousse and Sfax and the area on nearby Jerba Island had dry, sandy soil ideal for olive culture. Low-yield cereal crops and, at the northern edge of that region, some vegetable crops in newly constructed greenhouses could also be found. The central hinterlands supported only subsistence farming but produced large quantities of wild esparto grass, a base material for paper and cordage. Encouraged by the government, tree crop plantations (including olives, almonds, and apricots) were gradually transforming the steppe. The oases on the southern desert fringes produced olives, vegetables, dates, and palm by-products, such as fronds used in handicraft weaving. Irrigated agriculture existed mostly in the south. More than half of the irrigated land was used to grow vegetables, about 35 percent of it for fruit trees, 8 percent for fodder crops, and 7 percent for cereals and industrial crops such as sugar beets.

Two methods of farming existed in the mid-1980s: the modern approach that was adopted by cooperatives, state farms, and large private farms and the traditional, more prevalent method used on the numerous small private farms. Traditional agriculture was marked by heavy dependence on hand labor or at best the use of draft animals, including the camel, for plowing and hauling. Farm implements and equipment were rudimentary, and little use was made of crop rotation, fertilizers, or even primitive soil conservation techniques, such as terracing. Most of the small traditional farmers were displaced from the productive areas by the Europeans during the protectorate era and were consequently working land of marginal value unless improved by irrigation or other means.

The circumstances of the small farmers varied with the region in which they lived and with the crops they grew. Income was generally higher in the north, with its greater rainfall and emphasis on cash crops, than in central or southern Tunisia where land was dryer and successful cultivation (primarily grains) depended almost entirely on weather conditions. A comparatively small number of farmers, most of them employed in olive culture, were fairly well off and could employ seasonal labor. The average cereal farmer employed laborers only in good years, paying them in kind. At a lower economic level were those farmers whose holdings were so small or poor that they could not live by their own produce and who had to seek day or seasonal labor working at the olive presses, herding, or performing any jobs they could find. A drought year reduced most of them to penury. Sharecropping and tenant farming were also common practices in the traditional sector.

The seminomads of the steppe were little better off than the small sedentary landholders. Pasturage was poor, techniques of breeding were archaic, and as a consequence yields of meat and wool were low and of inferior quality. Even under these conditions the seminomads could be nearly self-sufficient by virtue of their small requirements for subsistence. Such income as was necessary could be earned by gathering esparto grass, making handicrafts, or hiring out camels for transport.

Land Tenure and Reform

A complicated system of land tenure existed when the French protectorate was imposed in the late nineteenth century. Some land was privately owned, mostly by the bey or by a few important families. Privately owned land was called *melk* land, and the owner had the right to dipose of it by sale, gift, or inheritance. Subject for centuries to the Muslim law of equal inheritance among heirs, *melk* land became highly fragmented and was held in joint ownership with uncertain title. Collectively owned tribal property, called *arch* land, found largely in the southern half of the country, gave the individual a right to share in the use of the land held by the village or tribe. The *arch* land was managed by elected councils for the benefit of members of the group.

Another kind of property holding, which represented most of the land tenure arrangements before the French arrived, was the *habus* (see Glossary). An old Islamic institution, the *habus* was a foundation from which the revenues were dedicated in perpetuity for a charitable purpose. Establishment of a *habus* was an irrevocable legal transaction, and property so endowed could not be expropriated and was inalienable. Any landowner, regardless of his kind of holding, whether *melk* or *arch* land, could render his estate inalienable (to prevent either squandering by his heirs or confiscation by the government) by transforming his land into a private *habus*. Private *habus* land was still used by the original tenants or their descendants, who paid a yearly rent to the religious institution. Although *habus* land was inalienable in principle, the French authorized the transfer of public *habus* land in 1898, after which date much of it changed hands. The area in public *habus* land was estimated to have declined from hundreds of thousands of hectares to less than 20,000 hectares by national independence in 1956. After independence steps were taken to make more land available. Because *habus* land was considered to be wasteful in production methods, the small remainder of public *habus* was nationalized in 1956, and the individuals who would have otherwise inherited it became the proprietors of the land, an event that gave rise to immediate disputes among the descendants involved.

The system of landownership hindered the acquisition of land by European colonists after the protectorate was established. The French met the situation by inducing the bey to decree in 1885 the registration of title under French law, specifying in full detail the location and size of the property. Land so registered came under the jurisdiction of French courts. The certificates of title issued under this system wiped out previous claims, and all future transactions had to be inscribed on the certificate to be valid. The new law provided legal measures for private acquisition of land by Europeans, who were generally able to get claims settled quickly in their favor. Thousands of Tunisian farmers also acquired land, but their farms were small in comparison with those of the French, Italian, and Maltese settlers.

Other legislative measures made large amounts of land available cheaply to French colonists. In 1890 it was decreed that all uncultivated bush lands were to be classified as state forests. Land not suitable for reforestation was made available for sale to the colons (settlers). This action was disastrous for the nomadic herders of the country because much of the land sold to the Europeans had traditionally been available to them for grazing purposes. The nomads were forced to graze their animals on less suitable land, and the erosion of this marginal land was greatly increased. By independence some 4,000 European farmers owned some 850,000 hectares of farmland, about 5,000 Tunisian farmers owned sizable holdings and operated modern farms as did the Europeans, and some 450,000 Tunisians owned or leased small properties and depended on subsistence farming and traditional methods of operation.

Both before and after the period of agrarian reform, a wide variety of tenant relationships existed. The most common method of tenancy encountered was that of a fixed rent paid for the land for a specific period of time. Few tenant farmers had official contracts and therefore little assurance of long-term use of the land and as a result had little incentive to invest in long-term improvement of the land. Absentee landlords were also seldom concerned. A somewhat similar but better form of tenancy was an increasingly prevalent arrangement known as share-tenancy, under which the landlord received a share of the crop—usually one-third—in return for participating in the costs of preparing the land. If the landlord did not participate, his share was smaller. An unusual aspect of sharecropping in Tunisia, particularly in the north, was the increasing number of small individual farmers renting their land under a sharecropping arrangement to much larger private operators. By the use of modern technology, the large farmer's income went up without his having to work the land himself.

A widespread movement into the cooperative program had its origin in the period after independence. From 1956 until 1964 the state had been acquiring European-owned farmland that had been either abandoned or sold to the government, although some land held by the French owners was confiscated in 1961 during the Bizerte crisis. These holdings were then operated as state farms or increasingly turned into cooperatives for the benefit of the former workers on the estates. These actions created a lack of confidence among the remaining European landowners, and farm investment and production decreased, a result the government attempted to counteract in 1963 by guaranteeing ownership for at least five more years. In May 1964, however, a law was suddenly passed nationalizing all farmland still held by foreigners. The state, in an attempt to manage the larger amounts of land it had acquired, resorted increasingly to the formation of cooperatives.

The historical basis for the government's role was the necessity, after the French withdrawal, of maintaining essential supplies of nourishment to the people and surpluses to the established export markets. Equally, there was the desire on the part of those whose opposition to the protectorate arrangement had been carried out on egalitarian principles to institute their beliefs at the grassroots level with a reform of the land tenure system. The method chosen to fulfill these goals was the cooperative, launched after careful studies to determine its feasibility. From a practical standpoint, the cooperative supplied a framework in which land could be consolidated, workers could be strictly organized, and management by agricultural technicians could be maintained as it had been under the French estate system. The cooperatives, however, gave their members nominal ownership of the land, a share in the profits, and the right to eventual control of it. Through their function as training and demonstration centers, the cooperatives were foreseen as the prime means of moving the rural population from the subsistence sector to the modernizing sector of the economy.

Between 1963 and 1969 new legislation had put in place elements of a comprehensive land reform program centered on cooperative agriculture. The intent of the cooperative movement was that of transforming the values and habits of rural residents by training them in modern farming methods using cadres of technicians to teach and managers to administer the farms. Decisionmaking was to be taken out of the hands of the farmer and placed in the hands of the government, and it was on this point that the movement foundered. A 1967 cooperative statute called for a transformation of all farmland in the country into cooperatives, private farmers becoming members of the cooperatives—largely against their wishes. The government never anticipated the opposition that resulted nor knew of the incompetence of the farm managers and the losses incurred on the farms until late 1969, when the entire cooperative movement was abandoned by order of Bourguiba. In September 1969, at the height of the movement, almost all the farmland in the country (about 92 percent) had come under state control and was in cooperatives.

Later analysis by social scientists revealed that so much local resistance to the implementation of cooperative policies was encountered that coercion by the authorities was necessary. The actual extent of coercion during the cooperative period was not adequately reported at the time and was made known only later. Apparently, farmers were threatened, sabotage occurred, and physical violence erupted between villagers and police backed by army units in many areas, particularly in the Sahil. During the two-year period of forced cooperativization between 1967 and 1969, farm output fell, most farms operated at a loss, and management was generally incompetent. The officials administering the cooperatives had little or no agricultural training and were mainly bureaucrats who continually falsified production figures in their reports to superiors, who in turn never checked on the true situation of the farms. It was later revealed that when profitable sales were achieved, the profit per hectare on many cooperatives was actually less than the profit made by the small farmers using traditional methods before their land became part of the cooperative.

After September 1969, farmers were given the option of remaining with the cooperative or taking their farms out of it and returning to private ownership. By January 1970 most farmers had chosen the option of returning to farming their own land. The cooperative movement still existed in the mid-1980s, albeit on a much smaller scale and on a voluntary basis.

A complete cadastre of the country had never been completed as of the early 1980s. Only partial surveys had been made with property titles issued by the land registrar. Properties without titles received a title of possession, which was not as negotiable as a property title. As much as one-half of the arable land was believed to lack clear titles. After many years of partial efforts, the government committed itself in 1985 to a comprehensive program of land reform and titling.

Land distribution in the mid-1980s was highly skewed. As little as 3 percent of the total number of farms encompassed about one-half of the cultivated land, and one-third of the farms accounted for practically all (99 percent) of the private land. The remaining two-thirds of the farms most often had land areas of less than five hectares each. More than half of the smaller landholdings of fewer than five hectares were situated in the north. Such minute holdings demonstrated the poverty in which the large majority of the rural population lived. By 1985 around 80 percent of the total cultivable land was privately owned. Only about 234,000 hectares of farm cooperatives remained on exclusively state-owned land. There were an additional 213,000 hectares in state farms. Most of the existing cooperatives were in areas of public irrigation projects where average per capita income was higher than in other rural areas. Irrigated public agricultural land also fell under special agrarian reform laws that specified maximum and minimum land-holdings permitted for each area.

Crop Production

Among crops, cereals predominated, covering almost one-third of all agricultural land in the mid-1980s. Durhum, or hard wheat, barley, and Mexican soft wheat were the major crops, in that order, accounting for about 97 percent of annual production. Oats, corn, and sorghum made up the remaining 3 percent of the total. Wheat, a nonperishable crop, was grown by all farmers—large, small, and subsistence farmers alike. Hard wheat was milled to yield semolina, the basic ingredient of pastas such as spaghetti and of the standard Tunisian dish, couscous. Soft wheat was used in bread-making. Cereal crops were concentrated in the north, where they covered 800,000 hectares of land, but were also found in the center of the country and in the south. Wheat was grown mostly in the northwest and barley, which can tolerate dryer conditions, in the central and southern areas of the country. To a limited degree, high-yielding new strains of Mexican soft wheat have been adapted to certain areas of Tunisia, but Mexican wheat requires much care in its cultivation; thus only the most modern of farms have profited from its introduction.

Tunisia had historically been a net exporter of cereals. Production in the mid-1980s, however, was unable to keep pace with population growth, particularly because it was still largely accomplished by traditional methods and remained dependent on adequate rainfall. Variation in climate from poor to favorable could result in a 30-percent increase in output. Drought conditions resulted in one of the lowest outputs ever in 1982–83. The output of 1983–84 was 14 percent higher and was more representative of an average annual yield. Ouput of hard wheat was 600,000 tons, barley 300,000 tons, and soft wheat 150,000 tons. Nevertheless, local demand was about twice the quantity produced. The United States supplied about three-quarters of Tunisia's import needs in hard and soft wheat during the mid-1980s.

In the mid-1980s cooperatives, state farms, and the large private farms that had adopted modern farming techniques accounted for the largest share of output. The modern subsector occasionally used various inputs, such as fertilizer and machinery, and had easy access to credit. The traditional subsector, which consisted of the small private holdings, had very limited access to credit and rarely used any inputs other than the seeds themselves. The government

173

estimated that the modern sector was only producing half of its potential and that the land cultivated by traditional methods was producing as little as 15 percent of its potential. Cereal production suffered from a lack of fertilizers, better seeds, herbicides, and mechanical preparation of the soil. Only 25 percent of the land in the north was supplied with the necessary modern inputs. Although mechanization greatly expanded the area under cultivation, it tended to increase the harmful effects of erosion. Some soils were being overexploited, and virgin foothills were being stripped of cover to expand growing areas. As it became aware of these abuses, the government took measures to fight the problem by teaching careful use of mechanization. Additionally, large amounts of funds went toward reclamation of at least 400,000 hectares of once cultivable land before the end of the 1982–86 plan. The problem of poor use of modern agricultural inputs was as much a result of financial affordability as of a primitive distribution network for the small farmers. The National Cereals Office, which purchased and marketed all cereals and set producers' prices, saw its duties expanded to include a large number of extension services that would provide farmers with seeds, fertilizers, and pesticides at subsidized prices. Effort and funds were also invested in upgrading the inadequate cereal storage facilities, which aggravated the problem of insufficient supply.

Fruit trees covered around 45 percent of the arable land, including one-third of the irrigated land, and contributed about one-third of all agricultural produce. Olive trees dominated, covering one-third of the land planted to trees. Other fruit production included grapes, citrus, date, almond, and apricot crops, all of which were relatively more productive than olive trees, producing higher yields per hectare. A reduction in the output from trees in the early 1980s was believed to be caused by the old age of most trees and an invasion of couch grass. Because tree crops were exportable, large funds were allocated in the mid-1980s to remedy the situation. To fight against erosion, new trees were planted, and the effort apparently was successful.

The olive tree is well suited to the Tunisian climate because it can survive long periods of drought. An essential feature of olive culture is the irregularity of the yield. Production has varied widely from year to year depending upon rainfall and care, and seldom are there two good years in a row. Traditionally, inheritance of olive holdings was limited to the trees and not the land. Each generation, an owner's trees were divided among all his heirs, a practice that greatly fragmented holdings. One farmer could own trees separated by several miles or share title to a single tree with several others. The system discouraged capital improvements to the olive groves and in many cases made adequate care impossible.

Tunisia had traditionally been one of the world's largest producers of olive oil, but production diminished steadily during the 1970s and the first half of the 1980s. The average annual yield had been 700 kilograms per hectare in the late 1960s but had fallen to 570 kilograms in the late 1970s, when a government survey showed that between 5 million and 9 million of the 55 million olive trees in the country were yielding too little to justify further cultivation. An extensive program of branch and root pruning and removing underproductive trees was undertaken. This, coupled with the planting of new olive trees to combat erosion, assured the authorities of an increase in production through the 1990s.

The olive industry provided as much as one-half of the agricultural jobs and supported nearly 1 million people. As a result of the new olive tree plantings, almost 80,000 additional farmers had been persuaded to shift from growing wheat and maize to growing olives. The trees would take about 15 years to bear fruit, and production was expected to reach 180,000 tons annually. Domestic consumption of olive oil, generally around 45,000 to 50,000 tons a year, would be growing at a much slower rate and was expected to remain significantly lower than the domestic supply. Meanwhile, Western Europe, Tunisia's traditional olive oil export market, would have reached self-sufficiency in that commodity. Since early 1986 competition from Spain and Portugal, new members of the EEC, made the future of Tunisian olive oil exports appear bleak. In the mid-1980s revenues from olive oil exports were equal to an average of US$70 million a year. In an effort to boost domestic demand, the government had imposed import restrictions on all competing vegetable oils, initiated trade negotiations with France to protect its sales, and started promoting its olive oil in new markets. In spite of these measures, the results of increased production and therefore lower world prices were bound to hurt the Tunisian national income by the end of the 1980s.

The land allocated to vineyards changed from a minimal share before the Europeans lived in Tunisia to large areas covering much of Cape Bon and the northern coastal hills by the time of Tunisian independence and reverted to a small amount as of the mid-1960s when Tunisia forfeited the French wine market. In the mid-1980s some 34,700 hectares were planted to grapes, and the yield from

Olive groves near Sfax
Courtesy Embassy of Tunisia, Washington

28,000 hectares was used for winemaking. The significant funds allocated to improving vineyards in the 1982–86 plan reflected renewed interest in the production of both quality table grapes and wines mainly for export.

Citrus fruit production was a relatively recent but expanding industry. The major citrus fruit areas were between Tunis and Cape Bon and in the vicinities of Nabeul and Hammamet. Most orchards were small—90 percent were under 10 hectares—but, being irrigated, were capable of steady production and were not drastically affected by drought. Having received significant funds and attention throughout the 1970s and the first half of the 1980s, citrus production was increasing rapidly. About 25 percent of the annual output was exported, and the remainder went either to the domestic market or to the growing food-processing industry. Despite Spain and Portugal's admission to the EEC, Tunisian oranges, described as unmatched in juiciness and flavor, would continue to be in demand in West European markets.

Date production was of prime importance to farmers living in the southern oases around Gabès, Medenine, and Gafsa, where

Tunisian farm workers
Courtesy International Labour Organisation

groves of date palms totaling 18,000 hectares offered the only possibility of commercial agriculture. Dates have high nutritional value and in drought years serve as a staple—sometimes as the only food—for much of the human and animal populations on the desert's edge. During average years more than two-thirds of the crop are consumed within the country, and date pits and inferior varieties are used as animal fodder. Superior strains are exported. Numerous date farmers have begun to adopt modern techniques of cultivation, and processing plants have been built at several oases. In the 1980s agronomists calculated that as little as one hectare of land in an oasis, if properly cultivated with a mix of dates and fruits, could generate a fairly large annual income for a farm family. An additional incentive to encourage date cultivation has been the increased international demand for dates.

Vegetable cultivation included items essential to the Tunisian diet—chick-peas, eggplant, artichokes, broad beans, turnips, and

Workers irrigating seedlings on a date plantation
at Nefta in southern Tunisia
Courtesy World Bank/William Graham

peppers—and enough of the more common European table vegetables, such as tomatoes, red peppers, potatoes, onions, peas, carrots, and melons, to support a small yet growing export industry. The total area in vegetables in the early 1980s was estimated at 105,000 hectares. Truck gardening had long been established on the northern and central coastal plains, and vegetables covered nearly one-half of the cultivated land in the northeast and slightly more than one-quarter of the central plains. They also accounted for nearly one-half of the crops on irrigated land. A network of experimental and demonstration farms had been established east of Tabarka along the northern coast to disseminate knowledge of advanced methods to the farmers of the area. Additionally, around 215 hectares of greenhouses and 895 hectares of small plastic tunnels were built near Monastir and Sfax as a first step toward more all-weather production. Early ripening vegetable strains would give Tunisia the opportunity to export profitably to West European fresh produce markets before the northern season.

Harvesting dates at El Hamma du Jerid
near Tozeur in southern Tunisia
Courtesy World Bank/William Graham

Sugar beets covered 2,000 hectares of land in the early 1980s. Production had expanded rapidly but not fast enough to satisfy local demand. The government planned to increase the land under cultivation to 11,000 hectares by 1986, a most ambitious and perhaps unrealistic target, or at least to stimulate production to meet as much as one-third of the national sugar requirements by 1986. In the first half of the 1980s, sugar production met only a tiny percentage of domestic requirements, and imports reached 70,000 tons a year. Tobacco was increasingly cultivated, but production remained below the domestic demand. Small amounts of cotton were grown until 1977, when a cotton expansion program was successfully launched by the government on state farms to meet the needs of the growing textile industry, which was having to import its raw materials. Figs, pears, apricots, apples, peaches, plums, cherries, and almonds were other crops grown profitably by Tunisian farmers.

179

Livestock, Fishing, and Forestry

Sheep were the predominant livestock, numbering about 4.5 million head in 1984. The numbers of sheep, goats, and cattle were all multiplying rapidly; cattle were estimated at 600,000 head in 1984 and goats at 800,000. The number of chickens had reached 14 million, and poultry production was on the rise. Nevertheless, livestock production was still short of the domestic demand in the mid-1980s. Rainfall was the critical variable in animal husbandry because most animals depended on natural vegetation. Because the government was concerned about Tunisia's increased reliance on food imports, the cultivated areas producing dry fodder were to be increased by three times to about 800,000 hectares by the end of the 1982–86 plan. Attempts were also under way to improve the quality of the herds by importing breeding stock and using better care and feeding methods. Tunisia also had about 173,000 camels, 205,000 donkeys, 70,000 mules, and 52,000 horses.

The fishing industry achieved notable growth during the 1970s, but production reached a plateau of around 65,000 tons—the volume of local demand—during the first half of the 1980s. The industry had a potential of at least 100,000 tons but suffered from inadequate equipment and from difficulties linked to the marketing of any larger catch. The National Fishing Office, which owned part of the trawler fleet, was responsible for supervision and development of the industry. In the mid-1980s it was involved in a major effort to increase production by supplying fishermen with more modern equipment, building more cold-storage rooms and warehouses in Tunisian ports, and operating larger distribution networks. Because Tunisian fishing waters had not been fully exploited, the country signed an agreement with Italy in 1976 permitting a limited number of Italian trawlers to fish within Tunisian territorial limits in exchange for an annual payment. But increasingly Italian fishermen were competing with the Tunisians in the mid-1980s and undermining Tunisian output. The National Fishing Office was also promoting the cultivation of shellfish, which were available not only on the coastline but also in the numerous lakes, and was optimistic that future production would be significant.

There were only about 800,000 hectares of land classified as forests in Tunisia; of these, about 296,000 hectares were actually wooded, mainly with pine, oak, cork oak, and eucalyptus. Firewood production was the major output of the forest industry, followed by timber and cork production. Esparto grass grew wild in the steppe and was collected and used as a raw material for the small paper industry and for cordage. Protective measures against erosion taken in the mid-1980s involved reforestation of around 11,000 hectares. Tunisians of the forest regions were expected to benefit from the large number of new jobs and the increased production, which should total about 11,000 tons of cork and 100,000 tons of esparto grass by the end of the 1982–86 plan.

Industry

Of all the sectors of the Tunisian economy, industry (including manufacturing, mining, construction, and energy production) has realized the greatest economic growth since 1956. Industrial expansion was particularly remarkable in the 1970s, when annual growth sometimes reached 10 percent. In the early 1980s growth slowed down considerably to about 2.5 percent but later picked up again, and industrial output was growing at nearly 6 percent a year in the mid-1980s. The reasons for the vigorous development of the industrial sector were numerous. Among the most important was the increasing support given by the Tunisian government to private investors in manufacturing in the form of various tax breaks, credit facilities, and other advantages (see Balance of Payments and External Finance, this ch.). Also of major importance to the industrial sector's growth was the rise in oil, gas, and phosphate prices that occurred in the early 1970s and lasted into the early 1980s.

Tunisian industry was quite well diversified, although phosphates and oil dominated the export revenue picture, followed increasingly more closely by the textile subsector. In the mid-1980s about 40 percent of total investment funds went toward modernizing, diversifying, and generally enhancing industry. Particularly favored were the mechanical industries, electricity generation, and consumer goods production. More than half of Tunisia's imports consisted of inputs for industry: equipment, raw materials, and semifinished products. The government believed that the problems of unemployment and the trade deficit would be largely reduced by continued industrial growth. Industry had indeed created about 65,000 jobs, most of them in manufacturing, between 1982 and 1985.

Hydrocarbons

Tunisia's hydrocarbons industry was small; Tunisian oil and natural gas output made up only a fraction of 1 percent of the total

181

world supply. But hydrocarbons have been indispensable to Tunisia's economic development. In just a little more than a decade, oil and gas production grew to contribute 12 percent of GDP, and petroleum exports alone earned 47 percent of all export revenues in the mid-1980s.

The first production of crude oil began in 1966 at El Borma oil field, which sits astride the Tunisian-Algerian border in the south. The two governments agreed in 1972 that two-thirds of the production from the field would be considered Tunisian and the remainder Algerian and that all production would be transported jointly to the Tunisian seaport of Sakhira for export. The El Borma field experienced loss of pressure in the early 1970s, and its output had started to drop; expensive water injection techniques used in 1977 and 1978 fully restored its production. In the late 1970s a second field, at Ashtart, came into production and soon became as productive as that at El Borma. Together the two fields accounted for 85 percent of Tunisian production. Other fields were exploited at Ad Douleb, Tamesmida, and Sidi Litayem. As of 1985, onshore reserves of petroleum were estimated at 1.7 million barrels but were being depleted quite rapidly. All of the mainland oil fields were dwarfed, however, by the deposits said to exist offshore in several places in the Gulf of Gabès. Full exploitation of the offshore fields had long been delayed because of a dispute with Libya over the extension of its border into the oil field area. The dispute was settled in 1982 in favor of Libya, but Tunisia was nevertheless able to open a number of fields to development, including those at Didon, Miska, Isis, Tazerka, Birsa, and Halk el Manzel.

All exploration in the offshore fields was done by foreign companies, mainly American, French, and Italian. Tunisian oil policies were more liberal than those of many other oil-producing countries, and it rarely entered into partnerships at the initial exploration stage. When exploration agreements did exist, they were easily converted into exploitation agreements if oil was found. Ownership was then split on a 50/50 basis as was the case for the El Borma field, but many fields were owned wholly by private firms or by companies under agreements in which the state had only a small interest. There was little intervention into the activities of the private oil companies. The major operating companies were the Franco-Tunisian Petroleum Exploiting Company (Société Franco-Tunisienne d'Exploitation Pétrolière—SOFRATEP) and the Italo-Tunisian Petroleum Exploiting Company (Société Italo-Tunisienne d'Exploitation Pétrolière—SITEP). The state company, the Tunisian Company for Petroleum Activities (Entreprise Tunisienne d'Activités Pétroliées—ETAP), coordinated all exploration, production, and trade. In 1985 Tunisia was not a member of the Organization of Petroleum Exporting Countries (OPEC), but it generally followed OPEC's pricing patterns.

Annual production was about 39 million barrels of light-grade petroleum. Tunisia was a net exporter of crude oil and, despite rapidly rising consumption at home, was expected to remain self-sufficient for a good number of years. Nevertheless, significant amounts of heavy low-grade crude oil were imported for domestic needs.

There was a major oil refinery at Bizerte with an annual output of about 1.8 million tons a year. In 1985 a project to expand that refinery's capacity to between 3 million and 4 million tons was under way. The increased capacity would significantly cut down on fuel oil and distillate imports supplied by Algeria.

The discovery of natural gas deposits had resulted from petroleum explorations. Gas was found in several locations in four different general areas: Cape Bon, El Borma, Sfax, and the Gulf of Gabès. Reserves were estimated in 1981 at 159 billion cubic meters. A rich quantity of gas, not included in this last estimate, was believed to exist offshore at Miska. The development of the Miska field awaited a financial assessment and the choice of exploitation companies. When exploited, the Miska field should triple present output levels. In the mid-1980s, production stood at around 43 million barrels a year, which was about equal to Tunisia's national gas consumption.

An additional source of natural gas for Tunisia came as a result of the Algerian-Italian gas pipeline, which crossed 360 kilometers of Tunisian territory. The pipeline also distributed 153 million cubic meters of gas to Tunisia in the mid-1980s and was to provide at least triple that quantity before the end of the decade.

Other Mining

Phosphate was the predominant mineral, and the phosphate industry was a vital element of the Tunisian economy. Tunisia was the world's fifth largest producer of phosphate rock, with a 4-percent share of the world's output. Its phosphate quality, however, compared poorly with that of its competitors. Annual production was around 5 million tons in the mid-1980s, of which a little less than one-half was used domestically.

Phosphate mines were located mostly in the west-central area and the southwest of the country. They were totally state owned and operated, which was true of all the mining industry. The Gafsa Phosphate Company (Companie des Phosphates de Gafsa—CPG)

Petroleum refinery at Bizerte
Courtesy Embassy of Tunisia, Washington

handled phosphate research, production, processing, and marketing. Studies forecasted a doubling of the outputs of phosphate rock and phosphoric derivatives as new mines were likely to be exploited at Oum Kecheb, Jellabia, Le Kef, Eddour, and Sra Ouertane before the end of the decade. However, the demand for phosphates in the world market was falling and with it revenues from exports of phosphate rock.

Tunisia had stepped up its production of phosphate derivatives because the demand for them was much less variable than that of phosphate rock. A number of phosphate processing plants existed in the country, the most important of which were located at Gabès and Sfax. In 1985 a large new plant was under construction by contract with a French firm at Sakhira. The construction of another large integrated complex to be located at Gafsa was to start in 1986, with 49 percent of the investment funds supplied by Kuwait. That complex would become the third such Kuwaiti-CPG joint investment in Tunisia. Kuwait and Tunisia were also partners in a plant located in Kuwait that processed Tunisian phosphate. In 1985 Tunisia and Kuwait entered into a similar arrangement with China involving the construction of a fertilizer complex there. Projects to build fertilizer complexes in Pakistan and Turkey were also under study.

Phosphate derivatives produced by Tunisia included ammonium nitrate, diammonium, and phosphoric acid. Tunisia was the world's third largest exporter of phosphoric acid, the production of which reached 600,000 tons a year in the mid-1980s. Average annual production of ammonium nitrate and diammonium amounted to 250,000 tons and 400,000 tons, respectively.

One of the causes for the reduced demand for phosphate abroad was the shortage of funds resulting from cuts in farm subsidies in importing countries. Knowing that, Tunisia entered into barter agreements as another way to dispose of its supply of phosphate rock. Such arrangements were made in 1984 when Tunisia and Romania agreed to exchange phosphate for timber and Tunisia and Britain exchanged phosphate for small-scale capital equipment.

The National Mines Office, founded in 1962, conducted research into mineral deposits that appeared to be commercially exploitable and in some cases carried out the exploitation itself. Other than phosphate, Tunisian mineral resources included iron ore, lead, zinc, fluoride, and mercury. Surface iron ore deposits were abundant, particularly in the north and in the central area near the Algerian border. All mines were of the open pit variety, and the ore was high grade. Average yearly production totaled 320,000 tons in the mid-1980s, of which a significant portion was used in the domestic steel industry and the remainder exported. About a dozen lead mines were operating; reserves of lead were estimated at 450,000 tons, and production reached 8,000 tons a year. Estimates of zinc reserves in the early 1980s were adjusted upward from previous figures. Reserves were placed at 550,000 tons; production of zinc had been increasing substantially and reached 13,700 tons a year in the mid-1980s. Output of fluoride and mercury was negligible. Increasing amounts of marble were quarried and met most of the national demand. Salt, obtained by open-air evaporation of seawater, met both domestic and export requirements. In the mid-1980s, Tunisia was exporting around TD390,000 worth of marine salt each year to the United States.

Manufacturing and Handicrafts

Manufacturing, formerly the smallest and least important sector of the Tunisian economy, had undergone the greatest expansion and provided 14 percent of GDP in 1984. Tunisian manufacturing included textiles, processed foods, shoes and other leather products, steel, automobiles, chemicals, small mechanical and electrical products, and traditional crafts.

Tunisia adopted import-substitution policies between the mid-1960s and the early 1970s but then reversed its economic policy to promote export industries. During the initial stage of industrialization, Tunisian manufacturing was protected from external competition and relied on the domestic market to sell its output. Consequently, it was often producing poor-quality items and producing them inefficiently, not being able to take advantage of large-scale operations. As of 1972 Tunisian authorities relaxed import restrictions, encouraged foreign investment, and directed national manufacturing toward producing goods over which Tunisia had a comparative advantage and could export (see Balance of Payments and External Finance, this ch.). Private investment quickly reacted and increased so much that the share of investment in manufacturing doubled between 1971 and 1983, when it reached 22 percent. Most of the public investment had been directed toward chemicals, construction materials, and food processing while the private sector invested mostly in textiles and the remaining smaller industries.

The Investment Promotion Agency, an autonomous institution, advertised foreign investment in Tunisia and also assisted both domestic and foreign investors in speeding up licensing agreements and obtaining financial assistance. The Industrial Land Agency, a subsidiary of the Investment Promotion Agency, acquired industrial landsites throughout the country (except for those in Tunis) and either rented or sold the land and buildings to industrial promoters for development and resale to enterprises at subsidized prices. Another agency controlled new industrial sites in and around Tunis in a similar manner. Market studies, sectoral studies, and project feasibility studies for prospective investors were carried out by yet another government agency. As of the late 1970s the Investment Promotion Agency and the Industrial Land Agency were offering more generous support to projects that would be located away from the Tunis area. The high concentration of manufacturing there conflicted with the later plans' objectives of reducing regional development disparities. Additionally, in the 1980s the government agencies started to support small crafts and artisans' enterprises that had long been neglected.

Manufacturing employed about 20 percent of the labor force. The large majority of manufacturing enterprises were small and employed very few people. Even larger enterprises often deliberately chose labor-saving techniques because of the nature of the Tunisian labor market. Most Tunisian laborers were unskilled and, backed by strong unions, overpaid in relation to their productivity. The small number of managerial and technical workers were hardly better remunerated, which discouraged the workers from seeking higher training. Few of those who did so remained in Tunisia. There was, therefore, less employment-generation from industrial growth than had been predicted in the government plans. Nevertheless, manufacturing did create at least 100,000 new jobs between 1975 and 1985.

The food-processing industry had been the most important segment of manufacturing until the mid-1980s, when lower agricultural output caused it to decline somewhat. Food processing made up a little less than one-quarter of Tunisia's manufacturing output. It produced mainly for domestic consumption with the exception of such items as olive oil and fish. Tunisia had the potential to become a net exporter of food products with increased investment in modernization of agriculture and the agro-processing plants. The cereal industry, which included both grinding grain and manufacturing related products, was government operated. Olive oil, one of the country's traditional exports, and other olive by-products were processed in over 2,000 small factories. Sugar was refined by two companies: a private enterprise in Tunis that made lump sugar and the government-owned Tunisian Sugar Corporation in Béja.

In the mid-1980s textiles constituted the most important manufacturing industry in production and employment. The industry still suffered from inefficient operation and quality control. Tunisia sent much of its output to Italy and France for the final finishing stage and had made a number of arrangements with its trade partners to receive technical advice. The industry was composed of state-owned plants, private Tunisian factories, and foreign-owned ventures, and the General Textile Industry Corporation (Sociètè Gènèrale de l'Industrie Textile—SOGITEX), one of the government-owned companies, was the dominant element. In line with the policy to liberalize the Tunisian economy, the government offered SOGITEX shares to the private sector, but only a few had been bought as of 1985. After a period of very rapid expansion, which fulfilled domestic needs, textile manufacturers turned to overseas markets. But they began to face serious problems beginning in 1977 and continuing into the 1980s as a result of import quotas imposed by the EEC, the main market for Tunisian textiles. Nevertheless, the textile industry had established itself as an important source of foreign exchange.

Ancillary to textiles was the leather and shoe industry. The main tannery was government-owned, but all leather products were made by the private sector. A broad range of shoes was produced, and the industry had grown from one that barely met domestic demand in the late 1970s to an export industry selling 30 percent of its output abroad in the mid-1980s.

The steel industry consisted of one government-owned iron and steel plant at El Fouladh near Bizerte, which produced billets, concrete rounds, steel structures, and galvanized products and operated at high capacity. Automotive assembly and parts manufacturing was one of the major import-substitution industries. The assembly of automobiles, trucks, and buses was handled by one firm, the government-owned Tunisian Automobile Industry Corporation (Sociètè Tunisienne de l'Industrie Automobile—STIA) located at Sousse. The STIA attempted to reduce its dependence on imported automotive parts by producing them domestically. Among such parts and equipment manufactured in Tunisia were batteries, spark plugs, and tires. It was estimated that a Peugeot factory at Sidi Abdelhamid produced about 16,000 vehicles per year. In 1985 construction began on a large Volkswagen plant with funds supplied by the parent company, Tunisian businessmen, and development banks. The plant was to start operating in 1988 and would produce about 5,000 vehicles a year and employ 400 people.

There was a growing chemical industry dominated by the production of fertilizers, which had received heavy government investment. State-owned and joint-venture chemical companies made additional products, such as pesticides, detergents, pharmaceuticals, paints, and perfumes. The chemical industry constituted 11.3 per-

An artisan embroidering a saddle blanket in the Tunis souk

cent of Tunisia's total manufacturing output. The electrical industries included plants assembling or manufacturing television receivers, radios, sewing machines, lamps, and other electrical equipment. A wide variety of mechanical equipment, such as boilers, radiators, and tools, was also produced. Numerous small plants made miscellaneous household and industrial goods. The electric and metallic industries formed 13.5 percent of manufacturing output. They offered some potential for additional and possibly alternative export products in the future as oil and gas exports tapered off. Together with the steel and automobile industry, they supplied 11 percent of the jobs in the private manufacturing sector. The mechanical and electric industries were, however, hampered by a number of production and marketing problems.

Construction of housing units, hospitals, and schools was a major goal of the 1982–86 plan, and consequently the demand for construction materials boomed during that period. Large investment funds went into the industries producing cement, bricks, and ceramics in an effort to reduce Tunisian reliance on foreign sources for these products. The construction industry made up about 17 percent of the total manufacturing output in the mid-1980s. To a large extent the construction industry was privately owned, and the number of large contractors employing modern equipment was increasing.

Artisanry and handicrafts held an important place in the economy because of the large number of people working their traditional trades. Exposure to different cultures and customs over the centuries had developed a distinctive and widespread handicrafts industry. Handicrafts could be divided into two varieties: the utilitarian and the artistic. The former rapidly became obsolete because of competing imports and cheaper products of the modern domestic manufacturing sector. The latter was an important part of the economy, which the government sought to preserve and promote for tourist and export purposes.

More than 100,000 people depended on handicrafts to provide all or part of their livelihood. They worked mostly on a family basis or in small workshops where the owner worked along with his assistants. There were, however, some individuals who worked independently and others, mostly women, who worked at home either for themselves or for a manufacturer or trader. Many craftsworkers still belonged to organized guilds as they did centuries ago.

In 1959 the National Handicraft Office was established to operate handicrafts shops, to supervise the quality of products for export, to promote marketing at home and abroad, and to help form cooperatives of craftsworkers. By the early 1980s the office owned and operated numerous workshops and retail stores in most towns that sold locally produced crafts of good quality at fixed prices. Dozens of cooperatives comprising several thousand members had also been formed. These cooperatives bought raw materials and sold the finished products. They helped alleviate shortages of credit and supplies, which traditionally threatened the artisans.

The major handicraft products included textiles, rugs and carpets, pottery and ceramics, leather goods, brasswork, copperware, jewelry, embroidery, and wrought iron. Certain areas specialized in the production of particular items. Fine tunics were made at Ksar Hellah in the Sahil. Jerba Island was noted for woolens and blankets, Kairouan for carpets, and Nabeul for table linen. The government helped to make modern equipment and technical training available for the weaving of carpets and rugs. A wool-washing center, dye factory, rug finishing plant, and training center had all

Solar energy power system experiment at
Hamman Biadha southwest of Tunis
Courtesy John Metelsky

been established on Jerba Island. Modern equipment had also been
acquired by the weavers of Kairouan.

Electricity

Since 1962 the state-owned Tunisian Electricity and Gas Company (Société Tunisienne de l'Électricité et du Gaz—STEG) has
been responsible for the production and transmission of electricity
and natural gas. About 14 percent of total electrical production,
however, was generated by large self-users like industrial plants
and the phosphate mines. Electricity potential was certainly underdeveloped; hydropower could be increased substantially if a fuller
and more efficient use of dams were implemented. The STEG operated four steam-power plants, four hydroelectric power plants,
seven combustion turbine plants, and a few small diesel plants.

About 90 percent of all electric power was thermally generated, 2 percent was hydraulic, and 8 percent was provided by other means.

The total production of electricity in 1986 was around 3.4 billion kilowatt hours. Estimates of installed capacity were not available, but it was believed that plants were generally operating at full power to meet requirements. Demand for electricity was increasing at an average rate of 13 percent in the 1970s and even faster in the 1980s. Between 1984 and 1985 alone, electricity consumption grew by an estimated 30 percent. The rise in consumption took place mostly in the cities, particularly in Tunis, and consequently put pressure on existing capacity, causing frequent voltage drops and occasional power failures. While urban areas were practically all fully electrified, more than two-thirds of the rural conglomerates were still not electrified, and there were numerous rural areas throughout the country that did not have access to electricity at all. The government hoped to be able to double the supply of electricity to all rural areas through the execution of the 1982–86 plan.

Several alternative sources of energy were under study. A nuclear reactor project to be located at Gabès was planned. A Belgian firm had begun manufacturing solar panels, and a project mounted by the United States Agency for International Development (AID) contributed to the study of solar energy use. (Tunisia has more than 3,500 hours of sunshine annually.) The government was giving serious consideration to using coal, even if it had to be imported, instead of fuel oil and natural gas, which produced more revenue as export products.

Tourism

The gentle climate of Tunisia, its lengthy beaches, impressive and well-restored historical sites, and geographic proximity to Europe have all contributed to the country's tourist appeal. Major attractions and sites include Jerba Island, oases in the Tunisian Sahara, the Sousse and Monastir fortresses, Phoenician and Carthaginian archaelogical ruins, the former Spanish port of Hammamet, the colosseum of El Jema, and the mosques at Mahdia, Zituna, and Kairouan. Jerba Island, in the Gulf of Gabès, is connected to the mainland by a causeway, the foundations of which were built by the Romans. Fabled as the home of the lotus eaters in *The Odyssey* of Homer, the island has miles of beaches, many small hotels, ancient ruins, mosques, and a Jewish colony believed to date from the seventh century B.C. with one of the oldest synagogues in the

Roman colosseum at El Jemaa, built at the beginning
of the third century A.D., is one of the largest
and best preserved of the Roman Empire ruins
Courtesy Embassy of Tunisia, Washington

world, which attracts about 40,000 pilgrims annually. In the mid-
1980s Tunisia also had modern international tourist complexes offering sports facilities, pleasure marinas, commercial areas, hotels,
villas, and apartment accommodations, such as the Port Kantaoui
complex. Other sites were under construction at Monastir, Upper
Ghammarth, and Tabarka.

Tourism had become one of the most important economic sectors, contributing about 4 percent to GDP and 17 percent to export
receipts; revenues totaled TD415 million in 1985. Additionally,
roughly 10 percent of the total Tunisian work force depended, directly or indirectly, on the tourism industry. The government
owned a chain of hotels that were operated under management contracts by private concerns and generally encouraged private investment in tourism by granting, for example, liberal tax concessions.

The 1982–86 development plan particularly encouraged investment in off-season attractions, such as commercial fairs, and investment in nonpriority tourist areas. An important problem of the tourism industry was the shortage of first-class accommodations. A number of West European tour companies had built their own hotels to accommodate the influx of tourists. The industry also suffered from inexperienced hotel operators and a shortage of trained staff. The 1982–86 plan was to add about 40,000 beds to the 80,000 that existed in 1982 and to invest in the training of about 2,000 young people, some of whom had trained at institutes specializing in tourism and hotel management.

Tourists came primarily from France and, in descending order, West Germany, Algeria, Libya, Britain, and Italy. The total number of visitors had slowed somewhat in the early 1980s but picked up again in 1984–85. The number of tourist arrivals was 2.2 million in 1981, 1.4 million in 1983, and roughly 2 million in both 1984 and 1985.

Foreign Trade

Tunisia has traditionally imported mostly capital goods, raw materials, and semifinished products (see table 7, Appendix). In the early 1980s it had to import increasing amounts of foods as a result of the drought. The country's traditional exports were unprocessed phosphate, phosphate-based chemicals, oil, and agricultural products. Textile exports increasingly became a source of foreign exchange in the 1970s. Exports of manufactured products grew by about 400 percent between 1971 and 1983 to form a 10-percent share of all Tunisian exports in the mid-1980s.

The tremendous growth in manufactured exports came as a result of a change in official Tunisian policy from the import-substitution followed until 1972 to export-promotion when Tunisian authorities realized the domestic market was too small to produce efficiently or absorb all the production of a single industry. A law passed in 1972 permitted the establishment of companies producing solely for export and to be exempt from customs duties, foreign exchange regulations, and fiscal regulations applicable to other firms. In 1973 a public organization, the Center for the Promotion of Exports (Centre de Promotion des Exports—CEPEX), was created to contribute to the development of Tunisian exports. It would assist exporters by conducting market surveys, encouraging trade fairs, and disseminating commercial information. The export-promotion policies were to be strengthened throughout the 1980s by the introduction of other institutions and laws. By 1985 new laws extended a number of important advantages to any company that exported even a small part of its output; included were reduced corporate taxes, significant reductions in social security payments, and access to simpler formalities for their input imports. Complex administrative procedures relating to export had often been cited as hindrances to greater trade volume. In 1984 the Export-Credit Insurance Company was created to cover exporters who did not have enough collateral to obtain bank loans. Export trading companies newly established in 1984 specialized in marketing Tunisian products abroad. The government was also helping potential exporters by offering easier export financing.

The trade balance was traditionally in deficit, as the country's import needs far exceeded its export capacities. The annual trade deficit in the early and mid-1980s was in the vicinity of US$700 million, considerably higher than that of the 1970s, which was about US$400 million. The major cause of the escalating deficit was a decline in exports in general but more particularly among exports of petroleum and of agricultural products. The deficit had a severe impact on the economy, representing about 9 percent of GDP. It was generally financed by borrowing abroad; remittances, tourism, transfers, and foreign investment offset only about one-third of the deficit.

For many years since independence France has been Tunisia's leading trading partner, not only because of the previous political and economic ties but also because French has remained the language of business, thus giving an edge to French suppliers and buyers. France's relative share of trade with Tunisia, however, has been declining as the latter has actively sought alternative markets. As a result the United States, Italy, and West Germany have also become important trade partners. The United States share of Tunisian exports was around 21 percent in the mid-1980s, or roughly US$400 million annually, almost equal to France's share of 22.5 percent. Imports from France represented 25 percent of total Tunisian imports. Italy, West Germany, and the United States were, in that order, the next most important sources of imports. Imports from the United States amounted to around US$300 million. Arms purchases from the United States between 1980 and 1984 were estimated at US$200 million; military purchases from other sources, mainly France, Italy, Brazil, and West Germany, totaled roughly US$425 million for the same period.

In 1969 Tunisia concluded a treaty of association with the EEC, and on January 7, 1976, the agreement with the EEC was elaborated to include economic cooperation. Under the agreement,

Tunisia was promised grants and loans, social security benefits for Tunisian immigrant workers, and increased access to EEC markets for Tunisian agricultural products. In 1982 more export credit was negotiated and granted. But the general attitude of the EEC in the 1980s has been restrictive. For example, it put lower quotas on the Tunisian exports consisting of products that were imported semifinished to Tunisia and then processed. Tunisian authorities were very concerned about the future of most of their exports to the EEC after Spain and Portugal entered the Community on January 1, 1986. The sales of citrus fruits, wine, fish, and olive oil were particularly threatened. In the early 1980s, the olive oil industry grossed about US$70 million per year and supported almost 1 million Tunisians. Olives were planted on one-third of Tunisia's arable land—an area that could not be used for other crops. Tunisia's best agricultural export prospects appeared to lay in certain fruits, such as apricots and oranges, which were generally available two weeks before that of South European countries' produce.

Trade with East European countries was marginal. It was carried out under special bilateral agreements that relied chiefly on barter rather than currency as the means of settlement. The Soviet Union and Poland were the main trading partners from Eastern Europe. As a member of the Maghrib, Tunisia has benefited from Maghribi efforts to coordinate the long-range development of certain sectors of their economies, particularly as applied to trade, transportation, communications, tourism, and light manufactures. Algeria and Libya were important trading partners in the late 1970s, but bilateral trade has decreased in the 1980s. Trade with other Arab countries was marginal.

Balance of Payments and External Finance

Since 1975 Tunisia's balance of payments has been regularly, albeit not severely, in deficit (see table 8, Appendix). A merchandise trade imbalance that had amounted to around US$700 million a year was largely the cause of the problem, and tourism receipts and workers' remittances, although significant, were not sufficient to offset it. In addition to tourism receipts and remittances, between US$250 million and US$350 million in foreign capital entered Tunisia yearly in the form of private foreign investment, and about $US20 million was secured in grants. Nevertheless, Tunisia had to borrow about US$400 million a year in the 1980s to balance its current account deficit. The country's international reserves were resorted to sparingly and had been maintained at around US$500 million.

The vigor of the United States dollar in the 1980s had made repayments on loans contracted in the late 1970s extremely costly. The total foreign debt outstanding at the end of 1984 was estimated at US$4 billion, equaling about TD3.2 billion or a ratio of 45 percent of GDP, and a debt service ratio of around 18 percent. In 1984 alone some US$500 million was raised in foreign loans, an amount 35 percent higher than the yearly average of the early 1980s and reflective of recent poor trade performance.

Despite hopeful official expectations of better agricultural production, larger tourism receipts, and incoming foreign investment, trade deficits were predicted by international economists until the early 1990s. Thus, Tunisia would be obliged to continue securing foreign loans for some time in the future. Furthermore, purchases of important military equipment from the United States began in the early 1980s. The United States Department of Defense estimated repayments to cover these purchases, often omitted from economists' assessments of Tunisian debt, at around US$41 million in 1985 and US$52 million in 1986.

The climate for foreign investment in Tunisia has been excellent since 1972. Before then, the nationalization in 1964 of foreign-owned lands and the lack of guarantees in the investment laws were the chief reasons for a low rate of private foreign investment in the country. A new investment code in 1972 granted complete foreign ownership for export-oriented industries as well as numerous concessions, such as tax advantages and the guaranteed right to repatriate capital and profit. In 1974 a law was enacted to promote employment-creating investments and investments in domestic-oriented industries. In 1976 offshore banking units were approved. These institutions were allowed to conduct business with nonresidents, grant credit to residents, and participate—with prior approval of the central bank—in the capital of resident companies. The 1974 law was revised in 1981 to offer further advantages to investment in the manufacturing industry—particularly the high-technology industry—and in projects promoting regional development and industrial decentralization. Economic and political stability in Tunisia, along with pleasant living conditions and efficient telecommunications, have traditionally encouraged overseas private investors to enter into Tunisian operations. Around TD600 million in direct foreign investment had been raised in the period from 1983 through the first half of 1985.

About 60 percent of all direct foreign investments in the mid-1980s was in oil and gas exploration and development. There were also large amounts of foreign investment in the textile industry and, since the early 1980s, in tourism and real estate. American business activity was concentrated in oil and gas, and the yearly expenditures of exploration operations were between US$150 million and US$200 million. American equity as of early 1985 was under US$10 million and limited to a joint-venture automobile and pickup truck assembly plant and a small food-processing plant. The amount of American equity investment in Tunisia may grow significantly, however, as a result of a focused effort directed at United States investors by AID, and Tunisian agencies, such as the Investment Promotion Agency, the Agricultural Investment Promotion Agency, and the Tunisian-Saudi Company for Investment and Development. Conferences held in Sousse and Hammamet have endeavored to stimulate investment in manufacturing, farming, and food processing as well as in constructing warehouses, which are to be used as transit points for the distribution of manufactured goods in the Middle East, Europe, and Africa. The main obstacle to American business in Tunisia as of 1985 was the absence of a dual taxation treaty between the United States and Tunisia. Negotiations between the two governments were held in 1983 and again in 1984 regarding a proposal to reduce income taxes on American employees and corporate taxes on foreign companies.

Tunisia has received foreign assistance from a variety of sources since 1956. Increasingly, however, it has resorted mainly to official governments rather than to private banks and commercial partners, although the latter still supplied about 30 percent of the total loans contracted in the 1980s. Foreign grants were in decline, as Tunisia was accepted more as a middle- rather than a lower-income country. Nevertheless, Tunisia's consistently efficient management of its modest resources had earned it an appreciable amount of soft loans.

Traditionally, Tunisia's most important creditors had been the United States, France, and increasingly, West Germany. Beginning in the mid-1970s credit from Arab countries (particularly Kuwait), and international organizations, such as the IMF, the World Bank, and the United Nations, increased significantly although never reaching the scale of American, French, and West German aid. In Western Europe, Italy was another important creditor. Communist countries—mainly the Soviet Union, China, Bulgaria, Romania, Yugoslavia, and Hungary—have extended minimal credit, often in the form of trade loans.

Transportation and Telecommunications

General control and management of all forms of transportation are the responsibility of the Ministry of Transport, which has coordinated road, rail, sea, and air services and has established rates. In the mid-1980s the transportation system was relatively well developed, particularly in the northeastern part of the country, where population and economic activity were concentrated (see fig. 9).

Railroads were the most important element of the transportation system. Trackage totaled about 2,152 kilometers, of which about 500 kilometers were standard gauge. The geographical distribution of the rail system reflected its commercial function in linking mining and main agricultural regions to the seacoast. Three narrow-gauge lines running southwest from the coast joined the phosphate regions west of Ebba Ksour, Fériana, and Gafsa to the port cities of Tunis, Sousse, and Sfax, respectively. A narrow-gauge coastal line linked Tunis to the eastern port chain as far south as Gabès. Standard-gauge trackage was confined to the northern quadrant defined by Tabarka, Bizerte, Tunis, and Nabeul. The section connecting Tunis to the Algerian border was the eastern extremity of the international rail link to Casablanca.

During the French protectorate period, the rail network was operated by a private organization. Nationalization after Tunisian independence brought the lines under a newly created state corporation, the Tunisian National Railroad Company (Société Nationale des Chemins de Fer Tunisiens—SNCFT). The bulk of revenues was provided by the transport of freight, particularly phosphates in the south of the country. The SNCFT directly employed about 10,000 workers.

Tunisia inherited a fairly extensive highway network and improved upon it; but the design characteristics were insufficient for the growing volume of traffic, and much rehabilitation was required to bring the system up to modern standards. As of 1985, there were about 23,695 kilometers of what were termed classified roads (first-, second-, or third-class roads) plus about 14,000 kilometers of seldom-used forest and agricultural roads. About one-half of the classified roads were paved. Almost 10,000 kilometers of the classified roads and an equal amount of the unclassified roads were further categorized as rural roads, defined as being outside the urban areas and carrying almost entirely agricultural traffic. The rural roads were poorly maintained, mostly unpaved, and almost impassable in wet weather.

The road system was used by about 90 percent of passenger and freight traffic. All coastal cities were linked to inland settle-

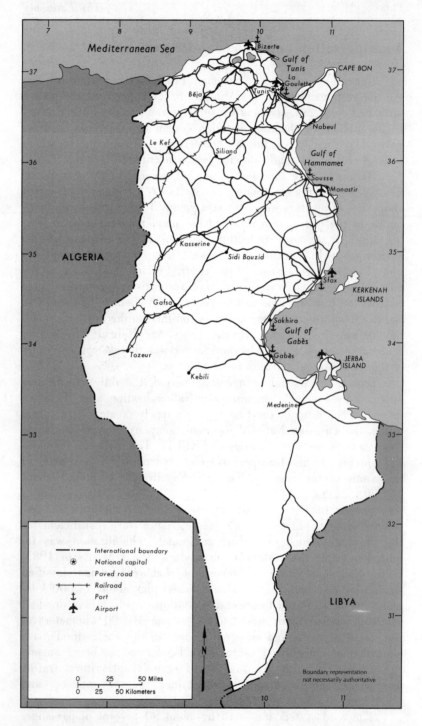

Figure 9. Transportation System, 1985

200

Modern equipment
on the rail line
from Tunis to Sfax
Courtesy of Embassy
of Tunisia, Washington

Loading cargo at the port
of Tunis-La Goulette
Courtesy World Bank
William and
Christine Graham

ments and were connected with the road networks of Algeria and
Libya. In the south the road system served a vital function in linking southern areas, notably the city of Medenine and Jerba Island
to the southernmost railhead at Gabès. Commercial road services
were managed by a series of 21 local and provincial public transportation companies that were created out of the hundreds of small
trucking and bus firms that had previously operated independently.
These local enterprises were organized into the National Transportation Company, which was attempting to standardize equipment
and coordinate interregional commercial transportation so that full-
est use could be made of existing units. Both the railroads and the
bus companies operated at a loss because fares were deliberately
kept low as a social policy.

The country had six major seaports—Tunis-La Goulette, Bizerte, Sfax, Sousse, Sakhira, and Gabès—as well as about 45
smaller ports, of which 23 were really only traditional fishing har-

bors. Sakhira handled Algerian and Tunisian petroleum exports, and Sfax held a monopoly on the export of olive oil and phosphates. Bizerte and Tunis-La Goulette handled most of the imports. In terms of volume of cargo handled, the ports of Sfax and Bizerte were the busiest. But both had reached their handling capacity, about 13 million tons of cargo, by the early 1980s, and expansion of their facilities was required to avoid congestion. Roughly 85 percent of the maritime traffic was international, mostly with countries in Western Europe, North Africa, and the Middle East.

There was one shipping concern as of 1985, the Tunisian Shipping Company (Companie Tunisienne de Navigation—CTN), established in 1958 with the controlling interest owned by the government. In the second half of the 1970s the CTN began to acquire additional vessels in an attempt to expand its fleet. By 1985 the merchant fleet consisted of 18 vessels, a small number in comparison with the national fleets of neighboring Arab countries. The fleet included oil tankers, multipurpose vessels, and car ferries, the latter connecting Tunisia with French and Italian seaports to facilitate tourism and the trucking of merchandise. By the mid-1980s the merchant marine had reached a stage where it faced a shortage of qualified personnel, and the Advanced Merchant Marine Institute was established to train several hundred students annually.

Major airfields were at Bizerte, Tunis, Monastir, Sfax, and on Jerba Island. Minor fields were at about 12 other locations throughout the country. The main international field was in suburban Tunis and was designated Tunis-Carthage. The airfield on Jerba Island was improved to accept international jet traffic, and the one at Monastir was similarly constructed in the hope of attracting direct jet service from Western Europe. In the early 1980s a new international airport at Tawzar, 110 kilometers southwest of Gafsa, began receiving traffic—most of it still domestic—in an endeavor to accommodate tourism in the southern part of Tunisia.

The national airline, Tunis-Air, was owned jointly by the Tunisian government, Air France, and private Tunisian investors; the state had the controlling interest. The company in the early 1980s owned 10 Boeing 727s, four Boeing 737s, and one Airbus 300. Tunis-Air had a monopoly on all domestic air traffic and operated scheduled service between Tunis and other Tunisian cities and to several foreign countries. In 1975 Tunis-Air founded a subsidiary company called Tunisavia to operate domestic charter flights, but in 1976 Tunisavia began some scheduled service, including flights to Malta.

All telecommunications were under the control of the Ministry of Transport and Communications. By 1985 almost 90 percent of the telephones in the country were automatic, a result of a long-range program to introduce gradually automated switchboards to cut telephone rates and improve service. Automated telephone links also existed with West Europe, and telex services connected Tunisia with several West European and neighboring Arab countries. Telecommunications facilities included open-wire lines, a coaxial cable to Algeria, and radio relays to Algeria, Libya, and Italy. Tunisia was a member of the International Telecommunications Satellite Consortium (Intelsat) with a major station at Dkhira. In the mid-1980s, an Arabsat satellite backup control station was also under construction.

*   *   *

Readers with a continuing interest in the Tunisian economy might want to consult recent issues of periodicals such as *Africa Research Bulletin, Marchés Tropicaux et Méditerranéens, Middle East Economic Digest, Financial Times,* and *Quarterly Economic Review: Libya, Tunisia, Malta.* For readers interested in investment in Tunisia, recent information on pertinent laws can be found in the International Monetary Fund's *Annual Report on Exchange Arrangements and Exchange Restrictions.* Analysis of particular sectors of the Tunisian economy are covered in the publications of the various United States government agencies, such as the Department of Agriculture, the Department of Labor, the Department of Commerce, and the Bureau of Mines. Also helpful are the official Tunisian government publications and the semi-official periodicals, *Conjoncture* and *Dialogue.* (For further information and complete citations, see Bibliography.)

Chapter 4. Government and Politics

Tunisia's state coat of arms

WITH THE APPROACH in 1986 of the thirtieth anniversary of their national independence, Tunisians could look back with satisfaction over their success in keeping peace with their neighbors and attaining a notable record of economic growth and social reform. Much credit for these achievements was due to President Habib Bourguiba, often called the Supreme Combatant, the country's incorruptible and inspirational leader who had remained at the forefront of Tunisian politics for more than half a century.

The goals and ideals imparted by Bourguiba in his messages to the Tunisian people and in his policies had for long set the country apart in the Arab world. Through his programs for health, higher education, cultural advancement, women's rights, and secularization of the state, the president labored to recast Tunisia as a modern nation. Impatient at first with the pace of development, he experimented for a time with socialism but swung back to a mixed economy when it became obvious that the socialist initiatives were producing resistance and disorder.

Staying clear of international conflicts, Bourguiba had for long felt secure enough to forgo a large military establishment, saving resources and averting military involvement in politics. His own political movement, the Destourian Socialist Party, with its monopoly over political activity, served as an instrument for mobilizing Tunisians on behalf of his policies.

By 1986, as the Bourguiba era drew nearer to its close, it seemed uncertain whether the solid political edifice identified with him would endure after he was no longer in command. Many of the doctrines of Bourguiba's program that had brought major advances during the first decades were being challenged. The program's secularist features and its emphasis on the Western aspects of Tunisia's cultural heritage were under attack from many Tunisians demanding a reassertion of traditional Islamic religious values. The inability of the economy to create jobs for the young—particularly the increasing numbers turned out by the universities—and the failure of wages to keep up with price increases had led to violent outbursts in 1978 and 1984 that the government was barely able to bring under control. Economic development had largely bypassed the poorer southern and western regions of the country.

Previously close to the government and the party, the labor movement in early 1986 was locked in a struggle with the regime. Bourguiba had decreed in 1981 that opposition parties should be recognized and allowed to compete against the Destourian socialists. Although given legal status and allowed their own publications, the other parties were obstructed in their efforts to contest both national and local elections. Only the government party and affiliated groups were represented in the submissive parliament. The government's reluctance to accept nonconformity and criticism contributed to public cynicism over Destourianism and the existing institutions of government.

Prime minister since 1980, Mohamed Mzali was a liberally inclined appointee and Bourguiba's prospective successor under the Constitution. Mzali had gradually consolidated his position under Bourguiba's patronage, although his own political strength remained untested. In early 1986 Bourguiba's fragile health had sapped him of the vigor of his earlier days, but he still wielded sufficient power to decree the downfall of any underling deemed to be presumptuous or imprudent in exercising authority. The fear of disapproval and disgrace discouraged ministerial initiative and left a sense of immobility in the face of pressing national problems.

The political personalities at the top of the Destourian movement were positioning themselves for the protracted struggle for power that might follow Bourguiba's departure from the scene. Even if the transition could be accomplished smoothly, preserving the institutions of government created by the 1959 Constitution, the new leadership would soon be called upon to defend itself in elections against other parties and interests. Above all, account would have to be taken of the growing appeal of the Islamic renewal and the power of the army, hitherto unpoliticized but unlikely to remain indifferent if the established political structure began to crumble.

Tunisia's traditional international posture—nonaligned but friendly to the West and moderate on Middle East issues—also seemed to be in jeopardy as it was being drawn closer to the vortex of Arab politics. The headquarters of the Palestine Liberation Organization near Tunis had been the target of an Israeli air raid in 1985. Libya, its well-armed neighbor, persisted in acting in a capricious and threatening manner. The Islamists attacked Tunisia's ties with the West, demanding that the country identify itself with the Arab world.

Bourguiba had endowed the Tunisian people with broad social and educational reforms, a compassionate and humanistic conception of the government's role, many years of stable growth, and a responsible course in its foreign affairs. But it was feared that, in perpetuating his paternalistic and authoritarian style of rule, Bourguiba had failed to establish a firm base for future progress, leaving his country ill equipped to deal with domestic discontent and the rising danger from abroad.

Constitutional Development

In 1857 the bey (ruler) of Tunisia, influenced by reform-minded European countries, promulgated the Fundamental Pact. The pact contained guarantees of basic human rights, property ownership, and freedom of religion. Four years later, after consultations with Napoleon III, a new bey promulgated the constitution of 1861, the first such document in the Islamic world. The constitution placed some limits on the bey's political prerogatives, divided legislative power between him and an appointed council, and provided for an independent judiciary. A revolt three years later caused the suspension of the constitution, but the symbolic importance of the document had been established and would later serve as the basis for the nationalist movement that developed in the early twentieth century.

The country's first political party, the Destour (Constitution) Party, emerged from the nationalist movement in 1920. Reacting against the elitism of much of the party's French-educated, middle-class membership and against its goal of limited legal reforms within the French protectorate, a group of young Destour members, led by Bourguiba, founded the Neo-Destour Party in 1934. Neo-Destourians led the independence movement that resulted in self-governing autonomy in 1955 and in complete Tunisian independence on March 20, 1956 (see Toward Independence, ch. 1).

Elections for the Constituent Assembly of 98 members followed, in accordance with a decree issued by the bey, who was to have no role in the drafting process and who was pledged to promulgate the constitution as written by the assembly. An electoral front, known as the National Union and controlled by the Neo-Destourians, won an overwhelming affirmative vote in the elections. Bourguiba became presiding officer of the Constituent Assembly but was forced to relinquish his position upon becoming the country's prime minister. Preparation of the draft constitution was an undertaking that stretched over three years, owing in part to Bourguiba's preoccupation with establishing an effective government and party apparatus and in part to the need to rework portions of the document when the decision was made to replace the monarchy with a republican form of government. The final text did not necessitate new institutions and procedures but rather legitimized those that Bourguiba had already introduced. On July 25, 1957, the assembly unanimously passed a resolution ending the beylicate and establishing Tunisia as a republic. It further provided for Bourguiba, as president of the republic, to assume the duties of head of state in addition to those of head of government, which he had held as prime minister. On June 1, 1959, the Constituent Assembly approved the draft constitution, which was promulgated by Bourguiba later the same day.

Rather than copy the constitution of the French Fourth Republic, with its strong parliament, the Tunisian Constitution imposed a presidential system inspired in part by that of the United States. It entrusts significantly greater powers to the office of the president, however, than does the American document, and the separation of powers is not as rigid. Like the constitutions of other North African states, it also establishes Islam as the official religion and Arabic as the official language, and it proclaims Tunisia's identification with the Maghrib (see Glossary) and the ideal of Maghribi unity.

The Constitution guarantees to the citizens of Tunisia several basic liberties, including equality before the law and presumption of innocence in legal proceedings; freedom of expression, the press, association, and assembly; inviolability of the home; the right of public worship; and the right to travel within and outside the country. Many of these liberties have been circumscribed in practice, however, based on the constitutional caveat that they may be limited by laws intended to protect the rights of others or to further law and order, national defense, and economic and social progress. The small Jewish and Christian communities in Tunisia worship freely, although proselytizing is discouraged and government employment is confined to Muslims.

All three branches of government—the executive, the legislature, and the judiciary—are dominated by the president. Although judicial independence is prescribed, the status of the judiciary is clearly regarded as inferior to that of the other two branches. The courts have no jurisdiction over disputes between the president and the legislature, nor may they interpret the Constitution. The Chamber of Deputies (formerly the National Assembly), a unicameral body, is given sole legislative authority and exercises formal powers to approve the budgets and development plans and to ratify treaties. These factors notwithstanding, the judiciary's lack of power to rule on the constitutionality of legislation and on the president's exercise of his powers and the chamber's subordination to the leadership of Bourguiba have precluded an effective system of checks and balances.

Either the president or a minimum of one-third of the members of the Chamber of Deputies may initiate amendment or revision of the Constitution. (The provision calling for a republican form of government is, however, exempt from amendment.) Adoption of an amendment requires two separate votes at least three months apart, each by a minimum of two-thirds of the assembly membership. To become effective, a constitutional amendment so adopted must be promulgated by the president.

The Constitution has been amended on several occasions since 1959. Legislative sessions have been reduced from two to one per year, and the provisions pertaining to presidential succession have been modified, as have the requirements for eligibility for presidential candidates. In 1969 the office of prime minister was instituted. The proclamation of Bourguiba as president for life was embodied in the Constitution in 1975. Broad revisions reducing the age requirement for service in the legislature and altering the composition of the Council of State were adopted in 1976. A national referendum procedure was added along with a procedure for the legislature to force the resignation of the government and ultimately the president through adoption of censure motions. The 1976 revision also introduced a differentiation between ordinary laws and organic laws (those involving constitutional articles, civil liberties, judicial powers, electoral affairs, and budgetary matters).

Structure of Government

In early 1986 all real governmental authority in the Tunisian presidential republic was concentrated in its executive branch headed by the nation's architect of independence, Bourguiba, and under him Prime Minister Mzali and a cabinet composed of about 30 ministers and secretaries of state known as the Council of Ministers. Regional and local organs of government were entrusted with a limited degree of autonomy by the central authorities; regional governors exercised considerable authority under ultimate supervision of the national leadership. The popularly elected Chamber of Deputies generally gave pro forma approval to legislative initiatives emanating from the president and his cabinet (see fig. 10).

The strength of the formal institutions of government had not been exposed to a major test since they were put into place nearly 30 years earlier. The chief determinant of the system's stability was Bourguiba's prestige and personal authority, secured by a single party whose functions overlapped those of the government.

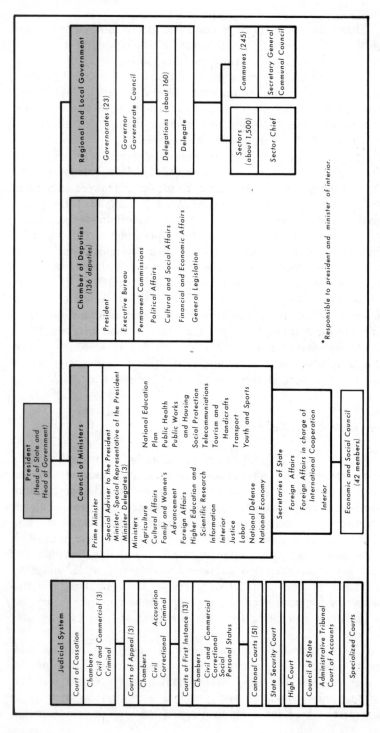

Figure 10. Government Structure, 1985

One of the few real modifications in the system was its opening in 1981 to permit opposition parties. Although acceptance of the multiparty model was far from an accomplished fact in 1986, its introduction could bring needed vitality to the system at all levels.

Executive

The Constitution vests decisive political power in the president of the republic, who is both head of state and head of government (the executive branch). The Constitution stipulates that the president is elected for a five-year term (concurrent with the term of the Chamber of Deputies) by direct universal suffrage. Bourguiba was Tunisia's first and, as of early 1986, the country's only president, having been elected unopposed on four occasions—after the Constitution was introduced in 1959 and subsequently in 1964, 1969, and 1974—and proclaimed president for life in 1975.

The president determines basic national policies and directs their implementation. He appoints high civil and military officers upon the recommendation of the cabinet, accredits Tunisian diplomats, receives foreign diplomatic representatives, ratifies treaties, is the supreme commander of the armed forces, exercises the right of pardon, and declares war and concludes peace with the consent of the Chamber of Deputies. The president shares the power to initiate legislation with the chamber, although his measures take precedence.

Unless he sends a bill back to the assembly, the president is called upon to promulgate laws within 15 days after having received them; he is responsible for their implementation and exercises general regulatory powers. If a bill is returned by the president for a second reading and is then readopted by a majority of two-thirds, he is obliged to promulgate the law. As of 1985 the legislature had never overruled a presidential veto. The president may submit to a national referendum any bill pertaining to the organization of public powers or the ratification of a treaty. The Chamber of Deputies may delegate to the president the right to issue decree-laws for a limited period and for a specific purpose. The president may also issue decree-laws when the chamber is not in session, with the permission of the permanent legislative committee concerned. In either case, the decree-law must later be submitted for ratification by the full chamber.

The Constitution extends sweeping emergency powers to the president in case of impending danger threatening the existence of the republic. In these circumstances, after consultation with the prime minister and the president of the Chamber of Deputies, the president may take whatever exceptional measures he deems necessary. During such an emergency period, the Chamber may not be dissolved, nor may censure motions be introduced against the government.

In cases of temporary disability the president may delegate his powers (except the power to dissolve the legislature) to the prime minister. The cabinet continues in existence during such period even if a censure motion should be voted against it. If the presidency were to be vacated because of permanent disability, death, or resignation, the prime minister would assume the office and all presidential functions for the remainder of the unexpired term.

The president appoints the prime minister and, upon the prime minister's recommendation, the other ministers. The president retains the right to terminate the tenure of the entire government or any member of it. He presides over meetings of the Council of Ministers and may delegate most of his powers to the prime minister. Members of the government may attend and address meetings of the Chamber of Deputies and its committees. Members of the chamber, in turn, have the right to put written and oral questions to the cabinet. The distinction between the two bodies is not, however, strictly observed. More than half of the cabinet members, including the prime minister, were elected to the chamber in 1981.

For several years after independence the highest government positions were those of the secretaries of state. There were no ministers, nor was there a prime minister, and members of the government were considered merely advisers to the president rather than executive department heads in their own right. Ministers were first designated in 1969, although some secretary of state positions were retained for certain ministries on a level junior to the ministers (see table 9, Appendix).

The prime minister has become increasingly important through the exercise of his responsibility for overseeing the execution of policies and for day-to-day governmental administration. The importance of the position is further accentuated by the constitutional amendment providing that the prime minister be first in line of presidential succession and complete the term of the president in case of his death or incapacity.

A censure procedure adopted by constitutional amendment in 1976 introduced the principle that the government should be responsible to the Chamber of Deputies as well as to the president. Three months after notifying the president of its intent, the cham-

Entrance to the Chamber of Deputies in Bardo Palace,
former residence of the beys, in Tunis; Berber guards
wear uniforms of the historical French Zouaves
Courtesy Jean B. Tartter

ber may adopt a censure motion by a two-thirds majority. The
president must respond, either by replacing the cabinet or by calling for new elections. If during its first session the new chamber
passes another censure motion criticizing the same conditions as
did the original, the president must resign along with the government. The prospect of the legislature's invoking these new powers
seemed implausible under the existing executive-dominated system.

The Economic and Social Council, established in 1961, is
composed of 42 members appointed by the government, representing salaried workers and wage earners in agriculture, industry, the
trades, and services as well as consumers and youth. Six economists and social scientists are included. Mohamed Ennaceur, head
of the governmental body then known as the Ministry of Social Af-

fairs, was named the council's chairperson in late 1985. The council's primary function is to examine draft economic and social legislation and to advise both the government and the Chamber of Deputies on such bills. It must be consulted on legislation that involves general economic planning, implementation of specific economic plans, and the national budget.

Legislature

The Chamber of Deputies is a unicameral body; the sixth legislature (1981–86) comprised 136 members. Deputies must be at least 28 years of age and must have been born of a Tunisian father. The five-year legislative term is under normal circumstances concurrent with that of the president.

The chamber sits in a single session beginning in October and lasting until July. Extraordinary sessions may be called by the president or by a majority of the deputies. The chamber passes ordinary laws by majority vote; organic laws require a two-thirds majority approval. Should the chamber fail to pass the national budget by December 31, financial measures may be put into effect by presidential decree.

Under the Constitution, subjects requiring legislative action by the chamber include rules of legal procedure; definitions of crimes and misdemeanors and penalties to be imposed; tax rates, except where such authority had been delegated to the president; loans and financial commitments of the state; procedures for implementing the Constitution; establishment of boards, public offices, and national companies; nationality; and general principles concerning ownership and title, education, public health, labor, and social security. The development plan must be approved, as must government revenues and expenditures, in accordance with the budget organic law.

The Chamber of Deputies elects from its membership an executive bureau headed by the president of the chamber and four permanent commissions, or committees, covering political affairs, cultural and social affairs, financial and economic affairs, and general legislation. The commissions study and report to the whole chamber on proposed legislation that falls within their areas of competence. The commissions continue to meet when the chamber is not in session.

Under the system prevailing before the election of the Chamber of Deputies in 1981, a deputy had to be a member of the Destourian Socialist Party (Parti Socialiste Destourien—PSD). As an important feature of the reforms introduced in 1981, other parties were permitted to run, but they did not gain a single seat (see Elections, this ch.). The PSD formed the National Front with the General Union of Tunisian Workers (Union Générale des Travailleurs Tunisiens—UGTT) to offer a common slate of candidates. Of the 136 seats at stake, 27 were secured by candidates affiliated with the UGTT.

In the nine-month legislative season ending in July 1985, the chamber assembled for 43 plenary sessions. A total of 103 laws proposed by the government were examined before being approved. Mzali's efforts to introduce a more liberalized climate since he took office in 1980 have encouraged the legislature to bestir itself to engage in sometimes lively debates. As a result of objections mounted in the chamber, the government has occasionally changed or withdrawn individual clauses of bills placed before the body. The UGTT deputies in the National Front abstained from voting on the 1982–86 development plan, an action seen as a significant departure from the previous practice of virtually unanimous assent for the government's major programs. Criticism of the government's harsh suppression of dissidents was also implied in private bills dealing with amnesty and abolition of the State Security Court—moves that were met by delaying tactics on the part of the government.

Elections

Before the 1979 election, Tunisian voters had no real choice among candidates for the national legislature because only one nominee was presented for each seat. Lists of candidates were compiled by the PSD, which had been the only legal party since the Tunisian Communist Party (Parti Communiste Tunisien—PCT) was banned in 1963.

After amendment of the election code earlier in the same year, two candidates were nominated for each seat in the November 1979 election, but the names submitted to the electorate were again drawn up by the PSD from PSD membership roles and others sympathetic to the party. Opposition groups abandoned the possibility of contesting the election after concluding that they would not be permitted to campaign in a normal manner.

At an extraordinary congress of the PSD in April 1981, Bourguiba announced his plan to allow "differing currents of opinion" to be represented in the Chamber of Deputies. A constitutional amendment was adopted providing for an election to be held before the end of the year—instead of the normally scheduled time in 1984—to give immediate effect to the party's decision. In spite of the government's commitment to political pluralism, it was decided that legal recognition of other parties would be withheld until after the election. As a condition of subsequent recognition, a party would be required to obtain at least 5 percent of the valid vote. An exception was made for the PCT, based on the premise that the party had been officially recognized until it was suspended in 1963.

When the election was held in November 1981, only the National Front of the PSD and affiliated groups offered slates of candidates for all 136 seats in the 23 electoral districts. Three opposition formations also entered lists of candidates. The Movement of Socialist Democrats (Mouvement des Démocrates Socialistes— MDS) submitted slates in 19 districts with a combined total of 116 names. The internal faction of the Movement of Popular Unity (Mouvement d'Unité Populaire—MUP) contested eight districts with 55 candidates, and the PCT entered lists in six districts totaling 37 names. Each group was given access to the government-operated television and radio services to explain its platform. Airtime was accorded on the basis of two minutes of television time and three minutes of radio time for each list filed.

According to the official returns of the 1981 election, the National Front achieved an overwhelming victory, gaining 94.6 percent of the valid votes cast and winning every seat in the chamber; it was claimed that 85 percent of all eligible citizens had gone to the polls. The MDS attracted only 3.3 percent of the vote, and the MUP gained 0.8 percent. The PCT could muster only 0.8 percent, and independents who had submitted lists in three districts won 0.5 percent. Bitter charges of irregularities in the conduct of the election were made by the losers. It was claimed that the opposition had been prevented from having observers present at the polling places and during the ballot counts. In addition, the voting was not entirely secret because individuals were required to select lists identified by color in a public area.

The government later rescinded its condition that parties must attract at least 5 percent of the total vote to qualify for recognition. Accordingly, the MDS and the MUP were recognized in November 1983. Nevertheless, when local elections were held in May 1985, the various opposition forces declared a boycott on the grounds that the minimal conditions were not present for a credible election process. They cited the persistent dominance of the single-party mentality among officials, the continued political trials and suspension of newspapers, the harassment of opposition politicians, the

Tunisian voters at the polls
Courtesy Embassy
of Tunisia, Washington

destruction of party offices, and the use of state agencies to serve the ruling party.

The Legal System

Traditional Tunisian law was based on sharia. Sharia (the revealed law of God, according to Muslims) is derived not only from the Quran but also from the teachings of the Prophet Muhammad, the interpretations of Islamic jurists, and analogical reasoning. Both the Hanafi and the Malikite schools of Islamic law were well-established in Tunisia before the advent of the French protectorate.

Temporal power was in the hands of the bey, who could issue regulations in conformance with Islamic principles but could not make laws. According to Muslim belief, laws could originate only from God. A secular court system existed to adjudicate cases outside the jurisdiction of sharia courts. The *qaid* (see Glossary), as

219

personal representative of the bey, exercised a judicial function for civil, criminal, and commercial cases in the governorates; in Tunis, officials of the beylicate heard these cases as well as appeals involving *qaids'* decisions. Cases involving personal status and family law and succession within Tunisia's sizable Jewish community were heard in rabbinical courts.

During the protectorate period the French left to the jurisdiction of the sharia courts, headed by Islamic judges *(qadis)*, cases of personal status, such as marriage, divorce, inheritance, and landownership. A new secular court system, staffed by French judges, was created to apply French legal principles in cases involving non-Tunisians or for commercial matters and crimes. Traditional elements were often incorporated in the new laws. The beylicate courts were modified to become part of the protectorate administrative system.

After attaining independence Tunisia immediately began to modernize and unify its legal system. In 1956 sharia courts were abolished, and the Code of Personal Status, far more liberal than corresponding codes in other Arab states, was adopted. A year later, application of the code to all Tunisians, regardless of religion, ended Judaic law as a separate legal source. At the same time an agreement was concluded with France providing that the French court system would cease to function by July 1, 1957. (An earlier agreement would have permitted the French courts to continue hearing cases involving French citizens until at least 1970.) Among the seven codes that completed the reform of the Tunisian legal system were the Code of Civil and Commercial Procedure adopted in 1959 and the General Revision of the Code of Criminal Procedure in 1968.

The Judiciary

The common law courts comprise, in ascending order of authority, cantonal courts, courts of first instance, courts of appeal, and the Court of Cassation (supreme court of appeal). At the base of the court hierarchy are the cantonal courts *(justices cantonales)*, whose criminal jurisdiction includes cases involving *contraventions* (petty offenses) and *délits* (misdemeanors). Heard by single magistrates, rulings involving *contraventions* cannot be appealed. Only those *délits* punishable by fines and imprisonment of not more than one year can be heard in the cantonal courts, and these cases may be appealed.

Above the cantonal courts are the courts of first instance *(tribunaux de première instance)*, found in the principal administrative centers. Each court comprises a civil and commercial chamber, a personal status chamber, a correctional chamber, and a social chamber. Decisions are rendered by a panel of three judges. The court of first instance is the last court to which decisions made in the cantonal courts can be appealed. Original jurisdiction applies to civil and commercial cases where more than minimal amounts are being litigated and to all cases involving *délits* that are outside the jurisdiction of the cantonal courts.

The three courts of appeal *(cours d' appel)* sit in Tunis, Sousse, and Sfax. Each court comprises one or more civil chambers, a correctional chamber, a chamber of accusation, and a criminal chamber. The civil and correctional chambers hear appeals from the courts of first instance on civil and criminal cases, respectively. The accusation chamber functions much like a grand jury in the United States legal system. It investigates cases involving a *crime,* the most serious category of criminal offense, which is punishable by a prison sentence of more than five years' duration. If the charge is substantiated, the case is turned over to the criminal chamber for trial. Decisions of the criminal chamber may not be appealed, but they are subject to the Court of Cassation's *pouvoir en cassation* (power of abrogation or annulment).

At the apex of the common court system is the Court of Cassation, which sits in Tunis. It is composed of three civil and commercial chambers and one criminal chamber. A panel of three judges considers decisions from lower courts through the court's *pouvoir en cassation.* In exercising its power to annul inferior court decisions, the Court of Cassation does not render a final verdict but rather returns the case to the lower court for a new ruling.

A number of specialized courts have jurisdiction over such matters as land, juvenile offenses, family allowances, and employer-employee relations. Their judgments are not ordinarily subject to appeal. The High Court hears cases of high treason against members of the government, a charge that is construed to include such offenses as acts against state security, systematic abuse of public authority, purposely misleading the head of state so as to damage the national interest, and commission of a *délit* or *crime* while in office. The court has been convened twice, once to sentence the disgraced economic tsar, Ahmed Ben Salah, in 1970 and again in 1984 for the case of former minister of interior Driss Guiga, who was tried in absentia for dereliction in his handling of antigovernment demonstrators (see The Riots of 1984 and Their Aftermath, this ch.). The court was constituted by the Chamber of Deputies, which selected four official members and three members from its own ranks.

The State Security Court, established in 1968, sits on an ad hoc basis with a career magistrate, who acts as president, and four assessors (two magistrates and two legislative deputies). The court was convened in 1978 to try a number of leading trade unionists for inciting strikes and demonstrations and again in 1980 to try 60 persons accused of participation in the attack on Gafsa (see Opposition and Unrest, ch. 1). Generally, cases with political overtones have been heard in the regular judicial framework, where normal safeguards have applied. Nineteen members of the armed forces were sentenced to imprisonment by a military court in 1984 for affiliation with an underground organization of a political character (the Islamic Liberation Party), and 11 civilians were found guilty by the same court of having incited the soldiers to join.

The Council of State, provided for under the Constitution, consists of the Administrative Tribunal and the Court of Accounts. The Administrative Tribunal hears cases by private individuals alleging abuse of powers by the state or public agencies. It has not been accorded an active place in the judicial system. The Court of Accounts functions as an audit agency for the accounts of the state, local and national public organizations, and public industrial and commercial enterprises, including private enterprises in which the state holds a share.

The Constitution also provides for the Higher Council of the Judiciary, which is charged with administering discipline as well as appointing, promoting, and transferring magistrates. The council's purpose is to safeguard the independence of the judiciary from interference in the judicial process by the executive branch.

Civil and Human Rights

The Constitution provides that "every accused person shall be presumed innocent until his guilt has been proven, following proceedings offering him the necessary conditions for his defense." Defendants are guaranteed counsel, and the courts appoint attorneys for anyone who does not have one for whatever reason. The whereabouts of a detained person must be made known to counsel and family. Access to prisoners has generally not been withheld for more than a few days. Under Tunisian law, anyone suspected of an offense punishable for no longer than one year and who has no previous record may be held in preventive detention for up to five days. Persons suspected of more serious offenses may be detained without trial for an unlimited investigative period before being charged or released. Rights of appeal are respected in civil courts and are frequently exercised, except for the High Court, where the judgment is final.

The appointment of Mzali as prime minister ushered in a more liberal legal climate and gave rise to a number of reforms intended to bolster the independence of the judiciary. All persons serving terms on politically related charges were released. But as a result of new prosecutions in subsequent years, mostly of Islamists (see Glossary), the number of political prisoners rose again to 102 in 1983 and then dropped back to 50 in 1984, according to the Tunisian League of Human Rights. The London-based human rights organization, Amnesty International, has appealed for the release of prisoners jailed for nonviolently exercising their freedom of expression and association. In a number of cases, persons serving long sentences for illegal political activities have been amnestied by the government.

The trial of 91 Islamic activists in 1981 was conducted publicly in a criminal court, although statements by officials and a campaign in the official media tended to prejudice the outcome. The accused were not permitted outside contact for a month, and their lawyers were given little time to prepare their defenses. According to the United States Department of State's *Country Reports on Human Rights Practices for 1984*, "political pressures are sometimes brought to bear on magistrates in cases involving political charges, and sentences in such cases often reflect these pressures."

Both Amnesty International and the Department of State have mentioned reliable evidence indicating that political detainees and common-law offenders had been subjected to torture and ill-treatment while in pretrial detention. The Department of State was critical of the behavior of the police in making arrests connected with the January 1984 bread riots, of the lengthy and incommunicado detention of some defendants, and of the irregularities by some judges during their trials.

Regional and Local Government

Under Tunisia's unitary system of government, all authority exercised by lower governmental units is delegated by the central government; they have no inherent or residual powers of their own. The single constitutional provision covering subnational government states simply that "the municipal and regional councils shall deal with matters of local interest as prescribed by law." Subsequent legislation has introduced a well-developed system of regional and local administration that stresses the interdependence of government and party.

The highest regional authority is the governorate. The number of governorates, totaling 13 when they were first created soon after independence, was increased several times and by 1984 numbered 23 (see fig. 1). The chief executive of the governorate is the governor, who is appointed by the president upon the recommendation of the minister of interior. The governor also serves as the regional director of the PSD and is a member of the party's Central Committee. He is assisted by the Governorate Council, which is composed of representatives from the national organizations, members of the party's regional coordination committee, and communal council presidents (see The Destourian Socialist Party, this ch.). The council's primary duties include examination of the governorate's finances and budget and consultation regarding social and economic requirements and regional planning. The governor's personal powers are extensive; he represents the president at the regional level and is concurrently the senior party official. He supervises and coordinates the activities of smaller administrative divisions, exercises control over the police, is responsible for the execution of court decisions, and controls local public bodies.

Beneath the governorate, the second level in the hierarchy is the delegation *(délégation)*, each of which is headed by a delegate *(délégué)*. The delegate, a civil servant appointed by the central government, is responsible to the governor. Each delegation is divided into several sectors *(secteurs* or *oumadaat;* sing., *oumada).* Sectors were created in 1969, replacing the traditional tribal-oriented subregional administrative unit known as the *shaykhat.* At the head of each sector is the *omda* (sector chief). The new system shifted the focus of the lowest rung of local power from that of the shaykh, who most often came from a traditionally prominent local family, to that of a militant of the PSD; the *omda* is appointed from members of the local party cell. The *omda* acts as a conduit between the citizens and the other tiers of government. He publicizes decisions and regulations promulgated by the governor and advises his superiors of local developments of political interest. The *omda* registers births, marriages, and deaths, and he issues various official certificates and permits. He concerns himself with matters such as the organization of basic food supplies, application of traffic rules, distribution of seed grains, and army recruitment. He is in charge of local police activities and ensures the execution of civil judgments.

The entire territory of the country is divided into sectors, which numbered more than 1,500 in 1985. About two-thirds of the sectors had within their boundaries only small villages of less than 4,000 population or, in some cases, simply hamlets consisting of extended rural families. In more populous areas, a degree of local self-government was accorded within the framework of another local unit, the commune. In larger communities, a single commune might be composed of several sectors. Created by decree of the central government, their number had risen from 69 after independence to 245 in 1985. The communes are administered by communal councils (often referred to as municipal councils), which are popularly elected at three-year intervals. The councils annually hold four 10-day sessions convened in February, May, July, and November. Under a 1985 revision of the law on municipalities, most council decisions were to be subject to approval only by the governor. The purpose was to consolidate the authority of the governor as the sole reviewing authority in local matters. More important actions, such as borrowings, would continue to be referred to the ministries of finance and interior.

In the communal elections of May 1985, all 3,540 candidates were nominated by the PSD. Their elections were assured by the boycott mounted by the other legal parties in the absence of guarantees that the election would be conducted in an impartial manner. The electoral lists were composed of PSD members—headed in many cases by a member of the PSD Political Bureau or otherwise high in the party hierarchy—as well as members of national organizations representing women, agriculture, commerce, and industry, along with some independents.

The members of the communal councils select presidents from their own ranks. An exception is the municipality of Tunis, whose head (called a mayor) is appointed from the elected council members by the president of the republic. The president of a communal council plays a preeminent role in directing the council's activity and superintending the execution of its decisions. With the exclusion of Tunis, the presidency of the council is intended to be a part-time office. The highest full-time official, the secretary general, is in charge of the administrative apparatus of the commune. Although the *omda* is still present, his role is considerably circumscribed in larger cities, being more a neighborhood representative of state and party. The *omda* is likely to be a loyal party worker in need of employment.

Political Dynamics

In spite of Bourguiba's fragile health and infirmities of advancing age (he was officially reported to be 83 in 1986), he had maintained to a remarkable degree his place at the head of the political order. On several occasions, it seemed that serious medical problems would force him to retire from active politics, and the maneuvering over the succession intensified correspondingly. The official media exploited every opportunity to portray Bourguiba as ceaselessly involved in the affairs of his country. Whether or not this remained true in 1986, his personal approval was still indispensable for any major policy decision or new initiative.

The philosophy guiding Tunisia's political course under Bourguiba has been one of limited democracy guided by mature, educated members of the elite; the nondogmatic acceptance of state economic planning and intervention; and the application of gradualism, pragatism, and rationalism (see Bourguibism and Destourian Socialism, this ch.). The element of pragmatism has been uppermost, making it difficult to trace a consistent approach by Bourguiba to his nation's problems other than a willingness to shift—sometimes abruptly—if a given policy is seen to be ineffective.

At successive stages of Bourguiba's rule, various high appointees have had a prevailing influence, causing him to follow new directions in policy or to adopt fresh concepts. During the 1960s centralized planning and the collectivization of agriculture and retail trade were emphasized during the ascendancy of the trade union leader and planning secretary, Ben Salah. Growing opposition, which gave way to violence among farmers, coupled with Bourguiba's misgivings over Ben Salah's accumulation of power, led to the latter's downfall and curtailment of his policies (see Intraparty Politics in the 1970s, ch. 1). During the decade of the 1970s, the government's economic policies were liberalized under Prime Minister Hedi Nouira, although its political grip was tightened. Several ministers who called for democratization of the PSD and more open political processes were forced out of government, and Bourguiba's control over party and state was reasserted in the PSD congress of 1974. Some of the leading politicians who were discarded by Bourguiba after his rejection of their policies became involved in opposition movements at home and abroad.

Increasing pressure for the relaxation of political life and the legitimation of organized opposition movements continued to be rebuffed by Bourguiba and Nouira. The violence kindled by a general strike in January 1978 dramatized the pent-up grievances that had been suppressed under a system inhospitable to dissenting

Prime Minister Mohamed Mzali
Courtesy Embassy
of Tunisia, Washington

opinions. The power of the unions, which were blamed for the riots, was curbed by arrests and imprisonment. The minor concession of allowing a choice between two candidates for each seat— both carrying the endorsement of the PSD—did little to mollify the public's resentment over the monopoly of political expression by the PSD.

The 1981 Election: Opposition Parties Sanctioned

When Nouira suffered a stroke in early 1980, Bourguiba grasped the opportunity to replace him as prime minister with the more liberally inclined Mzali. Acting with the advice of Mzali, the former minister of education, Bourguiba reconciled himself to the need for greater tolerance of political pluralism. Several ministers whose differences with Nouira's policies had earlier led to their departure from government were restored to the cabinet and the

227

party. Political prisoners were released, and nearly 1,000 trade union members convicted for their role in the 1978 riots were pardoned. When Bourguiba told an extraordinary congress of the PSD that he saw no objection to the emergence of other political parties, his announcement was greeted with approval by the delegates.

In the special parliamentary election that followed, some opposition forces were allowed to nominate lists of candidates and were permitted to express their views in their own publications. The Islamist group known as the Islamic Tendency Movement (Mouvement de la Tendance Islamique—MTI) was rejected as a religious organization legally precluded from participation in politics.

In spite of having to campaign in an atmosphere that was not free from intimidation, the other parties had believed they might win a substantial minority of the seats, an outcome that could have transformed the Chamber of Deputies from a virtual rubber stamp for Bourguiba's programs into one in which policy alternatives could be introduced and debated. Moreover, although the UGTT had combined with the PSD to form the National Front election coalition, the labor movement represented a separate power base that was soon at odds with the government on many issues. When the official results were announced, however, the opposition parties were crushed by the PSD-led National Front in every district. According to Richard B. Parker, a former senior United States diplomat in the Maghrib, at the last moment Bourguiba changed his mind about allowing a real opposition party to run and ordered his minister of interior to see to it that only Destourian candidates were elected.

In the period following the 1981 election, the momentum for liberalizing the political atmosphere slackened. Mounting economic difficulties contributed to a resurgence of social stress and unrest. In the absence of decisive leadership from the top, there was little incentive for other politicians to risk their futures by proposing the painful correctives that were needed. The uneasiness of the government in dealing with criticism was reflected in its suspension of several newspapers for expressing dissenting opinions. The PSD–UGTT coalition was strained when the labor federation's members in the Chamber of Deputies spoke out against the strategy of the 1982–86 development plan. Nonetheless, two opposition parties (the MDS and the MUP) were belatedly extended recognition in November 1983.

The country's economic fortunes and growth rates, which had been adequate during the 1970s to stay abreast of population pressures and rising consumer expectations, faltered during the early 1980s. More balanced in terms of resources than its Maghribi neighbors, boasting an industrious and better educated work force, Tunisia's liberal economic policies had helped to attract the foreign capital needed to expand its manufacturing sector. In spite of this, the economy came under mounting pressure from balance of payments deficits owing to lower market prices for its raw material and oil exports and its growing need for imported foodstuffs. With insufficient funds for job creation amid growing signs of poverty, resentment was fueled over the widening gap between the poor and the salaried workers and the wealthy elite. The 1983–86 development plan emphasized increased investment in agriculture to reduce the need for food imports and to stem migration to the cities. As a result of poor harvests and other unforeseen developments, these objectives could not be realized (see Development Planning, ch. 3).

The Riots of 1984 and Their Aftermath

One of the principal measures belatedly adopted by the government to bring an alarming balance of payments drain under control was to restrict imports and reduce subsidies on sales of basic food products, notably cereals. Bread prices were to double, while semolina (used in making couscous) and pasta were to go up by nearly as much. Although the government had made known its intentions three months in advance and had pledged itself to earmark compensatory payment to wage earners, it neglected to take account of the harsh impact on the unemployed and rural poor subsisting on the very foods most affected by the price increases.

Even before the price rises were announced officially on January 1, 1984, protest demonstrations had begun. In the south, the region least advanced economically, mobs attacked shops, vehicles, and public buildings. In similar outbreaks at Gafsa in the west and Gabés, the main industrial center of the south, protestors battled police with stones. Symbols of authority and wealth were targets of arson and looting. A state of emergency was declared on January 3, and army units used automatic weapons against crowds barricaded in the streets of Tunis when it became evident that the demoralized police were incapable of controlling the situation. Order was not restored until January 6, when Bourguiba appeared on radio and television to announce that in the face of the unrest the price rises would be rescinded and that he was directing the cabinet to submit a new budget to him that would avoid excessive price increases for food staples.

It was officially reported that 89 Tunisians had died in the disturbances, 938 others had been injured (including 348 members of the security forces), and over 800 had been arrested. Most of the demonstrators were unemployed youths, joined by students and Islamists. In its analysis of the cause of the riots, the Tunisian League of Human Rights alluded to the serious disparities among classes and regions, generating a gap between two worlds—one the idle and unemployed citizens without prospects and the other a class of entrepreneurs engaged in parasitic and speculative activity. The league's report noted that the promise of tangible reform of the political system had not been kept, producing a political vacuum in which the citizens were not involved in decisions affecting their daily lives. It forthrightly assailed the government's "determination to keep the legal opposition on the sideline of debates and decisions on major national issues and the continuance of political trials, suspensions of newspapers, and the monopoly of audiovisual media."

The restoration of order was followed by the dismissal of Minister of Interior Driss Guiga. A report by an official commission of inquiry later declared that Guiga had neglected his legal and security obligations, had been slow in summoning the forces at his command against the rioters, and had even tried to exploit the disturbances to further his own ambitions. Guiga had left the country after his dismissal, saying that he had been picked as a scapegoat; he called the commission report "unproven slander." He was subsequently tried in absentia in June 1984 and sentenced to a jail term.

Presidential Succession

By 1983 Mzali, Bourguiba's presumptive successor under the terms of the Constitution, had begun to solidify his authority. In that year he succeeded in replacing three key cabinet members—Minister of Planning and Finance Mansour Moalla, Minister of Information Tahar Belkhodja, and Minister of National Economy Abdelaziz Lasram—with officials more congenial to him. The prime minister's differences with Moalla and Lasram over tactics in dealing with the socially sensitive issue of lifting price ceilings that had kept basic foodstuffs at artificially low levels served as the motive for their removal. Although Mzali still had potential rivals in high places, he continued to strengthen his position during 1984–85. He was somehow able to escape censure for the abrupt rise in the price of staple foods that ignited the January 1984 riots and was even able to profit from the crisis by banishing Guiga, his main adversary. Guiga's portfolio was added to that of the prime minister, whose authority over that important ministry was reinforced by the appointment of Mzali's own cousin, Ameur Ghedira, as its deputy head. Mzali also succeeded in advancing several officers of his own choosing to high posts in the military and security services.

In March 1985 Bourguiba told the PSD Central Committee that "Mr. Mohamed Mzali has acquired experience over many years. . . . When the moment comes, he will not find himself incapable of taking charge." In the confrontation with Libya in August 1985 that sprang from the Libyan expulsion of Tunisian workers, the prime minister appeared to demonstrate his ascendancy over another potential contender, Foreign Minister Beji Caid Essebsi. Mzali also waged a relentless campaign over union wage demands and management of the UGTT against veteran labor leader Habib Achour, whom some thought Mzali might later face as a political opponent.

Among other prominent figures considered to be likely challengers to Mzali for the presidency, Minister of Public Works and Housing Mohamed Sayah was most often mentioned. Sayah was associated with a more authoritarian political style and was believed to be unsympathetic to the democratizing trends inspired by Mzali. He had headed the PSD over a span of 13 years and, while party director, had been responsible for the punishment of labor union members after the 1978 strikes and riots. He was said to have personal access to Bourguiba and was, moreover, considered to be a confidant of Habib Bourguiba, Jr., the president's son by his first wife, a woman of French origin. The younger Bourguiba had long been a member of the cabinet (special adviser to the president) but was removed from this position in early 1986. He was also president of the Tunisian Industrial Development Bank. Said to be in poor health, he was not thought to harbor personal ambitions for the presidency.

The president's second wife, Wassila Bourguiba, was accounted to be a factor in the maneuvering around the presidency, although her influence may have diminished after the disgrace of her ally, Guiga. She was said to be ill-disposed toward Sayah and Bourguiba, Jr., and was identified with the faction that included Essebsi and Minister of National Defense Slaheddine Baly. Hedi Baccouche, who had been called back from the important post of ambassador to Algeria to reinvigorate the decaying PSD apparatus, was yet another potential aspirant to the highest office.

Bourguibism and Destourian Socialism

Tunisia's philosophical and political heritage is a synthesis of the predominant values of earlier historical periods. The virtues of continuity, order, and stability developed during the period of Punic mercantilism. Roman law and custom, administered by a strong central government, reinforced Punic standards and values. Islam—particularly the urban strain of Islam in Tunisia—also attached importance to enterprise and order, and it prized the virtues of moderation, piety, and frugality. The beylical system provided another centralized political structure. The colonial period reaffirmed Tunisia's ties with the West and imparted both liberal humanitarianism and some authoritarian values found in French political philosophy. Most members of the Tunisian political elite, including Bourguiba, are French educated.

Bourguiba's fundamental ideas guiding his political thoughts and actions were propounded in speeches and writings, beginning with his newspaper columns in the early 1930s. His philosophical and ethical outlook—often referred to as Bourguibism—was founded on belief in human dignity, cultural modernism, rational use of resources, and social justice. He set realistic goals that could be attained by the application of reason. He saw people as basically good but needing to have their intellectual level raised to a stage where they would equate the public interest with their own.

Bourguiba concluded that if people were to fulfill their potential, then traditional social and religious constraints, as well as those imposed by material need, had to be eliminated. Thus, Bourguiba embarked on postindependence campaigns that advocated women's emancipation, opposed *habus* (see Glossary) property holdings and other conservative aspects of Islam, and stressed modernization through economic development.

The advance of democracy would have to go hand in hand with the spread of education, culture, and social progress. Bourguiba drew on nationalist feeling by stressing Tunisia's unique historic role. At the same time he insisted on the importance of retaining elements of French culture while seeking to model Tunisia's economic development on Western industrialized societies.

Bourguiba believed that the state had a positive role to play in channeling the energies of the people by providing guidance and technical and financial support in accomplishing national tasks. The unifying role of the state and the existing low level of political sophistication among the mass of the people were regarded as justifying the monolithic party structure and the party-state complex. Training and counsel in citizenship were to be provided by a small minority of party activists who would contribute to the diffusion of decisions and policies made at the highest levels of state and party. They would, in effect, form an elite group of political tutors to the masses.

Destourian socialism, a combination of Bourguibism in a somewhat formalized form and the concept of systematic planning and intervention, was introduced by Bourguiba in June 1961. An undogmatic, original creation linked to the "objective realities" of the country, Destourian socialism was free from imported ideologies, including Marxism. For Bourguiba, the issue was not the Marxist struggle between classes but how the individual could be educated and evolve from a preoccupation with personal welfare to contributing to the good of the community and to human betterment. In its elitism, gradualism, rejection of class struggle, view of the individual, and emphasis on the state's function in directing rather than taking over economic activity, Destourian socialism resembled British Fabian socialism. It was not a rigid ideology but served the same purpose of clarifying long-term objectives, imparting a sense of continuity, and legitimizing the state's role by mustering a consensus for its goals and methods.

Destourian socialism, when first introduced, was designed to correct the inadequacies of the first years of independence when private investment and economic liberalism had failed to produce expected growth. To increase the pace of economic development and break down social rigidities and immobility, a system of comprehensive planning was adopted. In 1964 the nationalization of foreign-owned land, chiefly French, was followed by a five-year period during which the formation of agricultural cooperatives was stressed, initially on the sequestered French estates but later extending to large domestic landholders. Industrial and commercial life was also brought within the scope of collectivist plans.

In 1969, when these policies were in turn acknowledged as having failed, Bourguiba curtailed the socialist experimentation and reduced state regulation, reverting to encouragement of domestic capitalism and foreign investment. Politically, Bourguiba briefly embraced democratization, but at the 1974 party congress he reasserted the concept of a monolithic structure with an overlapping of the PSD and the state. The PSD was supposed to represent the "assembly point" through which a reconciliation of all interests was to be achieved.

By 1986 economic distress and Bourguiba's weakened physical condition had divested Bourguibism and Destourian socialism of much of their meaning and promise. His acceptance of political pluralism, enabling other parties to contest the election of 1981, conceded that the PSD no longer need be seen as the unique force for national unity and the sole instrument for social and economic advancement. In reality, the party was an ossified institution, hollow at its base and no longer relevant to the needs and aspirations of the Tunisian public. Analyzing the sources of disenchantment with the Destourian ideal in his article "L'état Tunisien: de la tutelle au désengagement," French political scientist Michel Camau asserted that rather than creating a new model of the socially oriented citizen, development had brought a differentiation of interests marked by consumerism and individualism. Cleavages had sharpened between workers and enterprises and between wage earners and farmers. Regional divisions had intensified between the wealthier coastal cities and the western and southern sections of the country. The social "marginalization" of youth had been a prime determinant in the rising level of antisocial behavior and political radicalism, which had often turned to street violence. Camau warned that the vitality shown by Islamic renewal represented the gestation of a countersociety against the legally constituted state. In *Comparative Politics of North Africa*, John P. Entelis argues that it also implied a reaffirmation by the young of a deeply held sense of their Arabic and Islamic heritage and a decline in popularity of the notion of a French-Tunisian synthesis and of the secularist state.

As viewed by Camau, Destourianism had been overtaken by a new trend—one of relative disengagement by the state, which was reducing its social involvement and turning to the private sector to provide many public services. The state's role would be to intervene only to protect those citizens reduced to poverty as a result of the effects of market mechanisms. Camau interpreted the emergence of an opposition press and the lifting of the ban on opposition parties as part of the same evolution. Submitting to the law of the market in economic matters thus had as its counterpart the recognition of the existence of a plurality of political interests among the public.

The Destourian Socialist Party

In 1920 the Destour (Constitution) Party was created as part of the nationalist movement. Bourguiba and others broke from the Destour Party and in 1934 formed the Neo-Destour Party, which led the successful independence struggle against the French. With the acceptance of Destourian socialism as Tunisia's national ideology, the name of the party was changed in 1964 to the Destourian

Socialist Party (Parti Socialiste Destourien—PSD) (see Destourian Socialism: Tunisia in the 1960s, ch. 1).

The party has never had serious rivals. Between 1963 and 1981 it was the only legal political formation. The party's success in building a broad, popular base of support in the struggle against France contributed greatly to its durability as the primary political force of the country. With independence achieved, the party was charged with tutoring the masses and providing a framework within which they could learn to participate in politics. As the government became increasingly involved in economic planning, the party was assigned the role of mobilizing the masses and providing the vehicle through which the people and the republic's leaders could communicate. In 1974 Bourguiba defined the state as "the instrument implementing the party's historical message."

Membership in the PSD is open to anyone who is not a member of another party, who agrees to pay regular dues, and who adheres to the party's principles. Officially, the total membership was 750,000 in 1984, implying the near doubling of its strength within a decade and representing roughly one in three of all citizens eligible to vote. An active party role is considered indispensable for senior officials in government and quasi-government posts. Governors and delegates are invariably the responsible party officials in their local jurisdictions. The highest party body, the Political Bureau, is composed largely of cabinet members. It is possible for especially qualified individuals to rise to high positions without having been party activists, but in such cases correspondingly high party titles may be assigned to them. In spite of the association of the PSD with career success in many fields, the party has not been able to retain its early vigor and has had difficulty attracting better educated younger members. The steady erosion of its vitality at the local levels has been frankly acknowledged.

The party's hierarchical structure has as its base the cells, sometimes referred to as branches, which numbered about 4,000 in 1985 (see fig. 11). Fifty party members were the minimum needed to form a cell, which was originally organized geographically according to place of residence of its members. Beginning in 1964, emphasis shifted to the creation of professional cells that enrolled people working in a particular enterprise. The professional cell was expected to help motivate the work force, to analyze problems and suggest solutions in meetings with management, and to lead the battle against waste and theft. Party cells have also been established among Tunisian migrant workers, particularly in France. The cells do not function with the same secrecy associated with many European communist and socialist party counterparts. Their meetings are often open to the public. Local direction of the cell is the responsibility of an executive committee of 10 to 20 members elected every two years by and from the entire cell membership.

Above the cell is the circumscription, which is organized at the level of the delegations into which each governorate is divided. The circumscription coordinates the activities of the various cells; the presidents of the cells are included among the members of the circumscription's executive committee. The most important subnational party units are the regional coordinating committees, which numbered 28 in 1985—generally corresponding to one in each governorate, although Tunis had three. The coordinating committee is headed by a secretary general (appointed by the Political Bureau) and usually has 14 elected members. The secretary general is the chief full-time party functionary in the region, although the governor bears formal responsibility for party activities.

The National Congress, comprising up to 1,000 delegates elected by local executive committees, is usually held at five-year intervals. The regular congresses of 1974 and 1979 were, however, followed by an extraordinary congress in 1981. Regarded as the party's highest formal authority, it is in practice more of a consultative and advisory body that lends its endorsement to the policies introduced by the party executive, the government, and the president of the republic. The National Council functions as an interim congress between sessions. The National Congress elects the 80 members of the Central Committee, which meets periodically to develop and enunciate party doctrine.

The Political Bureau constitutes the main executive organ of the party. There are 22 bureau members, who are selected from among the Central Committee membership by the party president. Appointment to the Political Bureau is partly a matter of prestige, reflecting high standing in the party-state hierarchy. More sensitive policy issues and nominations for senior posts are likely to be raised in the Political Bureau, where views are exchanged more frankly than in the cabinet. Demotion from a senior government position or loss of presidential confidence is generally accompanied by removal from the Political Bureau as well. The newly appointed Political Bureau after the 1981 congress included 15 of the 21 government ministers, along with the heads of the leading organizations affiliated with the PSD (see table 10, Appendix). The highest position, that of president of the party, has been held exclusively by Bourguiba. The office of party secretary general is held by the prime minister. The official with day-to-day executive authority is the director; Baccouche replaced Mongi Kooli in this position in March 1984. It was agreed in 1979 to add to the Political Bureau

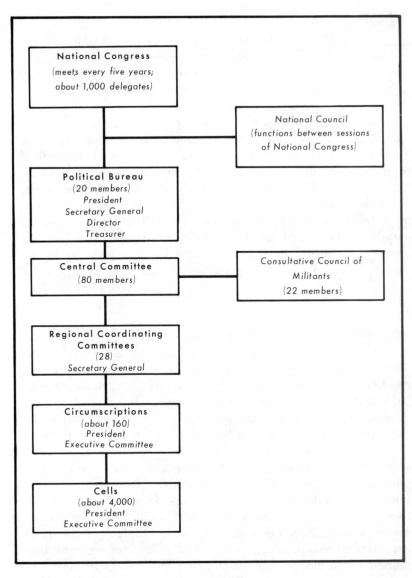

Figure 11.   Structure of the Destourian Socialist Party, 1985

the 22-member Consultative Council of Militants comprising many veteran party members who had not been active in political life. Bechir Zarg Layoun, a close associate of the president since the independence era, was placed at its head.

Opposition Groups

By the close of 1985, three opposition parties had been legally recognized by the government. Another significant political force, the MTI, representing the Islamic renewal movement, had been denied legalization by the government in 1981, and its followers were for a time subject to suppression. The government's plan to introduce legislation in 1986 on the organization of political parties was intended to relax the conditions for other opposition bodies to qualify. The MTI in particular was expected to benefit if it could show that it had been fashioned as a party based on "moral authority" rather than religious commitment. Nonetheless, the PSD remained closely identified with the state at every tier of government and was firmly established in official agencies and enterprises. It was far from clear whether responsible party officials would be prepared to adjust their outlook and practices to the extent that unqualified acceptance of a multiparty system would entail.

Movement of Socialist Democrats

Although credited with less than 4 percent of the vote in the 1981 election, the Movement of Socialist Democrats (Mouvement des Démocrates Socialistes—MDS) is considered to be the primary contender among the authorized opposition groups. Its secretary general, Ahmed Mestiri, previously a leading liberal within the ranks of the PSD, was expelled from the government party in 1975, having been accused of disruptive factionalism. In 1977 more than 160 liberals, including Mestiri and other former cabinet ministers, appealed to Bourguiba to end the deterioration of civil liberties and called a national conference—later banned by the authorities—for the same purpose. In June 1978 Mestiri announced his intention to form a separate political party. Many of his liberal associates were unwilling to carry their differences with the Destourian Party this far and in 1980 accepted an invitation to be reintegrated into the PSD. These persons included Essebsi and Sadok Ben Jomaa, both of whom were rewarded with new cabinet portfolios.

The first congress of the MDS was held in December 1983, shortly after its formal recognition. Its elected National Council of 81 members included the heads of the regional federations and the 10 members of the Political Bureau, consisting of Mestiri and nine deputy secretaries general.

The MDS is a reformist group that urges a true multiparty system, relaxation of the PSD grip on the administration of the country, a more open political dialogue, an end to the harassment of opposition parties and their members, and greater press freedom. Its outlook on economic issues is little different from that of the PSD. It advocates an economy blending public and private sector activity and a broader range of legislation aimed at ameliorating social conditions.

Popular Unity Party

Ahmed Ben Salah, the former secretary of state for planning and finance and architect of the country's centralized planning policies during the 1960s, joined other dissidents to form the Movement of Popular Unity in Paris in 1973. The group's manifesto, *Toward a New Tunisia,* published in 1975, advocated a totally planned economy under strict state control, social reform, and a nonaligned foreign policy. It did not hesitate to criticize Bourguiba personally nor to question the legitimacy of the PSD government. A rift developed between the external and the internal wings of the movement, Ben Salah and a majority of the political committee opposing the establishment of local units within Tunisia and efforts to become registered as a legal party. The internal faction also adopted a less intransigent attitude toward Bourguiba. The split became formalized when four internal members applied for authorization to found a party and a newspaper in January 1981. The more moderate internal group, although designating itself the Movement of Popular Unity, was often referred to as MUP-II to distinguish it from the Ben Salah faction. In 1985 it was renamed the Popular Unity Party (Parti d'Unité Populaire—PUP). Its secretary general, Mohamed Ben Hadj Amor, described the party as "socialist nationalist" in its outlook and appealed for a unification of all leftist ranks in a single national front. The MUP attracted little public support in the 1981 election, gaining less than 1 percent of the announced vote.

Tunisian Communist Party

The Tunisian Communist Party (Parti Communiste Tunisien—PCT) was founded in 1920 as an arm of the French Communist Party but became independent in 1934. It adopted orthodox pro-Soviet positions, although in its program for the 1981 election it softened its approach. Its call for a united opposition front was, however, rejected by the MDS. It assailed the government's economic policies as aggravating regional and social disparities and favoring the bourgeois classes but refrained from demanding the nationalization of the private sector. The PCT's foreign policy platform included peaceful coexistence and nonalignment, insisting on a firm stance against "imperialism—especially American imperialism." After Israel's invasion of Lebanon in 1982, the PCT called upon the government to freeze its relations with Washington and to dissolve the United States-Tunisian Joint Military Commission.

At the eighth congress of the PCT in 1981, a three-member Secretariat was elected, headed by Secretary General Muhammad Harmel, plus a Political Bureau of six members and a Central Committee of 12 members. The party was believed to have no more than 100 committed adherents. Its six candidates in the 1981 election attracted a vote of 15,000.

Islamic Political Organizations

The upsurge of orthodoxy and piety in the observance of religion in Muslim countries had had its resonance in Tunisian politics. The government, although initially tolerant of preaching and other activities of the Islamists, did not permit them to organize as a political party. Especially after their disruption of the University of Tunis in 1981 and their role in the 1984 rioting, the militant Muslims were liable to prosecution for sedition because their goals and methods were perceived as a threat to the stability of the state.

Bourguiba's secularist policies had been the object of complaints by more conservative elements of the Muslim community. They had never reconciled themselves to the reforms introduced by him in 1956—the suppression of religious courts and Quranic schools, the prohibition of polygyny, the restrictions on divorce, and the procedure used to calculate the beginning of Ramadan, the month of fasting. Wearing of Islamic garments by women was prohibited for students and for workers in government offices. Bourguiba's opposition to observance of the Ramadan fast by working people on the grounds of reduced productivity was a particular source of distress. Nevertheless, these differences did not bring the Islamists into direct conflict with the government until the late 1970s.

The Islamic renewal took a more militant turn after the Iranian revolution in 1979, led by Ayatollah Ruhollah Khomeini. Although the Tunisian Islamists drew encouragement from Khomeini's success in transforming Iran into a religious state, there was no direct link between the Shia activists in Iran and the Tunisians who adhered to the mainstream Sunni division of Islam. The

Islamic Revival Movement that formed in November 1979 soon split into a number of smaller groups, the only significant one being the MTI, which filed in June 1981 for recognition as a political party. Its application was refused by the government, and large-scale arrests of MTI sympathizers followed; charges included offending the dignity of the head of state, disseminating false information, and belonging to an unauthorized organization. Government officials blamed the MTI for violent incidents on university campuses and inflammatory sermons by dissident imams (see Glossary). About 70 of those arrested received prison sentences of one to 11 years.

Beginning in 1984, the government shifted to less suppressive tactics in dealing with the MTI. In August all 17 MTI leaders still in jail were pardoned, including the movement's president, Rachid Ghanouchi, and its secretary general, Abdelfattah Mourou. The group was still refused registration as a legal party, and its journals, *Al Maarifa* and *Al Mujtamaa*, continued to be banned. Permission to hold public meetings was not granted, and MTI activists—many of them civil servants or government-employed teachers—remained under surveillance. Nevertheless, in late 1985 Mzali met with the MTI leadership and hinted that an end to its political exclusion was a possibility.

The MTI calls for the application of Islamic principles to all forms of political, economic, and social life. It rejects the "cultural colonization" of the Islamic world by Western influence. It believes that the Islamic code of conduct as expressed in sharia should be the law of the land. Bourguiba's economic policies have been criticized as overly dependent on tourism from the West and on employment of Tunisian workers abroad. The MTI demands greater self-sufficiency for Tunisia by modernizing and raising the productivity of agriculture and by turning industry to the production of goods for domestic needs.

In June 1985 the MTI issued a declaration that was interpreted as an effort to help establish it as a popular movement and to make common cause with other opposition forces. The declaration urged respect for the independence of mass organizations (including the UGTT labor federation), a general amnesty for all those jailed or exiled for their views and political affiliations, a guarantee of the rights of expression and association, and an end to preventive detention and other violations of civil liberties. It was also announced that the MTI would be headed by a Political Bureau of five members including, in addition to Ghanouchi and Mourou, Hammadi al Jibali (political relations and organizations), Habib al

Lawz (Islamic religion and culture), and Habib al Suwaysi (information).

Leaders of the MTI attributed government repression of them to fear of MTI popularity if tested in an election. Although judged to be the most moderate and politically sophisticated of the Islamic groups, the MTI seemed saddled with contradictions, calling for progressiveness and political liberalization when the implications of this demand for a society guided by Islamic principles could only bring new restrictions to political life. A militant wing of the party was openly antidemocratic, standing for an authoritarian Islamic regime.

A smaller and less tolerant group, the Islamic Liberation Party, reportedly originated as a secret society in the Federal Republic of Germany (West Germany) but decided in early 1983 to mount a recruiting campaign inside Tunisia. Its efforts to gain a foothold among the Tunisian military resulted in the trial of 30 individuals before a military court in August of that year. The party has called for a return to the Islamic caliphate, embracing the concept of a nation rallying under a single leader embodying both spiritual and political authority.

Although the Islamic renewal had made the most headway among students, it had also gained a foothold in some labor unions and among the professions and the intelligentsia. Its message reached many others who felt that a strong Islamic orientation—if moderate and enlightened—could be a factor for stability and morality. In late 1984 a number of members of the Chamber of Deputies urged the government to convert compensation payments to imams into fixed government salaries and to fund education for the imams on the premise that these changes would qualify them to exercise greater freedom from official control in their choice of sermons. One deputy called for a prohibition on gambling, the sale of alcoholic beverages, and the adoption of Friday as the day of rest. In reply, a deputy representing the government claimed credit for actions that had already been taken to upgrade the status of the imams and to construct more mosques.

Other Groups

Other political organizations have been launched from time to time purporting to represent a range of viewpoints from Arab nationalism to various forms of socialism. None is known to have attracted any significant following. One of these, the National Arab Rally (Rassemblement National Arabe) was considered to be little more than a front for Libyan political doctrines and slogans. Its leader, Bechir Essid, was sentenced in 1984 to a two-year jail term for slandering the head of state and members of the government. Twelve members of the Popular Revolutionary Movement (Mouvement Populaire Révolutionnaire) connected with Syrian-supported dissidents of the Palestine Liberation Organization (PLO) were jailed in 1983 for planning attacks against Saudi Arabian and United States installations in Tunisia. The Progressive Socialist Rally (Rassemblement Socialiste Progressiste), formed in 1984 by Ahmed Neguib Chabi, framed its appeal in terms of radical social reform, drawing on Marxist principles.

Interest Groups

Several national groups having a semiofficial status have been created to represent the interests of various segments of Tunisian society. Most of the organizations were established during the independence struggle to contribute to the resistance effort against the French. Although autonomous from the PSD, these organizations were expected to act with the interests of the entire nation in mind and to contribute to national goals of social progress and economic modernization. Organized labor had been close to the PSD since the preindependence period and at times was regarded as one of the pillars of the Destourian movement. But by the mid-1980s the government was in bitter contention with the leaders of the labor unions and seemingly was determined to curb labor's efforts to become a separate political force. Students and youth tended to be among those most easily aroused to react to political events and had repeatedly been a source of social disruption. The official student organization was moribund, leaving most of the politically active students divided into antagonistic Islamic and leftist camps.

Other national organizations were concerned with women, traders, makers of handicrafts, and professional groups. They were not in the habit of openly confronting the government in the pursuit of their interests. The Tunisian Federation of Industry, Commerce, and Handicrafts (Union Tunisienne de l'Industrie, du Commerce, et de l'Artisanat—UTICA) represented employers in negotiations over wages and other conditions of work in pacts among government, industry, and labor that embodied long-range economic goals. The farmers' union, the National Union of Tunisian Farmers (Union Nationale des Agriculteurs Tunisiens—UNAT), has also been enlisted as a signatory in such social pacts.

The Tunisian League of Human Rights has succeeded in maintaining its independence from the government and has met regularly with government officials to discuss arrests and detention procedures. It has chapters in a number of cities and publishes a bulletin recording claimed abuses of human rights.

The Tunisian military has been called upon to deal with internal disturbances in situations where the police have proved to be inadequate. The military is unusual in the Arab world, however, in never having acted except as an arm of the civilian state. The buildup of the armed forces in reaction to the perceived threat from Libya and the need for help in dealing with recurrent civil unrest have projected the military into a more prominent role. The possibility of involvement by politically conscious younger officers in a succession crisis or during severe domestic turmoil no longer seemed entirely implausible.

Organized Labor

In 1946 Ferhat Hached, who later became a national martyr in the fight for independence, led other Tunisian members out of the communist-dominated French General Confederation of Workers (Confédération Générale des Travailleurs—CGT) to form the UGTT. After its rift with the French group, the UGTT joined the noncommunist International Confederation of Free Trade Unions (ICFTU) and established links with Western labor federations, including the American labor movement. The UGTT "froze" its relations with the ICFTU between 1982 and 1984 over the international body's failure to adopt a position of recognizing the Palestinians' right to self-determination after the Israeli invasion of Lebanon.

The UGTT had been strongly identified with Tunisia's independence struggle, serving as a front for Bourguiba's supporters when the Neo-Destour Party was banned by the French in the early 1950s. After Hached's assassination in 1952 by French colonial terrorists, Ben Salah aligned the UGTT with strongly socialist economic policies. Although later forced from the UGTT leadership, Ben Salah was able to see his views prevail for a period in the 1960s when he was the architect of the country's economic policies as secretary of state for planning and finance. The official relationship between the UGTT and the government and party remained cooperative into the early 1970s even though the UGTT, under the direction of Habib Achour, made greater efforts to chart an independent course. Strikes, almost nonexistent until 1970, increased in number and duration between 1974 and 1977, reflecting growing estrangement with the government. Violence broke out in January 1978 when the UGTT called a general strike in protest over the arrest of a union leader and alleged that attacks against union offices in several towns had been officially inspired. Many people were killed and injured as workers clashed with the police, the army, and the PSD militia. Among the hundreds of persons arrested were Achour and nearly all of the 13 members of the UGTT Executive Board.

With the exception of Achour, who was kept under house arrest, the labor leaders were gradually released. At a special congress of the UGTT in May 1981, a new Executive Board was elected, 11 of whose members had served on the pre-1978 board, with Taieb Baccouche as secretary general. Baccouche, regarded as being to the left of Achour, was the first head of the UGTT who was not a member of the PSD. Pardoned by Bourguiba on the eve of the national election in November 1981, Achour was immediately elected to the newly created post of UGTT president. Baccouche and Achour shared the leadership until Achour engineered his own election as secretary general and the election of a new Executive Board supportive of his policies at a UGTT congress in December 1984. The post of president was abolished. Baccouche, given responsibility for the weekly *Ach Chaab,* was dismissed in 1985 for articles of a leftist and anti-Muslim slant deemed likely to invite official retribution. He apparently kept his post as deputy secretary general of the UGTT.

The decision by the UGTT to participate with the PSD in a national front in the election of 1981, reached by a narrow majority, remained a source of dissension within the federation. The 27 members of the UGTT elected as deputies to the Chamber of Deputies included eight members of the Executive Board. In debating economic and social issues, the UGTT members found themselves in an awkward position when they were expected to support even those government programs that had been opposed by the federation.

A new labor body, the Tunisian National Workers' Union (Union Nationale des Travailleurs Tunisiens—UNTT), was founded in February 1984 by Abdelaziz Bouraoui and six other members of the UGTT Executive Board who had previously been expelled as a result of internal disagreements. The dissidents had been associated with the controversial decision to join the PSD in a common election front. They accused Achour of conducting the UGTT's affairs in an increasingly authoritarian manner after his release from arrest. The UNTT was in turn suspected of having been formed with the encouragement of the government in an effort to divide the labor movement. The UNTT subsequently cooperated with the

PSD in the 1985 communal elections, which were boycotted by the opposition parties as well as the UGTT.

In 1985 unionized workers represented only about 17 percent of the total work force. They were concentrated in the public sector, state-owned industries, and some of the larger private enterprises. Although agriculture absorbed 32 percent of the labor force, only 2 percent—those employed by large, state-owned cooperatives—were unionized. Before the formation of the UNTT, the UGTT claimed a membership of 400,000. The UNTT was reported to have 55,000 members in 1985, all from unions that had disaffiliated from the UGTT.

The government had traditionally been willing to ensure that workers would share in economic growth by steadily raising wages. Faced in the mid-1980s with converging strains on the economy, however, the government was unwilling to lift its wage freeze in spite of mounting inflation. The UGTT threatened general strike action in 1985 if its demands for halting the decline in real wages were not met. The government reacted by withdrawing the checkoff of union dues at the source—a serious threat to union finances—and the right to hold union meetings in the workplace. The labor newspaper was also banned for six months (see Politics and the Information Media, this ch.).

The struggle escalated later in the year when Mzali, abetted by the government media, embarked on a fierce campaign to bring about Achour's downfall. Achour was subjected to house arrest on charges of mismanagement, diversion of union funds, and sympathy for Libya. In December 1985 he and other union officials were sentenced to prison. Sadok Alouch was installed as the new secretary general. The government apparently had curbed the federations autonomy and had parried the threat of a new labor party sponsored by the UGTT.

Students

University campuses have been the scenes of repeated protests, strikes, and violence between students of the Islamic movement and Marxists. The majority of students are not aligned with either group and are generally not politically active, although they have been involved in demonstrations against policies imposed by educational authorities. The General Union of Tunisian Students (Union Générale des Étudiants Tunisiens—UGET), autonomous but historically connected to the PDS, had become moribund after the government removed its elected leaders during the 1970s. The new Mzali government had committed itself in 1981 to the revival of the student movement by permitting a national student congress and promised that it would recognize whatever leadership was properly elected. The turmoil created by extremists from the Islamic and leftist factions had, however, frustrated efforts to launch a new movement that would be more representative of the student population.

Founded clandestinely by the Neo-Destour Party in 1952, the UGET made significant contributions to the fight against the French. UGET strongly supported Bourguiba's domestic social and economic policies but criticized him for an approach deemed too conservative on some foreign policy matters. The relevance of the UGET as an instrument for focusing attention on student political concerns faded after 1971 when the government replaced the UGET executive bureau, elected by the student organization's national congress, with a pro-PSD faction. By the mid-1970s the contest for control of the UGET was overshadowed by mounting student dissatisfaction with the government over a wide range of issues.

Student unrest and disturbances, resulting in the suspension of classes, became virtually an annual phenomenon after 1978. Although in many cases student agitation was directed at specific grievances—the use of government "monitors" in classrooms, examination practices, or the detention of student activists—it also was a manifestation of alienation from what was perceived as an outmoded political and social system dominated by a declining Bourguiba. In 1982 Mzali maintained that, of a university student body of 35,000, only 5,000 were interested in politics. Most of these, he said, were Islamists inspired by Iran's Khomeini. Mzali attributed the recurrent unrest to a situation in which more and more young people were being offered an opportunity for education at the same time that the faltering economy was unable to absorb new graduates in meaningful employment.

Since 1981, student politics have crystallized into a power struggle between the Islamic militants and the Marxists. Clashes between the two groups practically paralyzed the university faculties and institutes between November 1984 and March 1985. To alleviate the crisis, the authorities endorsed the convocation of a general congress of students, a proposal both the leftists and the Muslims favored in principle. Differences over the specifics of launching such a congress and over the creation of a new student union prevented its realization. In 1984 a renewed effort was made to resuscitate the student wing of the PSD by forming party cells at each university faculty. Student moderates, however, were discouraged from attempting to meet and express themselves out of fear of encountering violence from the Islamists. In 1985 the PSD student movement issued an invitation to the non-Destourians to combine and form a new body to negotiate differences with the administration, but it was received negatively by the other factions, and physical attacks on the PSD students by the Muslims were renewed.

A troublesome source of potential destabilization, the student element had repeatedly proved difficult for the government to negotiate with or to control. Although bitterly divided ideologically, the students could at times join forces with other dissidents to protest social conditions or economic injustice. Many of the students supporting the MTI were not eager for a return to the Islamic orthodoxy but simply regarded the movement as the best organized opposition force to a regime that no longer commanded their allegiance.

Women

The emancipation of women has always been extremely important to Bourguiba. Legal equality between the sexes has been vigorously upheld by the Tunisian government in spite of Islamist pressures for a much more restrictive role for women. The Code of Personal Status of 1956, considered to be virtually unique in the Arab world, did much to place women on an equal social and economic level with men. Rights similar to those found in Western legal systems permit women to initiate divorce actions, ban the practice of polygyny, and protect women in child custody cases. Inheritance procedures remain more restrictive (see The Individual, the Family, and the Sexes, ch. 2).

Women are encouraged to vote and participate in the political process. Many women are in the labor force, and more and more are found in administrative positions or are teachers, lawyers, physicians, and civil servants. Relatively few are active in political life or hold high government office. The restraints of Arab and Islamic traditions, especially in rural areas, have inhibited women from insisting on the full expression of their legal rights.

Of 40,000 students enrolled in the 41 faculties and institutes of the University of Tunis in 1984, about 40 percent were women. Among the 132 deputies elected to the Chamber of Deputies in 1981, seven were women. In 1984, there were 478 women among the 3,540 PSD candidates elected to communal councils on the single electoral slate. A small number of female jurists are active among the country's magistrates. The first two women to sit in the Tunisian cabinet since independence were named by Bourguiba in 1983. Fathia Mzali, wife of the prime minister, was appointed minister of family and women's advancement. She had been politically active as a deputy and a member of the Political Bureau of the PSD. The other new female cabinet member was Souad Yacoubi, dean of the Faculty of Medicine at Sousse, who was designated minister of public health.

The National Union of Tunisian Women (Union Nationale des Femmes Tunisiennes—UNFT), founded in 1956, offers through its local branches instruction in literacy, civics, hygiene, family planning, sewing, and other courses. It also helps to operate nurseries, and it participates in public health campaigns. The UNFT has less of a political character than the UGTT or the student movements. Fathia Mzali was president of the UNFT at the time she was nominated to the cabinet.

Politics and the Information Media

In spite of strict supervision imposed by the government, the communications media have been an important and accepted feature of political life in Tunisia. As part of the liberalizing trend under Mzali, several opposition journals were licensed in 1980, and scrutiny of the press was relaxed. The tolerance shown for editorial independence proved to be only transitory, however. Especially after the strikes and demonstrations of January 1984, seizures and suspensions had a crippling effect on the opposition publications. Western and Arabic-language journals published abroad continued to be available, although those issues critical of the Tunisian leadership were likely to be seized. Radio and television stations were operated or controlled by the government. Television was the primary source of news and played a major role in forming the political opinions of most Tunisians.

Newspapers

During the period of the French protectorate (1881–1956), the press was dominated by French-owned, French-language newspapers. Bourguiba wrote for two years for the organ of the old Destour Party, *La Voix du Tunisien*, until in 1930 he founded his own newspaper, *L'Action Tunisienne*. Before the French suspended all nationalist publications in 1933, Bourguiba used his journal to appeal for solidarity among all Tunisians—not just among Muslims but also among Jews and poorer European workers.

After independence a press regulation law was passed requiring official approval for all domestic and foreign journals. In 1955

L'Action appeared as the organ of the Neo-Destourian Party. The independent *La Presse*, politically neutral but leaning toward the French administration, was suspended and reappeared as *La Presse de Tunisie*, a progovernment newspaper published by the official news agency, Tunis-Afrique Press (TAP). Another daily, *Al Amal*, was the Arabic-language counter part to *L'Action*. These three officially sponsored publications plus two independent newspapers constituted five of the six dailies published in 1985 (see table 11, Appendix).

Efforts to establish a genuine opposition press met with little success under the rigid stewardship of Prime Minister Nouira. The weekly *Ar Rai*, linked with the dissidents of the MDS, obtained permission to publish in late 1978, but editor Hasib Ben Ammar was among those who abandoned the movement when the decision was made to convert it into an opposition party. In 1980 the MDS weekly organs, *Al Mostakbal* and *L'Avenir*, were authorized, although the party itself had not yet been legalized. When permission was granted for the communist PCT to resume its activity in 1981, its weekly *Al Tariq Al Jadid* was also licensed to publish.

A press code adopted in 1975 required that all persons managing or financing publications in the country be Tunisian citizens. The code reaffirmed freedom of the press but prescribed limits where necessary "to protect society from anything injurious to tranquillity, security, and public order," as well as to "protect the state and the constituted agencies of government against anything liable to cause foreign or domestic disorders." Direct attacks against the president, senior members of the government, or the structure of the state were also forbidden. Formal censorship has not been practiced, but editors have generally been able to sense what would be tolerated. Criticism by the opposition press has been constant but has been expressed in guarded terms. Suspensions, usually of three to six months, have nevertheless been frequently imposed, sometimes for seemingly trivial lapses. The UGTT journal, *Ach Chaab*, was suspended for six months just after it began to appear on a daily basis in July 1985, ostensibly because it had printed untrue statements predicting a shuffle of regional governors found to be incompetent. It was believed, however, that the real reason for the government's curb was its sensitivity to an editorial that attacked an announced rise in bread prices. Among 10 suspensions or seizures recorded in 1984, the independent weekly *Réalités* was banned for six months for printing excerpts of an interview with an exiled politician. Even the PSD magazine, *Dialogue*, was suspended for three months, reportedly because it gave less prominence to Bourguiba's meeting with Algerian president Chadli Bendjedid than to Mzali's visit to India.

The government has also been in a position to influence the press by offering subsidies in the form of official advertising or by bringing pressure to bear against would-be advertisers in opposition journals. The government has maintained further control through its news agency, TAP, which edits news items supplied to the domestic media. No reporter may legally function without a press card issued by the Tunisian journalists' union. Although affiliated with the PSD, the union has protested against the suspension of newspapers and the detention and imprisonment of journalists. It has urged the government to amend the Press Code to make it more democratic in accordance with constitutional provisions on freedom of opinion, thought, and expression.

Because the two independent dailies, *As Sabah* and *Le Temps*, have observed official guidelines, their content has differed little from that of the three government-sponsored dailies. Government policy statements and Bourguiba's pronouncements or public appearances received generous treatment in all newspapers. After Bourguiba's recovery in 1985 from a heart attack suffered the previous year, photographs of him receiving visitors in his office or taking walks were featured on almost a daily basis. The unofficial publications have been somewhat more popular because they have reported more details and have expressed opinions more openly. Government newspapers have tended to adopt a friendly tone toward the United States—with the exception of Washington's policies on the Middle East and the Third World generally. The independent dailies, however, have made the United States a target of severe criticism whenever an opportunity presented itself.

The most influential foreign journal, especially among intellectuals and senior officials, has been the Paris newspaper *Le Monde*. Other French publications, as well as Arabic-language journals published in London and Paris, have also been widely read. The weekly *Jeune Afrique*, edited by Tunisian expatriates in Paris, has remained popular, especially among students. Its coverage of Tunisian events has frequently resulted in individual issues being seized and, in late 1984, an outright ban for three months.

Radio and Television

The broadcast media have been a state monopoly since independence, administered by a public corporation, Tunisian Radio and Television (Radiodiffusion Télévision Tunisienne—RTT), under the Ministry of Information. RTT operated radio stations broadcasting in Arabic and French from Tunis, as well as regional stations in Sfax and Monastir. It was estimated in 1984 that there were about 1.5 million radio receivers in the country.

Television had overtaken radio in popularity and was considered the most influential medium of information. In 1985 there were over 500,000 television receivers, of which 50,000 were located in community centers in villages and settlements. Virtually everyone in the country had access to television. According to a public opinion poll, 62 percent of the Tunisian population relied on television for their news and information used in forming their opinions.

When younger, Bourguiba made effective use of television and radio to explain his policies and maintain personal touch with the public. After his health declined, his earlier talks were widely rebroadcast as reminders of his importance to the nation's development and as lessons in Destourianism.

Three television channels were available in 1985. The Arabic-language channel operated in the late afternoon and evening for 47 hours per week. A second channel, which began broadcasting in mid-1983, had 90 percent of its programming in French and went on the air daily at 8:30 P.M. Financed by France, this channel carried a selection of programs from French, Belgian, and Swiss television. Protests that the second channel would have a negative effect on the Arabic-Islamic personality of the country were rejected by the minister of information, who reasoned that the "maturity of the Tunisian people and their attachment to Arab-Islamic authenticity" had protected them against French cultural domination in spite of 75 years of colonization. The third televison channel transmitted Italian and Eurovision programs by means of a microwave relay station built before RTT had its own television facilities.

Foreign Relations

In the conduct of its foreign affairs, Tunisian's primary concern is with the management of its manifold ties—political, economic, and social—with its neighbors of North Africa. Its relations with Algeria and Libya, the two stronger contiguous states, have alternated between periods of tension and periods of relative harmony. During the 1980s relations with Algeria have improved dramatically, but relations with Libya have been buffeted by recurrent crises.

In the past, Tunisia's moderation on the emotional issues of the Middle East at times caused misunderstandings with the more radical Arab countries. More recently, the republic's foreign policy has largely corresponded to the mainstream Arab position, emphasizing the need for a peaceful resolution of the Palestinian problem as part of an overall Arab-Israeli settlement.

Under Bourguiba, Tunisia has generally aligned itself with the West on major East-West questions and has played a constructive role in debates in Third World and Arab forums. The president has cultivated ties with the United States and has cooperated with Washington in efforts to find peace in the Middle East. United States economic and technical aid has accounted for one-third of total foreign economic assistance received by Tunisia. Sharp disputes with France in the early years of Tunisian independence were bridged during the 1970s. Bourguiba's affinity for France contributed to the continuing importance of that country in cultural and educational matters. France was also the North African republic's primary trading partner and the leading source of its tourist revenue.

Its many ties to the West notwithstanding, Tunisia has remained an active member of the major organizations of the Arab, Muslim, and African worlds. It has participated in the Nonaligned Movement and its economic counterpart, the Group of 77 (see Glossary); the League of Arab States (Arab League); and the Organization of the Islamic Conference. Tunisia was a founding member of the Organization of African Unity (OAU) in 1963 and associated itself with other moderate French-speaking African states when disputes threatened the cohesion of the OAU in the early 1980s.

Maghribi Affairs

The ideal of a unified Maghrib recalls the splendors of the past, and all of the states of northwest Africa pay homage to it. In spite of the similarity of societies, language, religion, and history, no meaningful steps have been taken in the postcolonial era to advance the unity to which each country subscribes.

In its Constitution, Tunisia proclaims that it "is part of the Great Arab Maghrib and shall work for its unity within the framework of common interests." Indeed, Tunisia has consistently supported initiatives to expand coooperation among the countries of the Maghrib. Tunisia was a founding member of the Maghrib Permanent Consultative Committee, established at Tunis in 1964 with the aim of eventually creating a Maghribi economic community. Bilateral difference prevented any real progress toward this goal, although a rudimentary secretariat was still in place in 1985. Various efforts have succeeded in reducing some of the formal barriers to trade among Maghribi countries, and joint projects have been initiated; but the prospects for much economic integration appear limited. Inter-Maghribi trade remained at a low level owing in part to the absence of complementary products. To a large extent the countries of the region saw one another as commercial rivals marketing similar agricultural products in Western Europe.

A preoccupying factor for Tunisia has been the need to neutralize periodic threats to its security from the unpredictable Libyan leader, Muammar al Qadhaafi, either by finding common grounds for cooperation with him or by seeking protection through alignments with other powers. It previously feared efforts on the part of Algeria to destabilize the Bourguiba regime, but since 1980 Tunisia and Algeria have gradually succeeded in harmonizing their political and economic relations, culminating in a joint security treaty in 1983. Division of the Maghrib into rival camps was formalized the following year when Morocco and Libya announced that they had secretly entered into an alliance. Officially, Tunisia adopted a positive tone regarding the new Morocco-Libya "union," professing to accept it as a step toward rapprochement and unity among Maghribi members. In reality, however, Tunisian officials were made uneasy by a pact that seemed directed against their friendly neighbor, Algeria, and that seemed to place the conservative Moroccan King Hassan's seal of approval on Qadhaafi's adventurism. During the first part of 1985, Tunisian diplomacy was directed at convening a summit meeting of the Maghribi heads of state to prevent the new alignments from hardening into separate power blocs and to rekindle the unification movement. But Qadhaafi's political unreliability and differences centering on Morocco's claim to sovereignty over the Western Sahara complicated all such initiatives designed to relieve tensions in the region.

Algeria

Tunisia contributed material support to the Algerian war of independence against the French (1954–61) and permitted the provisional Algerian government and its armed forces to operate on Tunisian soil. Diplomatic relations were briefly severed after Algeria was accused of involvement in the December 1962 plot to assassinate Bourguiba. Despite the fact that both countries gave sanctuary to the opponents of each other's regimes during the 1960s, political relations were normal, and economic ties were reinforced, notably in the energy sector. A long-standing disagreement over their mutual border was resolved in 1970, at which time a treaty of friendship and good neighborliness was also concluded, providing for a joint Algerian-Tunisian commission to meet annually.

Misunderstandings arose in 1974 after Tunisia signed an accord—quickly renounced—for a merger with Libya and again in 1980 when a group of Tunisian insurgents who were trained in Libya crossed Algerian territory in an unsuccessful attack against the city of Gafsa. The Algerian government denied any part, maintaining that local Algerian officials had acted on their own in facilitating the transit. In spite of its suspicions of higher-level complicity, Tunis chose to accept this explanation.

During the visit of Mzali to Algiers in September 1980 shortly after being named prime minister, the two neighbors affirmed their intent to give new impetus to their relationship. It was agreed that the two heads of government would meet every six months; that the joint commission, which had not come together for five years, would be revived; and that a number of jointly agreed upon projects and forms of cooperation that had not materialized would be relaunched.

The dramatic improvement in relations between the two countries was cemented in 1983 by a 20-year treaty of friendship and concord. Although widely interpreted as a precaution against the Libyan threat, this security pact was to remain open for other Maghribi states to join and was represented by its two signatories as a suitable framework for regional unity. Mauritania endorsed the treaty later in the same year. The three countries were pledged to respect one another's territorial integrity, to avoid resorting to force in settling differences, to reject alliances or coalitions hostile to any of them, and to deter activities by any group on their soil that threatened the security of another or that sought to change its government by violent means.

Several new forms of economic collaboration, including joint projects for the manufacture of cement and diesel engines, were subsequently announced by Algeria and Tunisia. Working groups were studying the joint manufacture of chemical fertilizers, tires, and trucks. Apartment construction in Algeria's border areas by Tunisian firms was foreseen. A pipeline through which Algerian natural gas flows to Italy across Tunisian territory and beneath the Mediterranean Sea was inaugurated in 1983.

Libya

Libya has often been a troublesome neighbor, especially since 1974, when a projected union between the two countries was aborted by Tunisia. The impulsive Qadhaafi has repeatedly sought to inject himself into the internal politics of Tunisia. It has been feared that should Tunisia become embroiled in a dispute over the succession to Bourguiba, Qadhaafi might well exploit the situation as a pretext to intervene. The Libyan-supported insurgent attack at Gafsa and the presence of about 2,000 Tunisian dissidents in Libyan training camps during the early 1980s were viewed as evidence of Qadhaafi's capacity for stirring unrest. In addition to its vastly greater military power, Libya also has held important economic cards. The two countries have staked competing claims to an oil-rich sector of the Gulf of Gabès. Repatriated earnings of Tunisian migrant workers in Libya have provided needed incomes for several hundred thousand of their dependents remaining in Tunisia.

In January 1974 Bourguiba surprisingly agreed to a merger with Libya in spite of the fact that only a year earlier he had rejected such an idea as unrealistic and had chided Qadhaafi for his youth and inexperience in suggesting it. Prime Minister Nouira, out of the country at the time, quickly returned home and apparently prevailed upon Bourguiba to retract his acceptance. Foreign Minister Mohamed Masmoudi, who was thought primarily responsible for the unity plan, was dismissed. In 1984 Masmoudi briefly became a renewed source of contention between the two countries when he accepted the post of Libyan permanent representative to the United Nations (UN). Threatened under a special law with the loss of his Tunisian citizenship, he relinquished the Libyan appointment.

The question of continental shelf oil reserves provoked another dispute with Libya. Eventually the two countries agreed to submit their cases to the International Court of Justice in The Hague, whose judgment on a line of demarcation in February 1982 favored Libya. The Court rejected Tunisia's plea that its relative poverty in oil and gas resources was a relevant factor. As of 1985 a treaty accepting the court's suggested boundary had not been concluded. The proposed delimitation left enough ambiguity to enable Tunisia to claim rights to exploit significant fields of oil and gas.

The attack on Gafsa in 1980, although mounted from Algerian territory, brought relations to a new low. Members of the captured raiding party confessed that the plot had been planned and organized in Libya on the initiative of the Libyan government, which had recruited the group from Tunisian migrant workers. Tunisia addressed complaints against Libya's role to both the Arab League and the OAU. Neither body specifically condemned Libya but offered mediation facilities to help normalize relations. Tensions eased somewhat after Mzali succeeded Nouira as prime minister; the Libyans had considered Nouira as hostile to them since Tunisia's reversal on the merger plan.

A further stage of reconciliation was reached in January 1981 when, during a visit to Tunis by the Libyan secretary of state for foreign affairs, agreement was reached on a three-stage program for improving relations. These stages included the resumption of diplomatic relations, which had been suspended over the Gafsa raid; the examination of possibilities for widespread economic cooperation; and the establishment of a joint commission to study political coooperation and the opening of borders. A cooperation agreement signed during Qadhaafi's visit to Tunis in February 1982 held out the promise of a wide-ranging partnership in industrial and financial activity, the linkage of road networks and an electric power grid, the abolition of tariffs and entry visas, and the adoption of common customs procedures. A supreme joint commission, composed of members of the Tunisian Council of Ministers and the Libyan General People's Council, held three sessions between March 1982 and December 1984.

In spite of the improved atmosphere for economic collaboration, several minor border incidents and continued sniping at Bourguiba in the Libyan press (described as an "elderly marionette in the hands of the Americans") continued to plague political relations. In a joint security committee, Libyan officials called upon Tunisia to expel anti-Qadhaafi Libyans. Tunisian officials, in turn, wanted Libya to close its training camps for dissident Tunisians. Tensions flared in August 1985 when Libya carried out the sudden deportation of some 30,000 migrant workers. The number of Tunisians working in Libya had gradually fallen from a peak of 200,000 in the mid-1970s to less than 25,000 by December 1985 as the result of an austerity program and a drop in oil revenues. The Libyans made half-hearted attempts to justify their 1985 eviction on economic grounds, but the brusque and harsh way in which it was carried out served to remind Tunisians of Qadhaafi's capacity for mischiefmaking. In retaliation, Tunisia severed diplomatic relations and expelled several hundred Libyan officials.

Morocco

Tunisian-Moroccan relations have rarely been disturbed by serious differences. Both countries have a tradition of friendship with the West, share similar views on major international issues, and are among the more moderate Arab voices on relations with Israel and the problem of the Palestinian Arabs. Tunisia refrained from openly criticizing Morocco's 1984 alliance with Libya, directing its efforts to the avoidance of further polarization in the Maghrib that could inflame the rivalry between Morocco and Algeria. The Moroccan-Libyan "union" did introduce a potentially complicating dimension to the relationship. In the event of an open clash between Libya and Tunisia, Morocco was committed under the terms of the alliance to stand by Libya. In reality, such an eventuality seemed highly improbable.

On the primary matter of contention among the Maghribi countries—Morocco's annexation of the Western Sahara—Tunisia had originally favored partition between Morocco and Mauritania. This placed the government in Tunis at odds with Algiers, which backed the anti-Moroccan independence movement that in 1976 declared itself the Saharan Arab Democratic Republic (SADR). Tunisia's Saharan foreign policy gradually shifted to one of strict neutrality and support for a referendum by the Saharawi people (residents of the Western Sahara) on self-determination. It joined with other members of the OAU, mostly moderate French-speaking states, to block Algeria's efforts in 1982 and 1983 to gain recognition for a SADR delegation at OAU summit meetings. In 1984, however, Tunisia did not oppose the near-unanimous vote for seating the SADR, which precipitated Morocco's withdrawal from the OAU.

Other Arab Countries

During the early years of its independence, Tunisia did not place high priority on its relations with the eastern Arab countries, whose disputes and preoccupations had little to do with the problems facing the new republic. It did not join the Arab League until 1958, and Tunisia boycotted its meetings between 1958 and 1961 because of differences with the Egyptian leader, Gamal Abdul Nasser. Tunisia generally allied itself with the conservative Arab oil states—first against Nasser's domination of the league and later against the radical policies of some of the organization's other members. Bourguiba adopted a relatively moderate position over the Arab-Israeli conflict. He advocated acceptance of the 1947 UN resolution that sanctioned the partition of the area, then called Palestine, into independent Arab and Jewish states as the basis for a negotiated settlement. His stand aroused ill-feeling among other Arab states, but differences were resolved with the outbreak of the Arab-Israeli June 1967 War. Tunisia organized a military expeditionary force, which did not see action, however, because of the brevity of the war. A small military contingent and matériel assistance were contributed to the Arab cause in the October 1973 War. Bourguiba's commitment to an eventual negotiated settlement based on the 1947 UN resolution remained unchanged by the two conflicts.

The gradual reconciliation between Tunisia's views on the Middle East and those of other Arab states made it possible for the headquarters of the Arab League to be transferred from Cairo to Tunis when Egypt was ostracized as a result of its peace treaty with Israel in 1978. A Tunisian, Chadli Klibi, was appointed secretary general of the league and was reelected for a second five-year term in 1984. The Organization of the Islamic Conference, a grouping of 45 Arab and non-Arab Muslim states, has had as its secretary general since 1979 another Tunisian, Habib Chatti.

The Tunisian leadership was active in the formulation of the peace plan at an Arab summit meeting at Fès, Morocco, in September 1982. The plan, which called for Israeli withdrawal from the territories occupied after the 1967 war and the dismantling of Israeli West Bank settlements seemed consistent with Bourguiba's long-held position, although it did not promise formal recognition of the state of Israel.

The Israeli invasion of Lebanon in 1982 was strongly criticized by Tunisia, as was United States aid to Israel, which was viewed as having made the Israeli attack possible. When the PLO forces were obliged to evacuate Beirut, their leader, Yasir Arafat, was permitted to shift his headquarters to Tunis. The move helped Tunisia's standing with other Arab nations but was later to entangle it more directly in Middle Eastern politics. In 1985 about 500 PLO officials and their families, as well as representatives of other Palestinian mass organizations, were lodged in various suburbs of Tunis. Most of the 1,000 or so PLO combatants who had been evacuated with Arafat had drifted back to Lebanon or Syria.

Tunisia was critical of Egypt's confrontation policy toward Israel during the late 1950s and 1960s and of Nasser's ardent pan-Arabism and his friendly relations with the Soviet Union. Anwar al Sadat's accession to the presidency after Nasser's death in 1970 brought a marked improvement in relations. Sadat's peace initiative toward Israel, beginning in 1977, was, however, regarded by Tunis as a unilateral action damaging to Arab solidarity. Tunisia joined the Arab consensus in severing formal relations with Cairo and in suspending Egypt's membership in the Arab League in protest over the Camp David Agreements with Israel in 1978. In practice, normal contacts were maintained.

Tunisia has generally found itself in harmony with the policies of the more moderate nations of the Mashriq, or eastern Arab world. Disappointed in its efforts to expand trade and investment ties with Western Europe, Tunis had courted participation in its economic development plans by the oil states of the Persian Gulf, with which it has shared an aversion to Arab extremism. Loans and grants from Kuwait, the United Arab Emirates, and Saudi Arabia have contributed significantly to Tunisia's economic infrastructure, major industrial projects, and development of tourism. Tunis has also maintained cordial ties with Iraq. Without directly supporting Baghdad after its attack on Iran in 1981, Tunisia denounced Iran's conduct, called for nonintervention by other Arab states to prevent further division, and appealed for peace negotiations under the auspices of the Organization of the Islamic Conference.

France and the European Community

Tunisia has maintained extensive historical, cultural, and economic ties with Western Europe. France has been by far the most prominent among the European powers as a result of the two countries' long common experience and of Bourguiba's determination after independence that his country's Gallic cultural heritage should not be weakened. The two states shared several political objectives—a peaceful Mediterranean, pacification in the Middle East, and a desire to resolve regional differences in North Africa in order to concentrate on economic development.

During the early years of Tunisian independence, cooperation was hampered by a succession of disputes. Relations were briefly broken in 1958 in the aftermath of a border incident provoked by Tunisian efforts to aid Algeria in its war of independence against France. The 1961 crisis over continued French use of the military airfield at Bizerte again resulted in a rupture of relations. Tunisian nationalization of French-owned property in 1964 produced a new period of strain resulting in the cancellation of French economic aid (see Relations with France, ch. 1).

In 1972 Bourguiba visited France for the first time in his official capacity as president of Tunisia. When French president

Valéry Giscard d'Estaing reciprocated by coming to Tunis in 1976, the communiqué at the conclusion of his stay described relations between the two countries as "exemplary." Some of the warmth was dissipated after socialist François Mitterrand became president of France in 1981. During Mitterrand's official visit to Tunisia in October 1983, however, progress was made in resolving a number of outstanding problems. Agreement was reached on a method for speeding up the unblocking of nearly US$50 million in French assets that had been frozen more than 20 years earlier. Mitterrand reiterated assurance of the well-being and security of 214,000 Tunisian residents in France who had felt threatened by attacks from right-wing groups.

Although France extended no formal commitments to Tunisia, it had by its gestures implied a readiness to come to the aid of the existing government. As a reminder of France's capacity to intervene at short notice, three French warships hastily sailed from Toulon on a "routine maneuver" after the attacks on Gafsa in 1980. Emergency shipments of wheat and other foodstuffs were announced after the disturbances of January 1984. The visit by the French foreign minister, Roland Dumas, to Tunis in September 1985 at a time of tensions with Libya was interpreted as symbolizing French concern for Tunisia's security and territorial integrity.

France has long been Tunisia's leading trade partner, but efforts to correct a persistent imbalance in France's favor have not been successful. Economic aid, mostly in the form of long-term loans at subsidized interest rates, has financed major industrial projects and encouraged small and medium-sized enterprises. The responsibility for equipping and training the Tunisian army has also been assumed primarily by France. Cultural and technical cooperation has been extensive, taking the form of support for a number of schools providing French-language education, the loan of professors of science and mathematics, and the supply of television and radio programs.

Tunisia has been associated with the European Economic Community (EEC) since 1969, when an agreement was concluded granting the republic free access to the community for most of its industrial products and extending preferences for certain agricultural exports. A broader agreement, ratified in 1978, closely matched the terms of similar agreements with Morocco and Algeria. The trade provisions, which had already entered into force in 1976, extended free access to the EEC for Tunisian raw materials and industrial products, with the important exception of clothing and other textiles. Tariff reductions were also granted for Tunisia's main agricultural exports to the EEC—olive oil, wine, fruits, and vegetables—although the benefits were restrained by quotas, safe-guards, and restrictions to certain periods of the year. Two five-year economic aid packages amounting to US$117 million and US$111 million were allocated between 1976 and 1986. These were supplemented by bilateral aid from individual EEC members; in addition to France, West Germany was a substantial donor.

The trade balance between the EEC and Tunisia was strongly favorable to the EEC. In 1984 Tunisian imports valued at US$1.9 billion were far in excess of EEC imports from Tunisia amounting to US$1.2 billion. Petroleum products were the main sources of export earnings. To some extent the Tunisian trade deficit was offset by remittances from Tunisian workers in EEC countries and receipts from well over 1 million European tourists who have vacationed at Tunisian beach resorts each year. Although the West European market for Tunisian products was indispensable, the future of this trade was made uncertain by the accession of Spain and Portugal to full membership in the EEC at the close of 1985. This could endanger Tunisia's exports because their competing Mediterranean-type crops would benefit from more liberal trading rules within the EEC.

United States

Official relations between Tunisia and the United States have been maintained for nearly two centuries since the arrival of the first American consul in 1797. A treaty was negotiated in the same year dealing with commerce, tariffs, and protection against attacks or extortions by Tunisian corsairs. In return, gifts and naval supplies were promised to the bey. The United States was the first foreign country to recognize Tunisia upon its independence in 1956. The cordiality that has since prevailed between the two countries has rarely been disturbed. Beginning in 1946, Bourguiba has paid numerous visits to the United States and has met with most of the presidents who have held office since World War II.

Tunisia has never accepted the radical Third World view of the United States as an imperialist, neocolonialist power. Bourguiba once characterized the United States as "the country of liberty and of generous ideas." Tunisia was nearly alone among non-aligned nations in not condemning the American war effort in Southeast Asia, a policy it eventually reversed after 1969. Subsequent to the Israeli invasion of Lebanon in 1982, Bourguiba has repeatedly criticized Washington's policy of close military and political cooperation with Israel. Tunisians reacted angrily when the

President Habib Bourguiba, speaking at White House
ceremonies in June 1985, after welcoming remarks
by President Ronald Reagan (right)
Courtesy White House/Pete Souza

United States initially appeared to condone the Israeli bombing
attack on the PLO headquarters near Tunis in October 1985 in retaliation for a terrorist attack against Israeli tourists in Cyprus.
Bourguiba's official protest conveyed his "profound regret and
great astonishment" over Washington's position, which he said was
contrary to international law and the existing state of relations between the two countries. Subsequent statements and actions by
American officials helped to repair the breach, although popular
feeling against the United States remained high.

The United States has expressed admiration for Bourguiba's
political courage on Middle Eastern issues and appreciation for
Tunisia's moderating influence in the Arab League. Although the
two governments were not linked by security accords, President
Ronald Reagan said during Bourguiba's visit to Washington in

June 1985 that the United States "remains firmly committed to the sanctity of Tunisia's territorial integrity and to the principle of noninterference in its internal affairs."

Since first agreeing to provide economic and technical assistance to Tunisia in 1957, United States aid has amounted to nearly US$1 billion. Development aid was suspended in United States fiscal year (FY) 1981 because Tunisia's per capita income had risen to a point where this was no longer justified. In FY 1985 and FY 1986, however, economic support funds totaling about US$20 million were earmarked by the United States Congress in recognition of Tunisia's worsening economic situation and its importance as a moderating factor in the Middle East peace process. Most of these contributions were dedicated to agricultural loans for small farmers, technical training in both Tunisia and United States, and family planning. Additionally, proceeds from surplus grain provided under Public Law 480 (Food for Peace) were used for development of the private sector. The Peace Corps, which had been active in Tunisia since 1961, had approximately 100 volunteers in 1984 participating in rural development, vocational education, and public health projects.

Although there were no United States military facilities in Tunisia, vessels of the Sixth Fleet, including nuclear warships, were welcomed for port calls. The United States-Tunisian Joint Military Commission has met annually to discuss Tunisia's defense modernization needs and broader security questions. United States military aid, which until 1979 had been on a modest level averaging about US$8 million annually, rose steeply in the early 1980s to support Tunisian efforts to upgrade its armed forces' firepower and mobility (see Foreign Military Assistance, ch. 5).

The United States ranked second (after France) as a market for Tunisian products, imports of petroleum products predominating. Its 8-percent share of Tunisia's imports ranked it behind France, West Germany, and Italy. Among the leading products exported by the United States to Tunisia were cereals, soybean oil, industrial equipment, and chemicals and pharmaceuticals. In spite of efforts by both countries to encourage American capital, activity by United States investors was still limited in 1985.

Communist Countries

Tunisia has cultivated normal relations with the Soviet Union and the countries of Eastern Europe, entering into numerous commercial, technical, and cultural agreements. Nevertheless, its political and economic links with the communist states were of far less significance than its ties with the industrialized West.

Formal relations between Tunisia and the Soviet Union were not established until 1960. Moscow subsequently strongly backed Tunisia in the UN debates on the Bizerte crisis and supported the Tunisian demand for French evacuation of the military base there. During the 1970s Tunisia expressed uneasiness over the mounting Soviet involvement in Africa, notably in the Horn of Africa dispute and its activities in several other African countries. The Tunisian government joined in the condemnation voted by the UN General Assembly and by the Nonaligned Movement in early 1980 over the Soviet invasion of Afghanistan. Tunisia is the only Maghribi country that has never accepted Soviet military equipment or training personnel. It regularly permits Soviet naval vessels to make port calls, use port facilities, and repair ships at the Bizerte drydocks.

A trade protocol covering 1986–90 had as its target a total exchange of goods valued at US$250 million during the period, a figure that would represent a doubling of trade over the previous five-year period. The exchange heavily favored Soviet exports consisting of machinery, ammonia, sulfur, and lumber. Tunisia's trade with the Soviet Union and Eastern Europe combined accounted for less than 1 percent of its total exports in 1984 and only 4 percent of its imports. According to the United States Department of State, Soviet and East European personnel providing various technical services in Tunisia numbered 600 in 1981. In addition, these countries had accepted over 1,000 Tunisian students for professional training.

Tunisian relations with China have been conducted in a generally favorable climate, although limited to certain spheres of activity. The decision to form the Tunisian-Chinese Commission of Economic, Commercial, and Technical Cooperation in September 1983 seemed to herald a greater degree of interchange between the two countries. At the first session of the commission in 1984, it was announced that Chinese medical teams, which had been operating in a provincial hospital since 1975, would be augmented. In addition, a project was outlined to produce phosphoric acid and chemical fertilizer in China using resources and technology from Tunisia and financing from Kuwait. Previously, the most significant form of cooperation had been the construction of a 120-kilometer canal to convey water to the Cape Bon area, a five-year project completed in 1984 with a contribution of TD23 million (for value of the Tunisian dinar—see Glossary) from China plus the services of 850 Chinese personnel.

*   *   *

As a general work on Tunisia's political evolution from the colonial period to the mid-1970s, Wilfred Knapp's *North West Africa: A Political and Economic Survey* is useful. Subsequent developments are examined in briefer studies, such as the section of Tunisia in *Comparative Politics of North Africa* by John P. Entelis (1980) and the chapter dealing with sources of power in Tunisia in Russell A. Stone's *Political Elites in Arab North Africa*. Mark Tessler's "Tunisia at the Crossroads" is a short appraisal of the balance of political forces after the riots of 1984. A concise overview of Tunisia's politics and foreign relations in the context of United States interests in the Maghrib can be found in *North Africa: Regional Tensions and Strategic Concerns* by Richard B. Parker, a former United States ambassador to both Algeria and Morocco.

Tunisia's moderate and pragmatic approach in its diplomacy is viewed in Robert Santucci's article, "La politique étrangère de la Tunisie." The Islamic revival is the subject of numerous studies; a relatively current and accessible study is "The Islamist Challenge in Tunisia" by Susan E. Waltz. An account of Tunisia's constitutional and juridical development is contained in *An Introduction to Law in French-Speaking Africa, II: North Africa* by Jeswald W. Salacuse (1975). Tunisia's record in the area of civil and legal rights is appraised annually in the series, *Country Reports on Human Rights Practices*, produced by the United States Department of State for the United States Congress.

Contemporary Tunisian political events are the subject of regular commentaries in *Jeune Afrique* and are also treated frequently in *Le Monde, Africa Research Bulletin*, and *Marchés tropicaux et méditerranéens*. (For further information and complete citations, see Bibliography.)

Chapter 5. National Security

Monolithic ribat (fort) at Monastir

ALTHOUGH IT HAD LONG been regarded as the most peaceful and stable of the Maghribi countries, Tunisia faced a series of challenges in 1985 that could conceivably threaten the viability and effectiveness of the political system built up by President Habib Bourguiba. At the same time that the national leadership was encountering increased international tension, it was facing a growing challenge from organized domestic opponents. Its ability to contend with these problems was complicated by political uncertainty brought on by the advancing age and questionable health of Bourguiba, who had dominated the national leadership for three decades.

Domestic security was threatened by causes deeper than the problems of presidential succession. Widespread riots that grew out of the general strike in January 1978 gave observers their first indication that the national consensus behind the leadership and policies of Bourguiba and Destourian Socialist Party was not as strong as it had once been. Estrangement between the government and the labor movement and the growth of Islamist opposition continued in the 1980s and concerned government officials. To a degree, the emergence of a strong, political opposition reflected the relative openness of Tunisian society. It also indicated the existence of widespread dissatisfaction with the ruling Destourian Socialist Party, the pace of economic growth and development, high unemployment, official corruption, and the apparent rejection of Islamic values by some of the top national leaders. The fact that limited government reforms had not sufficiently ameliorated the causes of dissent was emphasized in January 1984 by rioting throughout the country that was triggered by an increase in the price of bread and other staples.

The republic's domestic difficulties have been compounded by problems with neighboring states. Tunisia is flanked by Algeria and Libya, two much larger and militarily stronger states whose militancy on Third World and Pan-Arab issues contrasted with Bourguiba's more pro-Western attitudes. During the early 1980s relations with Algeria began to improve, and a treaty of friendship and concord made the countries virtual allies. At the same time, however, Libya has repeatedly posed a potential threat to the Bourguiba government. By periodically threatening Tunisia with greater military strength and by instigating at least one armed rebellion in Tunisia, Libyan leader Colonel Muammar al Qadhaafi has proved himself a dangerous neighbor. Tunisian vulnerabilities were also demonstrated by the October 1985 air raid by Israeli warplanes on the headquarters of the Palestine Liberation Organization near Tunis.

Lacking any hope of absolute defense and preferring to invest in domestic programs, the Tunisian government had long been content to maintain a military establishment of modest size and limited combat effectiveness compared with those of its neighbors. By the 1980s, however, even Tunisia's relatively small armed forces become extremely costly. In 1985 the defense force consisted of a predominant army of 30,000 officers and men, a small navy of 2,600, and an air force and 2,500; collectively these forces were designated the Tunisian National Army. The military and a largely paramilitary police system were key elements in a defense strategy that called on the security forces to provide credible deterrence against external aggressive threats and, failing that, to deal effectively with minor incursions until assistance arrived from friendly states.

International Security Concerns

Since the nation's formal independence from France in 1956, the Tunisian government has generally attempted to concentrate its efforts and resources on domestic development while maintaining harmonious relations with its neighbors and other powers. Despite these efforts, Tunisia's location between Algeria and Libya—two states long characterized by their oil wealth and revolutionary ethos—its identity as an Arab and Islamic state, and the generally pro-Western, modernist tendencies of Bourguiba's leadership have prevented the country from avoiding regional disputes.

In the first years after independence the Bourguiba government was concerned with clashes and threats from France and Egypt (then known as the United Arab Republic). France, occupied with the revolution in Algeria, had kept a large number of troops on Tunisian soil after 1956. Intent on limiting Tunisia's role as a sanctuary for Algerian revolutionaries or as a conduit for material assistance, the French on several occasions used force against Tunisians who were giving support to the Algerians. The most notable example was the French bombing in 1958 of the Tunisian border village of Sakiet Sidi Youssef. Later, Tunisian attempts to end the French military presence by mobilizing civilian demonstrators and irregular militias resulted in some 1,000 Tunisian deaths in the so-called Battle of Bizerte in 1961 (see Relations with France, ch. 1).

The Egyptian government, then led by radical Pan-Arabist president Gamal Abdul Nasser, presented even more of a threat to the Bourguiba government during this period than did the French. Although the French experienced major differences with Bourguiba over the war in Algeria, the presence of French troops and the disposition of French-owned assets in Tunisia, these issues were eventually resolved without a serious breach. The Egyptians, by contrast, were known to be active supporters of the domestic opposition linked to Bourguiba's Neo-Destour Party rival, Salah Ben Youssef. In October 1958 Tunisia broke diplomatic relations with Cairo over its alleged involvement in a "Youssefist" attempt to assassinate Bourguiba. Relations with Cairo remained strained for years because of Egypt's continued support for Youssefists and because of Nasser's criticisms of Tunisia's unwillingness to subscribe to the Egyptian leader's brand of Pan-Arabism.

After its independence from France in 1962, Algeria soon moved to the forefront of Tunisian external security concerns. Under the leadership of its first president, Ahmed Ben Bella, Algeria took an active role in supporting "progressive" and "revolutionary" forces in Africa and the Middle East, including Tunisian opponents of Bourguiba. In January 1963 the Tunisian government recalled its ambassador to Algiers because of alleged Algerian involvement in an aborted coup attempt the previous month involving Youssefists and army officers. The Tunisian government was not known to have supported any actions against the Algerian government, but Algerian dissidents found assistance and sanctuary in Tunisia.

Relations between Algeria and Tunisia improved somewhat after Ben Bella was replaced by Houari Boumediene, but sharp political disagreements over Tunisia's generally pro-Western ties and its moderation on the Arab-Israeli problem remained a source of tension. From the perspective of the Tunisian government, the significance of the dissension was magnified by Algeria's overwhelming military strength (see fig. 12). In 1980 the Algerian government was briefly suspected of seeking to foment a rebellion inside Tunisia when it became known that a group of Libyan-backed insurgents who attacked the Tunisian town of Gafsa had entered the country from Algeria. Subsequently, low-ranking Algerian officials were implicated in the operation, but Chadli Bendjedid, who had replaced Boumediene in 1979, made overtures to convince the Tunisians that he and his government were not involved.

In the early 1980s Tunisia and Algeria steadily strengthened their relationship into a de facto alliance. The treaty of friendship and concord signed by the leaders of the two countries in March

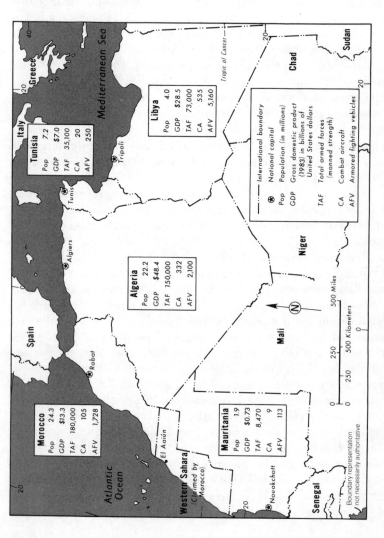

Figure 12. Balance of Power in the Maghrib, 1985

1983, hailed as the first step in forming a "Great Arab Maghrib," called for military liaison and consultation as well as economic cooperation and settlement of border issues. In late 1985, in the context of a Libyan troop buildup on the Tunisian border and the Israeli air attack, frequent discussions between Tunisian and Algerian officials appeared to indicate a further tightening of their security relationship.

Libya's destabilizing activities have troubled Tunisian leaders since the mid-1970s. Before the 1969 coup that brought Qadhaafi to power, Libya under the conservative King Idris I was regarded as a weak, sparsely populated wasteland whose friendship with Tunisia was symbolized by a 1957 treaty of good neighborliness. The military coup led by Qadhaafi and the increase in oil prices during the 1970s, however, gave rise to a more difficult security relationship between the two states. Relations chilled in 1974 when the Tunisian government hastily backed away from a merger agreement between the two countries, to which Bourguiba had earlier agreed. Abusive Libyan propaganda combined with military power—growing rapidly with new stocks of Soviet-supplied weapons—to induce the Tunisian government to begin the most extensive (although modest by regional standards) modernization of its armed forces undertaken since independence (see Armed Forces, this ch.).

The raid on the mining town of Gafsa focused attention on the potential danger from Libyan subversion or intervention. Early on January 27, 1980, a band of 50 or 60 armed Tunisians, equipped and trained in Libya, captured the police and army barracks in Gafsa, seized several hostages, and drove through the town calling on local Tunisians to rise up against the Bourguiba government. Accounts differed as to how much support they received from townspeople, but it was apparently not significant. Tunisian security forces were sent to Gafsa, and, in the heavy fighting that followed, official sources reported the 22 security personnel, 15 civilians, and four insurgents were killed. The attack, in concert with a sustained propaganda barrage from Libyan radio, was apparently intended to catalyze a popular uprising against the Bourguiba government. Its failure caused Tunisians from across the political spectrum to unite behind Bourguiba during the crisis. The Gafsa raid demonstrated for most Tunisians the magnitude of the threat posed by Libya and drew the immediate support of France and the United States, Tunisia's two closest Western allies. The French quickly dispatched a squadron of ships to the coast off Tunisia and Libya in a show of force, and the United States subsquently sent a military mission to evaluate Tunisian security needs.

After Gafsa, Qadhaafi made gradual moves to restore ties with Tunisia and was rewarded with the resumption of diplomatic relations, which had been broken at the time of the raid, and by agreements aimed at intensifying economic links. At the same time, however, he provided the Tunisian government with cause for continued concern. In the early 1980s some 2,000 Tunisians were reportedly receiving military training in Libyan camps. Members of the so-called Islamic Legion, they were purportedly being trained to liberate Palestine, but, given the precedent of Gafsa, officials in Tunis worried that they could be used against Tunisia. (In 1982 a small-scale attack on Kasserine, ostensibly supported by Libya, reminded Tunisians of this capability.) Although there was no direct evidence of Libyan involvement in the January 1984 riots, Qadhaafi's reputation led many Tunisians to suspect Libyan involvement. Tunisians were suspicious because at the time of the riots the price of Libyan bread was lowered, and major oil pipeline in Tunisian territory near the Libyan border was sabotaged. A concurrent Libyan offer to provide Tunisia with security assistance—which could be viewed either as an olive branch or a threat—was refused by Prime Minister Mohamed Mzali. Later in 1984 a Libyan show of force on the Tunisian border, the kidnapping of three Tunisian border guards in Tunisian territory, and ongoing rumors of Libyan arms shipments to Bourguiba's domestic opponents also kept Tunisian officials suspicious of their neighbor.

The basis for Tunisian-Libyan estrangement was reinforced in August 1984 when Qadhaafi and Morocco's King Hassan II announced a "merger" of their two countries. Rejected by the Tunisian-Algeria alliance (which had expanded to include Mauritania), it appeared that Morocco and Libya were directing their pact against Algeria and its allies. Despite the diplomatic efforts of the Tunisians to lessen regional tensions, the states of the Maghrib polarized into two contending blocs (see Maghribi Affairs, ch. 4).

The large-scale expulsions of Tunisian citizens from Libya in August and September 1985 appeared to bring Tunisian-Libyan relations to their most dangerous state since Gafsa. The expulsion of some 30,000 of the 90,000 to 100,000 Tunisian workers living in Libya threatened Tunisian security on two levels. First, the new arrivals exacerbated an already serious domestic unemployment problem, and, second, Tunisian officials feared the infiltration of dissidents who had received military training in Libya. Background checks on the returnees indicated that they were simply Tunisian workers forced to leave Libya when the Libyan economy could no longer afford their services. These expulsions were followed by Tunisia's ejection of some 300 Libyan officials and residents, the breaking of diplomatic relations and, according to Tunisian reports, the massing of Libyan troops on the border and flights of Libyan military aircraft into Tunisian airspace. The episode served to reaffirm Tunisian mistrust of the Qadhaafi regime and caused the government in Tunis to seek stronger security ties with the United States and Algeria.

Immediately thereafter, the raid by Israeli warplanes on the Palestine Liberation Organization (PLO) headquarters at Hamman-Lif on the outskirts of Tunis on October 1, 1985, raised new concerns in Tunis over national security. The raid, which killed as many as 20 Tunisians in addition to scores of Palestinians, demonstrated that Tunisia was not immune from involvement in the Arab-Israeli conflict although the Israeli government stated that it "had nothing against Tunisia" in striking "the headquarters of those who make the decisions, plan, and carry out terrorist actions." Bourguiba had previously sent small contingents of Tunisian troops and matériel to Egypt after the Middle East wars in 1967 and 1973, but the Arab-Israeli problem had always been on the periphery of Tunisian security concerns and outside the scope of Tunisian military planning. Beyond that, Bourguiba has long been considered the most moderate of the Arab leaders; his 1965 call for the recognition of Israel, which was based on the 1948 United Nations (UN) partition resolution, had led to difficulty for Tunisia in the League of Arab States (Arab League) during the Nasser era. Tunisian involvement in the issue intensified when Tunis was made the headquarters of the Arab League in 1979 and when the PLO moved its headquarters there in 1982 after being expelled from Beirut. Before the Israeli raid, however, the PLO presence—strictly limited by the Tunisian authorities—was a source of concern mainly as a potential threat to domestic stability (as it had been in Lebanon) rather than as a magnet for an Israeli attack.

Initially, the Israeli raid and the short-lived American support for it as a "legitimate response" to terrorist attacks made it appear that Tunisia had lost a friend and source of security assistance. The United States immediately adopted a more evenhanded approach to the issue and indicated a willingness to continue the two countries' longstanding security relationship. The Tunisian government, after initial shock and disbelief over the incident, also indicated that it did not intend to interrupt its security relationship with the United States (see Foreign Military Assistance, this ch.). It appeared, however, that Tunisian officials might become more circumspect and less inclined to advertise those ties because of sensitivity to criticism from both allies and enemies.

Domestc Security Issues and Policies

Between the 1960s and the mid-1980s, the Bourguiba government's vulnerability to perceived challenges from domestic opponents—and its methods of dealing with them—changed markedly. At the beginning of the period, Tunisia was a one-party state with a broad base of popular support where almost all opposition outside the Destourian Socialist Party (Parti Socialiste Destourien—PSD) was considered to be a threat to national security. In the 1970s the government continued to refuse to recognize the legitimacy of any critics outside the PSD, but the party's base of support was shrinking considerably even as opponents were becoming more numerous, more vocal, and more dangerous. In the period after 1980, Mzali, with Bourguiba's support, was apparently attempting to redefine what constituted a security threat. By taking steps toward allowing some of the opposition to vie for power through legitimate channels, it was thought that the prime minister was seeking to weaken and divide the government's most dangerous rivals while making government institutions (and the PSD itself) stronger, more vital, and more relevant to Tunisians. The Tunisian experiment was complicated, however, by a PSD leadership that was concerned about presidential succession and was divided over whether and how fast to proceed with liberalizaton of the political system. Even if the government did decide to hold elections that included broadly representative opposition groups, there were doubts as to whether the regime's strongest opponents, the Islamists (see Glossary), could be persuaded to participate.

Roots of Domestic Security Difficulties

During the 1960s a strong and popular party organization built on patronage and two-way communication with constituents served as the eyes and ears of the PSD leadership. In this environment, dissent was seldom expressed publicly except within the context of party loyalty, and civil disorders were kept to a minimum. Opposition was often placated by compromises on the part of the national leadership, but when this proved ineffective the government was able to act swiftly and effectively against dissidents. In the early years of independence, the most prominent opponents of the government were the supporters of Ben Youssef. Religious and cultural traditionalists objecting to the government's moves to build a more secular society occasionally demonstrated their contempt for the Bourguiba government, but they were a declining force during that time.

The roots of Tunisian stability were weakened somewhat during the 1970's. Despite unprecedented economic growth and a high standard of living by regional standards, popular dissatisfaction with the Bourguiba government increased as some of the structural shortcomings of the politico-economic system appeared to have become intractable. The gap between rich and poor Tunisians had grown since independence and showed no signs of narrowing. The citizens of the southern desert areas saw themselves excluded from the country's political elite and from sharing in the nation's economic growth. Partly as a result, large numbers of young unemployed Tunisian men flocked to the major cities, swelling the ranks of the urban poor. Ordinary crime, previously a negligible problem, increased with the influx of migrants, although reliable statistical data on the magnitude were not available. More important, the growth of a large mass of disaffected and disenfranchised young Tunisians had ominous implications for national security.

Government policies and the increasingly rigid and arbitrary style of Bourguiba's leadership also contributed to the growth of public discontent. In the early 1970s Bourguiba rejected the nation's socialist economic policies as well as new proposals to move toward the establishment of a multiparty democracy. In ousting officials most closely linked with those initiatives, the aging president indicated that he feared being overthrown by subordinates who had built up independent power bases. Political expression had always been limited in Tunisia, but the president and then-Prime Minister Hedi Nouria appeared to be unwilling to tolerate any dissent or accept any criticism, even from within the PSD. The regime's increasing remoteness combined with the rise in domestic criticism of its leadership to stifle the PSD's grass-roots dynamism, which had been the foundation of the government's security and effectiveness.

The 1970s were characterized as a decade of increasing civil unrest in Tunisia. At the beginning of the period, large numbers of students for the first time began to object publicly to the direction of government policies. Dominated by Marxist critics during this time, student dissent resulted in growing numbers of disturbances at Tunisian universities, unrest that continued despite the government's demonstrated willingness to arrest and impose strict prison sentences on offenders. At the same time, organized labor showed itself to be an important opposition force. The General Union of Tunisian Workers (Union Générale des Travailleurs Tunisiens— UGTT), which had long been closely allied with the PSD, became increasingly militant in demanding better working conditions and wages, criticizing growing unemployment, and protesting the economic gap between the affluent and poor elements in the society. Illegal strikes, rare before the mid-1970s, became more and more frequent, numbering approximately 600 between 1976 and early 1978 alone. When strike actions were joined by large numbers of unemployed urban youths and supplemented by the persistent dissidence of students who viewed the PSD as an outdated and increasingly ineffectual political party, they posed a direct challenge to the government.

The scope of Tunisia's discontent was first dramatically demonstrated by the violence connected with the general strike of January 26, 1978, a day Tunisians remenber as Black Thursday. The strike, coming after months of what observers called government intimidation of the UGTT leadership, was interpreted by the government as a direct threat to its authority. The violence was controlled after two days by army units equipped with infantry weapons and armored vehicles after police were overwhelmed by demonstrators. According to official Tunisian figures, 42 were killed and 325 were wounded before government forces restored order; other, unofficial, sources put the number of casualties far higher. Over 1,000 were arrested, and many, including the entire UGTT leadership, were brought before the State Security Court on charges of subversion. Even before the trials began, pro-PSD elements moved into positions of power within the UGTT. The new union leaders immediately expressed regret for the riots and pledged to cooperate with the government.

After the 1978 unrest, the national government increasingly found antigovernment dissidence expressed in religious terms. The conservative Muslim imams had long opposed Bourguiba's securlarist social reforms, but during the 1970s the authorities had supported Islamists as a counter to the influence of Marxist groups on Tunisian campuses. The Islamists only became regarded as a threat after the Iranian revolution of 1979 demonstrated that, even in the late twentieth century, Islam could generate great social and political upheavals. In the early 1980s a variety of Islamist groups came into existence, most of them drawing their strength from university students and other educated young Tunisians disaffected by the PSD and the secular Marxist alternative (see Opposition Groups, ch. 4). The largest and most important of these groups was the Islamic Tendency Movement (Mouvement de la Tendance Islamique—MTI), which was formed in 1981. Because of its leadership's political sophistication and calls for democratization of the political process, the MTI was considered to be among the most "moderate" of similar groups in existence throughout the Islamic world. The MTI's popularity, however, its calls for the rejection of Western values, and the militancy of some of its members (especially those on college campuses) made the government deeply concerned about the movement's potential as a threat to national security.

Government Security Policy under Mohamad Mzali

By early 1980, when militant Islam was beginning to be identified as a security problem in Tunisia, it was obvious that the government's hard line against dissidents had been unsuccessful in bringing back the order and stability that the country had known in the 1960s. Shortly after the shock of the Gafsa incident, then-Prime Minister Nouria—the person most closely associated with the government's strict security policies—reportedly became seriously ill and was replaced by Mzali. The new prime minister quickly made it clear that he would seek to deal with the regime's opponents in a different manner than had his predecessor. Forming a cabinet that included some of the PSD officials who had resigned in protest over the government's strict policies against the UGTT in 1977, Mzali in his first year in power released almost all Tunisian political prisoners and pardoned some 1,000 unionists who had been jailed for their participation in the 1978 riots. The UGTT was allowed a freer rein, press restrictions were eased, and the president and Mzali indicated that opposition parties would be allowed to compete against the PSD in elections.

It soon became clear that the moves to open the political system to opposition groups would be limited, cautious, and gradual. The Tunisian Communist Party—which had a very small popular following—was granted official recognition and allowed to contest the 1981 parliamentary elections. By contrast, the MTI—which probably was the country's most popular political grouping—had its application for recognition denied. In July 1981 the government arrested virtually the entire MTI leadership after a number of violent incidents blamed on Islamic extremists. In the trials that followed, 89 Islamist leaders were sentenced to prison for up to 11 years for offending the head of state, spreading disinformation, and belonging to an unauthorized organization. The severity of the sentences in what was thought to be a relatively liberal political environment was criticized by many, including the non-Islamist opposition parties. That the government was still not used to the concept of a loyal opposition was demonstrated in November 1981 when three opposition parties that had been allowed to contest the parliamentary election received only some 5 percent of the popular vote between them; widespread voting irregularities were reported (see The 1981 Election: Opposition Parties Sanctioned, ch. 4).

In the early 1980s other smaller Islamist and secular groups emerged and were perceived as threatening by Tunisian authorities. In 1982 and 1983 a number of dissidents linked to the Islamic Liberation Party, the Popular Revolutionary Movement, and the National Arab Rally—all of which were linked to Pan-Arab and Islamist causes—were arrested and convicted of criminal and political offenses (see Opposition Groups, ch. 4). During this period, the escalating conflict between Islamists and Marxists on University of Tunis campuses also worried the government insofar as the power and aggressiveness of the two radical groups resulted in the de facto suppression of student organizations affiliated with the PSD (see Interest Groups, ch. 4).

The January 1984 rioting, the most extensive in Tunisian history, clearly indicated that the government's political reforms had not removed the causes of popular discontent. The disturbances, which started in the south, spread nationwide and reportedly involved half a million Tunisians, 10 times the number in the 1978 violence. As in 1978, the police were overwhelmed by the protesters, and the army had to be called in to help restore order. The riots had heavy political overtones. Demonstrators, mostly young unemployed males, shouted slogans condemning Bourguiba, his wife Wassila, Mzali, and other PSD leaders and stoned the president's car in his hometown, Monastir. Although some observers suspected at the time that the riots were planned by regime opponents, later analyses indicated that they broke out spontaneously at the time of the price increases in bread and other staples. After the disturbances began, however, it appeared that government opponents, especially Islamists, were active in organizing antigovernment demonstrations. According to official sources, 89 Tunisians were killed in the disturbances and nearly 1,000 were injured. Over 1,000 others were arrested, some of whom were detained for as long as six months before being brought to trial.

The 1984 riots and their aftermath starkly revealed some of the regime's vulnerabilities. That the disturbances were completely unforseen showed the ineffectiveness of the PSD's local organization as a source of domestic intelligence. After the violence broke out, local PSD officials appeared to be unable or unwilling to stop the protesters or moderate their actions. Shortly after calm was restored, the PSD's internal disputes were also highlighted when the government's strongest reactions against the violence were reserved for one of Mzali's political rivals, Minister of Interior Driss Guiga. The minister and his director of the Sûreté Nationale were dismissed from their positions, tried, and convicted of treason and corruption. After Mzali and his appointees came to dominate the ministry, some observers criticized the prime minister for being more interested in finding scapegoats and consolidating his political position within the PSD than in addressing the root causes of the violence.

After the riots, some suspected that the government would toughen its stand against domestic opposition and return to the domestic security attitudes and policies of the 1970s. In January 1984 Mzali's appointment of Brigadier General Zine el Abidine Ben Ali, who had a reputation as a hardliner on security issues, as the director of national security within the Ministry of Interior appeared to confirm this view (see Internal Security Forces, this ch.). Mzali, however, continued to indicate that government attempts to integrate the opposition (including, perhaps, the MTI) into the political system would continue. The release from prison in August 1984 of the last of the Islamist leaders, jailed three years earlier, was the most tangible evidence that Mzali was still seeking to reshape the government's domestic security policies.

Despite the prime minister's assurances, government policy in 1984–85 had in many ways become more repressive. The government was accused of supporting divisive tendencies within the labor movement. Opposition parties that had been given legal sanction complained of renewed suppression (including attacks on members by groups of PSD loyalists), destruction of offices, unjustified arrests by police, and general harassment. Censorship of the information media, relaxed in 1980, again became increasingly prevalent and was directed against opposition publications (see Politics and the Information Media, ch. 4). The situation led the recognized opposition parties to boycott the 1985 local elections and Ahmed Mestiri of the Social Democratic Movement to conclude that "those responsible within the [Destourian Socialist] party are not yet ready for opposition."

In late 1985, after nearly six years of erratic moves to liberalize the political system, the party's and the regime's security did not appear to have been significantly improved. There was no sign that its most serious opponents—Islamists, unionists, the urban unemployed, southerners, and students—had moderated their attitudes toward the regime. There was cynicism in some quarters that the liberalization effort was simply a method for Mzali to enhance his status and eliminate potential rivals as he positioned himself to take power after Bourguiba's passing. Others noted that the prime minister's ability to recast Tunisian security policy had been frustrated by opposition from other elements within the PSD, notably Minister of Public Works and Housing Mohamed Sayah, who was reputed to favor a tougher attitude toward dissidence; by Bourguiba, who opposed Mzali's accumulation of too much political power; by those Tunisians who opposed Mzali as Bourguiba's successor; and by those PSD officials whose power would be diminished by the reforms. It was generally thought that as long as PSD leaders were more concerned with political maneuvering among themselves than with the potential threat posed by the country's disenfranchised opponents, disturbances such as those of 1978 and 1984 could become increasingly common, and the risk of domestic chaos or military involvement in the government might grow (see The Military and Politics, this ch.).

Armed Forces

The Tunisian National Army (Armée Nationale Tunisienne— ANT), which was divided into army, air force, and naval components, had a threefold mission: to defend the country's territorial integrity against hostile foreign powers, to assist the police as necessary in maintaining internal security, and to participate actively in government-sponsored civic action programs. The government has also sought to ensure, largely with success, that the ANT had little influence in the political sphere.

Since the late 1970s, all of the armed services have been undergoing expansion and modernization designed to improve their defenses against attack from potentially hostile states. Although the improvements have been extremely costly, the worsened relationship with Libya and the vulnerability demonstrated by the Israeli raid have heightened concern about Tunisia's military weaknesses. The president in 1985 therefore directed his government to explore with its friends and allies in the Arab world and the West the possibility of assistance in making new large-scale purchases of aircraft, armor, and naval vessels.

Military Tradition, Development, and Philosophy

Contemporary Tunisian society reflects little of the military tradition that permeates the national life of the other Maghribi countries. Many scholarly observers have attributed this anomaly partly to legacies of the era before Tunisia's protectorate period and to experiences encountered during the 75 years of French domination. Political scientist Jacob C. Hurewitz has also pointed to changes that have occurred within the society, including the virtual disappearance of traditional Berber culture (see The Social System, ch. 2). Thus Bourguiba and the PSD have not had to depend on the leverage of a preeminent military establishment to settle internal disputes between contending ethnic or regional groups as have leaders in other developing countries. Neither has it required military help in unifying the large homogeneous population behind the goals and aspiration that Bourguiba and his political elite have upheld as national objectives. Even so, the national life of the country has not been entirely devoid of military experience.

Early Development

While under French control, Tunisia served France as an important source of manpower. After establishing the protectorate, the French, under a beylical decree in 1883, were granted the authority to recruit local Muslims for the purpose of forming mixed French-Muslim military units. By 1893 all Muslim males in Tunisia became subject to military duty, although it was possible for those chosen for service to provide substitutes as long as induction quotas were fulfilled. As a result, most of the recruits came from the poorer classes of Tunisian society, and illiteracy was the norm among them. Conscripted Muslim Tunisians were required to serve for three years, as were French settlers, who were subject to the conscription laws of metropolitan France.

To assist in the pacification effort throughout the Maghrib, the French—as they had done in Algeria—formed Muslim infantry regiments of *tirailleurs* (riflemen) and spahis (cavalry) in Tunisia. In the late nineteenth century some of these units joined with their Algerian counterparts in aiding the French in military conquests south of the Sahara. Muslim Tunisian soldiers also formed regiments in the Foreign Legion and served in southern Tunisia as *méharistes* (camel corpsmen). Although Muslims served in all branches of the French army, strict segregation was normal. Few Tunisian soldiers—unless they were naturalized French citizens—were able to become officers, and of those only a small number rose beyond the rank of captain. In mixed units Muslim officers were not permitted command authority, and none were given high-level staff positions anywhere in the French military organization. The infantry and cavalry units were strictly divided on ethno-religious grounds; Muslim soldiers served under the command of French officers and noncommissioned officers (NCOs). More equality existed in artillery units, where Muslim soldiers were assigned as drivers as the French served as gunners. Most of the transportation corps consisted of Muslims under French command.

Although recruited chiefly for military service in Africa, Tunisian members of the French army were liable for service abroad and served with courage and distinction in such divergent spots as France and Indochina. It has been estimated that of the approximately 75,000 Tunisians who served France during World War I, some 50,000 experienced combat in the trenches on the western front, where they suffered a high casualty rate. Before France collapsed under the onslaught of Hitler's troops in World War II, many Tunisian soldiers and their counterparts from Algeria and Morocco were sent to Europe to aid the French in their fight against the Germans. As part of Hitler's June 1940 armistice agreement that accompanied German occupation, France was permitted to retain 15,000 troops in Tunisia, of which roughly 10,500 were Muslims. After Allied successes in the fight to liberate North Africa in 1943, Tunisian and other North African soldiers saw action in the Italian campaign and the eventual liberation of France.

After World War II the rise of Tunisian nationalism and the emergence of sporadic guerrilla warfare directed against French interests heralded the quest for independence (see Toward Independence, ch. 1). From early 1952 Tunisian guerrilla bands enjoyed considerable popular support and conducted operations primarily in the south. Their activities consisted mainly of acts of sabotage and coercion against the French community as well as against Tunisians who sympathized with the French authorities. The Tunisians involved in these demonstrations of militancy were labeled *fellaghas* (rebels) by the French press. As a result of an intense counterinsurgency campaign waged against them by the Foreign Legion, the *fellaghas* sought refuge in the central and southern mountains, buying time and increasing their strength and support from muslims who resented French administrative policies and practices. Although the *fellaghas* were able to strike occasionally against French authority, they were never able to muster a unified and cohesive force. It has been estimated that their strength never exceeded 3,000 men. By early 1956 most of their bands were deactivated as an act of cooperation aimed at enhancing the prospects of independence.

In April 1956 the French transferred responsibility for Tunisia's internal security to the new Tunisian government, including indigenous elements of the police services that had operated under

French control during the protectorate era. The new Tunisian government used them to track down militants connected with nationalist leader Ben Youssef, who challenged Bourguiba's leadership of the Neo-Destour Party and the country. Some of the agitators of this group were arrested, tried, and sentenced as an example of the government's intention to ensure a climate of acceptable public order for its development goals. Despite these efforts, however, the Youssefist threat was controlled only with the force of large-scale operations by the French army three months after Tunisian independence.

In the matter of responsibility for defense—and the building of a national military establishment—the transfer of authority was more difficult. To support its activities in suppressing the revolution in neighboring Algeria, the French government sought to maintain its military presence in independent Tunisia, espousing the notion that both countries would share in the new state's external defense needs. This form of interdependence, however, drew a less than sympathetic response from Bourguiba and his Neo-Destour Party hierarchy. It was only after long months of negotiations that in June 1956 the French government, beset with greater concerns for the Algerian conflict, agreed to assist Tunisia in the formation of its own military arm.

The nucleus of the new military force—the ANT—consisted of roughly 1,300 Muslim Tunisian soldiers, who were released from the French army, and some 600 ceremonial troops of the beylical guard, which the French had permitted the Tunisian bey to retain as a personal bodyguard throughout the protectorate era. These sources of military personnel were supplemented by volunteers—loyal party youth and politically reliable *fellaghas* of the earlier resistance movement. Key officer and NCO positions were filled by personnel carefully selected by the leadership of the Neo-Destour Party. Many of those selected had received training at Saint Cyr, the French military academy, or had served as NCOs in French Military units. All were loyal Neo-Destourians.

By the end of 1956 the force consisted of roughly 3,000 officers and men organized in a single regiment, but its effectiveness was limited by a shortage of qualified officers. Resolution of this problem was aided through a negotiated agreement with the French, who provided spaces for 110 Tunisian officer candidates to train at Saint Cyr. Meanwhile, a school for NCOs was established at Tunis with French help, and 2,000 enlisted men were enrolled to build up the needed cadre for the NCO corps. In addition to training Tunisian personnel, France provided a modest amount of military equipment and established a small liaison unit of French army officers, who were to advise and assist in matters of command and staff procedures.

Despite the assistance provided the new republic, independence did not remove frictions with the French. The war in neighboring Algeria and the continued occupation of bases in Tunisia by French forces—a concession of the independence agreement—served as unsettling factors for Tunisians. When the Bourguiba government pressed for the removal of its toops in mid-1957, France reacted with threats to terminate military assistance to the ANT. French intransigence led Bourguiba to turn to the United States, which had earlier concluded a bilateral agreement to supply the young republic with economic and technical assistance, and to Britain. Although they were allied with France in the North Atlantic Treaty Organization (NATO), Britain and the United States were willing to supply Tunisia with arms out of concern that Bourguiba might turn to Egypt for assistance.

After settlement of the issue over arms aid, Bourguiba asked the French to evacuate their bases earlier than had been agreed in the pre-independence protocol. Tunisian public support was generated for what Bourguiba termed the "battle for evacuation," and military skirmishes between French and Tunisian forces occurred sporadically. The most serious of these encounters came in 1961 after the French had consolidated their forces at the major military installation in Bizerte. Refusal to evacuate from Bizerte led to an attack on the French base by Neo-Destourian militants, students, and volunteers from the trade unions, youth organizations and women's unions. Organized and directed by the Garde Nationale, the Bizerte confrontation was an ill-conceived and militarily inappropriate venture against professional French troops that resulted in the loss of about 1,000 Tunisian lives, most of them civilians. Although few ANT regulars were involved—four battalions of 3,200 men had responded earlier to the UN appeal for a peacekeeping force in the Congo crisis of 1960—the defeat at the hands of the French was regarded by the Tunisian military establishment as a painful humiliation. Nonetheless, the so-called Battle of Bizerte sped the final withdrawal of French troops and ushered in a new era of strategic independence.

Strategic Philosophy

After the French withdrawal, Tunisia's relations with neighboring Algeria and nearby Egypt, far larger and stronger states, were at a dangerously low ebb, and ties with France were unstable at best. In this environment the government in the 1960s took steps to devise a defense policy tailored to protect Tunisia against stronger potential foes without sacrificing the national priority of promoting economic development. The Bourguiba government sought to construct a relatively low-cost military establishment— supported by a motivated and trained civilian population—capable of defending against a neighbor's attack until Tunisia's more powerful allies could assist.

Secretary of State for Defense Ahmed Mestiri first proposed a long-term plan that included military modernization and involvement of the civilian population in the country's defense in the aftermath of the Arab-Israeli June 1967 War. Greatly impressed by the Israelis' ability to defeat larger Arab forces in the brief encounter, Mestiri believed that Israel's defense strategy could be adopted by Tunisia. More important than the quantity of armaments, he pointed out, were the qualities of technical ability, leadership, the ingrained organizational structure of units, and the kind of faith that animates soldiers. He was greatly impressed by the concept of the Israeli citizen-soldier and advocated a program that would involve both the military and the civilian population in national defense. The program proposed by Mestiri seemed more economically feasible than joining a North African arms race, and the government approved it. An initial change in military policy involved amending the conscription law in an attempt to upgrade the quality of trained reserves (see Quality and Sources of Manpower, this ch.). The effort to improve the ANT's equipment and training, however, has proved more costly than expected; rising military costs and a continuing need for foreign military assistance have come to characterize Tunisia's military development.

Under pressures generated mainly by Libya, the Tunisian government in the late 1970s stepped up its program of military modernization and defined its strategy as one of "comprehensive people's defense." According to Minister of National Defense Abdullah Farhat in 1976, the republic's defense policy depended on two factors: a favorable external climate guaranteed by the leaders of friendly countries throughout the world and creation of a domestic climate that would make Tunisians feel they had something to defend. Further, the strengthening of the ANT was not only a question of quantity but also one of establishing cadres qualified in the modern technologies. "We have been able to provide these technologies and train the cadres to use them," Farhat said in a speech to the national legislature, "thanks to our relations and friendships. We are experiencing no difficulty in this connection at our schools or at schools abroad. We only need time to acquire the right training." Farhat went on to explain that Tunisian defense policy did not rely solely on the ANT. "Victory in this age comes through one or two elements," he pointed out, "the atomic weapon or comprehensive people's defense. Since we have no expansionist aims or nuclear ambitions, the only thing left for us is the second alternative."

The Tunisian government continued to emphasize the notion of a comprehensive people's defense in the mid-1980s, but in reality, defense policy was oriented more toward the modernization of the regular forces than to the building of reserve strength. Bourguiba in public statements still stressed "the need to ensure participation of civilians and all the people in defending the gains of the state" and called for "military preparation for all citizens." As a practical matter, however, programs and budgets focused on building the conventional forces and on acquiring sophisticated modern weaponry and associated training. In 1985, given the immediate impetus of a renewed chill in relations with Libya and the weaknesses highlighted by the Israeli air strike, it appeared that Tunisia's comprehensive defense would, more than before, emphasize the regular forces. As it had been since independence, the military was still designed and configured to be strong enough to deter an attack until stronger allies could intervene. But in view of the major military buildup in neighboring countries and the high cost of modern military equipment and training, even the strategy of minimum deterrence was proving extremely costly for Tunisia to maintain.

The Military and Politics

Since independence Bourguiba has sought to perpetuate a military relationship in Tunisia in which all elements of the armed forces would be apolitical in outlook and completely responsive to the needs and commands of the president and civilian authority. By and large, he has been successful, and with the exception of an aborted 1962 military coup supported by Algeria, which allegedly involved younger Youssefist officers, former members of the beylical guard, and Islamists, the military has never significantly threatened the civilian leadership. Given the strains in the civilian leadership and the society in the 1980s, however, the possibility of military intervention in Tunisian political affairs could no longer be discounted.

As premier of Tunisia at independence, Bourguiba, the son of a former lieutenant of the beylical guard, assumed personal responsibility for the country's defense policies and posture. Upon becoming president of the republic in 1957, he also took on the role of commander in chief of the armed forces as specified in the Constitution. Through Article 45 of the Constitution, Bourguiba has had the authority to make military appointments, a valuable prerogative that permitted close presidential control of the military establishment and its personnel.

His exclusive power to promote military officers has been among the strongest components of Bourguiba's control over the armed forces. From independence, high-ranking officers—general staff and senior commanders in particular—have been carefully selected for their party loyalty more than for their professional exprience and competence. This began in the late 1950s when the president dismissed those officers who had trained in the Middle East and who might therefore have been expected to sympathize with the militant Pan-Arab policies of Egypt's Nasser. The handpicked senior officers, in turn, carefully screened all officers who were considered for positions of authority in line units to ensure that antiregime elements did not pose potential threats at any level of the military establishment.

As a result of these promotion policies, the Tunisian officer corps took on a very homogeneous character that only began to break down in the 1970s. Senior officers have been generally representative of Tunisia's economically and politically dominant families from the north, the coastal areas, and the major cities. Although military men have been kept form operating major business ventures or holding political office while in uniform, it has been common for family members to be prominent in business or in the Destourian political movement. Generally Western and Francophile in outlook, tied by kinship to the country's upper socioeconomic stratum, and personally familiar with leading figures in the PSD, high-ranking Tunisian officers must be classed as part of the national elite.

In addition to the relatively small group of officers who have been elevated to senior military positions because of their political reliability, the military's expansion has brought into the services a growing number of younger officers from the less privileged segments of the society. Many of these young officers, along with enlisted men who have long been characterized as coming from the margins of society, have not been insulated from the political debate and social turmoil that has gripped Tunisian society since the 1970s. It is thought by observers of Tunisian affairs that many of the younger officers and enlisted men are more sympathetic than their leaders to the government's critics, including Islamists, leftists, and those opposed to the concentration of political power in the top echelons of the PSD. This threat was glimpsed in 1983 when 19 air force cadets linked to the Islamic Liberation Party were tried along with 10 other defendants by a military court where they were found guilty of having helped form a political organization. It has also been noted that many of these junior and mid-level officers—who were generally better educated than their elders and in many cases exposed to Western military training and practice—may have resented the policies that promoted politically "safe" officers of questionable competence and limited their own opportunities for advancement. The existence of pockets of dissatisfaction within the military has not of itself posed a threat to the PSD government. In 1985, however, it was clear that unease among mid-level and junior officers, which has been at the root of numerous changes of government in other parts of the Middle East and Africa, could not be ruled out as a potential source of trouble in Tunisia.

Bourguiba has also demonstrated his seriousness in limiting the overt participation of military personnel in the nation's political life. Most notably, when members of the ANT were involved in planning and acting as stewards at the 1979 PSD congress, Bourguiba refused to attend and soon dismissed Minister of National Defense Farhat, who had organized the event.

Beyond controlling military involvement in politics, Bourguiba has long sought to keep his troops quiescent by limiting the size of the armed forces, the quantity and quality of their armaments, and their operational responsibilities. Beginning in the late 1970s, however, domestic security concerns and problems with neighboring Libya caused the government to increase the size and capabilities of the military and domestic disorders, especially during the serious civil disturbances of 1978 and 1984.

Whether the government's increased dependence on the military will lead to officers demanding a greater role in shaping the policies they are being asked to implement remains uncertain. According to political scientist L.B. Ware, some Tunisians affiliated with the UGTT saw the appointment of a military man to the directorship of national security within the Ministry of Interior immediately after the 1984 disturbances as a step toward greater military influence in the affairs of state. (The officer, Brigadier General Ben Ali, has since moved on to become the minister delegate attached to the prime minister for national security.) Although a gradual increase in participation in political affairs seems a possibility, the Tunisian military's long apolitical tradition and widespread respect for Bourguiba militate strongly against the possibility that senior officers would move to overthrow the existing government. The country's political and economic crisis would have to grow considerably worse to warrant the intervention of senior officers, who are very much a part of the national elite. The younger officers are, however, much more of an unknown factor.

Although most observers believe that military intervention in politics is extremely unlikely as long as Bourguiba remains in control, few are as sanguine about military quiescence after Bourguiba passes from the scene. According to Ware, if post-Bourguiba Tunisia is characterized by economic decline and social tumult and if elite political forces long subsumed under the banners of "Bourguibism" and "Destourianism" break their facade of unity in a divisive struggle for control of the PSD and the country, the possibility of military intervention by senior military personnel is far more likely than was apparent in 1985. It was uncertain, however, whether the younger officers would be willing to support such a venture or whether some of them would seek to take it over to serve their own ends.

Defense Costs and the Economy

Throughout its history as an independent nation, Tunisia has maintained a record of having probably the smallest defense budget among all countries in the Arab world. Investment in impressive weaponry for the sake of prestige has never been a policy of the governing regime. In the 1980s, however, efforts to improve the armed forces' capabilities had strained a national budget oriented primarily toward economic and social development. Although spending increased to higher levels than Tunisian policymakers—and citizens—had been accustomed to, military spending as a percentage of total government expenditure or national income was still among the lowest in the region. Given continued political tensions in the Maghrib and the perceived need to modernize the relatively small armed forces, it appeared that military spending would continue to occupy a prominent place in the national budget.

The defense budget was drawn up annually by the national planning authorities in the Ministry of Finance and the president's office in consultation with the Ministry of National Defense. Although military officers historically have not exercised a major role in the process, greater military expenditures in the 1980s suggested that this pattern might be changing. In a shift from earlier approaches, most military spending in the early and mid-1980s came out of the capital budget. Capital expenditures in Tunisia included much of the new hardware being acquired during that time and

contrasted with current expenditures, which were primarily composed of the costs related to salaries, benefits, maintenance, and
fuel.

From independence until 1979 Tunisia had never devoted as
much as 2 percent of its estimated gross national product (GNP) to
defense expenditures. During this period the military's share of the
total government budget was consistently less than 5 percent, and
combined government expenditures on health and education normally accounted for more than five times the amount spent on defense. Beginning in 1979, however, when the country began to
order new equipment to modernize its armed forces, total defense
spending rose dramatically. From a level of TD36.8 million (for
value of the Tunisian dinar—see Glossary) in 1978 (4.4 percent of
the total national budget for that year), military spending skyrock-
eted to TD147.7 million (14.9 percent of the national budget). Defense costs as a percentage of central government expenditures
lessened over the next several years, except in 1982, when the
government made a large purchase of arms from the United States.

According to Tunisia's 1985 budget, TD102.6 million (9.9
percent of the government's current expenditures) was devoted to
defense. The Ministry of National Defense also received TD122.5
million (10.9 percent of the total) from the government's capital
budget. By contrast, government spending on education amounted
to nearly TD300 million (13.7 percent of the total government
budget). Public spending on health was somewhat less, accounting
for some 7.7 percent of the total 1985 budget.

To offset the cost of the military, the ANT since its formation
has lent its support to civic development programs. Much of this
effort has come from the engineering units and vast numbers of
conscripts who have labored on construction projects or in the
building of transportation facilities, mainly in the Sahara and other
remote areas of the country. In 1985 the minister of national defense announced the formation of a special army regiment that
would be devoted to developing the Sahara. Observers, however,
have reported that the younger soldiers at times have shown as
little enthusiasm for this tertiary mission as they have for their
role as surrogate policemen.

Under the National Service law, which operated in conjunction with military conscription requirements, Tunisian youth who
reached age 20 were expected to serve either in uniform for one
year or for a like period on programs such as building roads in
rural areas, laying railroad track, retimbering land, planting to control desert encroachment, or constructing rural housing units. The
program operated as a responsibility of the army, but various min-

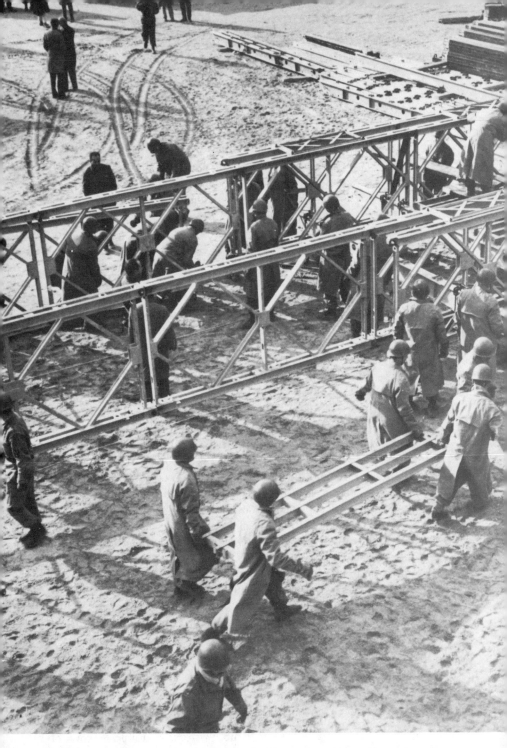

Army engineers restoring communications
after a natural disaster
Courtesy Embassy of Tunisia, Washington

istries provided technical planning and supervision of the work programs. In practice, the projects involving National Service conscripts were designed to avoid competition with workers in high unemployment areas. Almost all of the work, therefore, was located in remote rural regions of the country. In the mid-1980s it was thought that approximately 3,000 young people served in the National Service.

Quality and Sources of Manpower

The Tunisian military, a relatively small force, has never experienced difficulty in attracting adequate numbers of recruits for its needs. In the mid-1980s, according to United States government statistics, there were nearly 1.8 million males ages 15 to 49, of whom some 990,000 were considered fit for military service. Each year roughly 83,000 reached the age of 20, the age of eligibility for military service, indicating that basic manpower resources were more than adequate to meet military needs. Even with the addition of personnel needs for the paramilitary police units, manning of the ANT did not constitute a drain on the labor force. On the contrary, it was thought that any significant reduction in conscription requirements would only exacerbate the perennially high unemployment rate in the civilian sector.

Although the military has not faced any problems in filling numerical quotas, it has had more difficulty in attracting adequate numbers of technically trained personnel. The Tunisian people—especially educated citizens from the prosperous northern and coastal areas—have normally held those who volunteered for a military career in low esteem; this attitude persisted in the 1980s. In addition to the relatively low status of the job, engineers and technically trained Tunisians found the pay and benefits of the military to be less than what they could expect to attain in civilian life. Moreover, persons in these categories were able to obtain deferment if they were called up to serve under the conscription law. Although the technical competence of Tunisian soldiers was less than the high standards that the ANT expected of itself, the Tunisian military—which came from a society in which the literacy rate for people above the age of 15 was 50 percent—was considered to be among the better educated military forces in North Africa.

The Tunisian military in 1985 was built around a core of some 8,100 officers, NCOs, and enlisted men who volunteered for a military career. The regular establishment was strengthened by an annual quota of draftees, some 27,000 of whom were on active duty in 1985. The vast majority of the conscripts—about 26,000—served with the army while over 40 percent of the regular military served in the much smaller navy and air force.

Under the conscription law first introduced in 1959, all physically able male citizens reaching the age of 20 have been technically required to serve in the armed forces. Active military service normally has extended for one year without interruption, but students, teachers, civil servants, and certain technicians could be authorized to fulfill their obligations in stages if continuous service would interfere with their studies or occupation. A one-year deferment could be requested in peacetime by students and by those who had brothers currently serving in the ANT. Besides the physically unfit, exemptions could also be given, except in a national emergency, to those who had lost close relatives in the service of the country or to those who were the sole support of others. Through the years the number of physically qualified men has increasingly exceeded the number of troops the government has found necessary to train and equip. As a result, by 1985 only a third of those eligible were serving the year of active duty technically required of them by law.

In theory, the system of conscription was designed to provide a ready source of trained personnel, but in practice it did little to enhance the capability of the ANT. Exemptions allowed to potential draftees were extremely liberal, and consequently a preponderance of illiterate young men were inducted for training and service. Moreover, most of the conscripts were separated from the ANT just when their training and experience had turned them into useful members of service units.

As part of the program of comprehensive defense, Tunisian authorities in the 1960s sought to create a strong force of military reserves. After completing active military service, enlisted men and officers were required to become members of the reserves. Recruits were assigned to regional mobilization centers where they would be expected to report if they were called up in an emergency. Original plans had called for quotas of 9,000 reservists to be inducted annually for one year of military service. In reality, however, the reserve forces did not function effectively because the government focused its limited resources on active units. Although call-up exercises reportedly did take place, observers believed that even if a limited mobilization of reserve strength were possible, there would not be enough weapons, equipment, and support facilities to outfit and sustain the active-duty reservists.

Military Structure and Training

Although Bourguiba served as the commander in chief of the armed forces and remained the final arbiter on all major decisions, in the mid-1980s his day-to-day influence over the military was limited. The National Defense Council under the chairmanship of Prime Minister Mzali appeared to take a more active role in assessing security threats and directing the security forces. In addition to the prime minister, the council also included Minister of National Defense Slaheddine Baly, as well as the ministers of foreign affairs, finance, and interior (a spot also held by Mzali in 1985). Its staff work was directed by an ANT officer, army Colonel Abdel Massid Fehri in 1985.

The council had originally been formed in 1970 to provide counsel on the "application of the [security] policy defined by the President of the Republic," but by the early 1980s it had ceased to operate. It was recreated by presidential decree after the January 1984 riots to improve coordination between the military and the forces under the authority of the Ministry of Interior. Observers noted, however, that the reemergence of the council gave the prime minister more influence and undercut the power and independence of the minister of national defense, who was not considered to be a close political ally of Mzali.

The Ministry of National Defense was responsible for transmitting policy decisions to the uniformed services as well as for administrative, logistical, and personnel matters. In late 1985 the position of ANT chief of staff, generally filled by the senior ANT officer, had been vacant since Major General Fariq Abdel Hamid el Chiekh was transferred to become ambassador to Sudan in 1984. The chief of staff normally did not command troops but served as a policy coordinator among the three services and as the preeminent military adviser to the minister of national defense. It appeared that, with the reestablishment of the National Defense Council, the need for the position had lessened.

The Ministry of National Defense also included chiefs of staff for each of the three services, but, rather than acting as a unified general staff, each was considered to be the commander of his respective service. General Muhammed Said el Kateb, who was the senior active ANT officer in 1985, served as the inspector general of the armed forces. Under the authority of the minister of national defense, he was responsible for ensuring discipline and efficiency in all military units. Other elements of the general staff organization were charged with carrying out the plans involving budgeting, logistics, and various administrative support functions of their assigned areas of responsibility.

Army

Under the command of its chief of staff, General Youssef Baraket in 1985, the army was the largest and most developed branch of the armed forces. With a manned strength of 30,000 (of whom 26,000 were conscripts), the army was gradually continuing the expansion that had increased its size by two-thirds since 1979. More important, its units were absorbing new equipment that, it was hoped, would significantly improve the force's effectiveness.

According to *The Military Balance, 1985–1986*, published by the London-based International Institute for Strategic Studies, the army was tactically organized much as it had been in the late 1970s. At the core were two combined arms brigades (each of which included one armored battalion and two mechanized infantry battalions), one so-called paracommando brigade of elite troops, and the Sahara Brigade headquartered in Remeda that was trained to operate in the arid areas of the south. In addition to these units, which had been in existence for more than a decade, the army also included one newly formed armored reconnaissance regiment, one regiment of field artillery, one so-called antitank regiment, two air defense regiments equipped with antiaircraft guns and surface-to-air missiles, and an engineer regiment.

Although the army had undergone only slight organizational changes, the infusions of manpower and equipment received in the early 1980s were thought to have filled out what had long been an undermanned and ill-equipped force. Most striking was the addition to the armored units of over 50 M-60A3 tanks and 14 older but equally capable reconditioned M-48A5 tanks from the United States. Other newly acquired armored vehicles included a large complement of M-113 armored personnel carriers, some of which were armed with TOW anti-tank missiles. Artillery had been upgraded by the acquisition of new weaponry, and the force's air defense capabilities had been vastly improved by the addition of relatively sophisticated surface-to-air missile systems purchased from Sweden and the United States (see table 12, Appendix).

In earlier times Tunisian soldiers had an excellent fighting record, as demonstrated by their service in the French army before independence, but the modern army has been largely untested. The battalions that assisted in the UN peace-keeping forces in the Congo in the early 1960s saw little, if any, combat action. Similarly a cease-fire was declared during the Arab-Israeli June 1967 War before the symbolic contingent of army troops Bourguiba offered to the Arabs could be committed. The small military contingent contributed by Tunisia to the Arab cause in the October 1973 War with Israel may have gained valuable experience in terms of wartime planning, military deployment, and logistical support, but these forces did not gain combat experience.

In the 1970s and 1980s the army saw more action in internal security situations, where its record was mixed. The army was deployed in the Gafsa crisis of 1980 to put down the Libyan-supported insurgents. Although it was successful in the operation, shortcomings were pointed out by the army's delay in deploying troops to Gafsa and their difficulty in overwhelming some 60 rebels. Similarly, when it was used in support of the police in the major civil disturbances of 1978 and 1984, the army turned in a successful, but flawed, performance. Untrained in crowd control, the troops on both occasions used what observers considered to be excessive force to put down demonstrators. Reportedly, ANT officers and conscripts alike resented their role in these situations where their enemies were not foreign invaders but fellow countrymen.

Air Force

In the 1980s the air force was receiving new equipment and training to enable it to more adequately perform its principal missions. As the sole operator of military aircraft in Tunisia, the air force was responsible for the aerial defense of national territory, close air support of the army, air transport for the army and the police, and assistance to the navy in air-sea rescue operations. Under the command of Brigadier General Abdel Hamid el Farhi, who assumed the position of air force chief of staff in 1985, the force had a personnel strength of some 2,500, about 500 of whom were conscripts.

The last of the ANT elements to be established (in 1960), the air force has since received valuable assistance from a variety of Western sources. It commenced operations with the arrival of 15 Saab primary trainers and a contingent of instructors from the Swedish air force. In the mid-1960s a limited French training program coincided with the delivery of several French-built light fixed-wing aircraft and helicopters. In 1966 the Italians provided, along with training, eight Aermacchi M.B.326 trainer/light strike aircraft of a type still used in Tunisia. Subsequently, the United States agreed to assist in training, supplying equipment, and establishing the air force's technical support system. In 1969 Tunisia

Tunisian army unit on parade
Courtesy Embassy of Tunisia, Washington

took delivery of 12 F–86F Sabre jet fighters from the United States to establish the air force's first front-line combat squadron.

By the mid-1970s, however, aging equipment, shortages of highly trained technicians, and the low government priority given to defense had led to stagnation, if not deterioration, in the quality of the air force. The high costs of new equipment delayed efforts to modernize the force. Initially, when the Sabres were grounded at the end of the 1970s, they were replaced by new M.B.326s, which were relatively low-performance aircraft. Largely because of the high costs, a full decade passed after the Tunisian government first expressed an interest in purchasing Northrop F–5E and F–5F fighters, and they were finally delivered. By the end of 1985, however, the air force had largely completed the modernization begun in the late 1970s under the impetus of the Libyan threat.

The combat units of the air force included one fighter/attack squadron composed of 12 F–5s and one counterinsurgency/light strike squadron equipped with the M.B.326s. Two C–130Hs delivered in 1985 provide a transport capability, the need for which had been pointed out in 1980 by the army's difficulty in moving units to Gafsa to counter the attack on that town by Libyan-supported insurgents. The air force's training unit operated various types of aircraft, including 1940s vintage T–6 Texans delivered almost two decades earlier from France. The helicopter wing also used a wide variety of aircraft, mainly of French origin (see table 13, Appendix).

The air force units operated from facilities established by the French during the protectorate period and further developed by them for use by the Tunisian squadrons of the French air force during World War II. In the 1980s the main base was at Sidi Ahmed near Bizerte, but other air bases were located near Tunis, Sfax, and Gabès. The air force could also use the runways and support facilities of the country's major commercial airports (see Transportation and Telecommunications, ch. 3).

To protect its airspace, Tunisia in 1980 acquired from Sweden LM Ericcson Giraffe radar systems designed to be used in concert with fighter aircraft and surface-to-air-missiles. The air force had not been able to use its air defenses effectively to prevent reported incursions of Libyan aircraft or stop the Israeli warplanes that raided PLO headquarters at Hammam-Lif in 1985. In the latter instance, it was believed that not more than one F–5 was able to scramble, and this did not occur until the Israeli aircraft had left the area. It should be noted, however, that at the time of the raid the F–5s were newly delivered and that pilot and technical training were incomplete.

Navy

In the mid-1980s the navy had undergone a far more modest modernization than the other services, and much of its inventory was approaching obsolescence. The navy had a relatively limited mission concentrating on coastal protection, enforcement of customs regulations, rescue operations within territorial waters, and protection of the country's maritime boundaries. It was commanded by the chief of naval staff—Captain Habib Fadhila in 1985—and had a manned strength of 2,600 including 500 conscripts.

Established in 1959, the navy initially received French assistance, including advisory personnel and several small patrol vessels. In the mid-1980s the force included the frigate *President Bourguiba* (a World War II vintage destroyer escort transferred from the United States), two United States-built coastal minesweepers, and a variety of fast-attack and patrol craft. The most important additions to the fleet in the 1980s were three Combattante III fast attack craft armed with Exocet surface-to-surface missiles. Apart from these vessels, however, most of the fleet's units were old and capable of little more than coastal patrol duties (see table 14, Appendix).

During the 1960s and 1970s the navy was primarily involved in combating the smuggling of contraband, the illegal entry of undesirable aliens, and unauthorized emigration as well as other security activities affecting the coastal areas. In these matters the overall effort was shared with agencies of the Ministry of Interior, especially the customs agents and immigration personnel of the Sûreté Nationale.

Throughout the 1970s the navy also responded to government concerns over unauthorized use of Tunisian fishing waters through aggressive actions against encroaching foreign fishing fleets. In what many observers described as the "sardine war," armed patrol boats repeatedly engaged Italian vessels from Sicily, firing on them and forcing them into Tunisian ports for the imposition of heavy fines. During this period a longstanding dispute over the maritime border with Libya also resulted in shows of force by Tunisian naval vessels. Although the issue was later referred to international arbitration, its reemergence as a point of conflict could put the navy in the center of a future Tunisian-Libyan clash.

Training

Long-term absence of quality training programs for military personnel has resulted in a shortage of technically trained officers and enlisted specialists, hampering the development of the ANT as a credible fighting force. To a degree, the problem with ANT training resulted from official reluctance to increase defense expenditures over many years, thus restricting expansion of training facilities. Because of the relatively small size of the military elements and the scope of their technical requirements, the government has relied to a large extent on foreign assistance in matters of training.

In the mid-1980s basic training for conscripts normally lasted three months and was taught mainly at the army training center at Bizerte. After basic training, recruits received further specialized training with their units over the next three months. NCOs were trained at their own academy near Tunis in a one-year program.

This was followed by a six-month specialization course and six additional months of service as instructors for incoming recruits.

In December 1967 a national military academy was opened with French assistance at Fondouk Jedad, south of Tunis. The academy provided military leadership instruction to officer candidates of all three components of the ANT, although each service operated separate schools for specialized training. Admission was competitive among those who had achieved a baccalauréat degree recognized by the Tunisian education system. The academy's four-year course of instruction included university courses as well as coursework with specifically military content and was reportedly weighted toward engineering and scientific subjects. Beginning in the early 1980s academy graduates were rotated through an instruction center where they would spend a year assisting in recruit training—like the NCO school of graduates—honing their skills as leaders and educators. A year of specialized instruction or weapons training normally followed before the young officers joined a regular unit with the rank of second lieutenant.

Tunisian military officers continued to receive instruction throughout their careers. Junior staff training, called "the stage of captains," prepared Tunisian officers for command at the company level. Officers of major rank might qualify for the School of Superior Military Instruction, a junior staff college that prepared them to command large units, lead in interservice operations, and perform staff functions. Selected lieutenant colonels would be chosen to attend the Superior War College, after which they would qualify for the top command and staff positions in the ANT.

As an addition to the purely military schools, Bourguiba in early 1984 inaugurated the Institute of National Defense. The new institute was designed to operate as a forum for exchanges between high-level civilians and military personnel. In a scholarly atmosphere the fellows of the center were expected to conduct research, reflect, and help shape policy on the major issues of national defense and international relations facing Tunisia.

Uniforms, Ranks, and Insignia

The uniforms adopted by the ANT in 1956 basically reflected the French tradition, particularly those worn by units in the field. Modifications have occurred since then, however, and the modern uniforms of all services have a closer resemblance to those worn by eastern Arab military personnel, although the traditional French collar patches have been retained. By law the grades in the army rank structure ranged from basic private to lieutenant general (see fig. 13; fig. 14). Senior officer grades for the navy did not include officers of flag rank among their active-duty personnel in 1985 because of the small size of the service and the developing nature of its status within the ANT structure.

Foreign Military Assistance

Lacking a domestic arms industry, Tunisia since independence has remained dependent upon foreign sources for armaments and other defense-related equipment as well as for much of its military training. The United States and France, historically Tunisia's most important suppliers, continued to be predominant sources of aid in the 1980s when the country's military buildup caused a vast expansion in its arms imports. In the context of the ANT's growth, foreign military assistance has come to be an increasingly important military requirement and economic concern.

The United States began providing military assistance to Tunisia in 1957, and in 1967 a military liaison office attached to the United States embassy in Tunis was established. Throughout the first 20 years of Tunisian independence, however, United States military assistance remained modest, and the cost to Tunisia was low. Many of the most important items—including the F–86 fighters delivered in 1969—were surplus United States Air Force equipment supplied on a grant basis under the Military Assistance Program (MAP). ANT personnel were also trained through the International Military Education and Training (IMET) program, which was cost-free to the Tunisian government. Tunisian purchase of United States military equipment under the Foreign Military Sales (FMS) program never exceeded US$2.3 million in any year before United States fiscal year (FY) 1977 and were generally far less. In FY 1977, however, as Tunisia first began to modernize its armed forces, it placed some US$44 million in orders for United States equipment through the FMS program. The equipment it received included mainly transport helicopters and armored personnel carriers.

The Gafsa incident in 1980 and the specter of Libyan involvement served as an impetus for increased United States interest in supporting Tunisia's military needs. In early 1980 a survey team from the United States Department of Defense was dispatched to Tunisia to outline the country's defense capabilities and requirements. Its report found that the ANT was so poorly equipped that

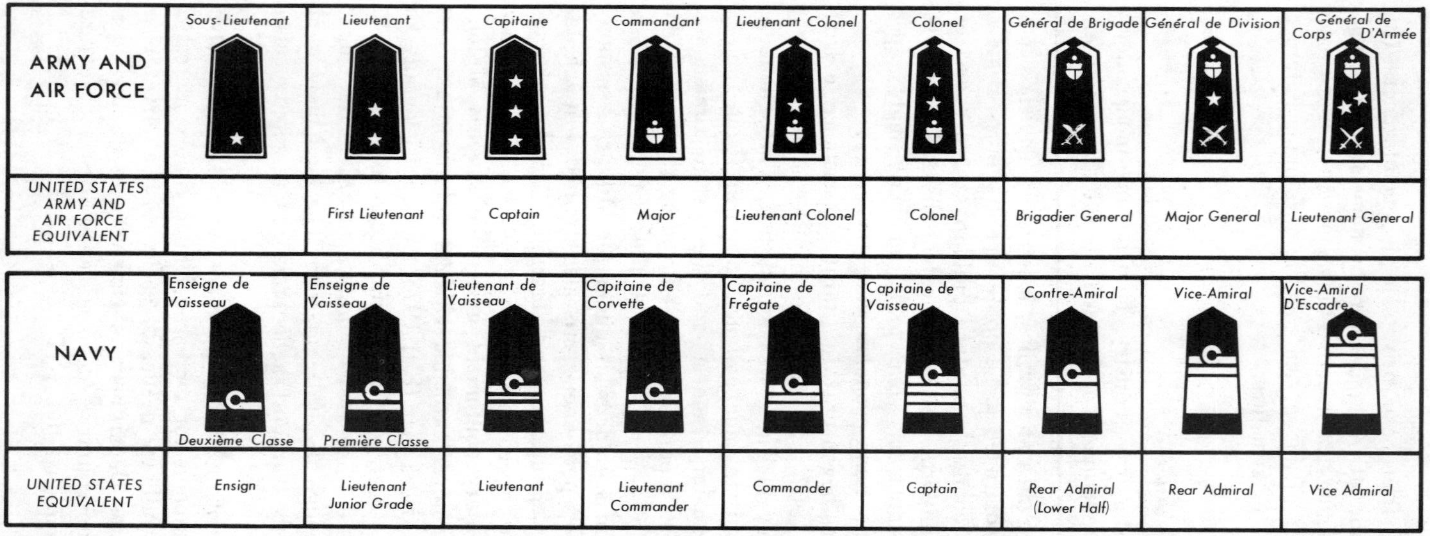

ARMY AND AIR FORCE	Sous-Lieutenant	Lieutenant	Capitaine	Commandant	Lieutenant Colonel	Colonel	Général de Brigade	Général de Division	Général de Corps D'Armée
UNITED STATES ARMY AND AIR FORCE EQUIVALENT		First Lieutenant	Captain	Major	Lieutenant Colonel	Colonel	Brigadier General	Major General	Lieutenant General

NAVY	Enseigne de Vaisseau Deuxième Classe	Enseigne de Vaisseau Première Classe	Lieutenant de Vaisseau	Capitaine de Corvette	Capitaine de Frégate	Capitaine de Vaisseau	Contre-Amiral	Vice-Amiral	Vice-Amiral D'Escadre
UNITED STATES EQUIVALENT	Ensign	Lieutenant Junior Grade	Lieutenant	Lieutenant Commander	Commander	Captain	Rear Admiral (Lower Half)	Rear Admiral	Vice Admiral

Figure 13. Officer Ranks, Insignia, and United States Equivalents, 1985

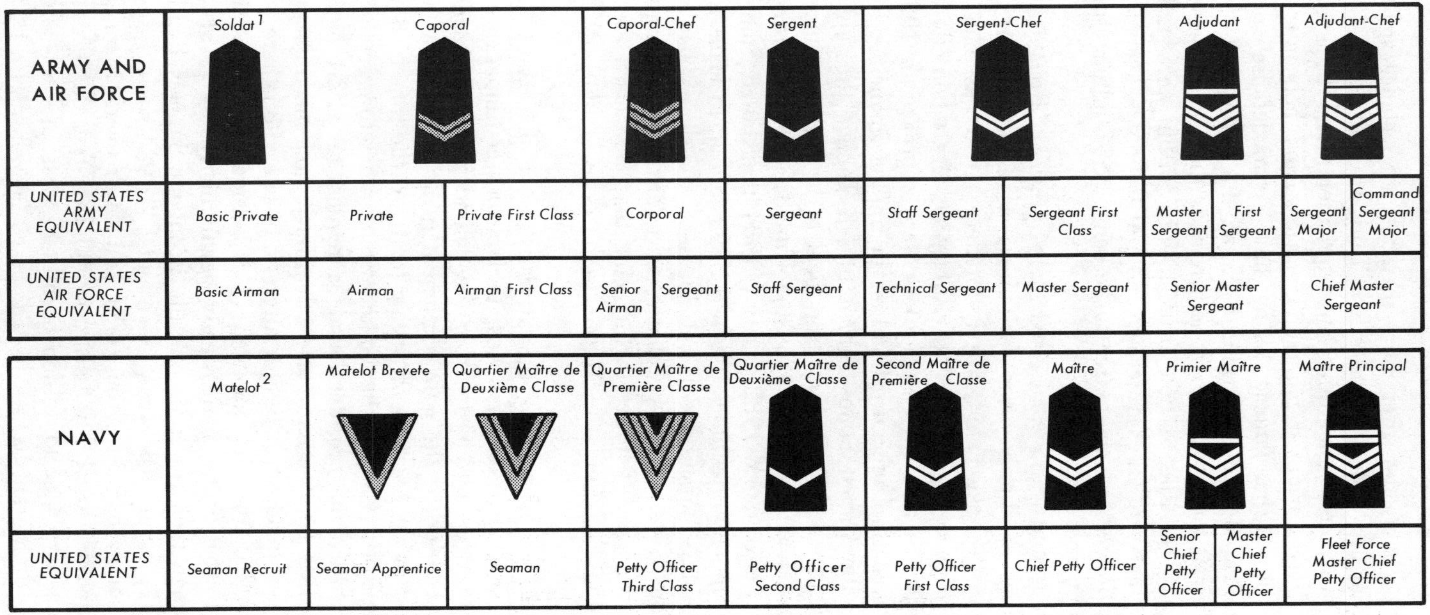

ARMY AND AIR FORCE

	Soldat[1]	Caporal	Caporal-Chef	Sergent	Sergent-Chef	Adjudant	Adjudant-Chef
UNITED STATES ARMY EQUIVALENT	Basic Private	Private First Class — Private	Corporal	Sergeant	Staff Sergeant — Sergeant First Class	Master Sergeant — First Sergeant	Sergeant Major — Command Sergeant Major
UNITED STATES AIR FORCE EQUIVALENT	Basic Airman	Airman First Class — Airman	Senior Airman — Sergeant	Staff Sergeant	Technical Sergeant — Master Sergeant	Senior Master Sergeant	Chief Master Sergeant

NAVY

	Matelot[2]	Matelot Brevete	Quartier Maître de Deuxième Classe	Quartier Maître de Première Classe	Second Maître de Deuxième Classe	Second Maître de Première Classe	Maître	Premier Maître	Maître Principal
UNITED STATES EQUIVALENT	Seaman Recruit	Seaman Apprentice	Seaman	Petty Officer Third Class	Petty Officer Second Class	Petty Officer First Class	Chief Petty Officer	Senior Chief Petty Officer — Master Chief Petty Officer	Fleet Force Master Chief Petty Officer

[1] Insignia for air force only; no insignia for army *Soldat*.
[2] No insignia.

Figure 14. Enlisted Ranks, Insignia, and United States Equivalents, 1985

it could probably not offer more than token resistance against an attack from Libya. In particular, the Tunisian military was lacking infantry weapons, communications equipment, and transport, including trucks, armored personnel carriers, and helicopters. The team also noted that Tunisia did not have an air defense capability or the ability to deter an armored thrust; the acquisition of interceptor aircraft and tanks would help remedy these deficiencies. Tunisian-American talks on new arms sales began but were stalled by the reluctance of the American administration to finance the costs—estimated by one source to be some US$1 billion—implied by these purchases.

The administration of United States president Ronald Reagan was willing to supply arms to Tunisia as a counter to Libyan strength in the region, but, like its predecessor, it was reluctant to bear the high costs of Tunisian military modernization. Purchases of M–60 tanks and F–5 jet fighters were approved in 1981 but were delayed by Tunisian difficulties in finding financing. Finally, in 1982, the United States agreed to sell Tunisia the tanks and aircraft in a US$293 million arms deal to be financed largely by commercial loans guaranteed by the United States Department of Defense. Between FY 1982 and FY 1984 the United States government annually guaranteed some US$90 million in loans for Tunisian military procurement but, because the loans had to be repaid, the costs of the purchases were difficult for Tunisia to meet. Continued difficulties in financing the sale caused the deliveries of the F–5s and the M–60s to be delayed until 1984 and 1985.

After the delivery of the aircraft and tanks, many United States officials believed that, despite Tunisia's continued problems with Libya, arms purchases from the United States would decline as Tunisia absorbed the new equipment in its military inventories and turned to the business of paying for it. At the time of Bourguiba's June 1985 visit to the United States, therefore, many were surprised when the president made a request for US$1 billion in grants to finance a second stage of military modernization, including another squadron of fighter aircraft. In late 1985 there was no indication that financing for such an expansion could be arranged, but the United States had already begun increasing grant assistance through the MAP program, the Economic Support Fund, and the IMET program. (Between 1957 and FY 1984 some 1,740 Tunisian students had been trained in Tunisia or overseas under the IMET program, nearly 600 after 1980.) In FY 1985 it was estimated that some US$36 million in military assistance was supplied to Tunisia on a grant basis. This compared favorably with US$22.5

million in arms agreements made between the two countries that year and US$50 million in loans directly from the United States government, half of which were made at concessional rates.

Apart from high costs, some observers anticipated that political difficulties linked to the initial United States reaction to the Israeli air raid on the PLO headquarters in late 1985 might weaken Tunisia's security ties with the United States. Although there were reports that negotiations over the proposed United States use of a bombing range in Tunisian territory had briefly stalled, there was no indication that any aspect of the military relationship had been significantly affected.

France also furnished considerable military assistance to Tunisia and has had a marked influence on the ANT's establishment at all levels. A French liaison unit within the Ministry of National Defense provided guidance in organizational, planning, and logistical matters, mainly for the army and the navy. Tunisian officers and NCOs have been trained at French military academies, and French officers have been assigned to ANT schools and units to assist in training. French equipment provided to Tunisia has included trainer and transport aircraft, helicopters, naval vessels, armored vehicles, artillery, small arms, and ammunition. Before the 1980s the French provided the bulk of the equipment used by the Tunisian army and navy, but after 1980 the United States became more prominent in equipping the army. Apparently, the French government of President François Mitterand has not been as willing as the Americans to furnish military equipment on a concessional basis, and a proposed purchase of Mirage F-1 fighters was never made. The most notable French arms sale to Tunisia in the 1980s involved the three missile-armed Combattante III fast-attack craft.

Although the United States and France have supplied Tunisia with the bulk of its military equipment, other countries have also provided the ANT with valuable assistance. Britain, Italy, and Sweden have been among the most important of these. Certain Arab countries—chief among them Kuwait and Saudi Arabia—have helped to finance Tunisian military purchases, and Tunisian officials were reportedly hoping that they could assist in paying for the proposed second round of military modernization. Algeria, an increasingly valuable ally in the 1980s because of the conflict with Libya, was also reportedly willing to give military aid to Tunisia. Its ability to furnish Tunisia with military equipment was limited, however, because the ANT was equipped almost exclusively with Western-made hardware, whereas the Algerian armed forces relied mainly on Soviet-type equipment. Tunisia, in keeping with its declared policy of nonalignment, has received some military equipment from communist countries. Notably, the Tunisian navy received two armed fast-attack craft from China in 1977. In addition, although the Soviet Union did not provide Tunisia with significant military assistance, Soviet naval and merchant vessels regularly called at Tunisian ports and occasionally used their ship repair facilities. Twenty-one Soviet naval vessels called at Tunisian ports in 1984, compared with six port calls by the United States Navy.

Internal Security Forces

Shortly after independence, responsibilities for maintaining public order and ensuring internal security were assigned to two separate police organizations: the Sûreté Nationale, an outgrowth of the administrative branch of its French counterpart of the protectorate era, and the newly established Garde Nationale. The Sûreté assumed responsibility for police duties in the urban areas; the Garde acted as a rural police force, much in the manner of the French gendarmerie units that had served this purpose in Tunisia until 1956. Since then the police system has been modified considerably as a result of experience gained during the decades since its creation and as domestic needs have dictated its expansion and upgrading.

Until 1967 the two police organizations operated autonomously, and the Garde was more related in its activities to the ANT, especially in matters such as exchange of officer and technical personnel, equipment, and training philosophy. Nonetheless, both police forces were under the supervision of the Ministry of Interior. After the anti-Jewish riots that occurred in Tunisia in the wake of the Arab-Israeli June 1967 War, the ministry was reorganized to centralize the control of domestic police functions and to clarify the separation of the Garde Nationale and the armed forces under the Ministry of National Defense. In this reorganization the two police forces were amalgamated under one Directorate of National Security, a section of the Ministry of Interior. The senior police administrative positions—director of the Sûreté Nationale and commandant of the Garde Nationale—still existed, but control over the operational use of all Tunisian police units was the responsibility of the director of the Directorate of National Security.

Minor reorganizations continued in the police and the Ministry of Interior over the next several years, but the personalities of the leaders have been more relevant to the operations of the internal security forces than the organizaton of institutions. In the late

1970s the director of national security, Colonel Ben Ali, also held the position of director of the Sûreté Nationale. The situation proved controversial for several reasons. Some Tunisians were concerned that holding both jobs made the incumbent too powerful, and the fact that Ben Ali was a military officer with long tenure as chief of military security concerned those who were interested in limiting military influence in the society. Ben Ali was also considered to be a protégé of Farhat, the former interior and national defense minister who fell from Bourguiba's favor in 1979. In 1980 after the Gafsa incident, Ben Ali was sent to Poland as ambassador and the director of national security in the Ministry of Interior remained vacant. His responsibilities were taken over by Abdelhamid Skhiri, who was named director of the Sûreté, and by Ahmed Bennour who was given the title of minister delegate attached to the prime minister for national security but who was not as closely involved in security operations as Ben Ali had been. The overall effect was to increase the direct influence of then-Minister of Interior Driss Guiga.

After the civil disturbances of January 1984, the leadership of the Ministry of Interior and the internal security forces was completely revamped. Bourguiba immediately dismissed Guiga, replacing him with Mzali, who held the interior post concurrently with the office of prime minister. Guiga, who left the country soon after his dismissal, was blamed for the relatively passive police performance during the rioting and for suggesting during the height of the crisis that Mzali should step down. Guiga was a political rival of Mzali, whose "personal interests had prevailed," according to Bourguiba, and had "threatened the superior interests of the nation." Guiga was tried in absentia by a special court and sentenced to 15 years in prison for treason.

As minister of interior, Mzali presided over a wholesale purge of the ministry's top leaders who had been closely linked to his predecessor. He immediately dismissed Skhiri as director of the Sûreté and abolished the Sûreté's Tunis prefecture, firing the prefect. Skhiri was later sentenced to a jail term on charges of treason and corruption. In May 1984 Bennour was eased out of his post and sent to Italy as Tunisia's ambassador.

To run the security forces, Mzali brought back Ben Ali, reappointing him to his old jobs and director of the Sûreté and director of national security within the Ministry of Interior. Reportedly, Mzali also wanted to appoint Ben Ali for his replacement as minister of interior. Bourguiba balked at this suggestion, but in October 1984 he consented to Ben Ali's being named minister delegate attached to the prime minister for national security. Because no one was appointed to replace him at the Directorate of National Security, Ben Ali was able to combine operational control of the internal security forces with subcabinet rank. Ben Ali, who had received training in the United States, was considered to be a tough and politically well-connected leader. Ameur Ghedira, a cousin of Mzali's who had been commandant of the Garde Nationale, was promoted after the 1984 riots to secretary of state within the Ministry of Interior charged with internal security; his position in the Garde Nationale was taken by Colonel Habib Ammar.

To perform its duties of maintaining internal security and administering the rural areas, the Ministry of Interior increased its budget significantly in the early 1980s. The bulk of the budget was devoted to current expenditures; this component rose from TD79.5 million in 1983 to TD106.5 million in 1985, representing 10.1 percent of the total current expenditures in the latter year. Spending by the ministry classed as capital expenditures was much less, fluctuating between TD11 million and TD25 million in the same years. The bulk of spending, some 80 percent of current expenditures, was devoted to the salaries of personnel.

The government has experienced little difficulty in its efforts to maintain adequate numbers of recruits for the police services. When formed initially, both elements conducted recruitment among politically reliable party members, *fellaghas*, and men who had served with French law enforcement agencies. Since this initial effort, pay and conditions of service have been maintained at levels that have continued to attract recruits who prefer the security of government jobs rather than the uncertainty many face in the civilian sector with its high unemployment rates.

Sûreté Nationale

In 1985 the Sûreté Nationale—in effect a national police force—remained the primary enforcement authority in the principal cities and other urban centers. It was charged with the maintenance of public order, protection of life and property, investigation of crimes, and apprehension of offenders. In addition it performed other routine policy functions, including traffic control. Total personnel strength of the Sûreté was not publicly available but has been estimated as being roughly 12,000 men and women.

The Sûreté was organized generally along the lines of its French counterpart and had operational and investigative branches and supporting services. The section best known to the public was made up of the uniformed urban police, segments of which were assigned to each of the 23 governorates. In the past, these elements have operated under the control of the individual governors, but in 1985 it was thought that they received orders primarily from Sûreté director Ben Ali in Tunis. Separate sections of the Sûreté handled functions that included border control, immigration services, political intelligence, presidential bodyguard responsibilities, and general information requirements. Other components were responsible for operations of the judiciary police, maintenance of criminal files, crime research laboratories, and licensing bureau, and the prison system.

In the late 1960s, particularly after the ineffectual performance of the Sûreté in coping with the anti-Jewish riots of 1967, the government established, with United States assistance, a unit of the Sûreté known as the Brigade of Public Order. Manned by some 3,500 policemen in 1985 and equipped with Fiat 6614 armored personnel carriers, the three battalions of this paramilitary unit specialized in tactics designed to be effective in controlling crowds and countering demonstrations and strike violence. The shortcomings of the brigade and other police elements were sharply pointed out by the riots of 1978 and 1984. In the former case, the police were generally criticized for being too aggressive. In the latter, the government's report of inquiry asserted that the police command was unprepared for the disturbances and did not deploy police units quickly and decisively enough to deter the rioters.

The Directorate of Territorial Surveillance was responsible for intelligence and counterespionage operation. Because of the clandestine methods used by its plainclothes personnel, this organization has engendered some fear and apprehension among the general public that it, in effect, has constituted a secret police of classic proportions. Tactics criticized by the United States Department of State's *Country Reports on Human Rights Practices for 1984* included the arresting of suspects on hearsay evidence without proper warrants during the 1984 violence. The police have also been noted for illegally detaining the relatives of fugitives in order to encourage them to surrender to the authorities. Veiled accusations have also persisted regarding possible police involvement in the 1961 murder in Western Europe of opposition leader Salah Ben Youssef and allegations of similar efforts against Ahmed Ben Salah during the years he spent in exile; the Tunisian government has vehemently denied such allegations. Overall, however, the security police have not displayed an obtrusive presence, although some observers were concerned that this might change under the aggressive leadership of Ben Ali.

Applicants accepted by the Sûreté were trained at its academy at Bir Bou Regba. The duration of their course varied with the service in which they were enrolled and was fixed for each applicant by the Sûreté director. Members of the force could be called upon at any time to take special training courses at the police academy, at a Tunisian institution of higher learning, or with a government agency. All those below the grade of superintendent could also be required to take any physical education or sports training the administrative section might organize.

Garde Nationale

The rural police force that was formed at independence—the Garde Nationale—assumed the investigative and internal security tasks formerly carried out by the units of French gendarmerie. The Garde was established in 1957 during the Algerian war of independence to give the Bourguiba government a strong border patrol force that could deter the infiltration of Youssefists and their supporters from Algeria. To man the Garde, former *fellaghas* were recruited, and the new paramilitary service began its operations with a personnel strength of roughly 3,000 officers and men. Its units suffered from shortages of small arms and other necessary military equipment, but its existence as a stopgap measure doubled the size of Tunisia's available security forces.

During the 1960s the Garde expanded its role from strictly border patrol duties and emerged as a major component of the police system. Eventually a large segment of the Garde consisted of a rural gendarmerie, which became active in all areas of the country where urban elements of the Sûreté did not exist. Other Garde units provided a highway patrol force, and still others served as presidential bodyguards and ceremonial troops for state occasions. In 1985 its personnel strength—including the rural gendarmerie elements—was estimated at roughly 6,000 officers and men.

Because of its size, training, equipment inventory, and tactical deployment capability, the Garde was thought to be a versatile paramilitary force. In operational terms it has been described as a combination rural security force and national guard always on active duty. In contrast with its Sûreté counterpart, the Garde was responsible for aiding the army in counterinsurgency tasks when needed. In times of emergency its mission has been to attempt, along with the Brigade of Public Order, to employ crowd control techniques. In addition to its paramilitary duties, the Garde has worked to create an improved environment through civic action, in-

Female members of the Tunis traffic police
Courtesy Embassy of Tunisia, Washington

cluding assisting public works projects and aiding the victims of natural disasters.

Personnel requirements of the Garde were met through recruitment in accordance with civil service regulations. In general most of the troop strength has consisted of former army enlisted men and junior NCOs who have completed their military training and tours of duty with ANT. Applicants selected for service with the Garde received instructions at the separate Garde training academy at Bir Bou Regba.

Prisons

The prison system, a responsibility of the Ministry of Interior, was administered by a department of the Sûreté Nationale. In 1985 it included central prisons at Tunis, Béja, Bizerte, Gabès, Gafsa, Kairouan, Le Kef, Sfax, Sousse, and Bardo as well as other smaller facilities at less populated centers. Habitual criminals, recidivists, were usually sentenced to hard labor at the agricultural penitentiary at Jabel Faqirin. Virtually all of the major prisons operating in 1985 had been established by the French during the protectorate era.

Attempts have been made to provide facilities and personnel to differentiate the kinds of offenders. Wherever possible, juveniles have been separated from adult prisoners, and most of the central prisons had segregated sections for men and women. Political prisoners were also normally separated from those jailed for ordinary crimes. For prisoners other than hardened criminals, attention has been given to rehabilitation programs in an effort to reduce recidivism. Selected prisoners serving sentences of less than five years could be transferred from the maximum security prisons to open camps called reeducation centers for social rehabilitation. Here they performed useful work inside or outside the camp and received a token wage. Industrial training has also been instituted in some prisons.

Prison conditions during the 75 years of colonial administration were generally grim, and the crowded institutions were usually the sources of labor crews used in construction projects, road maintainence, and general cleanup tasks. Reforms proceeded slowly in the three decades after independence, but, according to the United States Department of State's *Country Reports on Human Rights Practices for 1984*, "conditions in Tunisian detention centers and prisons are generally poor and in some cases injurious to health." There have also been numerous reports of torture in Tunisian penal facilities, including floggings. Although there were no indications that these actions were ordered or carried out by higher authorities, neither was there any evidence that police or prison officials have been punished for brutal treatment of prisoners in custody. The Tunisian League of Human Rights, an independent watchdog agency formed in 1977, has documented prisoner abuse and has brought its findings to the attention of higher officials within the Ministry of Interior. Reportedly, some improvements have resulted.

*   *   *

Although no single reference is devoted to describing and analyzing the entire range of Tunisian national security issues, relatively comprehensive knowledge and understanding can be gleaned from examining a number of sources, each of which deals with a specific aspect of Tunisia's security situation. A valuable contribution to an understanding of the early development of the Tunisian military and its role in Tunisian society is found in Jacob C. Hurewitz' *Middle East Politics: The Military Dimension*. A more recent treatment focusing upon the military's involvement in Tunisian politics is found in L.B. Ware's 1985 article "The Role of the Tunisian Military in the Post-Bourguiba Era."

Because relatively few books have been published on contemporary Tunisia since the early 1970s, periodicals provide an indispensable source of information on the government's security concerns and policies as well as on the military and police forces. Among the most consistently useful are the Paris daily *Le Monde* and the weeklies *Jeune Afrique* and *Marchés tropicaux et méditerranéens*. Another valuable reference on security developments is the Paris monthly *Afrique Défense*, which is also available in English translation as *Defense Africa*. Articles from a wide variety of other publications that deal with Tunisia are available as part of the *Near East/South Asia Report*, which contains translations by the Joint Publications Research Service. *The Military Balance*, produced annually by the London-based International Institute for Strategic Studies, is essential as a starting point for examining Tunisia's military inventory and order of battle. The detailed annual *Africa Contemporary Record: Annual Survey and Documents*, edited by the noted Africanist Colin Legum, and the quarterly journal *Maghreb-Machrek* are general works that often have useful sections, articles, or information relating to Tunisian security affairs. (For further information and complete citations, see Bibliography.)

Appendix

317

Table 1. Metric Conversion Coefficients

When you know	Multiply by	To find
Millimeters	0.04	inches
Centimeters	0.39	inches
Meters	3.3	feet
Kilometers	0.62	miles
Hectares (10,000 m²)	2.47	acres
Square kilometers	0.39	square miles
Cubic meters	35.3	cubic feet
Liters	0.26	gallons
Kilograms	2.2	pounds
Metric tons	0.98	long tons
	1.1	short tons
	2,204	pounds
Degrees Celsius (Centigrade)	9	degrees
	divide by 5 and add 32	Fahrenheit

Table 2. Population by Governorate, 1975 and 1984

Governorate	Population		Distribution in Percentage	
	1975	1984*	1975	1984*
Ariana	205,668	374,192	3.7	5.4
Béja	248,770	274,706	4.5	3.9
Ben Arous	152,011	246,193	2.7	3.5
Bizerte	343,708	394,670	6.1	5.7
Gabès	186,033	240,016	3.3	3.5
Gafsa	184,968	235,723	3.3	3.4
Jendouba	299,702	359,429	5.4	5.2
Kairouan	338,477	421,607	6.1	6.0
Kasserine	238,499	297,959	4.3	4.3
Kebili	69,684	95,371	1.2	1.4
Kef	233,155	247,672	4.2	3.6
Mahdia	218,217	270,435	3.9	3.9
Medenine	220,123	295,889	3.9	4.2
Monastir	223,150	278,478	4.0	4.0
Nabeul	368,114	461,405	6.6	6.6
Sfax	474,879	577,992	8.5	8.3
Sidi Bouzid	218,511	288,528	3.9	4.1
Siliana	192,668	222,038	3.4	3.2
Sousse	254,601	322,491	4.6	4.6
Tataouine	72,847	100,329	1.3	1.4
Tozeur	52,876	67,943	0.9	1.0
Tunis	692,665	774,364	12.4	11.1
Zaghouan	99,883	118,743	1.8	1.7
TOTAL	5,589,209	6,966,173	100.0	100.0

*Preliminary.

Source: Based on information from Tunisia, Ministry of Plan. National Institute of Statistics, *Recensement Général de la Population et de l'Habitat*, Tunis, March 30, 1984, 24.

Table 3. Population by Communes with Populations over 25,000 in 1984, Selected Years, 1956–84

Commune	1956	1975	1984*
Tunis	410,000	550,404	596,654
Sfax	65,636	198,872	231,911
Ariana	16,341	47,833	98,655
Bizerte	52,239	78,772	94,509
Jerba	13,456	70,217	92,269
Gabès	24,420	48,612	92,258
Sousse	48,172	69,530	83,509
Kairouan	33,968	54,546	72,254
Bardo	15,997	49,367	65,669
La Goulette	26,323	41,912	61,609
Gafsa	24,345	42,225	60,970
Ben Arous	7,248	27,001	52,105
Menzel Bourguiba	34,732	42,111	51,399
Zarzis	10,829	14,420	49,063
Kasserine	2,705	22,594	47,606
Hammam-Lif	22,060	35,634	47,009
Béja	22,668	39,226	46,708
M'saken	26,142	33,559	41,217
Nabeul	14,047	30,467	39,531
Marsa	14,225	35,124	38,319
Mahdia	10,842	26,007	36,828
Monastir	12,596	26,759	35,546
Le Kef	14,743	27,939	34,509
Moknine	17,699	26,035	31,783
Manouba	14,780	23,167	31,758
Kalaa Kebira	16,708	23,508	31,406
Hammamet	7,088	17,295	30,441
Tataouine	2,599	10,399	30,371
Rades	13,184	20,164	30,218
El Metaoui	1,052	17,748	29,850
Sakiet Ezzit	--	22,427	26,771

—nonexistent in 1956.
*Preliminary.

Source: Based on information from Tunisia, Ministry of Plan, National Institute of Statistics, *Recensement Général de la Population et de l'Habitat*, 1, Tunis, March 30, 1984, 26.

Table 4. *Gross National Product by Industrial Origin, 1981–84*

(in millions of Tunisian dinars)*

Economic Sector	1981	1982	1983	1984
Agriculture (including forestry and fishing)	568.8	629.9	688.8	823.0
Hydrocarbons	449.3	503.6	563.5	579.2
Other mining	64.9	52.7	65.0	74.5
Electricity	42.0	43.6	53.0	67.0
Textiles	121.0	142.8	164.9	187.8
Other manufacturing	372.9	412.0	484.1	586.2
Construction and public works	262.0	308.0	332.9	356.0
Tourism	160.6	184.6	191.6	215.0
Administrative services	442.4	564.3	676.3	752.0
Other sectors	1,129.6	1,345.2	1,542.2	2,594.3
TOTAL	3,613.5	4,186.7	4,762.3	6,237.0

*For value of the Tunisian dinar—see Glossary.

Source: Based on information from Economist Intelligence Unit, *Quarterly Economic Review of Libya, Tunisia, Malta*, 3, London, 1985, 2; and Economist Intelligence Unit, *Quarterly Economic Review of Libya, Tunisia, Malta: Annual Supplement 1984*, London, 1984, 27.

Table 5.   *Production of Selected Commodities, 1982–84*

Commodity	Unit	1982	1983	1984
Agriculture				
Cereals	Thousands of tons	1,255	921	1,023
Olives................................	-do-	400	275	700
Citrus fruit	-do-	165	138	200
Potatoes	-do-	110	150	135
Meat (including poultry)	-do-	193	181	190
Sugar beets	-do-	82	67	n.a.
Dates.................................	-do-	27	56	n.a.
Tomatoes...........................	-do-	260	360	n.a.
Eggs..................................	millions	830	940	970
Milk	thousands of tons	244	277	290
Olive oil	-do-	80	55	140
Fish...................................	-do-	63	67	74
Mining				
Petroleum...........................	-do-	5,102	5,531	n.a.
Natural gas.........................	millions of cubic meters	449	441	n.a.
Phosphate	thousands of tons	4,745	5,796	5,500
Iron ore.............................	-do-	275	316	320
Lead..................................	-do-	8.6	7.8	8.5
Zinc..................................	-do-	n.a.	13.7	13.5
Spar	-do-	n.a.	33.8	35.0
Manufacturing				
Cloth	millions of meters	64.8	71.7	76.0
Clothing	millions of pieces	60.6	62.9	61.6
Other textiles	thousands of tons	31.9	33.4	35.0
Footwear	millions of pieces	12.1	13.3	14.6

n.a.—not available.

Source: Economist Intelligence Unit, *Quarterly Economic Review of Libya, Tunisia, Malta: Annual Supplement 1984*, London, 1984, 29–31; and Economist Intelligence Unit, *Quarterly Economic Review of Libya, Tunisia, Malta*, 1, London, 1985, 20–23.

Table 6. Employment by Economic Sector, Selected Years, 1975–83

(in thousands)

Sector	1975	1980	1983
Agriculture	508.9	551.7	554.0
Mining and energy	38.1	46.7	48.8
Manufacturing	235.2	299.9	350.7
Construction	128.4	158.1	169.4
Transport and telecommunications	56.0	70.0	75.5
Commerce, banking, and insurance	124.3	119.8	135.1
Other services	213.3	271.6	315.6
Miscellaneous	62.3	59.1	59.1
TOTAL	1,366.5	1,576.9	1,708.2

Table 7. *Foreign Trade by Major Commodities, 1981–83*

(in millions of Tunisian dinars)*

Commodity	1981	1982	1983
Exports			
Hydrocarbons and derivatives	647.0	527.3	582.3
Textiles	181.3	215.2	248.3
Fertilizer	96.3	104.2	116.5
Chemicals	57.6	67.4	91.8
Olive oil	50.0	57.2	26.3
Phosphates	24.3	26.3	27.9
Fruit	24.7	13.6	19.9
Machinery (electrical)	14.5	16.8	27.6
Leather	15.8	20.1	22.0
Fish	8.1	14.4	24.3
Wine	4.4	4.2	3.2
Lead	3.2	4.6	1.1
Imports			
Machinery	261.3	276.8	n.a.
Mineral fuel and lubricants	466.7	258.0	225.9
Textile fibers	179.1	207.3	239.5
Metal goods	165.2	43.2	22.1
Automobiles	126.9	139.7	150.2
Cereals	86.5	84.2	124.1
Sugar	41.3	24.6	42.6
Cement	5.7	19.8	9.5
Animal and vegetable oil and fats	n.a.	n.a.	37.0
Dairy products	n.a.	n.a.	38.6

n.a.—not available.
*For value of the Tunisian dinar—see Glossary.

Source: Based on information from Economist Intelligence Unit, *Quarterly Economic Review of Libya, Tunisia, Malta: Annual Supplement, London, 1984,* 1984, 38.

Table 8. Balance of Payments, 1980-85

(in millions of United States dollars)

	1980	1981	1982	1983	1984*	1985*
Current Account						
Goods and services						
Exports	3,912.3	3,932.4	3,457.9	3,284.2	3,113.6	3,501.0
Imports	4,384.9	4,623.9	4,256.8	3,954.7	3,871.3	4,160.9
Net balance	-472.6	-691.5	-798.9	-670.5	-757.7	-659.9
Net Transfers	58.5	50.6	51.0	56.3	45.1	48.1
Current account balance...........................	-414.0	-640.9	-747.9	-614.2	-712.6	-611.8
Capital account						
Medium- and long-term loans						
Official..............................	263.0	247.4	277.6	248.8	367.6	423.3
Private	81.5	47.6	63.2	122.6	138.7	-5.8
Total loans	344.5	295.0	340.8	371.4	506.3	417.5
Direct private investment.......	236.0	387.4	420.5	223.9	219.1	215.6
Grants..................................	41.5	20.3	19.0	25.4	25.8	27.1
Other capital..........................	-143.1	28.3	-5.4	-21.2	-77.3	n.a.
Capital account balance......	478.9	731.0	774.9	599.5	673.9	611.8
Reserves						
Change in reserves.................	-64.9	-90.1	-27.0	14.7	38.7	-48.4
International reserves	412.4	502.5	529.5	514.8	553.5	601.9

*Estimated.
n.a.—not available.

Table 9. Council of Ministers, 1985

Position	Incumbent
President	Habib Bourguiba
Prime Minister	Mohamed Mzali
Special Adviser to the President	Habib Bourguiba, Jr.
Minister, Special Representative of the President	Mongi Kooli
Minister Delegate attached to the Prime Minister	Hedi Baccouche
Minister Delegate attached to the Prime Minister for Civil Service and Administrative Reform	Mezri Chekir
Minister Delegate attached to the Prime Minister for National Security	Zine el Abidine Ben Ali

Ministers
Agriculture	Lassaad Ben Osman
Cultural Affairs	Bechir Ben Slama
Family and Women's Advancement	Fathia Mzali
Finance	Salah Ben Mbarka
Foreign Affairs	Beji Caid Essebsi
Higher Education and Scientific Research	Abdelaziz Ben Dhia
Information	Abderrazak Kefi
Interior	Mohamed Mzali
Justice	Ridha Ben Ali
Labor	Noureddine Hached
National Defense	Slaheddine Baly
National Economy	Rachid Sfar
National Education	Mohamed Frej Chedli
Plan	Ismail Khelil
Public Health	Souad Yacoubi
Public Works and Housing	Mohamed Sayah
Social Protection	Ridha Hamza
Telecommunications	Ibrahim Khouadja
Tourism and Handicrafts	Ezzedine Chelbi
Transport	Mohamed Kraiem
Youth and Sports	Hedi Bouricha

Secretaries of State
Ministry of Foreign Affairs	Mahmoud Mestiri
Ministry of Foreign Affairs in charge of International Cooperation	Ahmed Ben Arfa
Ministry of Interior	Ameur Ghedira

Table 10.   Political Bureau of the Destourian Socialist Party, 1985

Members	Other Positions
President: Habib Bourguiba	President of the Republic
Secretary General: Mohamed Mzali	Prime Minister
Director: Hedi Baccouche	Minister Delegate attached to the Prime Minister
Treasurer: Rachid Sfar	Minister of National Economy
Slaheddine Baly	Minister of National Defense
Ferjami Belhaj Ammar	President, Tunisian Federation of Industry, Commerce, and Handicrafts
Sadok Ben Jomaa	Former Minister of Public Works and Housing
Zakaria Ben Moustapha	Mayor of Tunis
Bechir Ben Slama	Minister of Cultural Affairs
Habib Bourguiba, Jr	Special Adviser to the President
Mohamed Chaker	Former Minister of Justice
Mezri Chekir	Minister Delegate attached to the Prime Minister for Civil Service and Administrative Reform
Mohamed Ennaceur	Chairman, Economic and Social Council
Beji Caid Essebsi	Minister of Foreign Affairs
Mohamed Ghedira	President, National Union of Tunisian Farmers
Hamed Karoui	Not available
Mongi Kooli	Minister; Special Representative of the President
Mohamed Kraiem	Minister of Transport
Slaheddine Ben Mbarek	President, Arab Maghrib Cooperation Bank
Fathia Mzali	Minister of Family and Women's Advancement; President, National Union of Tunisian Women
Mohamed Sayah	Minister of Public Works and Housing
Bechir Zarg Layoun	President of Consultative Council of Militants

Table 11.   Selected Newspapers and Periodicals, 1985

Name	Language	Circulation	Sponsorship or Orientation
Dailies			
L'Action Tunisienne	French	50,000	Destourian Socialist Party
Al Amal...................................	Arabic	50,000	-do-
Ach Chaab[1]	-do-	n.a.	General Union of Tunisian Workers
La Presse de Tunisie................	French	40,000	Government
As Sabah	Arabic	80,000	Independent
Le Temps	French	30,000	-do-
Periodicals[2]			
L'Avenir[3]	French	6,000	Movement of Socialist Democrats
Dialogue	-do-	50,000	Destourian Socialist Party
Al Mawqif...............................	Arabic	n.a.	Socialist
Al Mostakbal	-do-	20,000	Movement of Socialist Democrats
Ar Rai....................................	-do-	20,000	Liberal Independent
Réalités...................................	French and Arabic	n.a.	Independent
Al Tariq Al Jadid	Arabic	n.a.	Tunisian Communist Party
Tunis Hebdo............................	French	25,000	Independent
Al Wahdah	Arabic	n.a.	Popular Unity Party

n.a.—not available.

[1]Converted from weekly to daily in July 1985; suspended for six months after eight issues.

[2]Weekly, except as indicated.

[3]Bimonthly.

Source: Circulation data based on information from *The Europa Year Book, 1984*, London, 1984, 2537.

Table 12. Major Army Weapons, 1985

Type	Estimated Number in Inventory	Country of Manufacture
Armored fighting vehicles		
M–60A3 main battle tank with 105mm gun	54	United States
M–48A5 main battle tank with 105mm gun	14	-do-
AMX–13 light tank	40	France
M–41 light tank	10	United States
Saladin armored reconnaissance vehicle	20	Britain
EBR–75 armored reconnaissance vehicle	30	France
AML–60 armored reconnaissance vehicle	10	-do-
EE–3 Jararaca armored reconnaissance	n.a.	Brazil
EE–9 Cascavel armored reconnaissance vehicle	n.a.	-do-
M–113A1 armored personnel carrier (APC)	50	United States
EE–11 Urutu APC	18	Brazil
Artillery		
M–109 155mm self-propelled howitzer	19	United States
M–114A1 155mm self-propelled howitzer	10	-do-
M–101A1 105mm towed howitzer	48	-do-
M–108 105mm self-propelled howitzer	48	-do-
25–pounder (88mm) towed field gun	6	Britain
M–106A2 107mm self-propelled mortar	12	United States
82mm mortar	n.a.	n.a.
81mm mortar	n.a.	n.a.
Antitank weapons		
STRIM–89 recoilless launcher	n.a.	n.a.
JPzSk–105 105mm self-propelled gun (tank destroyer)	54	West Germany
MGM–71A Tow antitank guided weapon (ATGW), 20 mounted on M–113 APCs	n.a.	United States
Milan ATGW	n.a.	France and West Germany
SS–11 ATGW	n.a.	n.a.
Air defense weapons		
RBS–70 surface-to-air missile (SAM)	n.a.	Sweden
MIM–72 Chaparral	62	United States

n.a.—not available.
Source: Based on information from *The Military Balance, 1985–1986*, London, 1985, 86.

Table 13. Major Air Force Weapons, 1985

Type	Estimated Number in Inventory	Country of Manufacture
Fighters		
Northrop F–5E Tiger II	8	United States
Northrop F–5F Tiger II (two-seat version)	4	-do-
Counterinsurgency/light-strike aircraft		
Aermacchi M.B. 326K..........................	5	Italy
Aermacchi M.B. 326L (two-seat version)	3	-do-
Transport aircraft		
Lockheed C–130H Hercules heavy transport..	2	United States
SIAI–Marchetti S.208M liaison aircraft...	4	Italy
Training aircraft		
SIAI–Marchetti SF.260	17	-do-
Aermacchi M.B. 326B..........................	7	-do-
North American T–6 Texan..................	12	United States
Saab–91 Safir.....................................	12	Sweden
Helicopters		
Aerospatiale Alouette III	5	France
Aerospatiale Alouette II.......................	7	-do-
Aerospatiale Puma...............................	1	-do-
Aerospatiale SA.365N Dauphin............	1	-do-
Bell UH–1H Iroquois	4	Italy and United States
Agusta-Bell AB 205, Bell 205..............	24	-do-

Source: Based on information from *The Military Balance, 1985–1986*, London, 1985, 86.

Table 14. Major Navy Weapons, 1985

Type	Date Built	Date Delivered	Number in Inventory	Country of Origin
Surface combatants				
Savage-class destroyer escort.....	1943	1973	1	United States
Combattante IIIM-class fast-attack craft (FAC) armed with eight Exocet surface-to-surface missiles (SSMs).........	1984	1984	3	France
P–48-class large patrol craft armed with eight SS–12SSMs................................	1970, 1975	1970, 1975	3	-do-
Shanghai II-class FAC armed with four 37mm, four 25mm guns	n.a.	1977	2	China
Patrol vessels				
Forgeux-type with one 40mm and two 20mm guns..............	1957	1969	1	France
Vosper Thorneycroft-type with two 20mm guns.....................	1977	1977	2	Britain
Adjutant-class coastal mine-sweeper (used as patrol vessel).....................................	1953 1977	1973,	2	United States
31.5-meter coastal patrol vessel.....................................	1957–67	1959–67	4	France
25-meter coastal patrol craft......	1961–63	1961–63	6	-do-
23-meter coastal patrol craft......	1981–82	1981–82	4	Spain

n.a.—not available.

Source: Based on information from *Jane's Fighting Ships, 1984–85,* London, 1984.

Bibliography

Chapter 1

Abun-Nasr, Jamil M. "The Beylicate in Seventeenth-Century Tunisia," *International Journal of Middle East Studies* [London], 6, No. 1, January 1975, 70–93.

_____. *A History of the Maghrib.* Cambridge: Cambridge University Press, 1971.

Ageron, Charles-Robert. *Politiques coloniales au Maghreb.* Paris: Presses Universitaires de France, 1972.

Ashford, Douglas E. *National Development and Local Reform: Political Participation in Morocco, Tunisia, and Pakistan.* Princeton: Princeton University Press, 1967.

_____. *The Politics of Planning in Morocco and Tunisia.* Syracuse: Syracuse University Press, 1965.

Bégué, Camille. *Le message de Bourguiba: Une politique de l'homme.* Paris: Hachette, 1972.

Bénabou, Marcel. *La résistance africaine à la romanisation.* Paris: Maspero, 1976.

Berque, Jacques. *French North Africa: The Maghrib Between Two World Wars.* New York: Praeger, 1967.

Bourguiba, Habib. "Nationalism: Antidote to Communism," *Foreign Affairs*, 35, No. 4, July 1957, 646–53.

_____. "The Tunisian Way," *Foreign Affairs*, 44, No. 3, April 1966, 480–88.

_____. *La Tunisie et la France.* Paris: Julliard, 1954.

Braudel, Fernand. *The Mediterranean and the Mediterranean World in the Age of Philip II.* 2 vols. New York: Harper and Row, 1972.

Brett, Michael. "The Arab Conquest and the Rise of Islam in North Africa." Pages 490–555 in J.D. Fage (ed.), *The Cambridge History of Africa, II (from c. 500 to A.D. 1050).* Cambridge: Cambridge University Press, 1978.

_____. "The Fatimid Revolution (861-973), and Its Aftermath in North Africa." Pages 589–636 in J.D. Fage (ed.), *The Cambridge History of Africa, II (from c. 500 to A.D. 1050).* Cambridge: Cambridge University Press, 1978.

————. "Ifriqiya as a Market for Saharan Trade from the Tenth to the Twelfth Century A.D." *Journal of African History* [London], 10, No. 3, 1969, 347–64.

————. "Problems in the Interpretation of the History of the Maghreb in the Light of Some Recent Publications," *Journal of African History* [London], 13, No. 3, 1972, 489–506.

Broughton, T.R.S. *The Romanization of Africa Proconsularis.* New York: Greenwood Press, 1968.

Brown, Leon Carl. *The Bizerte Affair.* New York: Institute of Current World Affairs, 1961.

————. *State and Society in Independent North Africa.* Washington: Middle East Institute, 1966.

————. *The Tunisia of Ahmad Bey, 1837–1855.* Princeton: Princeton University Press, 1974.

Brown, Peter, *Augustine of Hippo: A Biography.* Berkeley and Los Angeles: University of California Press, 1969.

Brunschvig, Robert. *La Berbérie orientale sous les Hafsides des origines à la fin du XV siècle.* 2 vols. Paris: Adrien-Maison-neuve and Librairie d'Amérique et d'Orient, 1940–47.

Bulliet, Richard. *The Camel and the Wheel.* New York: Columbia University Press, 1976.

Burke, Edmund, III. "Towards a History of the Maghrib," *Middle Eastern Studies* [London], 11, No. 3, October 1975, 306–23.

Chouraqui, André N. *Between East and West: A History of the Jews of North Africa.* New York: Atheneum, 1973.

Cleveland, William L. "The Municipal Council of Tunis, 1858–1870: A Study in Urban Institutional Change," *International Journal of Middle East Studies,* 9, No. 1, February 1978, 33–61.

Clissold, Stephen. *The Barbary Slaves.* London: Elek, 1977.

Courtois, Christian. *Les Vandales et l'Afrique.* Aalen, West Germany: Scientia Verlag, 1964.

Diehl, Charles. *L'Afrique byzantine: Histoire de la domination byzantine en Afrique, 533–709.* 2 vols. Philadelphia: Franklin, 1968 (reprint).

Field, James A. *America and the Mediterranean World, 1776–1882.* Princeton: Princeton University Press, 1969.

Fisher, Godfrey, *Barbary Legend: War, Trade, and Piracy in North Africa, 1415–1830.* Oxford: Clarendon Press, 1957.

Fisher, H.J. "The Eastern Maghrib and the Central Sudan." Pages 232–330 in Roland Oliver (ed.), *The Cambridge History of Africa, III (from c. 1050 to c. 1600).* Cambridge: Cambridge University Press, 1977.

Frend, W.H.C. "The Christian Period in Mediterranean Africa, c. A.D. 200 to 700." Pages 410–89 in J.D. Fage (ed.), *The Cambridge History of Africa, II (from c. 500 to A.D. 1050)*. Cambridge: Cambridge University Press, 1978.

_____. *The Donatist Church: A Movement of Protest in Roman North Africa*. Oxford: Clarendon Press, 1952.

Gallagher, Charles F. *Building a New Tunisia: Comments on an Address by Habib Bourguiba*. (American Universities Field Staff. Fieldstaff Reports. North Africa Series, 6, No. 1.) Hanover, New Hampshire: AUFS, January 1961.

_____. *Contemporary Islam: The Path of Pragmatism: The Human Modernization of Tunisia*. (American Universities Field Staff. Fieldstaff Reports. North Africa Series, 12, No. 3.) Hanover, New Hampshire: AUFS, June 1966.

_____. *Ramadan in Tunisia: Aspects and Problems of the Tunisian Republic*. (American Universities Field Staff. Fieldstaff Reports. North Africa Series, 4, No. 1.) Hanover, New Hampshire: AUFS, 1960.

_____. "Tunisia." Pages 11–86 in Gwendolen M. Carter (ed.), *Africa One-Party States*. Ithaca: Cornell University Press, 1962.

_____. *The Tunisian Way: Modernization and Progress in the Maghreb*. (American Universities Field Staff. Fieldstaff Reports. North Africa Series, 9, No. 11.) Hanover, New Hampshire: AUFS, 1963.

_____. *The United States and North Africa: Morocco, Algeria, and Tunisia*. Cambridge: Harvard University Press, 1963.

Ganiage, Jean. *Les origines du protectorat français en Tunisie*. Paris: Presses Universitaires de France, 1959.

Gautier, Emile-Félix. *Le passé de l'Afrique du Nord: Les siècles obscurs*. Paris: Payot, 1952.

Gordon, David C. *North Africa's French Legacy, 1954–1962*. (Harvard Middle Eastern Monographs, 9.) Cambridge: Harvard University Press for the Center for Middle Eastern Studies, 1964.

Green, Arnold H. *The Tunisian Ulama, 1873–1915: Social Structure and Response to Ideological Currents*. Leiden: Brill, 1978.

Hess, Andrew C. *The Forgotten Frontier: A History of the Sixteenth Century Ibero-African Frontier*. Chicago: University of Chicago Press, 1978.

Hill, Derek, and Lucien Golvin. *Islamic Architecture in North Africa*. London: Faber and Faber, 1976.

Hirschberg, H.Z. *A History of the Jews in North Africa, I: From Antiquity to the Sixteenth Century.* (2d ed., rev.) Leiden: Brill, 1974.

Hourani, Albert. *Arabic Thought in the Liberal Age, 1798–1939.* London: Oxford University Press, 1962.

Howe, George F. *United States Army in World War II, the Mediterranean Theater of Operations, North Africa: Seizing the Initiative in the West.* Washington: Department of the Army, 1957.

Irwin, Ray W. *The Diplomatic Relations of the Barbary Powers, 1776–1816.* New York: Russell and Russell, 1970 (reprint).

Johnson, Douglas. "The Maghrib." Pages 99–124 in John E. Flint (ed.), *The Cambridge History of Africa, V (from c. 1790 to c. 1870.)* Cambridge: Cambridge University Press, 1976.

Julien, Charles-André. *L'affaire tunisienne, 1878–1881.* Tunis: Dar El Amal, 1981.

————. *L'Afrique du Nord en marche: Nationalismes musulmans et souveraineté français.* Paris: Julliard, 1972.

————. *Études magrébines.* Paris: Presses Universitaires de France, 1964.

————. *Histoire de l'Afrique blanche des origines à 1945.* Paris: Presses Universitaires de France, 1966.

————. *Histoire de l'Afrique du Nord: Tunisie, Algérie, Maroc.* 2 vols. (2d ed., rev.) Paris: Payot, 1966.

————. *History of North Africa: Tunisia, Algeria, Morocco. From the Arab Conquest to 1830.* (Translation of Vol. 2, *Histoire de l'Afrique du Nord*, revised by Roger le Tourneau.) New York: Praeger, 1970.

Khayr al-Din al-Tunisi (Kherredin). *The Surest Path: The Political Treatise of a Nineteenth-Century Muslim Statesman.* (Ed., Leon Carl Brown.) Cambridge: Harvard University Press, 1967.

Knapp, Wilfrid. *North West Africa: A Political and Economic Survey.* (3d ed.) Oxford: Oxford University Press, 1977.

————. *Tunisia.* London: Thames and Hudson, 1970.

Lacouture, Jean. "Bourguiba: Portrait of a Non-Conformist," *New York Times Magazine,* June 6, 1965, 91–93.

————. *Cinq hommes et la France.* Paris: Éditions du Seuil, 1961.

————. *The Demigods: Charismatic Leadership in the Third World.* New York: Knopf, 1970.

Laroui, Abdallah. *The History of the Maghrib: An Interpretive Essay.* Princeton: Princeton University Press, 1977.

Law, R.C.C. "North Africa in the Hellenistic and Roman Periods, 323 B.C. to A.D. 305." Pages 148–209 in J.D. Fage (ed.), *The Cambridge History of Africa, II (from c. 500 B.C. to A.D. 1050).* Cambridge: Cambridge University Press, 1978.

"North Africa in the Period of Phoenician and Greek Colonization, c. 800 to 323 B.C." Pages 87–147 in J. D. Fage (ed.), *The Cambridge History of Africa, II (from c. 500 B.C. to A.D. 1050)*. Cambridge: Cambridge University Press, 1978.

Le Tourneau, Roger. *The Almohad Movement in North Africa in the Twelfth and Thirteenth Centuries*. Princeton: Princeton University Press, 1969.

_____. *Évolution politique de l'Afrique du Nord musulmane, 1920–1961*. Paris: Colin, 1962.

Lewis, Bernard. *The Arabs in History*. London: Hutchinson, 1966.

_____. *The Origins of Isma'ilism: A Study of the Historical Background of the Fatimid Caliphate*. New York: AMS, 1974 (reprint).

Ling, Dwight L. *Morocco and Tunisia: A Comparative History*. Washington: University Press of America, 1979.

_____. "Paul Camdon, Coordinator of Tunisia," *Historian*, 22, No. 4, October 1960, 449–55.

_____. "Planners of Protectorates: Camdon in Tunisia and Lyautey in Morocco," *Muslim World*, 44, No. 3, July 1974, 220–27.

_____. *Tunisia from Protectorate to Republic*. Bloomington: Indiana University Press, 1967.

Macksey, Kenneth. *Crucible of Power: The Fight for Tunisia, 1942–1943*. London: Hutchinson, 1969.

Mahjoubi, Ali. *Les origines du mouvement national en Tunisie*. Tunis: Université de Tunis, 1982.

Marriner, John. *The Shores of the Black Ships*. London: Kimber, 1971.

Marsden, Arthur. *British Diplomacy and Tunis, 1875–1902: A Case Study of Mediterranean Policy*. New York: Africana, 1971.

Micaud, Charles A., Leon Carl Brown, and Clement Henry Moore. *Tunisia: The Politics of Modernization*. New York: Praeger, 1964.

Montagne, Robert. *The Berbers: Their Political and Social Life*. London: Frank Cass, 1973.

Moore, Clement Henry. *Tunisia since Independence: The Dynamics of One-Party Government*. Berkeley and Los Angeles: University of California Press, 1965.

Moscati, Sabatino. *The World of the Phoenicians*. London: Weidenfeld and Nicolson, 1968.

Mzali, Mohamed Salah. *Les Beys de Tunis et le roi des français*. Tunis: Maison Tunis, 1976.

_____. *La situation en Tunisie à la vielle du protectorat*. Tunis: Maison Tunisienne de l'Édition, 1969.

Poncet, Jean. *La colonisation et l'agriculture européenes en Tunisie depuis 1881.* Paris: Mouton, 1962.

"Le mythe de la 'catastrophe' hilâlienne," *Annales économies, sociétés, civilisation,* [Paris], 22, No. 5, September-October 1967, 1099–1120.

_____. *La Tunisie à la recherche de son avenir: Indépendance ou néocolonialisme?* Paris: Éditions Sociales, 1974.

Rous, Jean. *Habib Bourguiba.* Paris: Didier, 1969.

Rudebeck, Lars. *Party and People: A Study of Political Change in Tunisia.* New York: Praeger, 1969.

Salem, Norma. *Habib Bourguiba, Islam, and the Creation of Tunisia.* London: Croom Helm, 1984.

Sallust (Gaius Sallustius Crispus). *The Jurgurthine War.* Baltimore: Penguin, 1964.

Smida, Mongi. *Khéredine: Ministre réformateur.* Tunis: Maison Tunisienne de l'Édition, 1971.

Spencer, William. "Ottoman North Africa." Pages 103–27 in William W. Haddad and William Ochsenwald (eds.), *Nationalism and the Non-National State: The Dissolution of the Ottoman Empire.* Columbus: Ohio State University Press, 1977.

Stone, Russell A. "Tunisia: A Single Party System Holds Change in Abeyance." Pages 144–76 in I. William Zartman (ed.), *Political Elites in Arab North Africa.* New York: Longman, 1982.

Talbi, Mohamed. *L'Emirat Aghlabide: Histoire politique.* Paris: Libraire d'Amérique et d'Orient, 1966.

Valensi, Lucette. *Fellahs Tunisiens: L'économie rurale et la vie des campagnes aux 18e et 19e siècles.* (Civilisations et Sociétés series, No. 45.) Paris: Mouton, 1977.

_____. *On the Eve of Colonialism: North Africa Before the French Conquest.* New York: Holmes and Meier, 1977.

Wansbrough, John. "The Decolonization of North African History," *Journal of African History* [London], 9, No. 4, 1968, 643–50.

Warmington, Brian Herbert. *Carthage.* New York: Praeger, 1969.

_____. *The North African Provinces from Diocletian to the Vandal Conquest.* Cambridge: Cambridge University Press, 1954.

Zartman, I. William. *Government and Politics in Northern Africa.* New York: Praeger, 1963.

Zartman, I. William (ed.). *Man, State, and Society in the Contemporary Maghrib.* New York: Praeger, 1973.

Zartman, I. William, et al. (eds.). *Political Elites in Arab North Africa.* New York: Longman, 1982.

Ziadeh, Nicolas A. *Origins of Nationalism in Tunisia.* Beirut: American University of Beirut, 1962.

Chapter 2

Allman, James. "Social Mobility and Educational Access in Tunisia." Pages 344–59 in C.A.O. Van Nieuwenhuijze (ed.), *Commoners, Climbers, and Notables: A Sampler of Studies on Social Ranking in the Middle East.* (Social, Economic, and Political Studies of the Middle East series, 21.) Leiden: Brill, 1977.

————. *Social Mobility, Education, and Development in the Middle East.* (Social, Economic, and Political Studies of the Middle East series, 28.) Leiden: Brill, 1979.

Ashford, Douglas E. *Second and Third Generation Elites in the Maghreb.* Washington: External Research Staff, Bureau of Intelligence and Research, Department of State, November 1963.

Barberis, Mary. "Tunisia: High Fertility Stalls Development." (Report No. 14.) Pages 15–16 in Sharon L. Camp, Mary Barberis, and Patricia Barnett (eds.), *Population Pressures: Signs of Stress.* Washington: Draper Fund, September 1985.

Beaujot, Roderic. "How LDC Fertility Declines Stall: The Case of Tunisia," *Population Today,* 12, No. 9, September 1984, 6–7.

Beaujot, Roderic, and Mongi Bchir. *Fertility in Tunisia: Traditional and Modern Contrasts.* Washington: Population Reference Bureau, August 1984.

Belhassen, Souhayr. "A Jerba, la bavure: des Juifs mourront," *Jeune Afrique* [Paris], No. 1293, Octoer 16, 1985, 46.

Berque, Jacques. *French North Africa: The Maghrib Between Two World Wars.* New York: Praeger, 1967.

Binsbergen, Wim M.J. van. "The Cult of Saints in North-Western Tunisia: An Analysis of Contemporary Pilgrimage Structures." Pages 199–239 in Ernest Gellner (ed.), *Islamic Dilemmas: Reformers, Nationalists, and Industrialization: The Southern Shore of the Mediterranean.* (Religion and Society series, 25.) Amsterdam: Mouton 1985.

Book of the Year, 1985. Chicago: Encyclopedia Britannica, 1985.

Brown, Leon Carl. "The Islamic Reformist Movement in North Africa," *Journal of Modern African Studies,* 2, No. 1, 1964, 55–63.

————. "The Role of Islam in Modern North Africa." Pages 97–122 in Leon Carl Brown (ed.), *State and Society in Independent North Africa.* Washington: The Middle East Institute, 1966.

_____. "Tunisia: Education, 'Cultural Unity,' and the Future." Pages 365–79 in I. William Zartman (ed.), *Man, State, and Society in the Contemporary Maghrib.* New York: Praeger 1973.

Camau, Michel. "L'État tunisien: de la tutelle au désengagement," *Maghreb-Machrek* [Paris], No. 103, January-February-March 1984, 8–38.

Chouraqui, André N. *Between East and West: A History of the Jews of North Africa.* New York: Atheneum, 1973.

Chourou, Bechir. *Educational Independence in a Developing Country: The Case of Tunisia.* Evanston; International TTT Project, School of Education, Northwestern University, 1973.

Dalby, David. *Language Map of Africa and the Adjacent Islands.* London: International African Institute, 1977.

Deshen, Schlomo. "The Social Structure of Southern Tunisian Jewry in the Early 20th Century." Pages 123–35 in Schlomo Deshen and Walter P. Zenner (eds.), *Jewish Societies in the Middle East: Community, Culture, and Authority.* Washington: University Press of America, 1982.

Dobbs, Michael. "Moslem Fervor Spreads at University in Tunis: Shift Reverses Bourguiba's Westernism," *Washington Post,* June 2, 1985, A16.

Durrani, Lorna. "Tensions and Role Conflict in the Tunisian Family," *Maghreb Review* [London], 2, No. 3, May-June 1977, 13–17.

Edwards, Mike, and David A. Harvey. "Tunisia: Sea, Sand, Success," *National Geographic,* 157, No. 2, February 1980, 184–217.

Entelis, John P. *Comparative Politics of North Africa: Algeria, Morocco, and Tunisia.* Syracuse: Syracuse University Press, 1980.

_____. "Reformist Ideology in the Arab World: The Cases of Tunisia and Lebanon," *Review of Politics,* 37, No. 4, October 1975, 513–46.

Faure, Adolphe. "Islam in North-West Africa (Maghrib)." Pages 171–86 in C.F. Beckingham and A.J. Arberry (eds.), *Religion in the Middle East: Three Religions in Concord and Conflict,* 2: *Islam,* Cambridge: Cambridge University Press, 1969.

Ferchiou, Sophie. "Women's Work and Family Production in Tunisia," *Feminist Issues,* 1, No. 2, 1981, 55–68.

Gallagher, Charles F. *Contemporary Islam: The Path of Pragmatism: The Human Modernization of Tunisia.* (American Universities Field Staff. Fieldstaff Reports. North Africa Series, 12, No. 3.) Hanover, New Hampshire: AUFS, June 1966.

————. *Ramadan in Tunisia: Aspects and Problems of the Tunisian Republic.* (American Universities Field Staff. Fieldstaff Reports. North Africa Series, 4, No. 1.) Hanover, New Hampshire: AUFS, June 1960.

Gordon, David C. *North Africa's French Legacy, 1954–1962.* (Harvard Middle Eastern Monographs, 9.) Cambridge: Harvard University Press for the Center for Middle Eastern Studies, 1964.

Guillaume, Alfred. *Islam.* (2d ed.) Harmondsworth, Middlesex, England: Penguin, 1956.

Hermassi, Mohamed El Baki. "La société tunisienne au miroir islamiste," *Maghreb-Machrek* [Paris], No. 103, January-February-March 1984, 39–59.

Hopkins, Nicholas S. "Tunisia: An Open and Shut Case," *Social Problems,* 28, No. 4, April 1981, 385–93.

Ismael, Tareq Y., and Jacqueline S. Ismael. *Government and Politics in Islam.* London: Pinter, 1985.

Joint Publications Research Service—JPRS (Washington).
The following items are from the JPRS series:
Near East/North Africa Report.
"Tunsia of the Uncertainties," *Le Monde,* Paris, February 17–19, 1982. (JPRS 80442, March 30, 1982, 40–49).
Near East/South Asia Report.
"Status of Maghreb Youth Assessed," *Le Monde,* Paris, July 10–13, 1984. (JPRS-NEA-84–124, August 13, 1984, 1–19).
"The Tunisian Elites," *Jeune Afrique,* Paris, August 1985. (JPRS-NEA-84–022–L, September 16, 1985, 20–29).
"The Tunisia of Frustrations," *Le Monde,* Paris, January 31, February 1 and 2, 1984. (JPRS-NEA-84–047, March 21, 1984, 23–34).

Jones, Marie Thourson. "Politics and Social Policy in Tunisia," *Maghreb Review* [London], 8, Nos. 5–6, September-December 1983, 131–40.

Legum, Colin (ed.). *Africa Contemporary Record: Annual Survey and Documents, 1982–1983.* New York: Africana, 1984.

Louis, André. *Nomades d'hier et d'aujourd'hui dans le sud tunisien.* (Collection Mondes Méditerranéens.) Aix-en-Provence: EDISUD, 1979.

McFerren, Margaret. *Arabization in the Maghreb.* Washington: Center for Applied Linguistics, January 1985.

————. *Country Status Report: Tunisia.* Washington: Center for Applied Linguistics, September 1984.

341

Tunisia: A Country Study

Majali, A.S. *The Development of Higher Education in the Arab World.* (Sixth Contreras Arab Lecture.) London: Longman's for the University of Essex, 1976.

Marshall, Susan E., and Randall G. Stokes. "Tradition and the Veil: Female Status in Tunisia and Algeria," *Journal of Modern African Studies* [Cambridge], 19, No. 4, 1981, 625–46.

Micaud, Charles A. *Tunisia: The Politics of Modernization.* New York: Praeger, 1964.

Moore, Clement Henry. *Tunisia since Independence: The Dynamics of One-Party Government.* Westport, Connecticut: Greenwood Press, 1982 (reprint).

Murdock, George. *Africa: Its People and Their Cultural History.* New York: McGraw-Hill, 1959.

Murphy, Dermot F. "Colonial and Post-Colonial Language Policy in the Maghreb," *Maghreb Review* [London], 2, No. 2, March-April 1977, 1–10.

Parker, Richard. *North Africa: Regional Tensions and Strategic Concerns.* New York: Praeger, 1984.

Pipes, Daniel. *In the Path of God: Islam and Political Power.* New York: Basic Books, 1982.

Ruedy, John. "The Maghreb: Another Arab World," *Journal of Defense and Diplomacy,* 2, No. 1, January 1984, 44–51.

Sadok, Sahli. "Le Couple entre l'union et la rupture," *Revue tunisienne de sciences sociales* [Tunis], No. 66, 1981, 117–30.

Salacuse, Jeswald W. *An Introduction to Law in French-Speaking Africa, II: North Africa.* Charlottesville: Michie, 1975.

Salem, Norma. *Habib Bourguiba, Islam, and the Creation of Tunisia.* London: Croom Helm, 1984.

Schissel, Howard. "Facing a Future Without Bourguiba," *Africa Report,* 29, No. 6, November-December 1984, 68–71.

Spencer, William. "Berber." Pages 99–109 in Richard V. Weekes (ed.), *Muslim Peoples: A World Ethnographic Survey.* Westport, Connecticut: Greenwood Press, 1978.

Stone, Russell A. "Tunisia: A Single Party System Holds Change in Abeyance," Pages 144–76 in I. William Zartman (ed.), *Political Elites in Arab North Africa,* New York: Longman, 1982.

Taamallah, Klemaies. "Structures Sociales en Tunisie," *Revue tunisienne de science sociales* [Tunis], No. 65, 1981, 183–90.

Tessler, Mark A. "Political Change and the Islamic Revival in Tunisia," *Maghreb Review,* 5, No. 1, January-February 1980, 8–19.

_____. "Tunisia at the Crossroads," *Current History,* 84, No. 502, May 1985, 217–20.

342

Tessler, Mark A., with Janet Rogers and Daniel Schneider. Pages 141–58 in Lois Beck and Nikki Keddie (eds.), *Women in the Muslim World.* Cambridge: Harvard University Press, 1978.

Tunisia. Ministry of Plan. National Institute of Statistics. *Recensement général de la population et de l'habitat,* 1. Tunis: March 30, 1984.

_____. *Statistiques: Les migrations internes et l'activité feminine.* Tunis: April-June 1984.

Udovitch, Abraham, and Lucette Valensi. *The Last Arab Jews: The Communities of Jerba, Tunisia.* New York: Harwood Academic, 1984.

United States, Department of Health, Education, and Welfare. *The Educational System of Tunisia.* (Education Around the World series.) Washington: GPO, 1974.

United States. Department of State. *Country Reports on Human Rights Practices for 1984.* (Report submitted to United States Congress, 99th, 1st Session, Senate, Committee on Foreign Relations, and House of Representatives, Committee on Foreign Affairs.) Washington: GPO, February, 1985.

United States. Department of State. Bureau of Public Affairs. *Background Notes: Tunisia.* (Department of State publication, No. 8142.) Washington: GPO, September 1984.

Vatin, Jean-Claude. "Revival in the Maghreb: Islam as an Alternative Political Language." Pages 221–50 in Ali E. Hillal Dessouki (ed.), *Islamic Resurgence in the Arab World.* New York: Praeger, 1982.

Voll, John Obert. *Islam: Continuity and Change in the Modern World.* Boulder, Colorado: Westview Press, 1982.

Waltz, Susan E. "Islamist Appeal in Tunisia." (Paper presented to Middle East Studies Association, New Orleans, November 1985).

_____. "The Islamist Challenge in Tunisia," *Journal of Arab Affairs,* 3, No. 1, Spring 1984, 99–114.

"Women's Equality Provokes Backlash," *Arabia: The Islamic World Review* [East Burnham, England], 4, No. 38, October 1984, 35.

Wright, Claudia. "Tunisia: Next Friend to Fall?" *Foreign Policy,* No. 46, Spring 1982, 120–37.

Wright, Robin. *Sacred Rage: The Wrath of Militant Islam.* New York: Simon and Schuster, 1985.

Chapter 3

ABECOR. "Tunisia." Paris: Banque Nationale de Paris, August 1984.

Abou Sada, Georges. "Return Migration and the Tunisian Labor Market." Pages 15–19 in Daniel Kubat (ed.), *The Politics of Return: International Return Migration in Europe.* New York: Center for Migration Studies, 1984.

"Budgets: Tunisia," *Africa Research Bulletin* [Exeter, England], 19, No. 12, January 31, 1983, 6700–6702.

"Budgets: Tunisia," *Africa Research Bulletin* [Exeter, England], 20, No. 12, January 31, 1984, 7129–30.

Camau, Michel. "L'État tunisien: de la tutelle au désengagement," *Maghreb, Machrek, Monde Arabe* [Paris], No. 103, January-February-March 1984, 8–37.

Cheema, G.S., and D.A. Rondinelli. *Decentralization and Development: Policy Implementation in Developing Countries.* Beverly Hills: Sage, 1983.

Cleaver, Kevin M. *Agricultural Development Experience of Algeria, Morocco, and Tunisia: A Comparison.* (World Bank Staff Working Papers, No. 552.) Washington: World Bank, 1982.

Economist Intelligence Unit. *Quarterly Economic Review of Libya, Tunisia, Malta* [London], No. 1, February 19, 1985, 4–26.

————. *Quarterly Economic Review of Libya, Tunisia, Malta* [London], No. 2, May 27, 1985, 2–26.

————. *Quarterly Economic Review of Libya, Tunisia, Malta* [London], No. 3, August 1985, 2–17.

————. *Quarterly Economic Review of Libya, Tunisia, Malta: Annual Supplement, 1983.* London: 1983.

————. *Quarterly Economic Review of Libya, Tunisia, Malta: Annual Supplement, 1984.* London: 1984.

Franco, Robert. "After Decade of Impressive Economic Growth Tunisia Aims at Diversifying Its Export Base, *IMF Survey*, No. 11, October 25, 1982, 340–43.

Hawley, David, and Juliet Broad McKee. "Tunisia Prepares for an Oil-less Future, *Middle East Economic Digest* [London], 26, No. 37, September 10, 1982, 12–14.

International Bank for Reconstruction and Development. *World Development Report, 1984.* New York: Oxford University Press, 1984.

International Monetary Fund. *Annual Report on Exchange Arrangements and Exchange Restrictions.* Washington: 1983.

_____. *Annual Report on Exchange Arrangements and Exchange Restrictions.* Washington: 1984.

"J.A.E. Fait Parler Habib Lazres," *Jeune Afrique Économie* [Paris], No. 44, July 19, 1984, 40–44.

Joint Publications Research Service—JPRS (Washington).
The following items are from the JPRS series:
Near East/South Asia Report.
"Corruption, Government Countermeasures Discussed," *Réalités,* Tunis, March 29, 1985. (JPRS–NEA–85–062, May 3, 1985, 8–9).
"Radical Steps Taken to Reform State Enterprises," *Le Temps,* Tunis, November 22, 1984. (JPRS–NEA–85–005, January 11, 1985, 32–47).

Lawless, Richard, and Allan Findlay (eds.). *North Africa: Contemporary Politics and Economic Development.* New York: St. Martin's Press, 1984.

Loumi, Hedi. "Emploi: La Promotion par la Solidarité Nationale," *Dialogue* [Tunis], No. 551, April 29, 1985, 32–59.

Mullen, Joseph. "Regional Planning as a Strategy for Integrated Rural Development in Central Tunisia," *Development Research Digest* [Brighton, England], No. 10, Winter 1983, 71–75.

Nellis, John R. "A Comparative Assessment of the Development Performances of Algeria and Tunisia," *Middle East Journal,* 37, No. 3, Summer 1983, 370–93.

_____. "Decentralization and Local Public Finance in Tunisia," *Public Administration and Development* [Chichester, England] (in press).

Nelson, Harold D. (ed.). *Tunisia: A Country Study.* (DA Pam 550–89, 2d ed.) Washington: GPO for Foreign Area Studies, The American University, 1979.

"Special Budget," *Conjoncture* [Tunis], No. 97, January 1985, 17–44.

Tirard, Jean-Marc. "Tunisia: An Overview of Its Tax System," *Bulletin for International Fiscal Documentation* [Amsterdam], 38, No. 1, January 1984, 27–33.

Tunisia. Ministry of Finance. *Economic Yearbook of Tunisia.* Tunis: 1984.

"Tunisia," *Financial Times* [London], March 16, 1984, 1–6 (Survey).

"Tunisia: Economy." Pages 691–707 in *Europa Yearbook, 1984: Middle East and North Africa.* London: Europa, 1984.

"Tunisia Hopes Sixth Five-Year Plan Brings Industrial Breakthrough," *An-Nahar Arab Report and Memo* [Beirut], No. 7, February 14, 1983, 8–10 (special survey).

"Tunisia: New Strategies Aim to Win Back Food Sufficiency," *Middle East Agribusiness* [Redhill, England], 3, No. 7, 1983, 14–17.

"Tunisia's Development Strategy: An Interview with the Economy Minister," *An-Nahar Arab Report and Memo* [Beirut], 7, February 14, 1983, 10–12.

"La Tunisie ou l'art de rester soi-même," *Le Monde* [Paris], No. 12053, October 28, 1983, 13–15.

United States. Central Intelligence Agency. *World Factbook, Nineteen Hundred and Eighty-Five.* Washington: 1985.

United States. Department of Agriculture. Economic Research Service. *Middle East and North Africa.* (Outlook and Situation Report, No. RS–84–3.) Washington: GPO, 1984.

United States. Department of Commerce. International Trade Administration. *Foreign Economic Trends and Their Implications for the United States.* Washington: GPO, 1985.

United States. Department of Labor. Bureau of International Labor Affairs. *Country Labor Profile: Tunisia.* Washington: GPO, 1980.

————. *Foreign Labor Trends: Tunisia.* Washington: GPO, 1984.

United States. Department of State. Bureau of Public Affairs. *Background Notes: Tunisia.* (Department of State publication, No. 8142.) Washington: GPO, September 1984.

United States. Department of the Interior. Bureau of Mines. *Mineral Industries of Africa.* Washington: GPO, 1984.

United States, Embassy in Tunis. *Foreign Labor Trends: Tunisia.* Washington: United States Department of Labor, 1984.

World Development Indicators. Washington: World Bank, 1983.

Wright, Marcus. "Tunisia Revives the Search for Oil and Gas," *Middle East Economic Digest* [London], 28, No. 4, January 27, 1984, 46–47.

————. "Tunisia: Sick Leader—Sick Economy," *Middle East Economic Digest* [London], 28, No. 45, November 9, 1984, 16–17.

(Various issues of the following publications were also used in the preparation of this chapter: *Africa Research Bulletin* [Exeter, England], January 1980–December 1985; *Conjoncture* [Tunis]; *Dialogue pour le progrès* [Tunis]; *Financial Times* [London], January 1982–January 1986; Foreign Broadcast Information Service, *Daily Report: Middle East and Africa,* January 1984–January 1986; *Jeune Afrique* [Paris], January 1983–November 1985; Joint Publications Research Service, *Near East/South Asia Report,* January 1983–December 1985; *Marchés Tropicaux et Mediterranéens* [Paris], *Le Monde* [Paris], January 1983–January 1986; *Quarterly Economic*

Review of Libya, Tunisia, Malta [London], 1983–85; and *Washington Post*, January 1981–January 1986.)

Chapter 4

Amalric, Jacques. "Les 'luttes pour la succession' pésent lourdement sur le fonctionnement du régime," *Le Monde* [Paris], March 8, 1985, 5.

Amnesty International Report, 1985. London: Amnesty International, 1985.

Barakat, Halim (ed.). *Contemporary North Africa: Issues of Development and Integration.* Washington: Center for Contemporary Arab Studies, 1985.

Bessis, Sophie. "Les tribulations d'un ex-parti unique," *Jeune Afrique* [Paris], No. 1233, August 15, 1984, 46–50.

Boyd, Douglas A. *Broadcasting in the Arab World: A Survey of Radio and Television in the Middle East.* Philadelphia: Temple University Press, 1982.

Camau, Michel. "L'État tunisien: de la tutelle au désengagement," *Maghreb-Machrek* [Paris], No. 103, January-February-March 1984, 8–38.

Castenera, Abdul Hasib. "Nobody's Man—But a Man of Islam," *Arabia: The Islamic World Review* [East Burnham, England], 4, No. 44, April 1985, 18–21.

Commission of the European Communities. *EEC-Tunisia Cooperation Agreement.* Brussels: 1982.

Dahmani, Abdelaziz. "Double pèlerinage présidentiel," *Jeune Afrique* [Paris], No. 1276, June 19, 1985, 46–48.

Damis, John. "Tunisia." Pages 69–70 in *Yearbook on International Communist Affairs, 1984*, ed., Richard F. Staar, Stanford: Hoover Institution Press, 1984.

Dhiaf, I. Ben. "Tunisie," Pages 655–713 in *Annuaire de l'Afrique du Nord, 1982.* Paris: Éditions du Centre Nationale de la Recherche Scientifique, 1984.

Dobbs, Michael. "Leader's Twilight Days Prompt Anxiety in Tunisia," *Washington Post*, May 26, 1985, A1.

Entelis, John P. *Comparative Politics of North Africa: Algeria, Morocco, and Tunisia.* Syracuse: Syracuse University Press, 1980.

————. "The Political Economy of North African Relations: Co-operation or Conflict." Pages 112–37 in Halim Barakat (ed.), *Contemporary North Africa: Issues of Development and Integration.* Washington: Center for Contemporary Arab Studies, 1985.

Europa Year Book, 1984: A World Survey. London: Europa, 1984.

Houidi, Fethi, and Ridha Najar. *Presse, radio, et télévision en Tunisie.* Tunis: Maison Tunisienne de l'Édition, 1983.

Joint Publications Research Service—JPRS (Washington).

The following items are from the JPRS series:

Near East/North Asia Report.

"Curtain Up on Tunisia Democracy," *8 Days,* London, October 24, 1981. (JPRS 79412, November 10, 1981, 104–106).

"Islamic Fundamentalism Reviewed," *Al Majallah,* London, September 19–25, 1981. (JPRS 79378, November 5, 1981, 50–61.)

Near East/South Asia Report.

"Circumstances Surrounding the Bread Riots Recounted," *Arabia: The Islamic World Review,* East Burnham, England, February 1984. (JPRS–NEA–84–038, March 7, 1984, 31–32.

"Dynamics of Change in Tunisia Analyzed," *Maghreb-Machrek,* Paris, January-February-March 1984. (JPRS–NEA–84–096, June 19, 1984, 1–64).

"Emancipated Islam," *Le Monde,* Paris, January 27, 1982. (JPRS–NEA–80–310, March 12, 1982, 8–11).

"Human Rights League Issues Report on December-January Events," *Le Temps,* Tunis, May 24, 1984. (JPRS–NEA–84098, June 21, 1984, 65–69).

"Islamic Tendency Leader Rached Ghannouchi Interviewed," *Arabia: The Islamic World Review,* East Burnham, England, April 1985, (JPRS–NEA–85071, May 24, 1985, 30–33).

"The Tunisia of Frustrations," *Le Monde,* Paris, January 31, February 1 and 2, 1984. (JPRS–NEA–84–047, March 21, 1984, 23–34).

"Un jour de sang et de colère," *Jeune Afrique* [Paris], No. 1293, October 16, 1985, 39–57.

Knapp, Wilfrid. *North West Africa: A Political and Economic Survey.* (3d ed.) London: Oxford University Press, 1977.

Legum, Colin (ed.). *Africa Contemporary Record: Annual Survey and Documents, 1980–1981.* New York: Africana, 1981.

————. *Africa Contemporary Record: Annual Survey and Documents, 1981–1982.* New York: Africana, 1981.

_____. *Africa Contemporary Record: Annual Survey and Documents, 1982–1983.* New York: Africana, 1984.

_____. *Africa Contemporary Record: Annual Survey and Documents, 1983–1984.* New York: Africana, 1985.

Nelson, Harold D. (ed.). *Tunisia: A Country Study.* (DA Pam 550–89, 2d ed.) Washington: GPO for Foreign Area Studies, the American University, 1979.

Nolan, Riall W. "Tunisia's Time of Transition," *Current History,* 80, No. 470, December 1981, 405–409.

Parker, Richard B. "Appointment in Oujda," *Foreign Affairs,* 63, No. 4, Summer 1985, 1095–1110.

_____. *North Africa: Regional Tensions and Strategic Concerns.* New York: Praeger, 1984.

Pope, Sterett. "Republic of Tunisia." Pages 1027–32 in George E. DeLury (ed.), *World Encyclopedia of Political Systems and Parties.* New York: Facts on File, 1983.

Salacuse, Jeswald W. *An Introduction to Law in French-Speaking Africa, II: North Africa.* Charlottesville: Michie, 1975.

Santucci, Robert. "La politique étrangère de la Tunisie: Continuité et pragmatisme," *Maghreb-Machrek* [Paris], No. 91, January-February-March 1981, 43–58.

Schissel, Howard. "Facing a Future Without Bourguiba," *Africa Report,* 29, No. 6, November-December 1984, 68–71.

Seddon, David. "Winter of Discontent: Economic Crisis in Tunisia and Morocco," *MERIP Reports.* (Report No. 127), 14, No. 8, October 1984, 7–16.

Stone, Russell A. "Tunisia: A Single Party System Holds Change in Abeyance." Pages 144–76 in I. William Zartman (ed.), *Political Elites in Arab North Africa.* New York: Longman, 1982.

Tekari, Bechir. *Du cheikh à l'omda: Institution locale traditionnelle et intégration partisane.* Tunis: Imprimerie Officielle de la République Tunisienne, 1981.

Tessler, Mark A. "Tunisia at the Crossroads," *Current History,* 84, No. 502, May 1985, 217–20.

Tunisia. *Constitution of the Tunisian Republic* (Text of Constitution of June 1, 1959, including amendments.) Tunis: n. d.

Tunisia. Ministry of Information. *Tunisian-American Relations.* Tunis: 1985.

Tunisia. Secretariat of State for Information. *Tunisia Moves Ahead.* Tunis: Ceres Productions, 1976.

"Tunisia." Pages 1102–04 in George Kurian (ed.), *World Press Encyclopedia.* New York: Facts on File, 1982.

"Tunisia." Pages 683–90 in *The Middle East and North Africa, 1984–85.* London: Europa, 1984.

"Tunisian Journalists Protest," *Index on Censorship*, 2, No. 2, April 1982, 41–42.

"Tunisia: Post Bourguiba Games," *Africa Confidential* [London], 23, No. 21, October 6, 1982, 2–5.

"Tunisia: Special Report," *Arabia: The Islamic World Review* [East Burnham, England], 4, No. 38, October 1984, 30–35.

"Tunisie: ce n'est pas fini," *Jeune Afrique* [Paris], No. 1202, January 18, 1984, 22–35.

United States. Department of Labor. Bureau of International Labor Affairs. *Country Labor Profile: Tunisia.* Washington: GPO, 1980.

United States. Department of State. *Country Reports on Human Rights Practices for 1984.* (Report submitted to United States Congress, 99th, 1st Session, Senate, Comittee on Foreign Relations, and House of Representatives, Committee on Foreign Affairs.) Washington: GPO, February 1985.

————. *Soviet and East European Aid to the Third World, 1981.* Washington: GPO, 1983.

United States. Department of State. Bureau of Public Affairs. *Background Notes: Tunisia.* (Department of State publication, No. 8142.) Washington: GPO, September 1984.

United States. Department of State. Embassy in Tunis. *Tunisia: Country Data Paper.* Washington: United States Information Agency, 1985.

United States. Embassy in Tunis. *Foreign Labor Trends: Tunisia.* Washington: Department of Labor, 1984.

Vatin, Jean-Claude. "Revival in the Maghreb: Islam as an Alternative Political Language." Pages 221–50 in Ali E. Hillal Dessouki (ed.), *Islamic Resurgence in the Arab World.* New York: Praeger, 1982.

Waltz, Susan E. "Islamist Appeal in Tunisia." (Paper presented to Middle East Studies Association, New Orleans, November 1985.)

————. "The Islamist Challenge in Tunisia," *Journal of Arab Affairs*, 3, No. 1, Spring 1984, 99–114.

Ware, L.B. "The Role of the Tunisian Military in the Post-Bourguiba Era," *Middle East Journal*, 39, No. 1, Winter 1985, 27–47.

Wilkinson, Ben. "Who Will Succeed Bourguiba?" *Middle East* [London], No. 130, August 1985, 41–44.

Wright, Claudia. "Tunisia: Next Friend to Fall?" *Foreign Policy*, No. 46, Spring 1982, 20–37.

(Various issues of the following publications were also used in the preparation of this chapter: *Africa Confidential* [London]; *Africa*

Research Bulletin [Exeter, England]; *Arabia: The Islamic World Review* [East Burnham, England]; *Christian Science Monitor; Dialogue pour le progrès* [Tunis]; *Financial Times* [London]; Foreign Broadcast Information Service, *Daily Report: Middle East and Africa; Jeune Afrique* [Paris]; Joint Publications Research Service, *Near East/South Asia Report; Keesing's Contemporary Archives* [London]; *Manchester Guardian Weekly* [London]; *Marchés Tropicaux et Méditerranéens* [Paris]; *Le Monde* [Paris]; *New York Times; Quarterly Economic Review of Libya, Tunisia, Malta* [London]; and *Washington Post.)*

Chapter 5

Amnesty International Report, 1985. London: Amnesty International, 1985.

Balta, Paul. "La Tunisie des incertitudes," *Le Monde* [Paris], 2 pts., February 17–18, 1982.

Barakat, Halim (ed.). *Contemporary North Africa: Issues of Development and Integration.* Washington: Center for Contemporary Arab Studies, 1985.

Belhassen, Souhayr. "Porquoi tant de morts?" *Jeune Afrique* [Paris], No. 1203, January 25, 1984, 28–32.

Buchet, Jean-Louis. "Tunisie: Pourquoi le procès Guiga?" *Jeune Afrique* [Paris], No. 1221, May 30, 1984, 44–50.

Camau, Michel. "L'État tunisien: de la tutelle au désengagement," *Maghreb-Machrek* [Paris], No. 103, January-February-March 1984, 8–38.

Castenera, Abdul Hasib. "Nobody's Man—But a Man of Islam," *Arabia: The Islamic World Review* [East Burnham, England], 4, No. 44, April 1985, 18–21.

"Chronique de Tunisie: Réactions contre une certain dégradation du climat politique," *Marchés Tropicaux et Méditerranéens* [Paris], No. 2062, May 17, 1985, 1219.

Combs-Schilling, M. Elaine. "Of Torn Veils and Revitalized Faith: Islam and Dissent in Morocco and Tunisia." (Paper presented at "Morocco Day" Conference at Johns Hopkins School for Advanced International Studies, Washington, April 1985.)

Couhat, Jean Labayle. "Middle Eastern, North African, and South Asian Navies," *United States Naval Institute Proceedings,* 110, No. 3, March 1984, 48–54.

Degenhardt, Harry (comp.). *Political Dissent.* New York: Longman, 1983.

Deuré, Michel. "Le Maghreb entre le modernisme et l'integrisme," *Le Monde* [Paris], January 27, 1982, 6.

Dwyer, Gwynne. "Tunisia." Pages 584–88 in John Keegan (ed.), *World Armies.* (2d ed.) Detroit: Gale Research, 1983.

Entelis, John P. *Comparative Politics of North Africa: Algeria, Morocco, and Tunisia.* Syracuse: Syracuse University Press, 1980.

Harris, D.R. "Tunisia." Pages 683–707 in *The Middle East and North Africa, 1984–85.* (31st ed.) London: Europa, 1984.

Heller, Mark (ed.). *The Middle East Military Balance, 1983.* Tel Aviv: Jaffe Center for Strategic Studies, Tel Aviv University, 1983.

Hermassi, Mohamed El Baki. "La société tunisienne au miroir islamiste," *Maghreb-Machrek* [Paris], No. 103, January-February-March 1984, 39–56.

Hewish, Mark, et. al. (eds.). *Air Forces of the World.* New York: Simon and Schuster, 1979.

Hurewitz, Jacob C. *Middle East Politics: The Military Dimension.* New York: Praeger, 1969.

International Monetary Fund. *Government Finance Statistics, 1983.* Washington: 1983.

Jane's Fighting Ships, 1984–85. (Ed., John Moore.) New York: Jane's, 1984.

Joint Publications Research Service—JPRS (Washington)
The following items are from the JPRS series:
Near East/North Africa Report.
"Islamic Fundamentalism Reviewed," *Al Majallah,* London, September 19–25, 1981. (JPRS 79378, November 5, 1981, 50–61).

"Role of Islamic Militants in University Unrest Explored," *Al-Sha'b,* Tunis, April 9, 1982. (JPRS 80975, June 3, 1982, 79–81).

"Defense Minister Inspects Saharan Brigade, Urges Support," *La Presse de Tunisie,* Tunis, August 16, 1985. (JPRS–NEA–85–124, September 25, 1985, 44–45).

"Director General of National Security Interviewed," *Al-Sabah,* Tunis, April 19, 1984. (JPRS–NAS–84–083, May 23, 1984, 46–50).

"Dynamics of Change in Tunisia Analyzed," *Maghreb-Machrek,* Paris, January-February-March 1984. (JPRS–NEA–84–096, June 19, 1984, 1–64).

"Human Rights League Issues Report on December-January Events," *Le Temps,* Tunis, May 24, 1984. (JPRS–NEA–84–098, June 21, 1984, 65–69).

"Released Ghannouchi Discusses Prison Life, Other Matters," *Al Mujtama*, Kuwait, September 11, 1984. (JPRS-NEA-84–170, November 27, 1984, 60–64).

"Report of Inquiry Commission of January Disturbances," *Le Press de Tunisie*, Tunis, April 19–20, 1984. (JPRS-NEA-84–084, May 24, 1984, 38–61).

"Status of Maghreb Youth Assessed," *Le Monde*, Paris, July 10–13, 1983. (JPRS-NEA-84–124, August 8, 1984, 1–19).

"Various Islamic Militants Discuss Policies, Objectives," *Al Ra'y*, Tunis, July 22, 1983. (JPRS-NEA-84–373, September 21, 1983, 39–41).

Kamin, Henry. "Islamic Group Claims Role in Tunis Riot," *New York Times*, January 9, 1984, A3.

Knapp, Wilfrid. *North West Africa: A Political and Economic Survey*. (3d ed.) London: Oxford University Press, 1977.

Lawless, Richard, and Allan Findlay (eds.) *North Africa: Contemporary Politics and Economic Development*. New York: St. Martin's Press, 1984.

Legum, Colin (ed.). *Africa Contemporary Record: Annual Survey and Documents, 1978–1979*. New York: Africana, 1980.

_____. *Africa Contemporary Record: Annual Survey and Documents, 1979–1980*. New York: Africana, 1981.

_____. *Africa Contemporary Record: Annual Survey and Documents, 1980–1981*. New York: Africana, 1981.

_____. *Africa Contemporary Record: Annual Survey and Documents, 1981–1982*. New York: Africana, 1981.

_____. *Africa Contemporary Record: Annual Survey and Documents, 1982–1983*. New York: Africana, 1984.

The Military Balance, 1985–1986. London: International Institute for Strategic Studies, 1985.

Nelson, Harold D. (ed.). *Tunisia: A Country Study*. (DA Pam 550–89, 2d ed.). Washington: GPO for Foreign Area Studies, The American University, 1979.

Nolan, Riall W. "Tunisia's Time of Transition," *Current History*, 80, No. 470, December 1981, 405–09.

"North African Navies," *Navy International* [Surrey, England], 86, No. 7, July 1981, 392–99.

Parker, Richard B. "Appointment in Oujda," *Foreign Affairs*, 63, No. 4, Summer 1985, 1095–1110.

_____. *North Africa: Regional Tensions and Strategic Concerns*. New York: Praeger, 1984.

Rondot, Pierre. "L'Afrique Arabe en 1984: Aperçu politique (de nombreux facteurs d'instabilité)," *Marchés Tropicaux et Méditerranéens* [Paris], 41, No. 2044, January 11, 1985, 59–65.

―――. "Tunisie et le Grand Maghreb Arabe," *Défense Nationale* [Paris], No. 39, June 1983, 105–20.

Santucci, Robert. "La Politique étrangère de la Tunisie: continuité et pragmatisme," *Maghreb-Machrek* [Paris], No. 91, January-February-March 1981, 43–58.

Schissel, Howard. "Facing a Future Without Bourguiba," *Africa Report*, 29, No. 6, November-December 1984.

Seddon, David. "Winter of Discontent: Economic Crisis in Tunisia and Morocco," *MERIP Reports* (Report, No. 127.) 14, No. 8, October 1984, 7–16.

"Spectre of Qaddafi Looms over Tunis Calculations," *Arabia: The Islamic World Review* [East Burnham, England], 4, No. 38, October 1984, 32–33.

Stone, Russel A. "Tunisia: A Single Party System Holds Change in Abeyance," Pages 144–76 in I. William Zartman (ed.), *Political Elites in Arab North Africa*. New York: Longman, 1982.

Tessler, Mark A. "Tunisia at the Crossroads," *Current History*, 84, No. 502, May 1985, 217–20.

Tunisia. Ministry of National Economy. "Budget Économique, 1985," *Conjoncture*, No. 97, January 1985, 17–44.

"Tunisia," *Financial Times* [London], March 16, 1984, 1–6 (Survey).

"Tunisia: Special Report," *Arabia: The Islamic World Review* [East Burnham, England], 4, No. 38, October 1984, 30–35.

United States. Arms Control and Disarmament Agency. *World Military Expenditures and Arms Transfers, 1985*. (ACDA Publication, No. 123.) Washington: 1985.

United States. Department of Defense. Security Assistance Agency. *Foreign Military Sales, Foreign Military Construction Sales, and Military Assistance Facts*. Washington: September 1984.

United States. Department of State. *Country Reports on Human Rights Practices for 1981*. (Report submitted to United States Congress, 97th, 2d Session, House of Representatives, Committee on Foreign Affairs, and Senate, Committee on Foreign Relations.) Washington: GPO, February 1982.

―――. *Country Reports on Human Practices for 1982*. (Report submitted to United States Congress, 98th, 1st Session, Senate, Committee on Foreign Relations, and House of Representatives, Committee on Foreign Affairs.) Washington: GPO, February 1983.

_____. *Country Reports on Human Rights Practices for 1983.* (Report submitted to United States Congress, 98th, 2d Session, House of Representatives, Committee on Foreign Affairs, and Senate, Committee on Foreign Relations.) Washington: GPO, February 1984.

_____. *Country Reports on Human Rights Practices for 1984.* (Report submitted to United States Congress, 99th, 1st Session, Senate, Committee, on Foreign Relations, and House of Representatives, Committee on Foreign Affairs.) Washington: GPO, February 1985.

Vandewalle, Dirk. "Bourguiba, Charismatic Leadership, and the Tunisian One-Party System," *Middle East Journal,* 34, No. 2, Spring 1980, 149–59.

Vatin, Jean-Claude. "Revival in the Maghreb: Islam as an Alternative Political Language." Pages 221–50 in Ali E. Hillal Dessouki (ed.), *Islamic Resurgence in the Arab World.* New York: Praeger, 1982.

Volman, Daniel. *A Continent Besieged: Foreign Military Activities in Africa since 1975.* (Institute for Policy Studies Report series.) Washington: 1981.

Waltz, Susan E. "Islamist Appeal in Tunisia." (Paper presented to Annual Conference of the Middle East Studies Association, New Orleans, November 1985.)

_____. "The Islamist Challenge in Tunisia," *Journal of Arab Affairs,* 3, No. 1, Spring 1984, 99–114.

Ware, L.B. "The Role of the Tunisian Military in the Post-Bourguiba Era," *Middle East Journal,* 39, No. 1, Winter 1985, 27–47.

Wilkinson, Ben. "Who Will Succeed Bourguiba?" *Middle East* [London], No. 130, August 1985, 41–44.

Wilson, George C. "U.S.-Tunisia Arms Deal Put on Hold," *Washington Post,* October 22, 1985, A25.

Wright, Claudia. "Tunisia: Next Friend to Fall?" *Foreign Policy,* No. 46, Spring 1982, 120–37.

(Various issues of the following publications were also used in the preparation of this chapter: *Africa Confidential* [London], January 1981-January 1986; *Africa Research Bulletin* [Exeter, England], January 1980-December 1985; *Afrique Défense* [Paris], January 1982-December 1985; *Arabia: The Islamic World Review* [East Burnham, England], January 1984-January 1986; *Christian Science Monitor,* January 1983-January 1986; *Dialogue pour le progrès* [Tunis], January 1983-November 1985; *Financial Times* [London], January 1982-January 1986; Foreign Broadcast Information Service, *Daily Report: Middle East and Africa,* January 1984-January

1986; *Jeune Afrique* [Paris], January 1983-November 1985; Joint Publications Research Service, *Near East/South Asia Report*, January 1983-December 1985; *Keesing's Contemporary Archives* [London], 1980-85; Maghreb-Machrek [Paris], January 1984-December 1985; *Manchester Guardian Weekly* [London], January 1983-January 1986; *Marchés Tropicaux et Méditerranéens* [Paris], January 1984-December 1985; *Le Monde* [Paris], January 1983-January 1986; *New York Times*, January 1983-January 1986; *Quarterly Economic Review of Libya, Tunisia, Malta* [London], 1983–85; and *Washington Post*, January 1981-January 1986.)

Glossary

al—Arabic definite article "the"; connotes family or belonging to. Also seen as el.

alim—*See* ulama.

bakshish—Gratuity or tip offered in exchange for a favor or service in many countries of the Middle East and North Africa. Derived from the old Persian word *bakhshidan* (to give), the term is often translated by foreigners as *bribe;* indigenous people of areas where the practice is common, however, do not regard it in this connotation.

baraka—The quality of special blessedness or grace characterizing marabouts *(q.v.)* or other divinely favored individuals in North African Islam; also, the charisma that endows the blessed with a special capacity to rule.

ben—Literally, "son of"; used before or as part of a proper name to indicate patrilineal descent. Also seen as *ibn. Bani* (also *banu* or *beni*) is literally "sons of" and is used to mean "tribe of" or "family of."

Bourguibism—Term used to describe the pragmatic methodology, humanistic philosophy, and political ethics advocated by Habib Bourguiba.

casbah—The native (Arab) quarter of a city, usually surrounding the fortress or stronghold. Also seen as *kasbah* and *qasbah.*

colons—French colonists; term *grands colons* (great colonists) refers to large European landholders.

Destourian socialism—Tunisia's official political ideology, which, in its synthesis of Bourguibism *(q.v.)* and the concept of centralized state economic planning and intervention, closely resembles British Fabian socialism.

évolué—Literally, "evolved one"; a gallicized Muslim educated in French schools.

fiscal year (FY)—Same as calendar year.

gross domestic product (GDP)—The total value of goods and services produced within a country's borders during a fixed period, usually one year. Obtained by adding the value contributed by each sector of the economy in the form of compensation of employees, profits, and depreciation (consumption of capital). Subsistence production is included and consists of the imputed value of production by the farm family for its own use and the imputed rental value of owner-occupied dwellings.

357

gross national product (GNP)—GDP (*q.v.*) plus the income received from abroad by residents, less payments remitted abroad to nonresidents.

Group of 77—A grouping of developing countries that functions as a caucus on economic matters in the United Nations and other international forums; membership has increased to well over 100 countries since its organization in 1964.

habus—Islamic religious endowment. Occurs also in Islamic countries as *waqf*. Sometimes seen as *habous*.

hadith—Literally, the right path; tradition based on the precedent of the words and deeds of the Prophet Muhammad that serve as one of the sources of Islamic law.

hajj—Pilgrim; title of honor conferred on a Muslim who has made the pilgrimage to Mecca.

imam—In general, a Muslim leader who is a recognized authority on Islamic theology and law; also the prayer leader of a mosque.

International Monetary Fund (IMF)—Established along with the World Bank (*q.v.*) in 1945, the IMF is a specialized agency affiliated with the United Nations and is responsible for stabilizing international exchange rates and payments. The main business of the IMF is the provision of loans to its members (including both industrialized and developing countries) when they experience balance of payments difficulties. These loans frequently carry conditions that require substantial internal economic adjustments by the recipients, most of which are developing countries.

Islamist—Proponent of Islamic religious renewal and integration of Islamic values into all aspects of national life; popularly referred to in many Western publications as Islamic fundamentalist.

jihad—According to Islamic doctrine, the permanent struggle for the triumph of the word of God on earth. This additional general duty of all Muslims has often been translated simply as holy war, but modern Muslims see it in a broader context of civic and personal action.

Maghrib—The western Islamic world (northwest Africa); distinguished from the Mashriq (*q.v.*). Literally, "the time and place of the sunset—the west." For its Arab conquerors the region was the "island of the west" (*jazirat al maghrib*), the land between the "sea of sand" (the Sahara) and the Mediterranean Sea. Traditionally includes Morocco, Algeria, Tunisia, and Tripolitania (*q.v.*); more recently some sources have treated Mauritania as part of the region. Also transliterated as Maghreb.

marabout (pl., *al murabitun)*—In North Africa an Islamic holy man and teacher thought to be touched by a special divine blessing; usually not a member of the ulama (*q.v.*). Transliteration of Arabic *murabit*; literally, a person of the *ribat*, a fortified camp occupied in some instances by a religious community. Understood figuratively as one who has made a religious conversion at a *ribat.*

Mashriq—Eastern Islamic world (the Middle East) in contrast to the Maghrib (*q.v.*).

Mauretania—Classical name for the ancient Berber kingdom in northwest Africa and Roman provinces that succeeded it. Cited in some sources as Mauritania but not to be confused with the modern Islamic Republic of Mauritania.

Nonaligned Movement—A grouping of countries that have deliberately chosen not to be associated politically or militarily with either the West or the communist states. Member countries are expected to pursue independent foreign policies, support national liberation movements, and refrain from participating in multilateral or bilateral military alliances with the major powers. The movement's seventh summit meeting, held in New Delhi in March 1983, was attended by 97 nations.

Punic—From the Latin *punicus*, generally describing any people speaking a Semitic language; more specifically applied to Carthage and Carthaginians.

qadi—Religious judge who interprets and administers sharia (*q.v.*). Also seen as *cadi.*

qaid—In modern Tunisia, the official who heads the local government structure in a district; formerly a tribal chief and representative of the bey and having broader judicial powers than the postindependence *qaid.* Primary historical function was that of collecting taxes. Also seen as *caid.*

Quran—Islamic scriptures believed by Muslims to be God's (Allah's) revelation to Muhammad. Derived from the Arabic verb *qaraa*, "to read." Commonly written as Koran.

Sahil—Region in eastern Tunisia. Literally, the shore or coast.

shahadah—Islamic statement of belief: "There is no god but God (Allah), and Muhammad is his Prophet."

sharia—The traditional code of Islamic law, both civil and criminal, based in part on the Quran (*q.v.*). Also drawn from the hadith (*q.v.*), consensus of Islamic belief (*ijma*, i.e., the faith as it is believed by the faithful at any given time), and *qiyas* (analogy, an elaboration on the intent of law).

Shia—The smaller of the two great divisions of Islam (literally, "party"). Adherents are referred to as Shias (also seen as Shiites). According to Shias, the Quran (*q.v.*) is not a closed body of revelation but is open to further elaboration by inspired imams (*q.v.*).

souk—A traditional market; also seen as *suq*.

the Sudan—Historical geographic region stretching across Africa and Cape Verde on the Atlantic coast to the Red Sea between 80° and 16° north latitude; characterized by savanna and semiarid steppe. Term derived from Arabic *bilad al sudan* (literally, country of the blacks). Not to be confused with the Democratic Republic of Sudan.

sunna—Body of Islamic customs and practices based on the Prophet's words and deeds.

Sunni—The larger of the two great divisions of Islam. Sunnis consider themselves the orthodox adherents of the *sunna (q.v.)*.

Tripolitania—Most populous of Libya's three historic regions, situated in the northwestern part of the country. Name derived from Tripolis (Three Cities).

Tunisian dinar (TD)—Unit of currency since 1968; divided into 1,000 millimes. The average exchange rate was TD0.68 to US$1 in 1983, TD0.78 to US$1 in 1984, TD0.81 to US$1 in August 1985, and TD0.76 to US$1 in December 1985.

ulama (sing., *alim*)—The highest body of religious scholars learned in Muslim theology, philosophy, law, and Quranic studies; it elaborated and interpreted sharia (*q.v.*). Derived from the Arabic verb *alama*, "to know."

World Bank—Informal name used to designate a group of three affiliated international institutions: the International Bank for Reconstruction and Development (IBRD), the International Development Association (IDA), and the International Finance Corporation (IFC). The IBRD, established in 1945, has the primary purpose of providing loans to developing countries for productive projects. The IDA, a legally separate loan fund but administered by the staff of the IBRD, was set up in 1960 to furnish credits to the poorest developing countries on much easier terms than those of conventional IBRD loans. The IFC, founded in 1956, supplements the activities of the IBRD through loans and assistance designed specifically to encourage the growth of productive private enterprises in the less developed countries. The president and certain senior officers of the IBRD hold the same positions in the IFC. The three institutions are owned by the governments of the countries that subscribe their capital. To participate in the World Bank group, members states must first belong to the International Monetary Fund (IMF—*q.v.*).

Index

Abbasid Dynasty: 14, 18
Abd al Mumin, Sultan (1130–63): 20
Abu Hafs, Mohamed ben (1207–21): 20
Ach Chaab: 245, 250, 329
Achour, Habib: 65–66, 69, 231, 244, 245, 246
Ad Douleb oil field: 182
Advanced Merchant Marine Institute: 202
Aeneid: 5
Afghanistan, Soviet invasion: 265
Aghlab, Ibrahim ibn: 14
Aghlabids: 14, 15–17, 18
Agricultural Investment Promotion Agency: 198
agriculture: 5, 163–80; cooperatives, 58, 59, 63, 170–72, 226, 233; cotton, tobacco, 164, 179; crops (cereals, olives, citrus trees, and other crops), xiv, xv, 76, 77, 163–80 *passim*, 187, 323 (table); development, 153, 164, 166, 174, 179, 228, 229, 264; droughts, xxiii, 58, 64, 78, 147, 148, 150, 154, 163, 173, 194; economic importance, 56, 63, 64, 163, 164, 322, 323 (tables); erosion, 164, 167, 174, 181; food shortages (*see also* food riots of 1984), 64, 147, 164, 173, 179, 228; French Protectorate, xix, 32, 37; irrigation, 16, 150, 166, 167, 168, 172, 173, 178, 179; labor, xv, 148, 161, 163, 168, 175, 324 (table); land use, 76–77, 165–68; limited arable land, 148, 165; marketing, mechanization, 63, 81, 147, 164, 174, 187; modern subsector, 167, 173–74; share-cropping and tenant farming, 168, 170; small-holdings, private, traditional, xv, 37, 58–59, 63, 64, 81, 164, 167, 168, 172, 173, 174; subsistence, 64, 73, 81, 92, 167, 168, 170; taxes, 156
Ahmed Bey: 25–27, 30
Air France: 202
Al Akzar University, Cairo: 124
Al Amal: 250, 329
Al Amin Bey (1943–57): 48, 50, 51
Al Maariafa: 241
Al Marsa Convention, 1883: 31, 33, 49

Al Mawqif: 329
Al Mostakbal: 250, 329
Al Mujtamaa: 241
Al Muquaddima: 21
Al Tariq Al Jadid: 250, 329
Al Wahdah: 329
Algeria (*see also* national security: Maghribi tensions and balance of power): Algerian rebel bases in Tunisia, 52, 53, 254, 270; economic relations, 196, 254–55; joint security treaty, 1983, 254, 255, 272; military aid, 307; preindependence, 21, 22, 24, 25–26; relations, 252, 254–55, 269, 271, 286, 288; road, railroad, and telecommunications links, 199, 202, 203; tourists, 194
Ali Bey (1759–82): 24–25
Ali Bey (1882–1900): 31
Almohads: 19, 20
Almoravids: 19
Alouch, Sadok: 246
American Federation of Labor (AFL): 48
Ammar, Habib: 310
Amnesty International: 223
Andalusia: 12
Ar Rai: 250, 329
Arab League. *See* League of Arab States
Arab-Israeli conflict (*see also* Israel): 287; Tunisian expeditionary forces, 259, 275, 297, 298; Tunisian moderation, 57, 58, 60, 208, 252–64 *passim*, 271, 275
Arabic language: forms and dialects, 87–88, 89–90; official language, xiv, 51, 86, 88, 210; personal names, meaning, xi–xii, 357
Arabs: amirates, 14, 16; Arab rule (*see also* Islam), 12–21, 84, 85, 118; Berber assimilation, xiv, xix, 13, 14, 84–85; *shurfa*, 18; urban elite, 13, 14, 23, 25, 27
Arafat, Yasir: 259
Aragon: 20
Ariana, population (tables): 320, 321
Aristotle: 5

civil liberties: xxii, 67, 209, 210
civil service: xx, 30, 40, 88, 93, 95, 161
climate: xiv, 78
Code of Civil and Commercial Procedure, 1959; and General Revision, 1968: 220
Code of Personal Status, 1956: xvi, 104–10 *passim*, 121, 220, 248
Commonwealth of Nations: 165
Congo, 1960: 287, 298
Congress of Berlin, 1878: 30
Constantius Africanus: 16
Constitution, 1861: 27–28, 29, 40, 209
Constitution, 1959: xxi, 52, 53, 68, 140, 210–11, 222, 289; amendments, 211; freedom of worship, 113–14; on "Great Arab Mahgrib," 253
Cordova: 20
Corsica: 6, 11, 23, 44
Council of Ministers (cabinet): xvi, 211, 212, 214, 230, 279; 1985, list of, 327; preindependence, 49, 50, 51
Crimean War: 27
Crusade, Eighth: 21
culture (*see also* Arabic language): xix, 3, 32; "golden age," ninth century, 14, 16–17; French elements, xix, 3, 32, 42, 232, 253, 260; Moorish, xix, 21, 81, 85
currency (Tunisian dinar): xv, 158, 360; foreign exchange, 159, 160
Cyprus: 30
Cyrenaica: 6, 8

Dahar: 82
Daladier, Edouard: 44
Darlan, Jean: 44
de Gaulle, Charles: 47, 53
Destour (Constitution) Party: 39–40, 41, 207, 234; *La Voix du Tunisien*, 249
Destourian Socialist Party (*see also* National Front coalition; politics), 3, 4, 234–37, 291; Congress of Destiny, 1964, 56; decline in power, 208, 233, 235, 269, 276, 278, 281; *Dialogue*, 250, 329; factionalism, xxv, 58–63, 230–31, 276, 281, 282; leaders of, 94–95, 237; membership, organization, 97, 224, 235–37; Political Bureau, 235, 236, 237, 238, 328 (table); political power, monopoly

of, xxi, 207, 226, 232, 233, 276; president, Bourguiba, 237, 328; sole legal party, 1963–81, xv, 234
Dialogue: 250, 329
Dido: 5
Didon oil field: 182
Din, Khair al: 21
Directorate of National Security: 308, 310
Djebel Tebaga: 45
Don Juan of Austria: 22
Doolittle, Hooker: 47
Dorsale mountains: xiv, 76, 78, 79
Dumas, Roland: 261

Ebba Ksour: 199
Economic Development Bank of Tunisia (BDET): 159–60
economy (*see also* agriculture; foreign investment, industry, mining, minerals; tourism); xv, 56–59, 147–203, 207, 228, 232; austerity, 1980s, xxiv, 147, 155, 229, 233, 246, 264; budget, 147, 154–57, 216; centralized state planning, 1960s, 55–59, 63, 207, 226, 244; development planning and investment, 152–54, 155, 162–63, 216, 226, 228, 232–34, 287; diversity 148, 152; domestic debt, xxiv, 156–57, 167–69; external debt, 197, 196–198; food subsidies (*see also* food riots, 1984), xxiv, 164, 229, 280, foreign aid, 56, 130, 131, 141, 142, 147, 153, 198, 260, 261, 264; French Protectorate. *See under* French Protectorate; gross domestic product (GDP), xv, 148, 181, 195, 357; gross national product (GNP), 322 (table), 357–58; growth rate, xiv–xv, 102, 103, 147, 148–50, 153, 154, 207, 277; historic, 20; inflation, xxiii, 147, 150, 152, 162, 207; market-dependent, xxiii, 147, 148, 175, 181, 184, 228; national income, 148–51; private sector, 60, 63–64, 166, 194, 233; remittances from workers abroad, xiii, 154, 163, 195, 196; taxation, 155–56; wage and price controls, 150, 155, 156
Eddour phosphate mines: 185
education: 4, 89, 96, 103, 127–40, 161; abroad, 92, 93, 131, 137, 265; adult,

Published Country Studies

(Area Handbook Series)

550-65	Afghanistan		550-151	Honduras
550-98	Albania		550-165	Hungary
550-44	Algeria		550-21	India
550-59	Angola		550-154	Indian Ocean
550-73	Argentina		550-39	Indonesia
550-169	Australia		550-68	Iran
550-176	Austria		550-31	Iraq
550-175	Bangladesh		550-25	Israel
550-170	Belgium		550-182	Italy
550-66	Bolivia		550-69	Ivory Coast
550-20	Brazil		550-177	Jamaica
550-168	Bulgaria		550-30	Japan
550-61	Burma		550-34	Jordan
550-83	Burundi		550-56	Kenya
5550-50	Cambodia		550-81	Korea, North
550-166	Cameroon		550-41	Korea, South
550-159	Chad		550-58	Laos
550-77	Chile		550-24	Lebanon
550-60	China		550-38	Liberia
550-63	China, Republic of		550-85	Libya
550-26	Colombia		550-172	Malawi
550-91	Congo		550-45	Malaysia
550-90	Costa Rica		550-161	Mauritania
550-152	Cuba		550-79	Mexico
550-22	Cyprus		550-76	Mongolia
550-158	Czechoslovakia		550-49	Morocco
550-54	Dominican Republic		550-64	Mozambique
550-52	Ecuador		550-35	Nepal, Bhutan and Sikkim
550-43	Egypt		550-88	Nicaragua
550-150	El Salvador		550-157	Nigeria
550-28	Ethiopia		550-94	Oceania
550-167	Finland		550-48	Pakistan
550-155	Germany, East		550-46	Panama
550-173	Germany, Fed. Rep. of		550-156	Paraguay
550-153	Ghana		550-185	Persian Gulf States
550-87	Greece		550-42	Peru
550-78	Guatemala		550-72	Philippines
550-174	Guinea		550-162	Poland
550-82	Guyana		550-181	Portugal
550-164	Haiti		550-160	Romania

550–84	Rwanda		550–89	Tunisia
550–51	Saudi Arabia		550–80	Turkey
550–70	Senegal		550–74	Uganda
550–180	Sierra Leone		550–97	Uruguay
550–184	Singapore		550–71	Venezuela
550–86	Somalia		550–57	Vietnam, North
550–93	South Africa		550–55	Vietnam, South
550–95	Soviet Union		550–183	Yemens, The
550–179	Spain		550–99	Yugoslavia
550–96	Sri Lanka (Ceylon)		550–67	Zaïre
550–27	Sudan		550–75	Zambia
550–47	Syria		550–171	Zimbabwe
550–62	Tanzania			
550–53	Thailand			
550–178	Trinidad and Tobago			

US GPO: 490-994 - 328/40007